Level 2 • Part 2
Integrated Chinese
中文听说读写
中文聽説讀寫

TEXTBOOK
Simplified and Traditional Characters

Third Edition

THIRD EDITION BY

Yuehua Liu and Tao-chung Yao
Yaohua Shi, Liangyan Ge, Nyan-Ping Bi

ORIGINAL EDITION BY

Yuehua Liu and Tao-chung Yao
Yaohua Shi and Nyan-Ping Bi

CHENG & TSUI COMPANY

Boston

Copyright © 2010, 2006, 1997 Cheng & Tsui Company, Inc.

Third Edition / Sixth Printing June 2016

20 19 18 17 16   6 7 8 9 10 11 12

Published by
Cheng & Tsui Company, Inc.
25 West Street
Boston, MA 02111-1213 USA
Fax (617) 426-3669
www.cheng-tsui.com
"Bringing Asia to the World"™
ISBN 978-0-88727-689-7— ISBN 978-0-88727-688-0 (pbk.)

Cover Design: studioradia.com
Cover Photographs: Man with map © Getty Images; Shanghai skyline © David Pedre/iStockphoto; Building with masks © Wu Jie; Night market © Andrew Buko. Used by permission.
Interior Design: Wanda España, Wee Design
Illustrations: Eloise Narrigan, www.eloisedraws.com
Editing: Kristen Wanner, Zheng-sheng Zhang, Laurel Damashek
Project Management: Laurel Damashek
Production: Victoria E. Kichuk
Manufacturing: JoAnne Sweeney
Proofreading: Karin Huang, Minying Tan, Eavan Cully, Victoria E. Kichuk, Laurel Damashek
Composition: Charlesworth
Printing and Binding: Transcontinental

Acknowledgments and copyrights can be found at the back of the book on page 407, which constitutes an extension of the copyright page.

Library of Congress Cataloging-in-Publication Data

Integrated Chinese = [Zhong wen ting shuo du xie]. Level 2, part 1 / third ed. by Yuehua Liu ... [et al.] ; original ed. by Yuehua Liu ... [et al.] -- 3d ed.
    <v. 1> cm.
  Chinese and English.
  Parallel title in Chinese characters.
  Includes index.
  Contents: [1]. Textbook --
  ISBN 978-0-88727-680-4 -- ISBN 978-0-88727-679-8 (pbk.)
  1. Chinese language--Textbooks for foreign speakers--English. I. Liu, Yuehua. II. Title: Zhong wen ting shuo du xie.

PL1129.E5I683 2009
495.1'82421--dc22

2009075151

The *Integrated Chinese* series includes books, workbooks, character workbooks, audio products, multimedia products, teacher's resources, and more. Visit **www.cheng-tsui.com** for more information on the other components of *Integrated Chinese*.

Printed in Canada

The Integrated Chinese Series

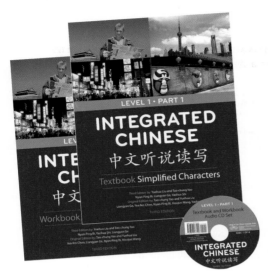

Textbooks Learn Chinese language and culture through ten engaging lessons per volume. Includes dialogues and narratives, culture notes, grammar explanations, and exercises.

Workbooks Improve all four language skills through a wide range of integrated activities that accompany the lessons in the textbook.

Character Workbooks Practice writing Chinese characters and learn the correct stroke order.

Teacher's Handbooks Create a successful language program with sample syllabi, lesson plans, classroom activities, sample tests and quizzes, and teaching tips.

Audio CDs Build listening comprehension with audio recordings of the textbook narratives, dialogues, and vocabulary, plus the pronunciation and listening exercises from the workbooks.

The Integrated Chinese Companion Site

www.integratedchinese.com

Find everything you need to support your course in one convenient place.

- FREE teacher resources
- Password-protected answer keys
- Image gallery

- Links to previews and demos
- Supplementary readings
- Sentence drills

Online Workbooks

Complete the exercises from the printed workbooks using a dynamic, interactive platform. Includes instant grading and intuitive course management.

eTextbooks

Display these downloadable versions of the printed textbooks on interactive whiteboards or your personal computer. Search, bookmark, highlight, and insert notes.

Textbook DVDs

Watch the *Integrated Chinese* story unfold with live-action videos of the textbook dialogues and cultural segments for each lesson.

BuilderCards

Reinforce and build vocabulary using flashcards. Features all essential vocabulary from Level 1.

To order call 1-800-554-1963 or visit www.cheng-tsui.com.

Contents

Lesson 11: 中國的節日 / 中国的节日
Chinese Festivals   1

Lesson 12: 中國的變化/中国的变化
Changes in China　　　　　　　　　　　　　　　　　37

Lesson 13: 旅遊/旅游
Travel　　　　　　　　　　　　　　　　　　　71

Lesson 14: 生活與健康／生活与健康
Life and Wellness   107

Lesson 15: 男女平等
Gender Equality   **139**

Lesson 17: 理財與投資/理财与投资
Money Management and Investing
211

Lesson 18: 中國歷史/中国历史
Chinese History
243

Lesson 19: 面試/面试
Interviewing for a Job   277

Lesson 20: 外國人在中國/外国人在中国
Foreigners in China   305

Let's Review! (Lessons 16–20)   337

Indexes   347

Publisher's Note

When *Integrated Chinese* was first published in 1997, it set a new standard with its focus on the development and integration of the four language skills (listening, speaking, reading, and writing). Today, to further enrich the learning experience of the many users of *Integrated Chinese* worldwide, Cheng & Tsui is pleased to offer this revised and updated third edition of *Integrated Chinese*. We would like to thank the many teachers and students who, by offering their valuable insights and suggestions, have helped *Integrated Chinese* evolve and keep pace with the many positive changes in the field of Chinese language instruction. *Integrated Chinese* continues to offer comprehensive language instruction, with many new features and useful shared resources available on our website at **www.cheng-tsui.com**.

The Cheng & Tsui Chinese Language Series is designed to publish and widely distribute quality language learning materials created by leading instructors from around the world. We welcome readers' comments and suggestions concerning the publications in this series. Please contact the following members of our Editorial Board, in care of our Editorial Department (e-mail: editor@cheng-tsui.com).

Professor Shou-hsin Teng *Chief Editor*
Graduate Institute of Teaching Chinese as a Second Language
National Taiwan Normal University

Professor Dana Scott Bourgerie
Department of Asian and Near Eastern Languages
Brigham Young University

Professor Samuel Cheung
Department of Chinese
Chinese University of Hong Kong

Professor Hong Gang Jin
Department of East Asian Languages and Literatures
Hamilton College

Professor Ying-che Li
Department of East Asian Languages and Literatures
University of Hawaii

Former members of our Editorial Board

Professor Timothy Light *(emeritus)*
Western Michigan University

Professor Stanley R. Munro *(emeritus)*
University of Alberta

Professor Ronald Walton *(in memoriam)*
University of Maryland

Preface to the Third Edition

It has been over ten years since *Integrated Chinese* (*IC*) came into existence in 1997. During these years, amid all the historical changes that took place in China and the rest of the world, the demand for Chinese language teaching-learning materials has been growing dramatically. We are greatly encouraged by the fact that *IC* not only has been a widely used textbook at the college level all over the United States and beyond, but also has become increasingly popular with Chinese advanced language students at the high school level. Over the years, regular feedback from the users of *IC*, both students and teachers, has greatly facilitated our repeated revisions of the series. Following its second edition published in 2006 that featured relatively minor changes and adjustments, this third edition of Level 2 is the result of a much more extensive revision.

Changes in the Third Edition

Revised Storyline

In the present edition, a new, cohesive storyline about a diverse group of characters connects together all the lessons in Level 2. The relationships among the main characters are carefully scripted. We hope that students will get to know the characters well and enjoy following their stories, and that by doing so, they will feel more of a personal involvement in the process of learning the language. In order to increase students' cultural competency and knowledge of Chinese society, in Level 2 Part 2 we have moved the setting of the storyline to China. The main characters in this volume are studying or working in China. The lesson topics have been designed to reflect students' interests and to be relevant to their lives.

Current Vocabulary

In Level 2, we have made a special effort to recycle many of the vocabulary items from Level 1. At the same time, we have accelerated the pace at which new vocabulary items and expressions are introduced, in the hope of enhancing students' ability to communicate. However, we are mindful of the number of vocabulary items introduced in this level and have tried to keep it manageable.

There are about 500 new vocabulary items in Level 2 Part 2. We have tried to limit the number of new words and expressions in each lesson to around 50. Where higher numbers of new words occur, they are necessitated mainly by the inclusion of proper nouns and specialized terms.

Most of the *pinyin* renderings and parts of speech of the vocabulary items are based on the fifth edition of the *Modern Chinese Dictionary* (現代漢語詞典第五版/现代汉语词典第五版) published by the Commercial Press (商務印書館/商务印书馆). For easy referencing, the Level 2 Part 2 vocabulary indexes also include vocabulary from Level 2 Part 1.

More Accessible Grammar and Usage Explanations

When learning to speak a foreign language, students typically go through several stages. The focus of the first stage is pronunciation. In the second stage, grammar is the main focus. In the third stage, expanding vocabulary and mastering important but difficult words and phrases become the primary goals. Ongoing attention to pronunciation and grammar, of course, remains a crucial part of improving students' language skills. Apart from adding new grammar points, we have made the following important changes in the grammar explanations in Level 2:

- We have further expanded explanations of some of the grammatical concepts that are first introduced in Level 1 and offered detailed, contrastive discussions of some language structures that are similar to each other, to help students differentiate among them.
- We have emphasized the use of linking words and phrases in order to improve students' ability to express themselves coherently in a series of sentences. Level 2 Part 2 also introduces a number of form words (虛詞／虚词) that are common in written and Classical Chinese.
- The usage of some of the more difficult but common words and phrases is discussed in a new section, "Words & Phrases." Those items are highlighted in green in the main text of each lesson.

Clear Learning Objectives and an Engaging Learner-Centered Approach

Ever since its inception in 1997, *IC* has been a communication-oriented language textbook which also aims at laying a solid foundation in language form and accuracy for students. The third edition holds fast to that pedagogic philosophy. It has adopted a task-based teaching approach, which is intended to intensify students' motivation and heighten their awareness of the learning objectives in each chapter. Each lesson includes "Learning Objectives" and "Relate and Get Ready" sections at the beginning to help students prepare and concentrate. At the end of each lesson, questions in "Self-Assessment" are to be used by students in self-testing their achievement of the learning objectives.

Additionally, we have introduced in Level 2 another set of new features, which delineates successive steps in building effective learning strategies: the section "Before You Study" helps students focus on the theme of the lesson and gives them opportunities to make predictions based on their own experience; the section "When You Study" encourages students to skim or scan the lesson for the main ideas or specific information; and the section "After You Study" allows the students to confirm their predictions, to recap what happens in the lesson, or to understand the organization of the text. These guidelines are student-centered and designed to be done independently by the students themselves. However, they can also be carried out in Chinese as part of the in-class activities if the instructor considers it appropriate to do so and if the students are linguistically ready.

Contextualized and Interactive Language Practice

The section "Language Practice" highlights the functions of the expressions in the current lesson and provides task-oriented classroom activities centered on those expressions. In particular, we have increased the number of interactive exercises as well as exercises that were designed for enhancing students' skills in oral communication and discourse formation. In at least one of the exercises, students are invited to link up a group of individual sentences and organize them in a coherent passage.

Similar changes are also present in the *Integrated Chinese* workbook, which offers new exercises that are more distinctly communication-oriented and more closely aligned with the learning objectives of each chapter. The exercises in the workbook cover the three modes of communication as explained in the "Standards for Foreign Language Learning in the 21st Century": interpretive, interpersonal and presentational. To help the user locate different types of exercises, we have labeled the workbook exercises in terms of the three communication modes.

Linguistically and Thematically Appropriate Cultural Information and Authentic Materials

In comparison with the earlier editions, there is more cultural information in the third edition. The revised texts provide a broader perspective on Chinese culture, and important cultural features and topics are discussed in the "Culture Highlights." In the meantime, more up-to-date language ingredients, such as authentic linguistic materials, new realia, and new illustrations, are introduced with a view towards reflecting cultural life in the dynamic and rapidly changing contemporary China. We believe that language is a carrier of culture and a second or foreign language is acquired most efficiently in its native cultural setting. Based on that conviction, we have attempted to offer both linguistic and cultural information in a coherent, consistent manner and simulate a Chinese cultural environment in our texts, especially those that are set in China.

A New, Colorful, and User-Friendly Design

Where design and layout are concerned, the third edition represents a significant improvement over the previous editions. We have taken full advantage of colors to highlight different components of each chapter, and have brought in brand-new illustrations and photos to complement the content of the text. The book has also been thoroughly redesigned for optimal ease of use.

Updated Audio Recordings

Throughout this book, an audio CD icon appears next to the main texts and vocabulary. This symbol indicates the presence of audio recordings, which are available on the companion audio CD set and as MP3 downloads.

It is our hope that these changes will enable students to learn Chinese in a more efficient and pragmatic way. By making these changes, we have attempted to place language acquisition in a real-world context and make *IC* all the more conducive to active use of the language, not only in the classroom, but more importantly, beyond it.

Acknowledgments

During the course of preparing for the third edition, we accumulated more academic and intellectual debts than any acknowledgment can possibly repay. We wish to express our deep gratitude to all those who helped us in so many different ways. In particular, our heartfelt thanks go to Professor Zheng-sheng Zhang of San Diego State University and colleagues and friends at Beijing Language and Culture University, as well as Kristen Wanner and Laurel Damashek at Cheng & Tsui.

As authors, we take great pleasure in the contributions that *IC* has made to Chinese teaching and learning, and we also feel the weight of responsibility to constantly improve on what has been done before. In retrospect, *IC* has traversed a long way since its earliest incarnation, yet we know its improvement will not end with the present edition. We promise to renew our efforts in the future, and we expect to continue to benefit from the invaluable comments and suggestions we receive from *IC* users.

An Overview of the New Features of the Third Edition

Chapter Opener

Each lesson opens with an illustration that highlights the theme for the lesson.

Learning Objectives for every lesson help students focus their study and envision what they will have accomplished at the end of the lesson. The self-reflective questions in **Relate and Get Ready** help students analyze similarities and differences between their native language and culture and Chinese language and culture.

LEARNING OBJECTIVES

In this lesson, you will learn to use Chinese to
1. Describe the sights and sounds of a major city;
2. Describe in basic terms some features of a historic tourist site;
3. Give a simple account of the growth of a city from the past to the present;
4. Express surprise at an unforeseen turn of events.

RELATE AND GET READY

In your own culture/community—
- What major changes have you seen in your city/town over the past few years?
- Is there any local landmark that has been demolished or transformed?
- Are there many tourists visiting your city/town?
- What places have remained unchanged and retained their local charm?

Before, When, and After You Study

Before You Study

Check the statements that apply to you.
- ☐ 1. I have visited my hometown recently.
- ☐ 2. I have seen changes in my hometown in terms of traffic and development.

When You Study

Listen to the audio recording and scan the text. Ask yourself the following questions before you begin a close reading of the text.

1. How do Zhang Tianming and Lisa get to Nanjing?

New in Level 2, **Before You Study** and **When You Study** are placed before the main text, whereas **After You Study** appears at the end of the main text. The trio assists students to use various strategies when studying.

Text Design

Each text begins with two illustrations depicting the scene, with traditional text on the left page and simplified text mirrored on the right.

Language Notes, Grammar Callouts, Words & Phrases

In the text, words or expressions with corresponding **Language Notes** are clearly marked and numbered in green circles, and the notes are placed at the bottom of the page for ease of reference. The **Grammar**

學期結束了，柯林決定到北京繼續學中文，而林雪梅想在北京實習和找工作。去北京前，他們先飛到杭州雪梅家看父母，在杭州待了幾天以後，來到了北京雪梅的舅舅家。

雪梅的舅舅是律師，舅媽是大學教授。他們把時間都放在自己的事業上，不想要孩子，生活在二人世界裏❶。他們住的

LANGUAGE NOTES

❶ Some married couples in China decide not to have children, preferring instead to live in a 二人世界 (two-person world). The term 丁克族 (Dīngkèzú, the DINK tribe) is from the English "DINK" (dual income no kids) couples.

Points are highlighted and numbered in red to draw students' attention to the language forms covered in the grammar section of each lesson. Words that are explained in more details in the **Words & Phrases** section are highlighted in green for ease of reference.

Culture Highlights

Culture Highlights

Photos or other authentic materials accompany the culture notes.

❶ The Spring Festival 春節/春节

Before 1911, when the last Chinese dynasty was overthrown and China became a republic, China's new year began with the Spring Festival. The Spring Festival begins on the first day of the first month of the lunar calendar, usually in late January or early February on the solar calendar. After 1911, with the adoption of the solar calendar in China, January 1 began to mark the beginning of the new year. Chinese New Year became known as the Spring Festival. However, it remains the most important holiday in China. People still refer to the activities surrounding the Spring Festival as 過年/过年 or "celebrating the New Year."

對聯/对联 (duìlián)

Legends abound about the origin of the Spring Festival. The one most widely told has to do with a fierce beast called 年. Every New Year's Eve the beast would prowl the villages preying on domesticated animals and people, who would flee in terror. One year an old beggar came to a village. A kindhearted old lady gave some food to the beggar and told him to seek refuge in the mountains. The beggar smiled and said, "Ma'am, if you'll let me stay

Language Practice

In addition to role plays and partner activities, this section also includes contextualized drill practice with the help of visual cues, as well as exercises to practice how to build a discourse. New sentence patterns are highlighted in blue.

Language Practice

A. Happy-Go-Lucky

Li Zhe has earned enough credits for graduation and is currently waiting for word about an internship opportunity, so he has been taking it easy and relaxing these past few weeks. Based on the pictures, describe Li Zhe's daily activities by using reduplicated verbs.

EXAMPLE: Early Morning:

→ 每天早晨李哲要麼打打籃球，   每天早晨李哲要么打打篮球，
　　要麼打打太極拳。　　　　　　　要么打打太极拳。

1. Morning:

English Text

English Text

Historically, China was a society that favored men over women. Women's status in the family and in society was much lower than that of men. After 1950 the situation changed gradually. Especially in the cities, girls and boys had equal access to education and employment. Women's social status also improved substantially.

However, since the Reform and Opening-Up [started], in certain for-profit and nonprofit enterprises, the phenomenon of gender inequity has resurfaced. For example, when looking for work, women tend to have more difficulty than men. Some factories and companies haven't implemented equal pay for equal work. Of course, there are some women who have surpassed men in terms not only of work achievement but also income, but in the final analysis their number among women is still few and far between.

Nowadays, in Chinese households, in Chinese households, many couples are considerate of and attentive to each other. Therefore, within the family is perhaps where men and women are most equal in Chinese society. Take Xuemei's uncle for example—he is a big soccer fan. The only time

The English translation of each text is added for students' reference at the end of the chapter, away from the main text, so that students will not be distracted when studying the main character text.

Self-Assessment

It is important for students to feel engaged and responsible for their own learning. At the end of each lesson, students are asked to check on their learning progress and evaluate whether they have achieved the learning objectives.

SELF-ASSESSMENT

How well can you do these things? Check (✓) the boxes to evaluate your progress and see which tasks you may need to practice more.

I can	Very Well	OK	A Little
Describe a scene in which people are busily engaged in all kinds of activities	☐	☐	☐
Describe some of the features of a clean environment	☐	☐	☐
Name commonly known green energy sources	☐	☐	☐
Give examples of practices that are friendly to the environment	☐	☐	☐

Let's Review

Let's Review! (Lessons 11-15)

I. Chinese Character Crossword Puzzles

You have learned many vocabulary items in Lessons 1–15. You may have noticed that some words and phrases share the same characters. Let's see whether you can recall these characters. The common character is positioned in the center of the cluster of rings. The block arrows indicate which way you should read the words. Work with a partner and see how many association rings you can complete. Of course, you may add more rings if you can think of additional words and phrases sharing the same characters, or you may create your own clusters of rings.

EXAMPLE:

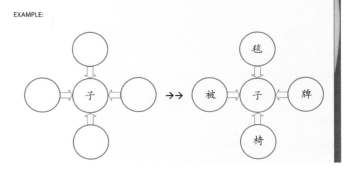

After every five lessons, there is a section to help the students review the language forms and language functions introduced.

Scope and Sequence

Lessons	Topics & Themes	Learning Objectives & Functions	Culture Highlights
11	中國的節日/ 中国的节日	1. Name the major traditional Chinese holidays and explain when they occur 2. Name the food that is most associated with each of the major traditional Chinese holidays 3. Express New Year's wishes 4. Describe the festivities during the Chinese New Year period 5. Wish others success or good health	1. The Spring Festival 2. The Lantern Festival 3. The Qingming Festival 4. The Dragon Boat Festival 5. The Mid-Autumn Festival
12	中國的變化/ 中国的变化	1. Describe the sights and sounds of a major city 2. Describe in basic terms some features of a historic tourist site 3. Give a simple account of the growth of a city from the past to the present 4. Express surprise at an unforeseen turn of events	1. High-Speed Rail in China 2. The City of Nanjing 3. Temples of Confucius
13	旅遊/旅游	1. Describe what costs may be covered in a package tour 2. Give a brief description of a Chinese sleeper car 3. Describe natural objects such as mountains, rivers, trees, and rocks 4. Discuss some things that tourists may expect to see or experience at a tourist site	1. The Stone Forest near Kunming 2. Famous Sights of Dali 3. The Old Town of Lijiang 4. Ethnic Diversity in Yunnan
14	生活與健康/ 生活与健康	1. Talk about your exercise routine 2. Outline some healthy eating habits 3. Describe habits that could make you age prematurely or harm your health	1. Housing in Beijing 2. Smoking in China 3. Morning Exercises in Chinese Cities

Forms & Accuracy	Words & Phrases
1. Adj/V + 著/着 + V 2. Reduplication of Measure Words 3. Preposition 以 4. Particle 嘛 5. (先)…再…	A. V 起來/起来 B. V 得出 (來)/V 得出 (来) (be able to tell) C. 氣氛/气氛 (atmosphere; ambiance) D. 傳統/传统 (tradition; traditional) E. 熱鬧/热闹 (lively; buzzing with excitement; bustling with activity)
1. Adverb 竟(然) 2. Particle 過/过 3. End-of-Sentence Particle 啊 4. 以 A 為/为 B 5. 一 + Reduplicated Measure Word 6. Adverb 可(是) Continued	A. 完全 (entirely; completely) B. 的確/的确 (indeed) C. 要不是 (if it were not for; but for) D. 從來/从来 (from past till present; always; at all times) E. 看來/看来 (it seems) F. 儘可能/尽可能 (as much as possible; do one's utmost)
1. Comparative Sentences 2. Numerals in Idioms 3. Multiple Attributives	A. 分別 (separately; respectively; to part from each other) B. 印象 (impression) C. 分享 (to share joy, happiness, benefit, or something pleasant or positive) D. 之前 (before; prior to) E. 只好 (have no choice but) F. 親眼, 親自, 親耳, 親手, 親身/亲眼, 亲自, 亲耳, 亲手, 亲身 G. 千萬/千万 (by all means; absolutely must) H. 不過/不过 (however; no more than)
1. Disyllabic Words Becoming Monosyllabic 2. Conjunction and Preposition 與/与 3. 有的…, 有的… 4. 使 and Pivotal Sentences	A. 顯得/显得 (to appear [to be]; to seem) B. 重視/重视 (to attach importance to; to think much of) C. 等於/等于 (to equal; to be equivalent to; to amount to) D. 只要…(就)… (only if; as long as) E. 隨便/随便 (casual; careless; to do as one pleases) F. 即使 (even if) G. 可見/可见 (it is obvious that; it can be seen that) H. 否則/否则 (otherwise)

Lessons	Topics & Themes	Learning Objectives & Functions	Culture Highlights
15	男女平等	1. Talk about how couples treat each other as equals 2. Discuss gender equality in the workplace 3. Summarize briefly the changes in Chinese women's social status in the twentieth century 4. Report the score and results of a sports game	1. China's Economic Reform 2. Traditional Preference for Boys 3. China's Women Athletes 4. Nuances of Various Gender Terms 5. Terms for Husband and Wife
Let's Review		Review Lessons 11-15	
16	環境保護與 節約能源/ 环境保护与 节约能源	1. Describe a scene in which people are busily engaged in all kinds of activities 2. Talk about indicators of a clean environment 3. List some green energy sources 4. Give examples of practices that are environmentally friendly	1. Ban on Plastic Shopping Bags 2. Green Power 3. Regulating Air-Conditioning Temperature
17	理財與投資/ 理财与投资	1. Describe if you're a saver or a spender 2. Identify ways to invest money 3. Talk about ways to purchase a big-ticket item 4. Describe your spending habits 5. Describe in basic terms the ups and downs of the stock market	1. China's High Savings Rate 2. Housing Reform 3. China's Stock Exchanges
18	中國歷史/ 中国历史	1. Name some of the most important dynasties in Chinese history 2. Describe briefly the historical significance of some major Chinese dynasties 3. Talk in basic terms about some of China's important historical figures	1. Confucius 2. *The Analects* 3. The Silk Road 4. Sun Yat-sen 5. The Revolution of 1911 6. China's Four Great Inventions 7. The Terracotta Army 8. Table of Chinese Dynasties

Forms & Accuracy	Words & Phrases
1. Pronoun 某 2. Adverb 畢竟/毕竟 3. 是…的 to Affirm a Statement 4. Complement 過來/过来	A. 逐漸/逐渐 (gradually; little by little) B. …以來/以来 (since) C. 拿…來說/拿…来说 (take…for example) D. 表現/表现 (to show; to display; to manifest; performance; manifestation) E. 看你説的/看你说的 (listen to yourself) F. 不得了 (extremely; exceedingly) G. 由 (by)
1. Chinese Character Crossword Puzzles 2. Matching Words 3. Put Your Thoughts into Words 4. Presentation 5. How Well Can You Speak?	
1. V1的V1, V2的V2 2. Adjectives That Can Be Reduplicated Like Verbs 3. …吧, …吧 4. (有益)於/(有益)于 5. Adj + 於/于 6. V著V著/V着V着	A. 想起(來)/想起(来) (to recall) vs. 想出(來)/想出(来) (to come up with) B. 環境保護/环境保护 (environmental protection) C. 可不是嗎/可不是吗 (Isn't that so? How true!) D. 造成 (to cause; to give rise to) E. 從…做起/从…做起 (to start with) F. 不堪設想/不堪设想 ([of consequences] too ghastly to contemplate; unimaginable; extremely bad or dangerous)
1. 一向 vs. 一直 2. Summary of the 把 Construction (I) 3. Reduplication of Verbs	A. 引起 (to give rise to; to lead to) B. 算(是) (to count as; to be considered as) C. 合 (to combine; to join) D. 終於/终于 (at last; in the end; finally; eventually) E. 接著/接着 (to follow; to continue) F. 突然 (sudden; unexpected)
1. 之一 2. 其中	A. 參觀/参观 (to visit; to look around) vs. 遊覽/游览 (to go sightseeing; to tour; excursion) B. 千千萬萬/千千万万 (thousands upon thousands) C. 在…基礎上/在…基础上 (on the basis of…; based on …) D. 在…方面 (in terms of; in the area of) E. 跟…有關(係)/跟…有关(系) (related to; having to do with) F. 再也沒/不 (no more; not anymore)

Lessons	Topics & Themes	Learning Objectives & Functions	Culture Highlights
19	面試/面试	1. Say one or two sentences to describe signs of nervousness 2. Explain in basic terms why China has been able to attract talent and foreign companies 3. Describe in basic terms your time management methods 4. Congratulate someone on his or her accomplishments	1. Multinational Companies in China 2. Qipao 3. Chinese Students Abroad
20	外國人在中國/ 外国人在中国	1. Welcome a visitor from afar at a welcoming party 2. Bid someone farewell at a farewell party 3. Pay homage to old-timers when joining a new community 4. Describe the ease or difficulty of adjusting to life in a different country	1. Expats in China 2. Welcome and Farewell Parties
Let's Review		Review Lessons 16-20	

Forms & Accuracy	Words & Phrases
1. Adverb 又 2. 越…, 越… 3. Conjunction 既然	A. 叫做 (to be called; to be known as) B. 好在 (fortunately; luckily) C. 善於/善于 (be good at; be adept in) D. 往往 (more often than not) vs. 常常 (often)
1. Word Order in Chinese 2. Summary of the 把 Construction (II)	A. 接受 (to accept; to take on; to undertake) B. 而已 (and no more) C. 在…下 (under) D. 你說呢？/你说呢？ (What do you say?; What do you think?)
1. Chinese Character Crossword Puzzles 2. Matching Words 3. Vocabulary Exercises 4. In Other Words 5. Put Your Thoughts into Words 6. Presentation 7. How Well Can You Speak?	

Abbreviations of Grammatical Terms

adj	Adjective
adv	Adverb
conj	Conjunction
interj	Interjection
m	Measure word
mv	Modal verb
n	Noun
nu	Numeral
ono	Onomatopoeia
p	Particle
pr	Pronoun
prefix	Prefix
prep	Preposition
pn	Proper noun
qp	Question particle
qpr	Question pronoun
t	Time word
v	Verb
vc	Verb plus complement
vo	Verb plus object

Cast of Characters

Back Row:

Xuemei's uncle and aunt

雪梅的舅舅、舅媽

雪梅的舅舅、舅妈

They are both in their mid-forties. He is a lawyer while she is a college professor. Both are very dedicated to their careers.

Mark

馬克/马克

is a European living in China. He also works as a part-time model, actor, language tutor and translator.

Zhang Tianming's older male cousin

天明的表哥

is in his early thirties and lives in Nanjing. He is very passionate about the history and traditions of his hometown.

Li Wen's parents

李文的父母

Li Wen's dad is sixty-five and her mom is sixty. Both are retired. They enjoy practicing tai chi.

Li Wen

李文

is about twenty-five and works in a museum as a guide. She is also Lisa's language partner and wants to go to graduate school.

Li Zhe

李哲

Zack Ruiz is a college friend of Zhang Tianming's. Li Zhe just graduated from college. At his brother's suggestion and with Tianming's encouragement, he is taking the opportunity to intern with a multinational company in China.

Front Row:

Lin Xuemei

林雪梅

is a graduate student from Hangzhou, China. She and Ke Lin are about four or five years older than Zhang Tianming and Lisa. Lin Xuemei and Lisa quickly became good friends. She is now back in China looking for a job.

Ke Lin

柯林

Al Collins is Lin Xuemei's boyfriend. He is also a graduate student. He is very warm and loves to help others. He is continuing his study of Chinese in Beijing.

Zhang Tianming

張天明/张天明

is an American-born Chinese. His parents immigrated to the United States from Nanjing, China. He is a sports fan and a computer whiz. He is very outgoing and has many friends, but his girlfriend thinks he spends too much time online. He is a college freshman. He and his girlfriend Lisa are spending a semester in China.

Lisha

麗莎/丽莎

Lisa Cohen is also a college freshman. She and Zhang Tianming were high school sweethearts. Lisa loves music and is interested in all things Chinese. She is also a fitness fan who especially enjoys yoga.

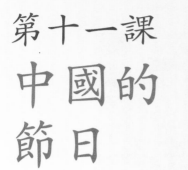

第十一课
中國的
節日

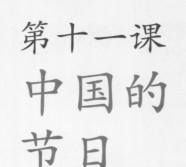

第十一课
中国的
节日

11

LEARNING OBJECTIVES

In this lesson, you will learn to use Chinese to

1. Name the major traditional Chinese holidays and explain when they occur;
2. Name the food that is most associated with each of the major traditional Chinese holidays;
3. Express New Year's wishes;
4. Describe the festivities during the Chinese New Year period;
5. Wish others success or good health.

RELATE AND GET READY

In your own culture/community—

• What are the major traditional holidays?
• How do people celebrate these holidays?
• What do people customarily eat during these holidays?
• Which holiday is associated with family reunions?

Before You Study

Check the statements that apply to you.

☐ 1. I can name the major traditional Chinese holidays.

☐ 2. I know what Chinese people customarily do to celebrate Chinese New Year.

When You Study

Listen to the audio recording and scan the text. Ask yourself the following questions before you begin a close reading of the text.

1. Why are Ke Lin and Xuemei in Beijing?

 學期結束了，柯林決定到北京繼續學中文，而林雪梅想在北京實習和找工作。去北京前，他們先飛到杭州雪梅家看父母，在杭州待了幾天以後，來到了北京雪梅的舅舅家。

雪梅的舅舅是律師，舅媽是大學教授。他們把時間都放在自己的事業上，不想要孩子，生活在二人世界裏❶。他們住的

LANGUAGE NOTES

❶ Some married couples in China decide not to have children, preferring instead to live in a 二人世界 (two-person world). The term 丁克族 (Dīngkèzú, the DINK tribe) is from the English "DINK" (dual income no kids) couples.

3. I can propose a toast in Chinese.
4. I can describe the number of rooms of my residence.

2. Where are they staying?
3. What do they do on this special night?

 学期结束了，柯林决定到北京继续学中文，而林雪梅想在北京实习和找工作。去北京前，他们先飞到杭州雪梅家看父母，在杭州待了几天以后，来到了北京雪梅的舅舅家。

雪梅的舅舅是律师，舅妈是大学教授。他们把时间都放在自己的事业上，不想要孩子，生活在二人世界里❶。他们住的小區②環境很好，房子是一套三房兩廳兩衛③的公寓，傢具都很新、很漂亮，每個房間都很乾淨，住起來很舒服。

今天是除夕，也就是春節的前一天。舅媽正在忙著①做年夜飯，舅舅在旁邊幫忙，看得出來，舅舅和舅媽的感情很好。

柯林看見牆上貼著一張不大的紅紙，紙上寫著一個漢字，他認識，那是"幸福"的"福"字，可是貼倒了。

★　★　★

柯林：	奇怪，雪梅，這個"福"字怎麼貼錯了，"福"字倒了。
雪梅：	沒貼錯。"福倒了"，"福到了"④，你想意思多好啊！
柯林：	噢，我懂了，懂了，真有意思！
舅舅：	雪梅，柯林，來、來、來，快坐下，吃飯了。
舅媽：	現在很多家庭過年過節都到餐館訂餐，又好吃、又方便。雪梅上個週末告訴我們你們要來，我本來也想在餐館訂餐，可是給幾家比較好的飯館打電話，家家②都說沒有位子了，沒辦法，只好在家裏吃了。
雪梅：	我媽媽常說舅媽菜做得好，我早就想吃舅媽做的菜了。
柯林：	在家裏吃才好呢，有家庭氣氛！
舅舅：	對，我同意你們的看法。大家都不喝酒，來，我們以③茶代酒，舉起杯來，歡迎你們來北京！
舅媽：	為你們在新的一年裏找工作順利、學習進步乾杯！
雪梅：	為舅舅、舅媽的事業成功乾杯！
柯林：	為舅舅、舅媽的身體健康乾杯！
舅舅：	看，電視上春節晚會開始了！我們一邊吃飯一邊看吧。

LANGUAGE NOTES

❷ 小區/小区 are planned and, almost always, gated urban residential developments that incorporate various convenience facilities such as grocery stores and beauty salons. Residents have to pay a maintenance fee. Upscale 小區/小区 have a clubhouse complete with a restaurant and a fitness center. 小區/小区 is 社區/社区 in Taiwan.

❸ 三房兩廳兩衛/三房兩厅兩卫 means "three bedrooms, a living room, a dining room, and two bathrooms."

小区②环境很好，房子是一套三房两厅两卫③的公寓，家具都很新、很漂亮，每个房间都很干净，住起来很舒服。

今天是除夕，也就是春节的前一天。舅妈正在忙着①做年夜饭，舅舅在旁边帮忙，看得出来，舅舅和舅妈的感情很好。

柯林看见墙上贴着一张不大的红纸，纸上写着一个汉字，他认识，那是"幸福"的"福"字，可是贴倒了。

★　★　★

柯林：　　奇怪，雪梅，这个"福"字怎么贴错了，"福"字倒了。

雪梅：　　没贴错。"福倒了"，"福到了"④，你想意思多好啊！

柯林：　　噢，我懂了，懂了，真有意思！

舅舅：　　雪梅，柯林，来、来、来，快坐下，吃饭了。

舅妈：　　现在很多家庭过年过节都到餐馆订餐，又好吃、又方便。雪梅上个周末告诉我们你们要来，我本来也想在餐馆订餐，可是给几家比较好的饭馆打电话，家家②都说没有位子了，没办法，只好在家里吃了。

雪梅：　　我妈妈常说舅妈菜做得好，我早就想吃舅妈做的菜了。

柯林：　　在家里吃才好呢，有家庭气氛！

舅舅：　　对，我同意你们的看法。大家都不喝酒，来，我们以③茶代酒，举起杯来，欢迎你们来北京！

舅妈：　　为你们在新的一年里找工作顺利、学习进步干杯！

雪梅：　　为舅舅、舅妈的事业成功干杯！

柯林：　　为舅舅、舅妈的身体健康干杯！

舅舅：　　看，电视上春节晚会开始了！我们一边吃饭一边看吧。

---

❹ 福倒了 (福 is upside down) is pronounced the same as 福到了 (福 has arrived). Many Chinese people are sensitive about words that sound similar or identical but have different meanings. For instance, the number "four" (四, sì) is often taboo because it sounds similar to 死 (sǐ) or death. That is why in some Chinese-speaking communities you may not find a fourth floor in a multi-story building. Many people like to have the number "eight" (八) in their phone and automobile license plate numbers because 八 (bā) rhymes with 發/发 (fā, to prosper; to strike a fortune). Some couples would avoid sharing a pear 梨, because to share a pear 分梨 sounds the same as 分離/分离, which means "to separate" or "to part ways."

雪梅： 柯林，現在很多很多中國家庭都像我們一樣，一邊吃年夜飯，一邊看春節晚會❺。

柯林： 是嗎？有好看的電視，又有好吃的菜，太棒了！舅媽做的清蒸魚又嫩又香，真好吃。

雪梅： 這才是地道的清蒸魚。你知道嗎？年夜飯一定要有魚，而且不能都吃了，要剩下一些。

柯林： 為什麼？那不是浪費嗎？

舅舅： 你沒聽說過嗎？"年年有魚，年年有餘"呀。"魚"跟"餘"發音一樣，"餘"有"剩下"的意思。

柯林： "年年有魚，年年有餘"，是"剩下錢"嗎？哈，中文真有意思。哎，中國還有好幾個傳統節日，吃的東西都不一樣，對吧？

舅媽： 對。農曆五月初五端午節…

柯林： 吃粽子！

舅舅： 八月十五中秋節…

柯林： 吃月餅。

雪梅： 中秋節有點像美國的感恩節，是一家人團圓的節日。還有正月十五元宵節…

柯林： 吃那個圓圓、白白的東西…

雪梅： 元宵節，吃元宵嘛④！

柯林： 對了，對了，我想起來了，元宵。

舅媽： 你們看，電視裏在倒計時了，"十、九、八、七、六、五、四、三、二、一。"十二點了，新的一年開始了！

雪梅： 舅舅、舅媽，我們給你們拜年了！

舅舅： 大家過年好！

柯林： 舅舅、舅媽過年好！恭喜發財！

舅舅： 發財、發財，大家發財。過年了，舅舅、舅媽給你們紅包。

LANGUAGE NOTES

❺ 春節晚會/春节晚会 is also colloquially known as 春晚. It is a hugely anticipated and popular five-hour long variety program aired on China's national TV broadcast station CCTV (China Central Television) on Chinese New Year's Eve.

雪梅： 柯林，现在很多很多中国家庭都像我们一样，一边吃年夜饭，一边看春节晚会❺。

柯林： 是吗？有好看的电视，又有好吃的菜，太棒了！舅妈做的清蒸鱼又嫩又香，真好吃。

雪梅： 这才是地道的清蒸鱼。你知道吗？年夜饭一定要有鱼，而且不能都吃了，要剩下一些。

柯林： 为什么？那不是浪费吗？

舅舅： 你没听说过吗？"年年有鱼，年年有余"呀。"鱼"跟"余"发音一样，"余"有"剩下"的意思。

柯林： "年年有鱼，年年有余"，是"剩下钱"吗？哈，中文真有意思。哎，中国还有好几个传统节日，吃的东西都不一样，对吧？

舅妈： 对。农历五月初五端午节…

柯林： 吃粽子！

舅舅： 八月十五中秋节…

柯林： 吃月饼。

雪梅： 中秋节有点像美国的感恩节，是一家人团圆的节日。还有正月十五元宵节…

柯林： 吃那个圆圆、白白的东西…

雪梅： 元宵节，吃元宵嘛④！

柯林： 对了，对了，我想起来了，元宵。

舅妈： 你们看，电视里在倒计时了，"十、九、八、七、六、五、四、三、二、一。"十二点了，新的一年开始了！

雪梅： 舅舅、舅妈，我们给你们拜年了！

舅舅： 大家过年好！

柯林： 舅舅、舅妈过年好！恭喜发财！

舅舅： 发财、发财，大家发财。过年了，舅舅、舅妈给你们红包。

柯林： 謝謝！謝謝！…外邊怎麼這麼熱鬧？

舅舅： 過春節要放鞭炮。我們也買了很多，咱們也出去放吧。

柯林： 雪梅，你給天明他們發個短信拜年吧。

雪梅： 好。不過，我想先給爸爸媽媽打手機拜年，再⑤給天明、麗莎發短信拜年。

柯林： 好吧。舅舅，舅媽，咱們走吧！

舅媽： 柯林，你和舅舅去吧。我去準備準備，等你們放完鞭炮回來，咱們一起吃餃子。

柯林： 什麼？還吃？

After You Study

Challenge yourself to complete the following tasks in Chinese.

1. Give a brief description of Xuemei's uncle's apartment.
2. Cite two examples of homophones mentioned in the text.

柯林：　　谢谢！谢谢！…外边怎么这么热闹？

舅舅：　　过春节要放鞭炮。我们也买了很多，咱们也出去放吧。

柯林：　　雪梅，你给天明他们发个短信拜年吧。

雪梅：　　好。不过，我想先给爸爸妈妈打手机拜年，再⑤给天明、
　　　　　丽莎发短信拜年。

柯林：　　好吧。舅舅，舅妈，咱们走吧！

舅妈：　　柯林，你和舅舅去吧。我去准备准备，等你们放完鞭炮回
　　　　　来，咱们一起吃饺子。

柯林：　　什么？还吃？

---

3. Name the special foods for different traditional Chinese holidays.

4. List the foods Xuemei and Ke Lin eat and describe the things they do on this Chinese New Year's Eve.

春节 —Spring Festival

年年有 yu

VOCABULARY

1.	節日	节日	jiérì	n	holiday; festival
2.	結束	结束	jiéshù	v	to end; to finish
3.	繼續	继续	jìxù	v	to continue; to go on with
4.	舅舅		jiùjiu	n	mother's brother; maternal uncle
5.	舅媽	舅妈	jiùmā	n	wife of mother's brother
6.	小區	小区	xiǎoqū	n	residential development; residential complex
7.	環境	环境	huánjìng	n	environment; surroundings
8.	除夕		chúxī	n	Chinese New Year's Eve
9.	年夜飯	年夜饭	niányèfàn	n	Chinese New Year's Eve dinner
10.	感情		gǎnqíng	n	feeling; emotion; affection
11.	牆	墙	qiáng	n	wall
12.	貼	贴	tiē	v	to paste; to glue
13.	幸福		xìngfú	adj/n	happy; happiness
14.	福		fú	n	blessing; good fortune
15.	倒		dào	v	to turn upside down; to go backwards
16.	奇怪		qíguài	adj	strange; odd
17.	意思		yìsi	n	meaning
18.	餐		cān	n	meal
19.	本來	本来	běnlái	adj/adv	original; originally; at first
20.	家		jiā	m	(measure word for families and commercial establishments such as restaurants, hotels, shops, companies, etc.)
21.	氣氛	气氛	qìfēn	n	atmosphere; ambiance

hóu nián Year of
扌侯关 Monkey 以茶代酒

22.	以		yǐ	prep	with [See Grammar 3.]
23.	代		dài	v	to replace; to substitute
24.	酒		jiǔ	n	alcohol; liquor
25.	舉	举	jǔ	v	to lift; to raise
26.	順利	顺利	shùnlì	adj	smooth; successful; without a hitch
27.	進步	进步	jìnbù	v/adj	to make progress; progressive
28.	乾杯	干杯	gān bēi	vo	to drink a toast; cheers!; bottoms up
29.	成功		chénggōng	v/adj	to succeed; successful
30.	晚會	晚会	wǎnhuì	n	evening gathering; soiree
31.	剩（下）		shèng (xia)	v(c)	to leave a surplus; to be left (over)
32.	浪費	浪费	làngfèi	v/adj	to waste; to squander; wasteful
33.	餘	余	yú	v	to surplus; to spare
34.	傳統	传统	chuántǒng	n/adj	tradition; traditional
35.	農曆	农历	nónglì	n	traditional Chinese lunar calendar; lit. "agricultural calendar"
36.	初		chū		first
37.	粽子		zòngzi	n	pyramid-shaped dumplings of glutinous rice wrapped in bamboo or reed leaves
38.	月餅	月饼	yuèbǐng	n	moon cake
39.	團圓	团圆	tuányuán	v	to reunite (as a family)
40.	正月		zhēngyuè	n	first month of the lunar year; first moon
41.	元宵		yuánxiāo	n	night of the fifteenth of the first lunar month; sweet dumplings made of glutinous rice flour

佶统

kǒu yīng 口音 accent

42.	嘛		ma	p	(particle used to emphasize the obvious) [See Grammar 4.]
43.	計時	计时	jì shí	vo	to count time
44.	拜年		bài nián	vo	to wish somebody a happy Chinese New Year; to pay a Chinese New Year's call
45.	恭喜		gōngxǐ	v	to congratulate
46.	發財	发财	fā cái	vo	to get rich; to make a fortune
47.	紅包	红包	hóngbāo	n	red envelope containing money to be given as a gift
48.	熱鬧	热闹	rènao	adj	(of a place or a scene) lively; buzzing with excitement; bustling with activity
49.	鞭炮		biānpào	n	firecracker

Proper Nouns

50.	春節	春节	Chūnjié	Spring Festival; Chinese New Year
51.	端午節	端午节	Duānwǔjié	Dragon Boat Festival
52.	中秋節	中秋节	Zhōngqiūjié	Mid-Autumn Festival; Moon Festival
53.	感恩節	感恩节	Gǎn'ēnjié	Thanksgiving
54.	元宵節	元宵节	Yuánxiāojié	Lantern Festival

Enlarged Characters

繼 續 舅 牆 舉 傳 農 曆 團 鞭
继 续 舅 墙 举 传 农 历 团 鞭

春节是中国的新年，有很多传统。

Culture Highlights

❶ The Spring Festival 春節/春节

Before 1911, when the last Chinese dynasty was overthrown and China became a republic, China's new year began with the Spring Festival. The Spring Festival begins on the first day of the first month of the lunar calendar, usually in late January or early February on the solar calendar. After 1911, with the adoption of the solar calendar in China, January 1 began to mark the beginning of the new year. Chinese New Year became known as the Spring Festival. However, it remains the most important holiday in China. People still refer to the activities surrounding the Spring Festival as 過年/过年 or "celebrating the New Year."

對聯/对联 (duìlián)

Legends abound about the origin of the Spring Festival. The one most widely told has to do with a fierce beast called 年. Every New Year's Eve the beast would prowl the villages preying on domesticated animals and people, who would flee in terror. One year an old beggar came to a village. A kindhearted old lady gave some food to the beggar and told him to seek refuge in the mountains. The beggar smiled and said, "Ma'am, if you'll let me stay overnight, I'll chase the beast away."

Around midnight 年 showed up at the old lady's door. The beast found it decorated with red paper and the inside brightly lit with torches. It was about to enter the house when it heard a loud explosion. Greatly startled, 年 took off as fast as it could. It turned out that 年 was mortally afraid of the color red, fire, and loud noises. Dressed in red, the beggar burst out laughing.

From then on every household would decorate its door with auspicious couplets on red paper and light firecrackers. Every family would light torches and candles and stay up for the New Year. On New Year's Day, people would visit families and friends and wish one another a happy new year. Children would receive cash gifts wrapped in red envelopes. These customs spread far and wide, making the holiday the most important in China.

In the past, the holiday season lasted from the first to the fifteenth day of the first month of the lunar calendar. Today, people have three days off. Combined with the preceding and following weekends, the holiday break can last seven to eight days. Traditionally, people sent New Year wishes by paying a brief visit in person. Nowadays it is increasingly common to send New Year wishes by cell phone.

鞭炮

紅包/红包

In northern China people eat dumplings on Chinese New Year; in southern China glutinous rice cakes are popular.

❷ The Lantern Festival 元宵節/元宵节

The Lantern Festival falls on the fifteenth day of the first month of the lunar calendar. Its origin can be traced to the Han dynasty (202 BCE–220 CE). 元宵, which literally means "first night," marks the first full moon of the lunar new year.

元宵 is also the name given to a glutinous rice dessert eaten on that day. Its filling consisting of sesame seeds, red bean paste, etc., is usually sweet. Many

元宵

花燈/花灯

streets are decorated with colorful paper lanterns, some with riddles written on them. In the evening people will go out to admire the lanterns and guess the riddles. Other festive activities include dragon and lion dances.

❸ The Qingming Festival 清明節/清明节

Traditionally, the Qingming Festival fell on the first two weeks after the vernal equinox. Today the holiday is observed around April 5. All over China people make offerings to deceased relatives. Roads to cemeteries are often clogged for miles with traffic. In rural areas, there are elaborate ceremonies of ancestor worship. The holiday is also associated with the beginning of spring. Some people go on spring excursions or fly kites.

❹ The Dragon Boat Festival 端午節/端午节

The fifth day of the fifth month of the lunar calendar (usually in late May or early June) is the Dragon Boat Festival. According to a popular legend, the holiday started as a way to commemorate the death of a famous poet, 屈原 (Qū Yuán) (ca. 340 BCE–278 BCE), who drowned himself in the Miluo River (汨羅江/汨罗江, Mìluójiāng). Every year, boat races are held all over China during the festival to commemorate the recovery of Qu Yuan's body. Often each dragon-shaped boat has a drummer to cheer the rowers on. To keep the fish away from his body, people threw 粽子, pyramid-shaped steamed dumplings wrapped in bamboo leaves, into the river. There is a wide variety of fillings in the 粽子 that people eat today, including plain sticky rice and different combinations of sticky rice with red beans, pork, salted duck eggs, and so on.

粽子

The Mid-Autumn Festival 中秋節/中秋节

The fifteenth day of the eighth month of the lunar calendar (in September or October) marks the Mid-Autumn Festival. It is a day for family reunion, which is symbolized by the full moon. The traditional holiday pastry is called the moon cake. There are many regional styles of moon cakes. They are usually baked with sweet fillings including nuts or preserved fruit, or even with salted duck egg yolks. In Suzhou and Shanghai, fresh and hot moon cakes with minced pork are also very popular.

月餅/月饼

Grammar

1. Adj/V + 著/着+ V

In this kind of structure, the second verb phrase indicates the reason for the first action or state:

❶   快放寒假了，小王正忙著準備考試。

快放寒假了，小王正忙着准备考试。

(It's almost the winter break. Little Wang's busy preparing for exams.)

[i.e., Little Wang is busy because he's preparing for his final exams.]

❷   他急著去見朋友，沒吃晚飯就走了。

他急着去见朋友，没吃晚饭就走了。

(He was in a rush to see a friend, so he left without having dinner.)

[i.e., He was in a hurry because he needed to see a friend.]

❸   妹妹哭著要我跟她玩電腦遊戲。

妹妹哭着要我跟她玩电脑游戏。

(My younger sister burst into tears asking me to play a computer game with her.)

[i.e., My younger sister cried because she wanted me to play a computer game with her.]

2. Reduplication of Measure Words

A measure word can be reduplicated to mean "without exception, all-inclusive."

❶   過年了，孩子們個個都非常高興。

过年了，孩子们个个都非常高兴。

(It's Chinese New Year, and every child is very happy.)

❷   張天明的衣服，件件都是名牌。

张天明的衣服，件件都是名牌。

(Every piece of clothing in Zhang Tianming's entire wardrobe is name brand.)

人, 年, 月, 天, etc. can also be reduplicated in this way:

❸   我們班人人都是網迷。

      我们班人人都是网迷。

      (Everyone in our class is an internet addict.)

Note that this kind of reduplication cannot occur when the measure word forms part of the object:

❹   我認識這裏的每個人。

      我认识这里的每个人。

      (I know everyone here.)

It is incorrect to say:

(4a) *我認識這裏的人人。

      *我认识这里的人人。

3. Preposition 以

以, which has its origin in Classical Chinese, is used as a preposition in modern Chinese. It has many meanings. In this lesson 以茶代酒／以茶代酒 means "to use tea to replace alcohol." 以 means "to use" or "with."

❶   他選課，只以興趣做標準，不考慮將來是不是容易找工作。

      他选课，只以兴趣做标准，不考虑将来是不是容易找工作。

      (He chooses his classes using his interests as his only criteria. He doesn't consider whether [these classes] will make it easier to find a job.)

❷   老師以自己的生活經驗教育學生。

      老师以自己的生活经验教育学生。

      (The teacher uses his life experience to teach his students.)

4. Particle 嘛

嘛 is a particle suggesting that the reasoning behind a statement is self-evident or "the way it should be."

❶   你不喜歡他，不想讓他天天來找你，就告訴他嘛。
你不喜欢他，不想让他天天来找你，就告诉他嘛。
(If you don't like him and don't want him to come looking for you every day, then why don't you just tell him?)

❷   你説這句英文不難，那你翻譯出來給我看看嘛。
你说这句英文不难，那你翻译出来给我看看嘛。
(You say that this English sentence is not difficult. Then translate it and prove it to me.)

❸   **A:**   我最不願意跟病人打交道，可是媽媽非讓我上醫學院不可。
我最不愿意跟病人打交道，可是妈妈非让我上医学院不可。
(There's nothing I dislike more than dealing with patients, but my mom insists that I go to medical school.)

    B: 你跟媽媽説清楚嘛，要是上了醫學院再想換專業，就難了。
你跟妈妈说清楚嘛，要是上了医学院再想换专业，就难了。
(Then tell your mom clearly. It'll be difficult to switch majors once you're in medical school.)

5. (先)…再…

The "(先)…再…" pattern can be translated as "(first)…then…." Like 才, 再 can link two clauses. However, unlike 才, 再 indicates that the action described in the first clause is a desired condition for the action in the second clause. In other words, the speaker would like to postpone the second action until the first action has occurred.

❶   **A:**   我們今年去雲南旅遊，怎麼樣?
我们今年去云南旅游，怎么样?
(Let's take a trip to Yunnan this year. How about it?)

B: 我今年不想去，等明年拿到碩士學位以後再去。

我今年不想去，等明年拿到硕士学位以后再去。

(I don't want to go this year. I'd like to wait until I receive my master's degree next year.)

❷   明年暑假我想先待在這兒打工賺點錢，然後再回紐約看父母。

明年暑假我想先待在这儿打工赚点钱，然后再回纽约看父母。

(Next year during the summer break I will stay here to make a bit of money by taking a part-time job, and then go back to New York to see my parents.)

❸   這個問題我們應該先好好兒討論討論再做決定。

这个问题我们应该先好好儿讨论讨论再做决定。

(We should discuss this question thoroughly before we make a decision.)

Words & Phrases

A. V 起來/起来

"V 起來/起来" can mean to look at, discuss, or comment on something from the point of view of "V." For example,

❶   這個手機用起來很方便。

这个手机用起来很方便。

(This cell phone is so convenient to use.)

[Here "convenient" is viewed in terms of "using it."]

❷   餃子吃起來好吃，做起來不太容易。

饺子吃起来好吃，做起来不太容易。

(Dumplings are delicious to eat, but not easy to make.)

[That is, in terms of taste, dumplings are delicious. However, in terms of actually making them, it's not so easy.]

❸   這把椅子搬起來很重。

这把椅子搬起来很重。

(This chair is very heavy to lift.)

potential or 不
outcome

B. V得出(來)/V得出(来) (be able to tell)

V得出(來)/V得出(来) can be used after verbs such as 看, 聽/听, 吃, 聞/闻 (wén, to smell), and 分辨 (fēnbiàn, to distinguish) to mean that one can judge or tell the nature of something through sensory experience, e.g., 看得出(來)/看得出(来) (be able to tell by looking):

❶ 林雪梅看得出(來)麗莎有心事。
林雪梅看得出(来)丽莎有心事。
(Lin Xuemei can tell that something is bothering Lisa.)
[Lin Xuemei can tell that something is bothering Lisa from her body language and expression.]

❷ 小李病得很重，可是他每天都還是很高興的樣子，大家都看不出(來)他有病。
小李病得很重，可是他每天都还是很高兴的样子，大家都看不出(来)他有病。
(Little Li is seriously ill, but he seems very happy every day. No one can tell that he's ill.

聽得出來/听得出来 (be able to tell by listening):

❸ 外邊有人叫我，(從聽聲音)我聽得出(來)是弟弟。
外边有人叫我，(从听声音)我听得出(来)是弟弟。
(Someone is calling me outside. I can tell [from the voice] that it's my younger brother.)

吃得出來/吃得出来 (be able to tell by eating/through taste):

❹ 我吃不出(來)這是南方菜還是北方菜，你吃得出(來)嗎？
我吃不出(来)这是南方菜还是北方菜，你吃得出(来)吗？
(I can't tell if this is southern or northern cooking, can you?)

C. 氣氛/气氛 (atmosphere; ambiance)

氣氛/气氛 is an abstract noun. It can be used as a subject or object:

❶   感恩節快到了，你可以感覺到節日的氣氛了。[object]
感恩节快到了，你可以感觉到节日的气氛了。
(Thanksgiving is around the corner. You can feel the holiday atmosphere.)

❷   在中國，春節的時候，你能感覺到到處都是節日的氣氛。[object]
在中国，春节的时候，你能感觉到到处都是节日的气氛。
(During Chinese New Year in China, you can feel the holiday atmosphere all around you.)

❸   今天她一走進教室就覺得氣氛不對，原來班上發生了一件大事。
[subject]
今天她一走进教室就觉得气氛不对，原来班上发生了一件大事。
(Today as soon as she walked into the classroom she sensed that there was something wrong in the air. It turned out that something major had happened to the class.)

D. 傳統/传统 (tradition; traditional)

傳統/传统 is an adjective as well as a noun.

❶   我們在中國歷史課裏學了不少中國的傳統文化。[adjective as attributive]
我们在中国历史课里学了不少中国的传统文化。
(We learned a lot about traditional Chinese culture in our Chinese history class.)

❷   他這個人很傳統，不會做這樣的事情。[adjective as predicate]
他这个人很传统，不会做这样的事情。
(He is a very traditional man. He wouldn't do such a thing.)

Other examples: 傳統方法/传统方法 (traditional method), 傳統思想/传统思想 (traditional thinking), 傳統道德/传统道德 (dàodé) (traditional morality), 傳統制度/传统制度 (zhìdù) (traditional system), etc.

❸ 這個學校有什麼傳統？ [noun]

这个学校有什么传统？

(What traditions does this school have?)

❹ 不浪費是這個家庭的好傳統。[noun]

不浪费是这个家庭的好传统。

(Being frugal is a good tradition in this family.)

E. 熱鬧/热闹 (lively; buzzing with excitement; bustling with activity)

熱鬧/热闹 is an adjective. It can be used as a predicate or attributive.

❶ 開學了，宿舍裏來了很多新同學，大家都在忙著搬家，很熱鬧。
[predicate]

开学了，宿舍里来了很多新同学，大家都在忙着搬家，很热闹。

(The semester has started. Many students have arrived at the dorm and everyone is busy moving in. There is a whirl of activity and excitement.)

❷ 我喜歡安靜，可是妹妹喜歡熱鬧。[predicate acting as the object of
喜歡/喜欢]

我喜欢安静，可是妹妹喜欢热闹。

(I like peace and quiet, but my younger sister prefers excitement and activity.)

❸ 我一到熱鬧的地方就頭疼。[attributive]

我一到热闹的地方就头疼。

(Whenever I am in a noisy and bustling place, I get a headache.)

可一可好

emphasize a dj=

倍北京
北京

Language Practice

A. Shifting Perspectives

Take turns with a partner to complete the following statements.

1. 粽子吃起來容易，
   做起來_____。

2. 這套公寓很大，住起來很舒服，
   但是整理起來很_____。

3. 毛筆字看起來很美，
   但是寫起來很_____。

1. 粽子吃起来容易，
   做起来_____。

2. 这套公寓很大，住起来很舒服，
   但是整理起来很_____。

3. 毛笔字看起来很美，
   但是写起来很_____。

B. Can You Tell?

Ask your friend to help identify the following items.

EXAMPLE:

→   你吃得出來這是什麼粽子嗎？
    你吃得出来这是什么粽子吗？

1.

2.

3.

C. Each and Every One of Them

Let's talk about Little Chang by using reduplication of measure words.

EXAMPLE:　　　　　　　今年

→ 小常的傢具件件都是新的。　　　小常的家具件件都是新的。

1.

2.

3.

D. Follow the Boss's Orders

Imagine you're a sous chef. You have a habit of confirming your work orders with your boss before you do anything.

EXAMPLE:　1. cook the rice　2. make the dumplings

→ A: 我應該先做餃子還是先做米飯？ A: 我应该先做饺子还是先做米饭？
　 B: 你應該先做餃子，再做米飯。 B: 你应该先做饺子，再做米饭。

1. 1. add sugar　　　　　2. add vinegar

→

2. 1. make hot and sour soup　2. make family-style tofu

→

3. 1. learn to make *zongzi*　2. learn to make moon cakes

→

4. 1. prepare fruit　　　　2. wash dishes

→

E. Name That Holiday

Make sure that your partner knows when the following holidays take place before filling in the table. Don't forget to include the lunar calendar in your answers if applicable.

English	Chinese	Date
1. Mother's Day	母親節/母亲节	五月第二個星期日/五月第二个星期日
2. Father's Day		
3. Thanksgiving		
4. Chinese New Year		
5. Lantern Festival		
6. Dragon Boat Festival		
7. Mid-Autumn Festival		
8. (Your Own Choice)		

F. Don't Get the Wrong Food

a. Connect with a line each of the holidays on the left with the name of the food that holiday is most associated with, and then connect the name of that food with the appropriate image on the right.

感恩節/感恩节	粽子	
春節/春节	火雞/火鸡	
元宵節/元宵节	月餅/月饼	
端午節/端午节	元宵	
中秋節/中秋节	餃子/饺子	

b. Report your answers to your partner.

G. Happy New Year to You All!

a. Work with a group of classmates and list all the Chinese New Year wishes that you can think of. See if your group can come up with more wishes than the other groups. Ask your instructor for assistance to make sure that you use 祝你 with the right wishes, and then take turns wishing others in your group a happy new year.

_____

_____

_____

_____

_____

_____

b. Using one or two wishes from the list above, prepare a Chinese New Year's card for your teacher or friend.

H. Well-Wishing

What would you say to wish someone well on the following occasions?

EXAMPLE: on Chinese New Year

→   恭喜發財!   恭喜发财!

　　or 過年好!   or 过年好!

　　or 祝你春節快樂!   or 祝你春节快乐!

1. on his or her birthday

→

2. your grandfather is celebrating his 80th birthday

→

3. your friend is wondering if he'll find a good job without too much difficulty

→

4. your classmate is going to study in China and wonders if his or her studies will go smoothly

→

5. your colleague is going to open a business and wonders if the business will be a success

→

I. When and Where to Hang Out

a. Walk around the classroom to find out what places your classmates like to go to because they are lively or quiet.

EXAMPLE:　**A:** 你喜歡去什麼地方？　　**A:** 你喜欢去什么地方？
→　　**B:** 我(不)喜歡熱鬧，所以　　**B:** 我(不)喜欢热闹，所以
　　　　我(不)愛去_____。　　　　我(不)爱去_____。

b. Then ask your classmates the following questions.

1. 這個城市什麼地方最熱鬧？　　**1.** 这个城市什么地方最热闹？

2. 你們家什麼時候最熱鬧？　　**2.** 你们家什么时候最热闹？

c. Tally everyone's answers for questions 1 and 2, and report to the instructor whose answers are the same as yours.

J. Don't Miss Out!

To ensure you won't miss out on any of the festivities during the Chinese New Year when you visit China,
a. list the activities that the Chinese do according to the time line.

除夕

1._____

2._____

3._____

4._____

正月初一

1._____

2._____

3._____

4._____

b. Based on the lists above, work with a partner to create a narrative about the Chinese New Year
festivities.

K. Writing Practice

Connect the following sentences into a paragraph incorporating the words and expressions in parentheses. Pay special attention to the use of appropriate pronouns and linking devices.

1. 除夕的晚上，雪梅和柯林在舅舅家吃年夜飯。
2. 雪梅的舅媽做了很多菜。
3. 舅媽做的菜很好吃。
4. 雪梅、柯林和舅舅、舅媽一邊吃飯一邊看春節晚會。
5. 十二點的時候，雪梅、柯林給舅舅、舅媽拜年。
6. 拜了年以後舅舅帶著柯林去外邊放鞭炮。(然後)
7. 雪梅給爸爸媽媽打電話拜年。(先)
8. 雪梅給麗莎和天明發短信拜年。(然後)
9. 這一天夜裏他們還要吃餃子。(…以後，…又…)
10. 除夕的晚上他們都很高興。

1. 除夕的晚上，雪梅和柯林在舅舅家吃年夜饭。
2. 雪梅的舅妈做了很多菜。
3. 舅妈做的菜很好吃。
4. 雪梅、柯林和舅舅、舅妈一边吃饭一边看春节晚会。
5. 十二点的时候，雪梅、柯林给舅舅、舅妈拜年。
6. 拜了年以后舅舅带着柯林去外边放鞭炮。(然后)
7. 雪梅给爸爸妈妈打电话拜年。(先)
8. 雪梅给丽莎和天明发短信拜年。(然后)
9. 这一天夜里他们还要吃饺子。(…以后，…又…)
10. 除夕的晚上他们都很高兴。

Pinyin Text

Xuéqī jiéshù le, Kē Lín juédìng dào Běijīng jìxù xué Zhōngwén, ér Lín Xuěméi xiǎng zài Běijīng shíxí hé zhǎo gōngzuò. Qù Běijīng qián, tāmen xiān fēi dào Hángzhōu Xuěméi jiā kàn fùmǔ, zài Hángzhōu dāi le jǐ tiān yǐhòu, lái dào le Běijīng Xuěméi de jiùjiu jiā.

Xuěméi de jiùjiu shì lǜshī, jiùmā shì dàxué jiàoshòu. Tāmen bǎ shíjiān dōu fàng zài zìjǐ de shìyè shang, bù xiǎng yào háizi, shēnghuó zài èr rén shìjiè li❶. Tāmen zhù de xiǎoqū❷ huánjìng hěn hǎo, fángzi shì yí tào sān fáng liǎng tīng liǎng wèi❸ de gōngyù, jiājù dōu hěn xīn, hěn piàoliang, měi ge fángjiān dōu hěn gānjìng, zhù qi lai hěn shūfu.

Jīntiān shì chúxī, yě jiù shì Chūnjié de qián yì tiān. Jiùmā zhèngzài máng zhe① zuò niányèfàn, jiùjiu zài pángbiān bāng máng, kàn de chū lái, jiùjiu hé jiùmā de gǎnqíng hěn hǎo.

Kē Lín kàn jiàn qiáng shang tiē zhe yì zhāng bú dà de hóng zhǐ, zhǐ shang xiě zhe yí ge Hànzì, tā rènshi, nà shì "xìngfú" de "fú" zì, kěshì tiē dào le.

* * *

Kē Lín: Qíguài, Xuěméi, zhè ge "fú" zì zěnme tiē cuò le, "fú" zì dào le.

Xuěméi: Méi tiē cuò. "Fú dào le", "fú dào le"❹, nǐ xiǎng yìsi duō hǎo a!

Kē Lín: Ō, wǒ dǒng le, dǒng le, zhēn yǒu yìsi!

Jiùjiu: Xuěméi, Kē Lín, lái, lái, lái, kuài zuò xia, chī fàn le.

Jiùmā: Xiànzài hěn duō jiātíng guò nián guò jié dōu dào cānguǎn dìng cān, yòu hǎochī, yòu fāngbiàn. Xuěméi shàng ge zhōumò gàosu wǒmen nǐmen yào lái, wǒ běnlái yě xiǎng zài cānguǎn dìng cān, kěshì gěi jǐ jiā bǐjiào hǎo de fànguǎn dǎ diànhuà, jiā jiā② dōu shuō méiyǒu wèizi le, méi bànfǎ, zhǐhǎo zài jiā li chī le.

Xuěméi: Wǒ māma cháng shuō jiùmā cài zuò de hǎo, wǒ zǎo jiù xiǎng chī jiùmā zuò de cài le.

Kē Lín: Zài jiā li chī cái hǎo ne, yǒu jiātíng qìfēn!

Jiùjiu: Duì, wǒ tóngyì nǐmen de kànfǎ. Dàjiā dōu bù hē jiǔ, lái, wǒmen yǐ③ chá dài jiǔ, jǔ qi bēi lai, huānyíng nǐmen lái Běijīng!

Jiùmā: Wèi nǐmen zài xīn de yì nián li zhǎo gōngzuò shùnlì, xuéxí jìnbù gān bēi!

Xuěméi: Wèi jiùjiu, jiùmā de shìyè chénggōng gān bēi!

Kē Lín: Wèi jiùjiu, jiùmā de shēntǐ jiànkāng gān bēi!

Jiùjiu: Kàn, diànshì shang Chūnjié Wǎnhuì kāishǐ le! Wǒmen yìbiān chī fàn yìbiān kàn ba.

Xuěméi: Kē Lín, xiànzài hěn duō hěn duō Zhōngguó jiātíng dōu xiàng wǒmen yíyàng, yìbiān chī niányèfàn, yìbiān kàn Chūnjié Wǎnhuì❺.

Kē Lín: Shì ma? Yǒu hǎokàn de diànshì, yòu yǒu hǎochī de cài, tài bàng le! Jiùmā zuò
            de qīngzhēngyú yòu nèn yòu xiāng, zhēn hǎochī.

Xuěméi: Zhè cái shì dìdao de qīngzhēngyú. Nǐ zhīdào ma? Niányèfàn yídìng yào yǒu
            yú, érqiě bù néng dōu chī le, yào shèng xia yì xiē.

Kē Lín: Wèishénme? Nà bú shì làngfèi ma?

Jiùjiu: Nǐ méi tīngshuō guo ma? "Nián nián yǒu yú, nián nián yǒu yú" ya. "Yú" gēn
            "yú" fāyīn yíyàng, "yú" yǒu "shèng xia" de yìsi.

Kē Lín: "Nián nián yǒu yú, nián nián yǒu yú", shì "shèng xia qián" ma? Hā, Zhōngwén
            zhēn yǒu yìsi. Āi, Zhōngguó hái yǒu hǎo jǐ ge chuántǒng jiérì, chī de dōngxi
            dōu bù yíyàng, duì ba?

Jiùmā: Duì. Nónglì wǔ yuè chū wǔ Duānwǔjié...

Kē Lín: Chī zòngzi!

Jiùjiu: Bā yuè shí wǔ Zhōngqiūjié...

Kē Lín: Chī yuèbǐng...

Xuěméi: Zhōngqiūjié yǒu diǎn xiàng Měiguó de Gǎn'ēnjié, shì yì jiā rén tuányuán de
            jiérì. Hái yǒu zhēngyuè shí wǔ Yuánxiāojié...

Kē Lín: Chī nà ge yuán yuán, bái bái de dōngxi...

Xuěméi: Yuánxiāojié, chī yuánxiāo ma④!

Kē Lín: Duì le, duì le, wǒ xiǎng qi lai le, yuánxiāo.

Jiùmā: Nǐmen kàn, diànshì li zài dào jì shí le, "shí, jiǔ, bā, qī, liù, wǔ, sì, sān, èr, yī."
            shí èr diǎn le, xīn de yì nián kāishǐ le!

Xuěméi: Jiùjiu, jiùmā, wǒmen gěi nǐmen bài nián le!

Jiùjiu: Dàjiā guò nián hǎo!

Kē Lín: Jiùjiu, jiùmā guò nián hǎo! Gōngxǐ fā cái!

Jiùjiu: Fā cái, fā cái, dàjiā fā cái. Guò nián le, jiùjiu, jiùmā gěi nǐmen hóngbāo.

Kē Lín: Xièxie! Xièxie!...Wàibian zěnme zhème rènao?

Jiùjiu: Guò Chūnjié yào fàng biānpào. Wǒmen yě mǎi le hěn duō, zánmen yě chū qu
            fàng ba.

Kē Lín: Xuěméi, nǐ gěi Tiānmíng tāmen fā ge duǎnxìn bài nián ba.

Xuěméi: Hǎo. Búguò, wǒ xiǎng xiān gěi bàba māma dǎ shǒujī bài nián, zài⑤ gěi
            Tiānmíng, Lìshā fā duǎnxìn bài nián.

Kē Lín: Hǎo ba. Jiùjiu, jiùmā, zánmen zǒu ba!

Jiùmā: Kē Lín, nǐ hé jiùjiu qù ba. Wǒ qù zhǔnbei zhǔnbei, děng nǐmen fàng wán
            biānpào huí lai, zánmen yìqǐ chī jiǎozi.

Kē Lín: Shénme? Hái chī?

English Text

The semester has ended. Ke Lin has decided to go to Beijing to continue studying Chinese while Lin Xuemei would like to intern and look for a job in Beijing. Before they go to Beijing, they fly first to Xuemei's family in Hangzhou to see [Xuemei's] parents. After staying in Hangzhou for a few days, they arrive at Xuemei's uncle's home in Beijing.

Xuemei's uncle is a lawyer, and her uncle's wife is a university professor. They devote all their time to their careers, choosing not to have children and to live instead in a "two-person world." The surroundings of their residential subdivision are very nice. Their apartment has three bedrooms, a living room and a dining room, and two bathrooms. The furniture is all new and very beautiful. Every room is very clean and very comfortable to live in.

Today is New Year's Eve—that is, the day before the Spring Festival. Xuemei's aunt is busy making New Year Eve's Dinner. Xuemei's uncle is at her side helping. It is obvious that Xuemei's uncle and aunt are very fond of each other.

Ke Lin sees a medium-sized piece of red paper pasted on the wall. On the paper is a Chinese character. He recognizes it as the 福 in the word 幸福 (fortune), but it is pasted upside down.

*   *   *

Ke Lin: How strange, Xuemei. How come this 福 character is pasted incorrectly? 福 is upside down.

Xuemei: It isn't pasted incorrectly. 福倒了 (fortune is upside down) , 福到了 (fortune has arrived). Think how great the pun is!

Ke Lin: Oh, I get it. I get it. How interesting!

Uncle: Xuemei, Ke Lin, come, come, please sit down. Time to eat.

Aunt: Nowadays many families make dinner reservations at restaurants during the Chinese New Year and other holidays. Not only is [the food] delicious but it is also convenient. Last weekend Xuemei told us that you were coming. I originally wanted to make a reservation at a restaurant, but when I called a few of the better restaurants, each and every one of them said that there were no seats left. There is nothing we can do except to eat at home.

Xuemei: My mom says Auntie cooks very well. I've wanted to eat Auntie's food for a long time.

Ke Lin: Nothing is better than eating at home. It has more of a family atmosphere.

Uncle: That's right. I agree with you. None of us drinks alcohol. Come, let's have tea instead. Let's raise our cups to welcome you to Beijing.

Aunt:	Let's wish that, in the new year, your search for work goes smoothly without a hitch and that you make [a lot of] progress academically. Bottoms up!
Xuemei:	Let's drink to Uncle and Aunt's success at work.
Ke Lin:	To Uncle and Aunt's health.
Uncle:	Look, the Spring Festival Evening Show has started on TV. Let's eat and watch.
Xuemei:	Ke Lin, right now many, many Chinese families are like us, having New Year's Eve dinner and watching the Spring Festival Evening Show.
Ke Lin:	Is that so? There's good TV to watch and delicious food to eat. Couldn't be any better! Auntie's steamed fish is both tender and tasty. It's simply delicious.
Xuemei:	That's [what I call] authentic steamed fish. Did you know? You've got to have fish for the New Year's Eve dinner, *and* you can't eat all of it. You have to leave some of it uneaten.
Ke Lin:	Why? Isn't that wasteful?
Uncle:	Haven't you heard? "When you have fish every year, you'll have a surplus every year." "Fish" and "surplus" are pronounced the same. "Surplus" means "excess left over from what is needed."
Ke Lin:	"When you have fish every year, you'll have a surplus every year." Does that mean "having money left over?" Chinese is really interesting. Oh, China has quite a few other traditional holidays. The food associated with them is all different, right?
Aunt:	That's right. On the fifth day of the fifth month of the lunar year during the Dragon Boat Festival...
Ke Lin:	People eat pyramid-shaped dumplings in bamboo leaves.
Uncle:	On the fifteenth day of the eighth month of the lunar calendar during the Mid-Autumn Festival...
Ke Lin:	People eat moon cakes.
Xuemei:	The Mid-Autumn Festival is a bit like America's Thanksgiving. It is a holiday for family reunion. There is also the Lantern Festival on the fifteenth day of the first month on the lunar calendar when...
Ke Lin:	People eat those round, white things...
Xuemei:	During the Lantern Festival (元宵節/元宵节) you eat dumplings of the same name (元宵).
Ke Lin:	Right, right. I remember now—元宵.
Aunt:	Look, the countdown has started on TV, "Ten, nine, eight, seven, six, five, four, three, two, one." Twelve o'clock. The new year has started!
Xuemei:	Uncle, Auntie, we wish you a Happy New Year!

Uncle:　　Everybody, "Happy New Year!"

Ke Lin:　　Uncle, aunt, Happy New Year! Best wishes for a prosperous new year!

Uncle:　　A prosperous new year for everyone. It's New Year. Uncle and Auntie have some red envelopes for you.

Ke Lin:　　Thanks, thank you very much. … How come it's so lively outside?

Uncle:　　Setting off firecrackers to celebrate the New Year is a must. We've also bought many [firecrackers]. Let's go out and set them off.

Ke Lin:　　Xuemei, why don't you send Tianming [and Lisa] a New Year text message?

Xuemei:　　OK, I'd like to first call Mom and Dad on my cell phone to wish them a happy Chinese New Year and then send Tianming and Lisa a New Year text message.

Ke Lin:　　OK. Uncle and Auntie, let's go.

Aunt:　　Ke Lin, you and Uncle go. I'll make some preparation. When you are back from lighting the firecrackers, we'll eat dumplings together.

Ke Lin:　　What, more food?

SELF-ASSESSMENT

How well can you do these things? Check (✔) the boxes to evaluate your progress and see which tasks you may need to practice more.

I can	Very Well	OK	A Little
Name the major traditional Chinese holidays and the dates on which they occur	☐	☐	☐
Name the foods associated with traditional Chinese holidays	☐	☐	☐
Express New Year wishes	☐	☐	☐
Describe some of the festivities during the Chinese New Year period	☐	☐	☐
Wish another person success or good health	☐	☐	☐

第十二課
中國的
變化

第十二課
中国的
变化

 LEARNING OBJECTIVES

In this lesson, you will learn to use Chinese to

1. Describe the sights and sounds of a major city;

2. Describe in basic terms some features of a historic tourist site;

3. Give a simple account of the growth of a city from the past to the present;

4. Express surprise at an unforeseen turn of events.

RELATE AND GET READY

In your own culture/community—

• What major changes have you seen in your city/town over the past few years?

• Is there any local landmark that has been demolished or transformed?

• Are there many tourists visiting your city/town?

• What places have remained unchanged and retained their local charm?

Before You Study

Check the statements that apply to you.

☐ 1. I have visited my hometown recently.

☐ 2. I have seen changes in my hometown in terms of traffic and development.

When You Study

Listen to the audio recording and scan the text. Ask yourself the following questions before you begin a close reading of the text.

1. How do Zhang Tianming and Lisa get to Nanjing?

張天明和麗莎上個學期末申請到中國學中文，原來以為時間會來不及，沒想到學校竟①很快就同意了。兩個人可以在中國學習、生活三、四個月，這讓他們非常高興。

張天明和麗莎先到上海，然後坐高速火車去南京。火車很快，兩個小時就到了。天明的表哥開車去火車站接他們。他們就住在姑媽家。

來中國前，天明的爸爸要他們一定去南京看看他以前的中學，拍幾張照片發給他。於是到南京的第二天，一吃過②早飯，

☐ 3. I have visited a tourist site that is famous for its historic architecture.
☐ 4. I enjoy sampling local snacks when I visit a new place.

2. What does Tianming's father ask Tianming to do in Nanjing?
3. What surprises Tianming when he first strolls down the streets of Nanjing?
4. What worries Lisa when she takes in Nanjing's sights?

　张天明和丽莎上个学期末申请到中国学中文，原来以为时间会来不及，没想到学校竟①很快就同意了。两个人可以在中国学习、生活三、四个月，这让他们非常高兴。

　　张天明和丽莎先到上海，然后坐高速火车去南京。火车很快，两个小时就到了。天明的表哥开车去火车站接他们。他们就住在姑妈家。

　　来中国前，天明的爸爸要他们一定去南京看看他以前的中学，拍几张照片发给他。于是到南京的第二天，一吃过②早饭，表哥就帶他們去找那個中學。沒想到那兒已經變成❶了一個購物中心，完全不是爸爸説的那個樣子了。表哥問了好幾個人，誰也説不清楚那個中學搬到哪兒去了。天明想，爸爸總説自己是南京人，可是實際上他熟悉的那個南京已經沒有了，今天的南京對他來説其實是一個完全陌生的地方。

　　雖然沒找到爸爸的中學，但表哥很高興地説願意當導遊，帶他們繼續在街上走走，讓他們好好看看南京。

★　★　★

張天明：	爸爸常常説南京是個很安靜的城市，沒想到這麼熱鬧！你看到處都是新蓋的高樓，大街上擠滿了汽車。
表哥：	這些年南京的變化的確很大，我以前騎自行車上班，現在也開起車來了。
麗莎：	這跟我以前想像的中國完全不一樣。在上海的時候，要不是到處都是中文，我還以為是在美國呢。
張天明：	我爸爸説，他小時候在南京很少看到外國人，可是現在，你看到處都有外國遊客啊③！
麗莎：	咱們不也是兩個"老外"嗎？哈哈！你看馬路對面，美國快餐店，日本銀行，法國服裝店…
張天明：	中國的大門打開了，中國融入世界了，這是件好事。
麗莎：	可是我擔心，這樣下去❷，有中國特色的東西會不會越來越少呢？
表哥：	不會的。南京還是保留了很多有中國特色的東西。比如説建築，南京最有中國特色的是夫子廟，那兒還有吃的、喝的、玩兒的…
張天明：	那咱們現在就去夫子廟，嚐嚐南京小吃❸吧。

LANGUAGE NOTES

❶ 變/变 is a transitive verb: 水變顏色了/水变颜色了 (The water has changed its color.) It's often followed by the complement 成: 那個中學變成了一個購物中心/那个中学变成了一个购物中心 (That middle school turned into a shopping center.) 變化/变化 is an intransitive verb and is used on its own as a predicate: 天氣變化得很快/天气变化得很快. (The change in weather was very abrupt.)

表哥就带他们去找那个中学。没想到那儿已经变成❶了一个购物中心，完全不是爸爸说的那个样子了。表哥问了好几个人，谁也说不清楚那个中学搬到哪儿去了。天明想，爸爸总说自己是南京人，可是实际上他熟悉的那个南京已经没有了，今天的南京对他来说其实是一个完全陌生的地方。

虽然没找到爸爸的中学，但表哥很高兴地说愿意当导游，带他们继续在街上走走，让他们好好看看南京。

★　★　★

张天明：	爸爸常常说南京是个很安静的城市，没想到这么热闹！你看到处都是新盖的高楼，大街上挤满了汽车。
表哥：	这些年南京的变化的确很大，我以前骑自行车上班，现在也开起车来了。
丽莎：	这跟我以前想像的中国完全不一样。在上海的时候，要不是到处都是中文，我还以为是在美国呢。
张天明：	我爸爸说，他小时候在南京很少看到外国人，可是现在，你看到处都有外国游客啊③！
丽莎：	咱们不也是两个"老外"吗？哈哈！你看马路对面，美国快餐店，日本银行，法国服装店…
张天明：	中国的大门打开了，中国融入世界了，这是件好事。
丽莎：	可是我担心，这样下去❷，有中国特色的东西会不会越来越少呢？
表哥：	不会的。南京还是保留了很多有中国特色的东西。比如说建筑，南京最有中国特色的是夫子庙，那儿还有吃的、喝的、玩儿的…
张天明：	那咱们现在就去夫子庙，尝尝南京小吃③吧。

變化/变化 can also be a noun acting as a subject or an object: 天氣有變化/天气有变化 (There has been a change in the weather).

❷ As you may recall, 下去 after a verb suggests continuation. 這樣下去/这样下去 means "if it goes on like this."

❸ 小吃, literally "small eats," is what the Chinese call quick, light informal food such as 粽子, 元宵 and 油條/油条 (Chinese crullers). There is an endless variety from region to region.

表哥：	好啊！不管中國怎麼變，南京怎麼變，肚子餓了要吃沒變。你們聽説過 "民以食為天" ❹④ 這句話吧？
麗莎：	啊❺？什麼？從來沒聽説過。
張天明：	這句話的意思，簡單地説就是，"吃" 是老百姓生活中最重要的事兒。
麗莎：	好像挺有道理的。哎，天明，你看，那是什麼地方？人那麼多，旁邊好像還賣吃的、玩兒的，五顏六色，真好看，真熱鬧！
表哥：	那就是夫子廟啊。
麗莎：	看來，南京人真的是想儘可能保留老南京的特色，老南京的傳統啊。
張天明：	南京一邊是一棟棟高樓大廈，一邊是一座座⑤傳統建築，站在這兒，我好像聽到了一種聲音。
麗莎：	什麼聲音？
張天明：	歷史的腳步聲。晚上我給爸爸發一個電子郵件，告訴他中學已經找不到了，再把今天拍的照片發給他看看，不知道他看了會高興還是會難過。
表哥：	哎，我也聽到了一種聲音。
麗莎、張天明：	什麼聲音？
表哥：	肚子咕嚕咕嚕叫的聲音。走了這麼多路，你們好像不累不餓，我這個導遊可⑥又渴又餓了。別忘了，"民以食為天" 啊！走，吃飯去！

After You Study

Challenge yourself to complete the following tasks in Chinese.

1. Explain why Tianming can't fulfill his father's request.
2. Give three examples of Nanjing's transformation.

LANGUAGE NOTES

❹ 民以食為天/民以食为天 is the second half of a famous saying from a Han dynasty (202 BCE–220 CE) text: 王者以民為天, 而民以食為天/王者以民为天, 而民以食为天 (Those who rule regard the people [to be as important] as the sky; the people regard food [to be as important] as the sky.) 以 here means 把.

表哥：	好啊！不管中国怎么变，南京怎么变，肚子饿了要吃没变。你们听说过"民以食为天"❹④这句话吧？
丽莎：	啊❺？什么？从来没听说过。
张天明：	这句话的意思，简单地说就是，"吃"是老百姓生活中最重要的事儿。
丽莎：	好像挺有道理的。哎，天明，你看，那是什么地方？人那么多，旁边好像还卖吃的、玩儿的，五颜六色，真好看，真热闹！
表哥：	那就是夫子庙啊。
丽莎：	看来，南京人真的是想尽可能保留老南京的特色，老南京的传统啊。
张天明：	南京一边是一栋栋高楼大厦，一边是一座座⑤传统建筑，站在这儿，我好像听到了一种声音。
丽莎：	什么声音？
张天明：	历史的脚步声。晚上我给爸爸发一个电子邮件，告诉他中学已经找不到了，再把今天拍的照片发给他看看，不知道他看了会高兴还是会难过。
表哥：	哎，我也听到了一种声音。
丽莎、张天明：	什么声音？
表哥：	肚子咕噜咕噜叫的声音。走了这么多路，你们好像不累不饿，我这个导游可⑥又渴又饿了。别忘了，"民以食为天"啊！走，吃饭去！

3. Recap what the characters see and plan to do near the Temple of Confucius.

❺啊, on its own in the second tone, is an interjection indicating surprise, often used to make a further inquiry.

變化很大

VOCABULARY

1.	變化	变化	biànhuà	n/v	change; to change
2.	末		mò	n	end
3.	來不及		lái bu jí	vc	not have enough time to do something; too late to do something
4.	竟(然)		jìng(rán)	adv	unexpectedly; contrary to one's expectation [See Grammar 1.]
5.	表哥		biǎogē	n	older male cousin of a different surname
6.	站		zhàn	n/v	station; stop; to stand
7.	姑媽	姑妈	gūmā	n	father's sister
8.	拍		pāi	v	to take pictures; to shoot film; to clap; to pat
9.	變	变	biàn	v	to change
10.	總	总	zǒng	adv	always
11.	熟悉		shúxi	v/adj	to know something or someone well; to be familiar with; familiar
12.	陌生		mòshēng	adj	unfamiliar; strange; unknown
13.	街		jiē	n	street
14.	蓋	盖	gài	v	to build; to construct
15.	的確	的确	díquè	adv	indeed
16.	騎	骑	qí	v	to ride
17.	自行車	自行车	zìxíngchē	n	bicycle
18.	上班		shàng bān	vo	to go to work; to start work; to be on duty

19.	想像		xiǎngxiàng	v/n	to imagine; to visualize; imagination
20.	要不是		yàobúshì	conj	if it were not for; but for
21.	遊客	游客	yóukè	n	tourist
22.	老外		lǎowài	n	foreigner
23.	對面	对面	duìmiàn	n	opposite side
24.	快餐		kuàicān	n	fast food; quick meal
25.	服裝	服装	fúzhuāng	n	clothing; apparel
26.	融入		róngrù	v	to merge into; to meld into
27.	特色		tèsè	n	distinguishing feature or quality; characteristic
28.	保留		bǎoliú	v	to remain as before; to retain
29.	建築	建筑	jiànzhù	n/v	architecture; to build
30.	嚐	尝	cháng	v	to taste
31.	小吃		xiǎochī	n	small and inexpensive dishes; snacks
32.	不管		bùguǎn	conj	no matter; regardless of
33.	民以食為天 民以食为天		mín yǐ shí wéi tiān		the people think of food as important as heaven
34.	啊		á	interj	eh? what? [See Language Note 5.]
35.	從來	从来	cónglái	adv	from past till present; always; at all times
36.	老百姓		lǎobǎixìng	n	common folk; (ordinary) people
37.	儘可能	尽可能	jǐn kěnéng		as much as possible
38.	廈	厦	shà		mansion; tall building
39.	座		zuò	m	(measure word for buildings and mountains)
40.	聲音	声音	shēngyīn	n	sound; voice

保留

jǐ shì

41.	腳步	脚步	jiǎobù	n	footstep
42.	難過	难过	nánguò	adj	sad; hard to bear
43.	咕嚕	咕噜	gūlū	ono	rumbling sound

Proper Nouns

| 44. | 法國 | 法国 | Fǎguó | | France |
| 45. | 夫子廟 | 夫子庙 | Fūzǐmiào | | Temple of Confucius |

到处 everywhere
處 dù

Enlarged Characters

變 熟 蓋 確 裝 融 築 嚐 儘 嚕 廟
变 熟 盖 确 装 融 筑 尝 尽 噜 庙

這些是北京小吃，不是南京小吃。
这些是北京小吃，不是南京小吃。

Culture Highlights

❶ High-speed railways have come of age in China. CRH (China Railway High-Speed) was launched in 2007. CRH1, CRH2, and CRH5 are capable of traveling at 200 kilometers (120 miles) per hour. The fastest CRH3 trains run between Beijing and Tianjin at 350 kilometers (about 219 miles) per hour, cutting down the travel time between the two cities to twenty-six minutes. By comparison, Acela Express, Amtrak's fastest train, can only reach 240 kilometers per hour or about 150 miles per hour. Railroad construction is a high priority for the Chinese government, which plans to build the world's largest high-speed rail network by 2020.

❷ Nanjing straddles the Yangtze River, although the historical core lies on the south bank. It was the capital of six ancient dynasties. From 1927 to 1949, Nanjing served again as the capital of the Republic of China before the Nationalist government was overthrown. Today Nanjing is the capital of Jiangsu province and a popular tourist city. Some of the important historic sites in Nanjing include remains of the city wall, which total some twenty-four miles, the Temple of Confucius area along the Qinhuai River, the Sun Yat-sen Mausoleum, and examples of Republican architecture.

中山陵 (Zhōngshānlíng, Sun Yat-sen Mausoleum)

❸ Temples dedicated to Confucius were common in many Chinese towns. The most important ancient Chinese educator and philosopher 孔子 (Kǒngzǐ) (551–479 BCE) was colloquially known as 孔夫子 (Kǒngfūzǐ); hence his Latinized name Confucius in European languages. Confucian temples are called 孔廟/孔庙 (Kǒngmiào), 夫子廟/夫子庙 (Fūzǐmiào) or 文廟/文庙 (Wénmiào, literary temple). Aspiring scholars in imperial China would visit the temples and pray for success at the all-important imperial civil service examinations. Even today one might find high school seniors seeking good luck at the temples for their college-entrance examinations.

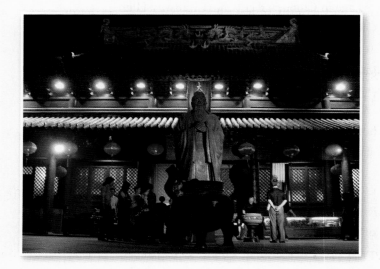

南京夫子廟(一)
南京夫子庙(一)

南京夫子廟(二)
南京夫子庙(二)

夫子廟旁的秦淮河(Qínhuáihé)
夫子庙旁的秦淮河(Qínhuáihé)

Grammar

1. Adverb 竟（然）

竟 is an adverb often occurring in formal Chinese. It suggests that something is unexpected from the speaker's point of view. For example,

❶ 早上天氣還非常好，沒想到中午竟下起大雨來。

早上天气还非常好，没想到中午竟下起大雨来。

(The weather was still beautiful this morning. Unexpectedly, it started to rain heavily around noon.)

❷ 昨天回到我熟悉的家鄉，竟找不到自己的家了。家鄉的變化太大了!

昨天回到我熟悉的家乡，竟找不到自己的家了。家乡的变化太大了!

(Yesterday I returned to my hometown, which I knew so well. Who'd have thought that I wouldn't be able to find my own home? My hometown has changed so much!)

❸ 我晚上要做功課，電腦竟不見了。

我晚上要做功课，电脑竟不见了。

(I had to do homework last night, but to my surprise the computer had disappeared.)

竟然 is interchangeable with, but more formal than 竟.

2. Particle 過/过

One usage of 過/过 is as a complement indicating completion.

❶ **A:** 老師叫你去辦公室找他，你快去吧。

老师叫你去办公室找他，你快去吧。

(The teacher asked you to go see him in his office. You'd better go quickly.)

B: 我去過了。

我去过了。

(I've already gone [there].)

❷ **A:** 你看看這本雜誌吧，很有意思。

你看看这本杂志吧，很有意思。

(Take a look at this magazine. It's really interesting.)

B: 什麼雜誌？噢，這本，我看過了，的確不錯。

什么杂志？噢，这本，我看过了，的确不错。

(Which magazine? Oh, this one. I've already read it. Indeed, it's quite good.)

❸ 別急，我洗過澡就走。

別急，我洗过澡就走。

(What's the big rush? I'll leave as soon as I take a shower.)

This usage of 過/过 is similar to the dynamic particle 了. However, there are also several differences. When 過/过 is used as a complement, the verb before it (e.g., 去, 看, in ❶ and ❷) must refer to a known action. Actions that are expected in certain given circumstances are considered known information and can also be used with 過/过 in this way, as in ❸.

As a complement, 過/过 must be used with 了 when occurring at the end of a sentence, as in ❶ and ❷. However, if there is an object, 了 can be omitted, as in ❸.

過/过 as a complement is interchangeable with 了, as seen in (**3a**). If there's 了 after 過/过, 過/过 can be omitted without changing the meaning, as seen in (**1a**) and (**2a**).

(1a) A: 老師叫你去辦公室找他，你快去吧。

老师叫你去办公室找他，你快去吧。

(The teacher asked you to go see him. You'd better go quickly.)

B: 我去了。

(I've already seen him.)

(2a) A: 你看看這本雜誌吧，很有意思。

你看看这本杂志吧，很有意思。

(Take a look at this magazine. It's really interesting.)

B: 什麼雜誌？噢，這本，我看了，是不錯。

什么杂志？噢，这本，我看了，是不错。

(Which magazine? Oh, this one. I've already read it. It is quite good.)

(3a)   別急，我洗了澡就走。

(What's the big rush? I'll leave as soon as I take a shower.)

過/过 as a complement is different from 過/过 as a dynamic particle:

First, they have different meanings. As a complement, 過/过 signifies completion. As a dynamic particle, 過/过 indicates experience.

Second, 過/过 as a complement can be used with 了; 過/过 as a dynamic particle cannot.

3. End-of-Sentence Particle 啊

A Chinese sentence can end in a particle expressing emotion. This is especially characteristic of spoken Chinese. The emotions conveyed by these particles are quite complex. In this chapter, there are several examples of end-of-sentence particle 啊 in neutral tone.

A. At the end of an exclamatory sentence:

❶   看來，南京人真的是想儘可能保留老南京的特色，老南京的傳統啊。

看来，南京人真的是想尽可能保留老南京的特色，老南京的传统啊。

(It seems that people in Nanjing do really want to preserve as much as possible the character and traditions of old Nanjing.)

This is an exclamatory sentence. Exclamatory sentences express the feeling of the speaker and often use 啊 to heighten the effect. More examples:

❷   雨下得多大呀！

(Wow, it's really pouring.)

❸   你的字寫得多好哇 (wa)！

你的字写得多好哇 (wa)！

(What great handwriting you have!)

❹   這裏的青菜好新鮮哪 (na)！

这里的青菜好新鲜哪 (na)！

(The vegetables are really fresh here!)

❺ 你聽，鞭炮多響啊！

你听，鞭炮多响啊！

(Listen, the firecrackers are really loud!)

The pronunciation of 啊 can be influenced by the preceding syllable. For instance, after "-i," "-a," and "-o" 啊 becomes 呀 (ya); see example ❷. After "-ao" it changes to 哇 (wa) as in ❸. After "n" it changes to 哪 (na) as in ❹. After "-ng" it is pronounced "ŋ" as in ❺.

B. At the end of a declarative sentence to explain or remind, e.g.,

❻ 可是現在，你看到處都有外國遊客啊！

可是现在，你看到处都有外国游客啊！

(But now, you see foreign tourists everywhere!)

❼ 那就是夫子廟啊。

那就是夫子庙啊。

(That *is* the Temple of Confucius.)

❽ 別忘了，"民以食為天"啊！

别忘了，"民以食为天"啊！

(Don't forget, "To ordinary people food is as important as the sky.")

C. At the end of a question:

One kind of yes-or-no question expresses request for confirmation because of the speaker's skepticism or surprise. 啊 serves to moderate the tone of voice.

❾ 明天你給我們上課啊？

明天你给我们上课啊？

(Tomorrow *you* are going to teach us?) [Indicating surprise.]

❿ 小馬不去哈爾濱哪？

小马不去哈尔滨哪？

(Little Ma *isn't* going to Harbin?) [The speaker thought otherwise.]

⓫ 你說的是這本書啊？

你说的是这本书啊？

(You were talking about *this* book?) [The speaker thought it was another one.]

啊 can also soften a definite question:

⑫　誰呀？

誰呀？

(Who is it?)

⑬　咱們什麼時候走啊？

咱们什么时候走啊？

(When are we leaving?)

⑭　你怎麼不説話呀？

你怎么不说话呀？

(How come you aren't saying anything?)

In alternative questions to soften the tone of voice:

⑮　咱們是看電影還是聽音樂呀？

咱们是看电影还是听音乐呀？

(Are we going to watch a movie or listen to music?)

⑯　你到底來不來呀？

你到底来不来呀？

(Are you coming?)

⑰　快説，你同意不同意呀？

快说，你同意不同意呀？

(Say it, do you agree?)

D. 啊 can tone down an imperative sentence:

⑱　小心點兒啊，別看錯了！

小心点儿啊，别看错了！

(Be careful, won't you, look carefully so that you don't make any mistakes!)

⑲　注意(zhùyì)啊，比賽馬上開始了！

注意(zhùyì)啊，比赛马上开始了！

(Pay attention, will you? The competition is about to begin!)

⑳　我只是開個玩笑，別急呀！

我只是开个玩笑，别急呀！

(I was just joking. Don't get upset now.)

㉑　明天你可早點來啊！

明天你可早点来啊！

(Tomorrow [don't forget to] come early.)

E. Sometimes 啊 can convey urgency:

㉒　大家都等着聽你的意見，你怎麼不說話，說呀！

大家都等着听你的意见，你怎么不说话，说呀！

(Everyone is waiting to hear your opinion. How come you're not talking? Say something!)

---

4. 以 A 為/为 B

"以 A 為/为 B" means to "regard or treat A as B." It is a written usage.

❶　民以食為天。（老百姓把吃飯當作天大的事。）

民以食为天。（老百姓把吃饭当作天大的事。）

(The people think of food as important as heaven.)

❷　這位老師以校為家。(這位老師把學校當作自己家一樣。)

　　这位老师以校为家。(这位老师把学校当作自己家一样。)

(This teacher views the school as his home.)

❸　我姐姐以幫助別人為自己最大的快樂。(姐姐把幫助別人當作自己最大的快樂。)

　　我姐姐以帮助别人为自己最大的快乐。(姐姐把帮助别人当作自己最大的快乐。)

(My older sister regards helping others as her greatest joy.)

5. 一 + Reduplicated Measure Word

"一 + reduplicated measure word" describes a large grouping of identical or similar, yet distinctly individual objects. For example,

❶　桌子上擺著一盤盤水果，一瓶瓶可樂。

　　桌子上摆着一盘盘水果，一瓶瓶可乐。

(On the table there is plate after plate of fruit and bottle after bottle of cola.)

❷　我家門前有一座座高山，風景特別漂亮。

　　我家门前有一座座高山，风景特别漂亮。

(In front of my house there are mountains upon mountains. The landscape is really pretty.)

This kind of construction differs from 很多 in terms of both meaning and usage. If the speaker's focus is on describing quantity alone, as in ❸ and ❹, then this kind of construction would not be appropriate, as shown in (3a) and (4a):

❸　書架上有很多書。

　　书架上有很多书。

(On the bookshelf are many books.)

(3a) 書架上有一本本書。

　　　书架上有一本本书。

❹ 教室裏坐著很多學生。

教室里坐着很多学生。

(Many students are sitting in the classroom.)

(4a) 教室裏坐著一個個學生。

教室里坐着一个个学生。

6. Adverb 可(是) Continued

The adverb 可(是) can mean "indeed," "very true" in a conversation to affirm or emphasize a fact. 是 can be left out. This usage typically occurs in spoken Chinese.

❶ 你出生的地方已經變成了一個大城市，這可是沒錯的。

你出生的地方已经变成了一个大城市，这可是没错的。

(Your birthplace has been transformed into a big city. There's no mistake.)

❷ **A:** 你說張天明的表哥是外國人？

你说张天明的表哥是外国人？

(Did you say that Zhang Tianming's cousin is a foreigner?)

B: 我可沒那麼說，他怎麼可能是外國人呢！

我可没那么说，他怎么可能是外国人呢！

(Not I, I never said that. How could he possibly be a foreigner?)

❸ 那個景點太遠，走路可走不到。咱們還是打車吧！

那个景点太远，走路可走不到，咱们还是打车吧！

(That scenic spot is too far away. We can't walk there. Let's take a cab.)

在旅遊景點新蓋的古式建築
在旅游景点新盖的古式建筑

Words & Phrases

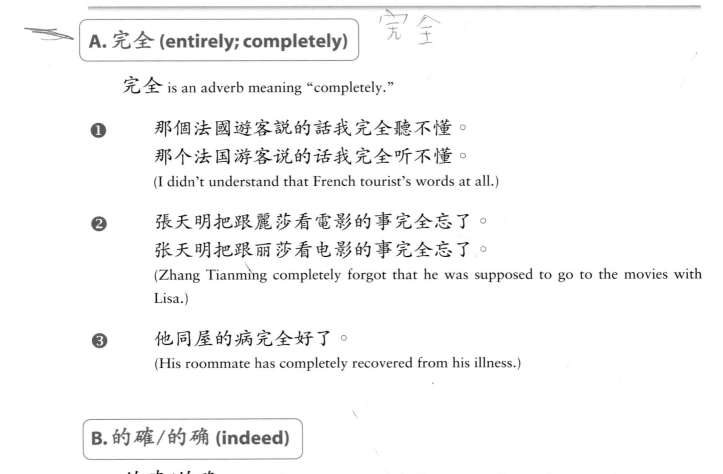

A. 完全 (entirely; completely)

完全

完全 is an adverb meaning "completely."

❶ 那個法國遊客說的話我完全聽不懂。

那个法国游客说的话我完全听不懂。

(I didn't understand that French tourist's words at all.)

❷ 張天明把跟麗莎看電影的事完全忘了。

张天明把跟丽莎看电影的事完全忘了。

(Zhang Tianming completely forgot that he was supposed to go to the movies with Lisa.)

❸ 他同屋的病完全好了。

(His roommate has completely recovered from his illness.)

B. 的確/的确 (indeed)

的確/的确 is an adverb meaning "completely true" used to confirm a previous statement or fact:

❶ **A:** 你真的不知道小張在哪兒嗎？

你真的不知道小张在哪儿吗？

(You really don't know where Little Zhang is?)

B: 我的確不知道，如果知道還會不告訴你嗎？

我的确不知道，如果知道还会不告诉你吗？

(I truly don't know. If I did, wouldn't I tell you?)

❷ **A:** 中國的春節真熱鬧。

中国的春节真热闹。

(The Spring Festival in China is really lively.)

B: 不錯，的確熱鬧，特別是除夕晚上。

不错，的确热闹，特别是除夕晚上。

(You're right. It is indeed very lively, especially the night before the festival.)

❸ **A:** 她真的給你道歉了？

她真的给你道歉了？

(Did she really apologize to you?)

B: 她的確給我道歉了，態度特別好。

她的确给我道歉了，态度特别好。

(She did indeed apologize to me, and she was very sincere.)

C. 要不是 (if it were not for; but for)

要不是 is spoken Chinese meaning "if it weren't for."

❶ 要不是麗莎叫天明跟她去看電影，天明根本不進電影院。

要不是丽莎叫天明跟她去看电影，天明根本不进电影院。

(If Lisa hadn't asked Tianming to go to the movies with her, he would have never stepped into a movie theater.)

❷ 要不是看到報紙上的新聞，大家都不知道那棟大廈已經蓋好了。

要不是看到报纸上的新闻，大家都不知道那栋大厦已经盖好了。

(If we hadn't seen that news story in the paper, no one would have known that that building had been finished.)

❸ 要不是有獎學金和政府貸款，他恐怕拿不到碩士學位。

要不是有奖学金和政府贷款，他恐怕拿不到硕士学位。

(If it hadn't been for his scholarship and government loan, he probably wouldn't have been able to get his master's degree.)

D. 從來/从来 (from past till present; always; at all times)

從來/从来 is an adverb. It's often followed by a word of negation such as 不 or 没.

1   我的外國朋友從來没過過端午節，也從來没吃過粽子。
　　　我的外国朋友从来没过过端午节，也从来没吃过粽子。
(My foreign friends have never celebrated the Dragon Boat Festival and never eaten any *zongzi*.)

2   小王上課從來不遲到，老師們都很喜歡他。
　　　小王上课从来不迟到，老师们都很喜欢他。
(Little Wang is never late for class. The teachers all like him very much.)

3   林太太買衣服從來不在乎牌子。
　　　林太太买衣服从来不在乎牌子。
(Mrs. Lin never cares about brand names when she shops for clothes.)

Sometimes 從來/从来 can be used in an affirmative sense.

4   **A:**　没想到你的房間這麼乾淨。
　　　　没想到你的房间这么干净。
(I didn't think that your room would be this clean!)

　　　B:　我的房間從來就很乾淨。
　　　　我的房间从来就很干净。
(My room is always very clean.)

你從來没看見過這種車吧？
你从来没看见过这种车吧？

看来

E. 看來／看来 (it seems)

看來／看来, meaning "it seems" or "it appears," introduces a conclusion or opinion based on a previously stated fact or previously described situation:

❶ 你心情這麼好，看來一定有什麼好事。

你心情这么好，看来一定有什么好事。

(You're in such a good mood. There must be a really good reason.)

❷ 聽你剛才那麼説，看來你兒子暑假的活動你都已經安排好了。

听你刚才那么说，看来你儿子暑假的活动你都已经安排好了。

(From what you just said, it seems you have made all the arrangements for your son's summer activities.)

❸ 我還得學五門課，看來這個學期畢不了業了。

我还得学五门课，看来这个学期毕不了业了。

(I have to take five more classes. It doesn't seem possible that I'll be able to graduate [at the end of] this semester.)

F. 儘可能／尽可能 (as much as possible; do one's utmost)

❶ 別着急，我們會儘可能幫你找到鑰匙。

别着急，我们会尽可能帮你找到钥匙。

(Don't worry. We'll do our best to help you find your keys.)

❷ 張天明認為旅行的時候儘可能要少帶東西，可是麗莎喜歡帶很多東西。

张天明认为旅行的时候尽可能要少带东西，可是丽莎喜欢带很多东西。

(Zhang Tianming thinks that when you travel you should pack as lightly as possible. However, Lisa likes to pack many things.)

❸ 你明天儘可能早點來學校，別又遲到。要不然老師會生氣。

你明天尽可能早点来学校，别又迟到。要不然老师会生气。

(Come to school tomorrow as early as you can. Don't be late again, or the teacher will be angry.)

這樣的傳統建築保留得多不多？
这样的传统建筑保留得多不多？

Language Practice

A. This Is Totally Unexpected!

Use 竟(然) to express your surprise when confronted with something unexpected:

EXAMPLE:

→　五月竟然下雪。

1.

2.

3.

4.

B. I Try My Best!

Suppose you are leaving home for college and you want to alleviate your parents' concerns about your lifestyle on campus by pledging to do more or less of the following.

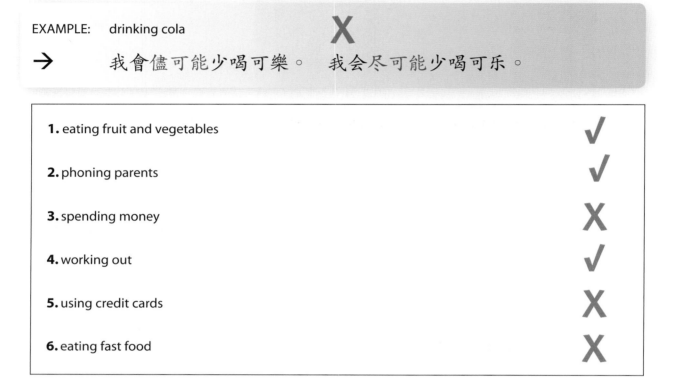

EXAMPLE: drinking cola   X

→   我會儘可能少喝可樂。   我会尽可能少喝可乐。

1. eating fruit and vegetables   ✓

2. phoning parents   ✓

3. spending money   X

4. working out   ✓

5. using credit cards   X

6. eating fast food   X

這兒賣什麼?
这儿卖什么?

這兒賣什麼地方的小吃?
这儿卖什么地方的小吃?

C. Little Sis

Suppose you have a little sister just starting college. Based on each of the scenarios below, express your concern about your sister's life on campus by using 擔心/担心.

EXAMPLE:　Her dorm is noisy.

→　　她的宿舍很吵，我擔心她　　她的宿舍很吵，我担心她
　　　晚上睡不好覺。　　　　　晚上睡不好觉。

1. She is a vegetarian, but most of the food at the cafeteria has meat in it.

2. She is a late riser, but her first class this semester starts at 8:00 a.m.

3. She is majoring in a subject that won't make her very competitive on the job market.

4. She has not called or text-messaged for two weeks.

5. She planned to study in China over winter break, but submitted her application a bit too late.

D. What Do You See?

a. Working with a partner, list in Chinese the things you might see in a busy downtown area.

1._____

2._____

3._____

4._____

5._____

b. Then, based on the list, describe city life to someone in a rural area.

E. A Memorable Place

What is the most memorable city or town that you have ever visited? What was it like? Recap what you heard (or didn't hear) and what you saw (or didn't see) during your visit there.

1._____

2._____

3._____

4._____

5._____

F. Taking a Stroll Down Memory Lane

a. Share with a partner the changes that your hometown has gone through in the past few years.

1._____

2._____

3._____

4._____

b. Explain the reasons why you like or dislike these changes.

G. Visiting A Popular Tourist Destination

a. What would you expect of a popular historic tourist site in China? Don't forget to mention the sights, the sounds, and the food.

1.＿＿＿

2.＿＿＿

3.＿＿＿

4.＿＿＿

5.＿＿＿

b. Tell a partner if you know of or have visited such a historic tourist site.

c. Talk about the location of a tourist site of your choice and the best time of the year to visit it.

H. Writing Practice

Below are some sentences and phrases that describe the changes in Nanjing based on the text of the current chapter. Connect them to form a paragraph. One way to organize the sentences is to use 第一, 第二, 第三···. Don't forget to introduce the paragraph with a general statement.

1. 張天明爸爸的中學搬家了，那兒變成了購物中心	1. 张天明爸爸的中学搬家了，那儿变成了购物中心
2. 新蓋了很多高樓大廈	2. 新盖了很多高楼大厦
3. 南京過去很安靜，現在街上人多，車多，很熱鬧	3. 南京过去很安静，现在街上人多，车多，很热闹
4. 街上有一些外國商店、銀行	4. 街上有一些外国商店、银行
5. 街上有很多外國遊客	5. 街上有很多外国游客

Pinyin Text

Zhāng Tiānmíng hé Lìshā shàng ge xuéqī mò shēnqǐng dào Zhōngguó xué Zhōngwén, yuánlái yǐwéi shíjiān huì lái bu jí, méi xiǎng dào xuéxiào jìng① hěn kuài jiù tóngyì le. Liǎng ge rén kěyǐ zài Zhōngguó xuéxí, shēnghuó sān, sì ge yuè, zhè ràng tāmen fēicháng gāoxìng.

Zhāng Tiānmíng hé Lìshā xiān dào Shànghǎi, ránhòu zuò gāosù huǒchē qù Nánjīng. Huǒchē hěn kuài, liǎng ge xiǎoshí jiù dào le. Tiānmíng de biǎogē kāi chē qù huǒchē zhàn jiē tāmen. Tāmen jiù zhù zài gūmā jiā.

Lái Zhōngguó qián, Tiānmíng de bàba yào tāmen yídìng qù Nánjīng kàn kan tā yǐqián de zhōngxué, pāi jǐ zhāng zhàopiàn fā gěi tā. Yúshì dào Nánjīng de dì èr tiān, yì chī guo② zǎofàn, biǎogē jiù dài tāmen qù zhǎo nà ge zhōngxué. Méi xiǎng dào nàr yǐjīng biàn chéng❶ le yí ge gòuwù zhōngxīn, wánquán bú shì bàba shuō de nà ge yàngzi le. Biǎogē wèn le hǎo jǐ ge rén, shéi yě shuō bù qīngchu nà ge zhōngxué bān dào nǎr qù le. Tiānmíng xiǎng, bàba zǒng shuō zìjǐ shì Nánjīng rén, kěshì shíjìshang tā shúxi de nà ge Nánjīng yǐjīng méiyǒu le, jīntiān de Nánjīng duì tā lái shuō qíshí shì yí ge wánquán mòshēng de dìfang.

Suīrán méi zhǎo dào bàba de zhōngxué, dàn biǎogē hěn gāoxìng de shuō yuànyì dāng dǎoyóu, dài tāmen jìxù zài jiē shang zǒu zou, ràng tāmen hǎo hāo kàn kan Nánjīng.

* * *

Zhāng Tiānmíng:	Bàba chángcháng shuō Nánjīng shì ge hěn ānjìng de chéngshì, méi xiǎng dào zhème rènao! Nǐ kàn dàochù dōu shì xīn gài de gāo lóu, dà jiē shang jǐ mǎn le qìchē.
Biǎogē:	Zhè xiē nián Nánjīng de biànhuà díquè hěn dà, wǒ yǐqián qí zìxíngchē shàng bān, xiànzài yě kāi qi chē lai le.
Lìshā:	Zhè gēn wǒ yǐqián xiǎngxiàng de Zhōngguó wánquán bù yíyàng. Zài Shànghǎi de shíhou, yàobúshì dàochù dōu shì Zhōngwén, wǒ hái yǐwéi shì zài Měiguó ne.
Zhāng Tiānmíng:	Wǒ bàba shuō, tā xiǎo shíhou zài Nánjīng hěn shǎo kàn dào wàiguó rén, kěshì xiànzài, nǐ kàn dàochù dōu yǒu wàiguó yóukè a③!
Lìshā:	Zánmen bù yě shì liǎng ge "lǎowài" ma? Hā hā! Nǐ kàn mǎlù duìmiàn, Měiguó kuàicān diàn, Rìběn yínháng, Fǎguó fúzhuāng diàn.

Zhāng Tiānmíng:	Zhōngguó de dà mén dǎ kāi le, Zhōngguó róngrù shìjiè le, zhè shì jiàn hǎo shì.
Lìshā:	Kěshì wǒ dānxīn, zhèyàng xia qu❷, yǒu Zhōngguó tèsè de dōngxi huì bú huì yuè lái yuè shǎo ne?
Biǎogē:	Bú huì de. Nánjīng hái shì bǎoliú le hěn duō yǒu Zhōngguó tèsè de dōngxi. Bǐrú shuō jiànzhù, Nánjīng zuì yǒu Zhōngguó tèsè de shì Fūzǐmiào, nàr hái yǒu chī de, hē de, wánr de…
Zhāng Tiānmíng:	Nà zánmen xiànzài jiù qù Fūzǐmiào, cháng chang Nánjīng xiǎochī❸ ba.
Biǎogē:	Hǎo a! Bùguǎn Zhōngguó zěnme biàn, Nánjīng zěnme biàn, dùzi è le yào chī méi biàn. Nǐmen tīngshuō guo "mín yǐ shí wéi tiān"❹④ zhè jù huà ba?
Lìshā:	Á❺? Shénme? Cónglái méi tīngshuō guo.
Zhāng Tiānmíng:	Zhè jù huà de yìsi, jiǎndān de shuō jiù shì, "chī" shì lǎobǎixìng shēnghuó zhōng zuì zhòngyào de shìr.
Lìshā:	Hǎoxiàng tǐng yǒu dàoli de. Āi, Tiānmíng, nǐ kàn, nà shì shénme dìfang? Rén nàme duō, pángbiān hǎoxiàng hái mài chī de, wánr de, wǔ yán liù sè, zhēn hǎokàn, zhēn rènao!
Biǎogē:	Nà jiù shì Fūzǐmiào a.
Lìshā:	Kàn lai, Nánjīng rén zhēn de shì xiǎng jǐn kěnéng bǎoliú lǎo Nánjīng de tèsè, lǎo Nánjīng de chuántǒng a.
Zhāng Tiānmíng:	Nánjīng yìbiān shì yí dòng dòng gāo lóu dà shà, yìbiān shì yí zuò zuò⑤ chuántǒng jiànzhù, zhàn zài zhèr, wǒ hǎoxiàng tīng dào le yì zhǒng shēngyīn.
Lìshā:	Shénme shēngyīn?
Zhāng Tiānmíng:	Lìshǐ de jiǎobù shēng. Wǎnshang wǒ gěi bàba fā yí ge diànzǐ yóujiàn, gàosu tā zhōngxué yǐjīng zhǎo bú dào le, zài bǎ jīntiān pāi de zhàopiàn fā gěi tā kàn kan, bù zhīdào tā kàn le huì gāoxìng háishi huì nánguò.
Biǎogē:	Āi, wǒ yě tīng dào le yì zhǒng shēngyīn.
Lìshā, Zhāng Tiānmíng:	Shénme shēngyīn?
Biǎogē:	Dùzi gūlū gūlū jiào de shēngyīn. Zǒu le zhème duō lù, nǐmen hǎoxiàng bú lèi bú è, wǒ zhè ge dǎoyóu kě❻ yòu kě yòu è le. Bié wàng le, "mín yǐ shí wéi tiān" a! Zǒu, chī fàn qù!

English Text

At the end of last semester Zhang Tianming and Lisa applied to go to China to study Chinese. They had originally thought that it might be too late. To their surprise, the school very quickly agreed. The two of them could study and live in China for three or four months. This made them very happy.

Zhang Tianming and Lisa arrived in Shanghai first, and then took a high-speed train to Nanjing. The train was very fast, reaching their destination in only two hours. Tianming's cousin drove to the train station to pick them up. They would stay with Tianming's aunt.

Before their trip to China, Tianming's dad wanted them to make sure to go to Nanjing to see his former middle school, take some photographs, and send them to him. So the day after they arrived in Nanjing, as soon as they finished breakfast Tianming's cousin took them to look for that middle school. They never imagined that place had been turned into a shopping center. It didn't look anything like what Tianming's father talked about. Tianming's cousin asked more than a few people, but none could say clearly where the middle school had moved. Tianming thought his dad always said that he was from Nanjing, but in reality the Nanjing that he was familiar with had already disappeared. The Nanjing of today would actually be a totally strange place to him.

Although they didn't find his dad's middle school, Tianming's cousin happily said that he'd be willing to act as a tour guide and keep on taking them around on the streets so that they could get a good look at Nanjing.

*   *   *

Zhang Tianming:	My dad often says that Nanjing is a very quiet city, so I never imagined it would be so lively! Look, there are new tall buildings everywhere, and the streets are crowded with cars.
Cousin:	Over the last few years the changes in Nanjing have indeed been great. I used to bike to work. Now I've started driving, too.
Lisa:	This is completely different from the China of my imagination. When we were in Shanghai, if it hadn't been for the Chinese characters everywhere, I'd have thought that I was in America.
Zhang Tianming:	My dad says that when he was little Nanjing saw very few foreigners, but now you see foreign tourists everywhere.
Lisa:	Aren't we two foreigners, too? Haha! You see on the other side of the street, American fast food, a Japanese bank, a French clothing store…

Zhang Tianming:	China's gate has been opened. China has melded into the world. This is a good thing.
Lisa:	But I worry that if it continues like this there will be fewer and fewer distinctly Chinese things.
Cousin:	That won't happen. Nanjing has preserved many things with a distinct Chinese character. Take architecture, for example—what is most distinctly Chinese in Nanjing is the Temple of Confucius. There are also food and drinks and amusements there....
Zhang Tianming:	Then let's go to the Temple of Confucius and try Nanjing's local snacks.
Cousin:	No problem! No matter how much China changes, no matter how much Nanjing changes, when you are hungry, you've got to eat. That hasn't changed. You have heard the saying, "To mortals nothing matters as much as food," right?
Lisa:	Huh? What? Never heard of it.
Zhang Tianming:	The meaning of this saying, to put it simply, is that the most important thing in ordinary people's lives is food.
Lisa:	That seems to make sense. Tianming, look, what place is that? There are so many people there. Nearby there is food and entertainment. It's so colorful. Really beautiful and lively!
Cousin:	That's the Temple of Confucius.
Lisa:	It seems that people in Nanjing really want to preserve old Nanjing's character and tradition as much as possible.
Zhang Tianming:	Nanjing has on the one hand row after row of tall buildings, and on the other row upon row of traditional buildings. Standing here, I seem to hear a sound.
Lisa:	What sound?
Zhang Tianming:	The footsteps of history. Tonight I'll send my dad an email message. I'll tell him that his middle school is nowhere to be found. I'll also send him the pictures that I took today for him to look at. I don't know if he'll feel happy or sad after he sees those.
Cousin:	I've also heard a sound.
Lisa and Zhang Tianming:	What sound?
Cousin:	The rumbling sound of my stomach. We've walked such a long way, but you don't seem tired or hungry. I, as your tour guide, am both thirsty and hungry. Don't forget, "To ordinary people nothing matters as much as food." Let's go and eat!

SELF-ASSESSMENT

How well can you do these things? Check (✓) the boxes to evaluate your progress and see which tasks you may need to practice more.

I can	Very Well	OK	A Little
Describe some of the sights and sounds of a city	☐	☐	☐
Describe some basic features of a historic tourist site	☐	☐	☐
Describe briefly a city's development over time	☐	☐	☐
Express surprise at an unforeseen turn of events	☐	☐	☐

第十三课　　第十三课

旅遊　　旅游

LEARNING OBJECTIVES

In this lesson, you will learn to use Chinese to

1. Describe what costs may be covered in a package tour;
2. Give a brief description of a Chinese sleeper car;
3. Describe natural objects such as mountains, rivers, trees, and rocks;
4. Discuss some things that tourists may expect to see or experience at a tourist site.

RELATE AND GET READY

In your own culture/community—

• Do tourists prefer to travel by airplane, car, bus, or train?
• Do many people like to keep a journal when they travel and post it on their blogs?
• Do people prefer to plan their own travel itinerary or join a tour group?
• What kinds of hotel accommodations are there? How do they vary?

Before You Study

Check the statements that apply to you.

☐ 1. I like to travel by train.

☐ 2. I have traveled on a sleeping car.

When You Study

Listen to the audio recording and scan the text. Ask yourself the following questions before you begin a close reading of the text.

1. Where do Tianming, Lisa, Ke Lin, and Xuemei meet up with one another?

新學期開始前，張天明、麗莎和柯林、雪梅一起去雲南旅遊。他們約好星期五晚上分別從南京和北京出發，星期天在昆明見面。從星期一開始，他們在雲南旅遊了一個星期。

中國的火車、導遊和雲南美麗的風景，都給天明留下很深的印象。

張天明每天寫博客，讓朋友們分享自己的快樂。

☐ 3. I have visited an ethnic minority region.

☐ 4. I like to purchase souvenirs when I travel.

☐ 5. I have stayed at a bed-and-breakfast.

2. Overall, what do Tianming and Lisa like about their train ride? What do they dislike?

3. Do they think their tour guide has done a good job?

4. Do Tianming and Ke Lin enjoy souvenir shopping?

 新学期开始前，张天明、丽莎和柯林、雪梅一起去云南旅游。他们约好星期五晚上分别从南京和北京出发，星期天在昆明见面。从星期一开始，他们在云南旅游了一个星期。

中国的火车、导游和云南美丽的风景，都给天明留下很深的印象。

张天明每天写博客，让朋友们分享自己的快乐。

- 去雲南之前，我們在網上報名參加了一個旅行團。團費包括^❶交通、旅館、三餐、和景點門票。

- 我們是坐火車去的雲南，為了能跟別的旅客練習說中文，我們買了硬臥^❷票，因為硬臥車廂每個“房間”都沒有門，容易找人聊天兒。我在上鋪，上鋪比下鋪和中鋪安靜一點，晚上可以睡個好覺。床上有毯子和枕頭，很乾淨。

硬臥/硬卧

- 我也去軟臥車廂看了看。那裏每個小房間裏有兩個上鋪，兩個下鋪，床比較軟也比較大，房間的門可以關上。我們沒有買軟臥票，還因為怕別人睡覺打呼嚕。你想想，在這麼小的房間裏，關上門，如果有人不停地打呼嚕，你還能睡得著覺^❸嗎？

- 這是餐車。我們在餐車上吃了一頓飯，那裏的飯，我覺得又貴又難吃，不如^①買盒飯^❹或者方便麵^❺。

餐車/餐车

- 我和麗莎在昆明下車後，等了兩個多小時，雪梅和柯林他們的火車才到。我們一見面，大家就高興地擁抱起來，雖然才分別幾天，可是好像好久不見了。我們一起走出火車站，看到導遊正舉著牌子找我們，牌子上寫的是我們四個人的名字。我們的導遊說話很幽默，常逗得大家哈哈大笑。不過有時^❻他說的話我們三個人都聽不懂，雪梅只好給我們當翻譯。

LANGUAGE NOTES

❶ 包括 can also be pronounced "bāoguā" in Taiwan.

❷ 臥/卧 here is short for 臥鋪/卧铺 (sleeping bunk).

❸ 睡得着覺/睡得着觉 (shuì de zháo jiào) means "be able to fall asleep."

- 去云南之前，我们在网上报名参加了一个旅行团。团费包括❶交通、旅馆、三餐、和景点门票。

- 我们是坐火车去的云南，为了能跟别的旅客练习说中文，我们买了硬卧❷票，因为硬卧车厢每个"房间"都没有门，容易找人聊天儿。我在上铺，上铺比下铺和中铺安静一点，晚上可以睡个好觉。床上有毯子和枕头，很干净。

軟臥/软卧

- 我也去软卧车厢看了看。那里每个小房间里有两个上铺，两个下铺，床比较软也比较大，房间的门可以关上。我们没有买软卧票，还因为怕别人睡觉打呼噜。你想想，在这么小的房间里，关上门，如果有人不停地打呼噜，你还能睡得着觉❸吗？

- 这是餐车。我们在餐车上吃了一顿饭，那里的饭，我觉得又贵又难吃，不如①买盒饭❹或者方便面❺。

- 我和丽莎在昆明下车后，等了两个多小时，雪梅和柯林他们的火车才到。我们一见面，大家就高兴地拥抱起来，虽然才分别几天，可是好像好久不见了。我们一起走出火车站，看到导游正举着牌子找我们，

昆明火車站/昆明火车站

牌子上写的是我们四个人的名字。我们的导游说话很幽默，常逗得大家哈哈大笑。不过有时❻他说的话我们三个人都听不懂，雪梅只好给我们当翻译。

---

❹ In Taiwan, instead of 盒飯/盒饭 the corresponding word is 便當/便当 (biàndāng), which is Japanese in origin.

❺ Instant noodles, 方便麵/方便面, literally means "convenient noodles." In Taiwan the corresponding word is 泡麵/泡面 (pàomiàn, soaked noodles).

❻ 有時/有时 is short for and slightly more literary than 有(的)時候/有(的)时候 (sometimes).

- 導遊介紹説雲南是一個省，在中國的西南部，省會是昆明。雲南自然風景很美，有山有水，這裏住著很多少數民族。來雲南旅遊，可以親眼看看不同民族的建築、服裝、飲食，了解各個民族的風俗習慣。

- 第一天我們遊覽了石林。這是一張石林的照片。石林有很多顏色很深的石頭，遠看就像樹林一樣。石頭的樣子千奇百怪②。我們在石林裏一邊走，一邊聽導遊講那些石頭的故事，非常有意思。石林給我們留下了很深的印象。

石林

- 這是大理三塔，建築很古老，很有名。大理城裏有很多賣紀念品的商店，導遊把我們帶到那兒，希望大家多買東西。雪梅和麗莎很高興，買了不少紀念品，而我跟柯林受不了，就抱怨説太浪費時間了。下次你們到中國旅遊找旅行團，一定要先問清楚，千萬別找有"購物"的團。你們可以自助遊❼，那樣就自由多了。

大理三塔/大理三塔

- 第三天，到了有名的麗江古城❽，我們非常喜歡這裏。這個古城不大，從東邊走到西邊不過一兩個小時。最特別的是有一條非常乾淨的小河③從城中間流過。小河兩邊有很多商店、茶館、小飯館。那天晚上，我們在一個很有雲南特色的茶館裏喝茶，看著外邊的小河，門旁的紅燈籠，還有來來往往的遊客，都不想回旅館去睡覺了。

LANGUAGE NOTES

❼ 自助遊/自助游 is literally "self-assisted travel." 自 is short for 自己 (self), while 助 is short for 幫助/帮助 (help). The term 自由行, short for 自由旅行, is now also very common.

- 导游介绍说云南是一个省，在中国的西南部，省会是昆明。云南自然风景很美，有山有水，这里住着很多少数民族。来云南旅游，可以亲眼看看不同民族的建筑、服装、饮食，了解各个民族的风俗习惯。

- 第一天我们游览了石林。这是一张石林的照片。石林有很多颜色很深的石头，远看就像树林一样。石头的样子千奇百怪②。我们在石林里一边走，一边听导游讲那些石头的故事，非常有意思。石林给我们留下了很深的印象。

石林

- 这是大理三塔，建筑很古老，很有名。大理城里有很多卖纪念品的商店，导游把我们带到那儿，希望大家多买东西。雪梅和丽莎很高兴，买了不少纪念品，而我跟柯林受不了，就抱怨说太浪费时间了。下次你们到中国旅游找旅行团，一定要先问清楚，千万别找有"购物"的团。你们可以自助游⑦，那样就自由多了。

大理三塔/大理三塔

- 第三天，到了有名的丽江古城⑧，我们非常喜欢这里。这个古城不大，从东边走到西边不过一两个小时。最特别的是有一条非常干净的小河③从城中间流过。小河两边有很多商店、茶馆、小饭馆。那天晚上，我们在一个很有云南特色的茶馆里喝茶，看着外边的小河，门旁的红灯笼，还有来来往往的游客，都不想回旅馆去睡觉了。

---

⑧ 古 in 古城 is short for 古老, and 城 is short for 城市.

- 在麗江，我們住了兩天家庭旅館。房間雖然很小，但是很乾淨，也能上網。房東還給我們做了些家常菜，辣辣的，味道很不錯。

- 雲南各個地方的風景不一樣，還有很多好玩的地方。我們明天要去遊覽大雪山。我過幾天會把拍好的照片放在博客上。

家庭旅館/家庭旅馆

After You Study

Challenge yourself to complete the following tasks in Chinese.

1. List the pros and cons of traveling in a sleeper car.

2. List the places that Tianming, Lisa, Xuemei, and Ke Lin visited and the distinguishing features of those places.

- 在丽江，我们住了两天家庭旅馆。房间虽然很小，但是很干净，也能上网。房东还给我们做了些家常菜，辣辣的，味道很不错。

麗江古城/丽江古城

- 云南各个地方的风景不一样，还有很多好玩的地方。我们明天要去游览大雪山。我过几天会把拍好的照片放在博客上。

雪山

3. Summarize the tour guide's introduction to Yunnan.
4. List the place that they are going to visit next.

VOCABULARY

1.	分別		fēnbié	adv/v	separately; respectively; to part from each other
2.	出發	出发	chūfā	v	to set out; to depart
3.	美麗	美丽	měilì	adj	beautiful
4.	留(下)		liú (xia)	v(c)	to leave behind; to stay behind
5.	深		shēn	adj	profound; deep; dark (color); intimate (of relations or feelings)
6.	分享		fēnxiǎng	v	to share (joy, happiness, benefit, etc.)
7.	之		zhī	p	(literary counterpart of 的)
8.	報名	报名	bào míng	vo	to sign up; to register
9.	參加	参加	cānjiā	v	to participate; to take part; to attend
10.	團	团	tuán	n	group; organization
11.	包括		bāokuò	v	to include; to consist of
12.	交通		jiāotōng	n	transportation; traffic
13.	門票	门票	ménpiào	n	admission ticket; admission fee
14.	旅客		lǚkè	n	passenger; voyager; traveler
15.	硬		yìng	adj	hard
16.	臥鋪	卧铺	wòpù	n	sleeping berth or bunk on a train
17.	車廂	车厢	chēxiāng	n	railway carriage
18.	枕頭	枕头	zhěntou	n	pillow
19.	軟	软	ruǎn	adj	soft
20.	關	关	guān	v	to close; to turn off
21.	打呼嚕	打呼噜	dǎ hūlu	vo	to snore

22.	頓	顿	dùn	m	(measure word for meals)
23.	盒飯	盒饭	héfàn	n	box lunch
24.	麵	面	miàn	n	noodles
25.	擁抱	拥抱	yōngbào	v	to embrace; to hug
26.	幽默		yōumò	adj	humorous
27.	逗		dòu	v/adj	to tease; to play with; amusing
28.	省會	省会	shěnghuì	n	provincial capital
29.	美		měi	adj	beautiful; good
30.	親眼	亲眼	qīnyǎn	adv	(to see) with one's own eyes
31.	飲食	饮食	yǐnshí	n	diet; food and drink
32.	風俗	风俗	fēngsú	n	custom
33.	習慣	习惯	xíguàn	n/v	habit; to be accustomed to
34.	遊覽	游览	yóulǎn	v/n	to go sightseeing; to tour; excursion
35.	石頭	石头	shítou	n	stone; rock; pebble
36.	樹林	树林	shùlín	n	woods; forest
37.	講	讲	jiǎng	v	to speak; to tell
38.	故事		gùshi	n	story; tale
39.	塔	塔	tǎ	n	tower; pagoda-shaped structure
40.	古老		gǔlǎo	adj	ancient; old
41.	紀念品	纪念品	jìniànpǐn	n	souvenir; keepsake; memento
42.	千萬	千万	qiānwàn	adv	by all means; absolutely must
43.	河		hé	n	river
44.	茶館	茶馆	cháguǎn	n	teahouse
45.	燈籠	灯笼	dēnglong	n	lantern

| 46. | 來往 | 来往 | lái wǎng | v | to come and go; to have dealings with |
| 47. | 房東 | 房东 | fángdōng | n | landlord or landlady |

Proper Nouns

48.	昆明		Kūnmíng		Kunming (capital of Yunnan Province)
49.	石林		Shílín		The Stone Forest
50.	大理		Dàlǐ		Dali
51.	麗江	丽江	Lìjiāng		Lijiang

Enlarged Characters

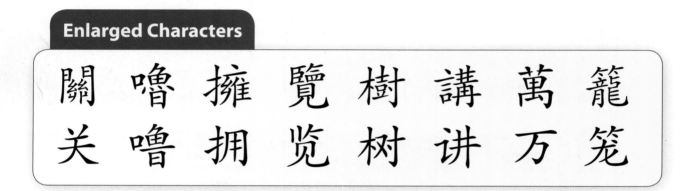

關 嚕 擁 覽 樹 講 萬 籠
关 噜 拥 览 树 讲 万 笼

Culture Highlights

1 石林, the Stone Forest, lies about 53 miles south of Kunming, the capital of Yunnan Province. Part of South China's karst topography, the Stone Forest is a UNESCO Natural World Heritage Site. It is one of the most photographed scenic sights in Yunnan, covering an area of about 160 square miles. The name 石林 derives from the forest-like rock formations in the geological park. The core of the scenic area consists of a group of fantastically shaped rocks. Because of their unusual forms, many of these rocks have become associated with popular legends and have been given fanciful names.

2 Dali is the capital of Dali Bai Autonomous Prefecture in central Yunnan. The local Bai people are one of the province's main ethnic groups. 大理三塔/ 大理三塔, the Three Pagodas of Dali, are the only remnants of an extensive ninth-century Tantric or Esoteric Buddhist temple complex built by the royal family of the ancient Nanzhao Kingdom. The three pagodas form an equilateral triangle. The central and tallest pagoda, at about 207 feet, has sixteen stories

大理城裏賣紀念品的商店
大理城里卖纪念品的商店

大理三塔
大理三塔

and bears a close resemblance to the famous Small Goose Pagoda in Xi'an. However, unlike most pagodas in the Chinese hinterland, the Three Pagodas of Dali have an even number of floors. The two ten-story pagodas are about 126 feet tall. The whitewashed pagodas fronting a beautiful blue lake are one of the most memorable sights of Yunnan.

3 Surrounded by snow-capped mountains and dotted with pristine lakes, 麗江/丽江, Lijiang, is located in northwestern Yunnan. 麗江古城/丽江古城, the Old City of Lijiang, is one of the best preserved in China. It survived a major earthquake in 1996 and has since become an extremely popular tourist city. The streets are paved with blue-gray flagstones, and small streams and rivulets ripple through the city. Most of the low-lying houses in Lijiang feature tiled roofs and carved wooden windows. Most of the city's residents belong to the Naxi ethnic minority.

麗江古城/丽江古城

麗江的小河、茶館、紅燈籠/丽江的小河、茶馆、红灯笼

❹ Yunnan is home to twenty-five officially recognized national minorities, who make up about a third of the province's population. About fifteen nationalities, including the Bai, Hani, Yi, Naxi, and Dai, are indigenous to Yunnan. Many of these minorities have their own distinct languages, cultures, and religious traditions. The Dai, for instance, practice Theravada Buddhism, and are linguistically related to Laotians and the Shan people of Burma. The Yao and Miao are famous for their embroidery and their elaborate silver headdresses and jewelry. The largest and most widely dispersed minority are the Yi, who practice an animist religion.

少數民族/少数民族

Grammar

1. Comparative Sentences

There are several forms of comparative sentences in Chinese. They can be summarized as follows.

A. Comparisons to indicate either sameness or difference:

跟/和···(不)一樣/(不)一样 (+ Adj/Mental Verb) can be used to suggest that two things are identical or different.

❶ 雲南跟上海的天氣不一樣。

云南跟上海的天气不一样。

(Yunnan's weather is different from Shanghai's weather.)

一樣/一样 can be followed by an adjective, or by a mental verb such as 想 or 喜歡/喜欢.

Note: unlike regular verbs, mental verbs may be preceded by 很. 想 (would like), 喜歡/喜欢 (to like), 想念 (to yearn for), 希望 (to hope), 愛/爱 (to love), 討厭/讨厌 (tǎoyàn, to dislike), 反對/反对 (to oppose), 同意 (to agree), and 贊成/赞成 (zànchéng, to approve) are just some of the verbs that convey mental states or activities, emotions, desires, attitudes, and so on.

❷ 這棟樓跟那棟樓不一樣高。

这栋楼跟那栋楼不一样高。

(This building and that building are not the same height.)

[高 specifies the difference in terms of height.]

❸ 麗莎和雪梅一樣喜歡買紀念品。

丽莎和雪梅一样喜欢买纪念品。

(Lisa likes souvenir shopping as much as Xuemei does.)

Remember that it is incorrect to use 比 to mark this kind of comparison. Instead we should use 跟 or 和:

(2a) *這棟樓比那棟樓不一樣高。

*这栋楼比那栋楼不一样高。

B. Comparison to indicate difference only

a. Using 比 as a comparison marker

A + 比 + B + Adj/Mental Verb

❹　張天明比表哥馬虎。
　　张天明比表哥马虎。
　　(Zhang Tianming is more careless than his cousin.)

❺　我的家教比我喜歡上網。
　　我的家教比我喜欢上网。
　　(My tutor likes to go online more than I do.)

Alternate patterns to indicate degree of difference:

A + 比 + B + Adj + 一點兒/得多/多了
A + 比 + B + Adj + 一点兒/得多/多了

❻　四川菜比廣東菜油一點兒。
　　四川菜比广东菜油一点儿。
　　(Sichuanese cooking is a little bit oilier than Cantonese cooking.)

❼　他同屋比他時髦得多。
　　他同屋比他时髦得多。
　　(His roommate is much more fashionable than he is.)

❽　舅舅的性格比媽媽開朗多了。
　　舅舅的性格比妈妈开朗多了。
　　(My uncle is much more outgoing than my mother.)

Note that first, we cannot modify the adjectives or mental verbs with 很 or similar adverbs expressing degree or extent.

＊我比你很高。

Second, "A + 不比 + B + Adj/Mental Verb" means A ≤ B:

⑨   **A:**   麗莎的獎學金比雪梅多吧?

丽莎的奖学金比雪梅多吧?

(Lisa's scholarship is bigger than Xuemei's, right?)

B: 麗莎的獎學金不比雪梅多，她倆一樣多。

丽莎的奖学金不比雪梅多，她俩一样多。

(Lisa's scholarship is not any bigger than Xuemei's. They are the same.)

C: 不，麗莎比雪梅少一些。

不，丽莎比雪梅少一些。

(No, Lisa's is smaller than Xuemei's.)

b. Using 沒有 to compare

A + 沒有 + B + Adj/Mental Verb

⑩   我們的導遊沒有他們的導遊幽默。

我们的导游没有他们的导游幽默。

(Our tour guide is not as humorous as theirs.)

c. Using 不如 to compare

不如 means more or less the same thing as 沒有, except that the adjective after 不如 is usually positive in meaning.

⑪   用電子郵件不如發短信方便。

用电子邮件不如发短信方便。

(Emailing is not as convenient as sending text messages.)

⑫   你做的盒飯不如我做的好吃。

你做的盒饭不如我做的好吃。

(The box lunch you made was not as tasty as the one I made.)

When the context is clear, the adjective after 不如 can be omitted.

⑬   我讀書不如你。(好)

我读书不如你。(好)

(I am not as good as you are academically.)

⑭ 我們去那麼遠的地方旅行，坐火車當然不如坐飛機。(快)

我们去那么远的地方旅行，坐火车当然不如坐飞机。(快)

(We are traveling to such a distant place. Taking the train, of course, can't compare with taking the plane [in terms of speed].)

2. Numerals in Idioms

Some idioms in Chinese contain two numerals, which are usually consecutive. These idioms usually have set meanings. For instance, "千⋯百⋯" can be interpreted to mean "myriad" or "many," e.g., 千奇百怪 (strange in all sorts of ways) and 千嬌百媚/千娇百媚 (qiān jiāo bǎi mèi, charming in myriad ways). Another example would be 千 and 萬/万 to emphasize "a large quantity," as in 千變萬化/千变万化 (protean; constantly changing), 千軍萬馬/千军万马 (a large and powerful army), 千家萬戶/千家万户 (hù) (tens of thousands of families and households). Similarly, there is 五顏六色/五颜六色 (very colorful; variegated). 一 and 二, on the other hand, mean "straightforward" and "clear-cut" as in 一乾二淨/一干二净 (quick and clean; complete), 一清二楚 (crystal clear). 七 and 八 suggest "messy" and "chaotic," as in 七上八下 (at an utter loss, feeling unsettled), 亂七八糟/乱七八糟 (at sixes and sevens; messy), 七手八腳/七手八脚 (too many cooks spoiling the broth), 七嘴八舌 (shé)(all talking in confusion).

Some expressions involve non-consecutive numbers: 五光十色 (dazzlingly colored), 五花八門/五花八门 (all manner of; every kind of). There are also expressions in which the numbers go from large to small: 三番兩次/三番两次 (repeatedly), 三心二意 (half-hearted).

3. Multiple Attributives

A noun can take several qualifiers or attributives. The order of these attributives follows certain rules. In Lesson 11, we have 一套三房兩廳兩衛的公寓/一套三房两厅两卫的公寓 (an apartment with three bedrooms, a living room, a dining room, and two bathrooms) and 一張不大的紅紙/一张不大的红纸 (a not-too-large piece of red paper). 一套 and 一張/一张 are numeral-measure words, whereas 三房兩廳兩衛/三房两厅两卫 and 不大的 and 紅/红 are descriptive modifiers. In this lesson, we have 一條非常乾淨的小河/一条非常干净的小河 (a very clean river), and 一個很有雲南特色的茶館/一个很有云南特色的茶館 (a teahouse with distinct Yunnan characteristics). Numeral-measure words normally precede descriptive modifiers, e.g., 一件漂亮的毛衣 (a pretty sweater), 一位有名的教授 (a famous professor), 一個大紅"福"字/一个大红"福"字 (a big red 福 character), 兩個感情很好的朋友/两个感情很好的朋友 (two close friends), 五個性格不同的研究生/五个性格不同的研究生 (five graduate students with distinct personalities), etc.

Sometimes descriptive modifiers can be placed before numeral-measure words for emphasis, e.g.,

❶   一房一廳的一套公寓就要一百萬，太貴了。
一房一厅的一套公寓就要一百万，太贵了。
(Even a one bedroom, one living-room apartment costs as much as a million. That's too expensive.)

❷   三歲大的一個孩子就能認識兩千個漢字，太厲害了。
三岁大的一个孩子就能认识两千个汉字，太厉害了。
(A three-year-old child can already recognize two thousand Chinese characters. That's incredible.)

Words & Phrases

A. 分別 (separately; respectively; to part from each other)

The adverb 分別 is usually used before action verbs.

❶ 他們星期五分別從南京和北京出發。[adverb]

他们星期五分别从南京和北京出发。

(They departed separately on Friday from Nanjing and Beijing.)

❷ 這個週末我們要開晚會，我給朋友們分別打了電話，他們都說
會參加。[adverb]

这个周末我们要开晚会，我给朋友们分别打了电话，他们都说
会参加。

(This weekend we are having a party. I called my friends one by one, and they all said
that they would come.)

分別 is also a verb meaning "to separate" or "to part from each other."

❸ 我跟他分別已經十年了，一直沒有見面。[verb]

我跟他分别已经十年了，一直没有见面。

(He and I went our separate ways ten years ago. We haven't seen each other since.)

❹ 我們分別以後，幾乎天天打電話，發電郵。[verb]

我们分别以后，几乎天天打电话，发电邮。

(Since we parted from each other, we have been phoning and emailing each other almost
daily.)

B. 印象 (impression)

印象 often appears in the following constructions:

1. A 對/对 B 的印象很好/不好/很深…

   (A has a very good [or bad, or very deep...] impression of B.)

2. B 給/给 A 留下很好/不好/很深…的印象

(B gave A a very good [or bad, or very deep...] impression.)

3. 有/沒有印象 (have [no] impression or recollection)

❶ **A:** 你跟那個人第一次見面，對他的印象怎麼樣？

你跟那个人第一次见面，对他的印象怎么样？

(This is the first time you've met that person. What's your impression of him?)

B: 那個人說話幽默，性格開朗，我對他的印象不錯。

那个人说话幽默，性格开朗，我对他的印象不错。

(That person is very humorous and outgoing. My impression of him is rather good.)

❷ **A:** 中國的哪一個城市給你留下的印象最深？

中国的哪一个城市给你留下的印象最深？

(Which city in China gave you the deepest impression?)

B: 北京古老的建築給我留下的印象最深。

北京古老的建筑给我留下的印象最深。

(The ancient architecture in Beijing left me with the deepest impression.)

❸ **A:** 聽說你去過雲南，你對那兒的印象好嗎？

听说你去过云南，你对那儿的印象好吗？

(I hear you have been to Yunnan. Do you have a good impression [of that place]?)

B: 雲南的風景美，少數民族的飲食、服裝、風俗習慣都很特別，給我的印象很好。

云南的风景美，少数民族的饮食、服装、风俗习惯都很特别，给我的印象很好。

(Yunnan has beautiful scenery, and the foods, costumes, customs and habits of the national minority groups are very unique. They gave me a very good impression.)

❹　這件事已經過去很多年了，我沒有印象了。

這件事已经过去很多年了，我没有印象了。

(This thing happened many years ago. I've no recollection of it anymore.)

C. 分享 (to share joy, happiness, benefit, or something pleasant or positive)

The object is usually an abstract noun. When used intransitively, the verb often occurs in this pattern: "跟/和 someone 分享."

❶　知道自己考上研究生院，他非常高興，馬上打電話告訴朋友們，讓他們分享自己的快樂。

知道自己考上研究生院，他非常高兴，马上打电话告诉朋友们，让他们分享自己的快乐。

(After learning that he had gotten into graduate school, he was very happy. He called his friends right away to share his happiness with them.)

❷　我當然願意跟家人分享自己的幸福。

我当然愿意跟家人分享自己的幸福。

(Of course I want to share my good fortune with my family.)

❸　他有什麼好事都讓女朋友跟自己分享。

他有什么好事都让女朋友跟自己分享。

(He shared with his girlfriend every positive thing in his life.)

D. 之前 (before; prior to)

之 means 的 in Classical Chinese. 之前 means "before such and such a time." If the time is specified, the preposition 在 can be used. When used alone at the beginning of a sentence, 之前 means "beforehand" or "previously," as in ❷.

❶　(在)畢業之前，我還得實習兩個月。

(在)毕业之前，我还得实习两个月。

(Before graduation, I have to intern for two months.)

❷ 之前沒人給我講過石林的故事。

之前没人给我讲过石林的故事。

(No one had told me stories about the Stone Forest before.)

雲南石林

云南石林

E. 只好 (have no choice but)

---

❶ 我今天很想看籃球賽，可是晚上到球場的時候，票賣完了，我只好以後再看了。

我今天很想看篮球赛，可是晚上到球场的时候，票卖完了，我只好以后再看了。

(I wanted very much to watch a basketball game today, but tonight when I got to the stadium, the tickets were all sold out, so I'll just have to wait till another time.)

❷ 小張的父母不給他零用錢了，他只好去打工。

小张的父母不给他零用钱了，他只好去打工。

(Little Zhang's parents stopped giving him an allowance, so he has to work part-time.)

F. 親眼, 親自, 親耳, 親手, 親身/亲眼, 亲自, 亲耳, 亲手, 亲身

All these are adverbs. 親/亲 is short for 親自/亲自 (oneself). 親眼/亲眼 and 親耳/亲耳 suggest firsthand experiences, whereas 親身/亲身 and 親自/亲自 convey personal attention and special care because the person considers it important to do so.

❶ 這頓年夜飯是奶奶親手做的，快吃吧。

这顿年夜饭是奶奶亲手做的，快吃吧。

(Grandma made this New Year's Eve dinner with her own hands. Please dig in.)

[The dinner is important to Grandma.]

❷ 她和男朋友分手了，我親耳聽她說的。

她和男朋友分手了，我亲耳听她说的。

(She broke up with her boyfriend. I heard her say that with my own ears.)

[It's not hearsay.]

❸ 這件事很重要，你一定要親自去辦。

这件事很重要，你一定要亲自去办。

(This is a very important matter. You'd better attend to it yourself.)

[You have to take it seriously.]

❹ 這些是我親身經歷過的。

这些是我亲身经历过的。

(I experienced these things first-hand.)

[It's not hearsay.]

G. 千萬/千万 (by all means; absolutely must)

千萬/千万 means "to make certain." It occurs in imperative sentences to advise or to urge.

❶ 明天考期末考，你千萬別遲到了。

明天考期末考，你千万别迟到了。

(Tomorrow is the final exam. Make sure that you aren't late.)

❷   這件事你千萬別告訴媽媽，要不然她會着急的。

這件事你千万别告诉妈妈，要不然她会着急的。

(Make sure that you don't tell Mom about this. She'd be very worried.)

> ## H. 不過/不过 (however; no more than)

As you may recall, 不過/不过 can be a conjunction indicating a turn in thought:

❶   南京夏天很熱，不過房間裏有空調，就不那麼難受了。

南京夏天很热，不过房间里有空调，就不那么难受了。

(Nanjing's summers are very hot, but the rooms have air conditioning, so it's not so unbearable.)

In this lesson, 不過/不过 is used as an adverb meaning "only, no more than," and it can be modified by 只.

❷   這個古城不大，從東邊走到西邊不過一兩個小時。

这个古城不大，从东边走到西边不过一两个小时。

(This ancient town is not big. It only takes a couple of hours to go from the east to the west side.)

麗江古城的小河
丽江古城的小河

❸   我不過是跟你開個玩笑，你怎麼哭了？

我不过是跟你开个玩笑，你怎么哭了？

(I was only joking with you. Why are you crying?)

Language Practice

A. I Know It by First-Hand Experience...

Make each of the following statements more convincing by using 親眼/亲眼, 親耳/亲耳, 親口/亲口, 親自/亲自, or 親手/亲手.

EXAMPLE:

這次去雲南，我看到了雲南
美麗的自然風景。

这次去云南，我看到了云南
美丽的自然风景。

→ 這次去雲南，我親眼看到了
雲南美麗的自然風景。

这次去云南，我亲眼看到了
云南美丽的自然风景。

1. 這次去雲南，我們看到了
有名的石林。

→

1. 这次去云南，我们看到了
有名的石林。

2. 他告訴我他今年冬天肯定
去哈爾濱。

→

2. 他告诉我他今年冬天肯定
去哈尔滨。

3. 舅媽教我做清蒸魚。

→

3. 舅妈教我做清蒸鱼。

4. 這件衣服是我奶奶做的。

→

4. 这件衣服是我奶奶做的。

5. 我聽她説她買的是硬臥票。

→

5. 我听她说她买的是硬卧票。

6. 那位老教授開車送我去機場。

→

6. 那位老教授开车送我去机场。

B. You Mustn't Do It!

Based on each of the scenarios below, advise your friend against doing something by using 千萬別/千万別.

EXAMPLE:

火車上的東西又貴又不新鮮，
→ 千萬別在火車上買東西吃。

火车上的东西又贵又不新鲜，
千万別在火车上买东西吃。

1. 那個家庭旅館又不乾淨，
   又不能上網，
   →

1. 那个家庭旅馆又不干净，
   又不能上网，

2. 雲南南部八月非常熱，
   →

2. 云南南部八月非常热，

3. 對面茶館賣的茶貴極了，
   →

3. 对面茶馆卖的茶贵极了，

4. 河邊的那個景點這幾天人
   太多，擠死了，
   →

4. 河边的那个景点这几天人
   太多，挤死了，

5. 那個旅行社的旅行團每個
   紀念品商店都進，
   →

5. 那个旅行社的旅行团每个
   纪念品商店都进，

C. A Frugal Traveler

Imagine that you are planning a trip on a modest budget.

a. Discuss with a partner the things you are willing to spend money on and the things you are not.

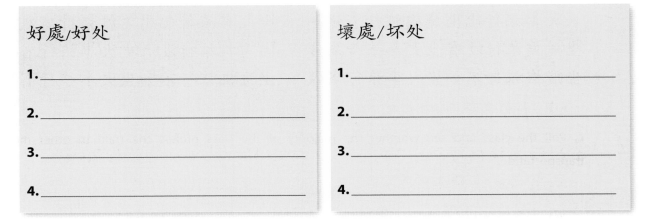

願意/愿意	不願意/不愿意
1._____	1._____
2._____	2._____
3._____	3._____

b. Consider the possibility of traveling on your own instead of joining a tour group. Talk about the pros and the cons of a 自助遊/自助游 with your partner.

好處/好处	壞處/坏处
1._____	1._____
2._____	2._____
3._____	3._____
4._____	4._____

c. After looking at both sides, explain to your partner whether you would like to join a tour group or travel by yourself.

D. Should We Travel by Train?

How would you convince your friends that they should or should not take the train for a long-distance trip in China? You may want to mention the price, speed, comfort level, food, hard vs. soft sleeper, opportunities to communicate with other travelers, etc.

a. Discuss with a partner the pros and the cons of traveling by train.

好處/好处

1. 省錢/省钱 _____

2. _____

3. _____

4. _____

壞處/坏处

1. _____

2. _____

3. _____

4. _____

b. Based on the list, make comparisons with other means of transportation using 比, 不如, and 沒有.

EXAMPLE:

坐火車旅行比坐飛機旅行省錢。　坐火车旅行比坐飞机旅行省钱。

坐飛機旅行沒有坐火車旅行省錢。　坐飞机旅行没有坐火车旅行省钱。

坐飛機旅行不如坐火車旅行省錢。　坐飞机旅行不如坐火车旅行省钱。

c. Poll the class and see whether the majority of the class prefers the train to other means of transportation.

E. A Nature Lover

a. What would a nature lover say about some of the most beautiful things in the natural landscape? Let's start with the basics by listing some adjectives to describe each of the following.

1. 山 : _____

2. 河 : _____

3. 樹/树 : _____

4. 石頭/石头 : _____

5. 風景/风景 : _____

b. Ask a partner to list the nature reserves or national parks (國家公園/国家公园) that he or she has visited:

我遊覽過   我游览过

1. _____ **2.** _____ **3.** _____

Ask your partner:

你對 (the nature reserves or national parks from above) 的印象怎麼樣?   你对 (the nature reserves or national parks from above) 的印象怎么样?

c. Ask your partner to describe his or her impressions of what he or she has seen.

EXAMPLE: 山

→ **A:** 那兒的山怎麼樣?   **A:** 那儿的山怎么样?

  B: 那兒的山真_____ 。   **B:** 那儿的山真_____ 。

1. 河   **2.** 樹/树   **3.** 石頭/石头   **4.** 風景/风景

d. Switch roles.

F. What Kind of Tourist Are You?

a. In addition to appreciating natural and architectural beauty, select from the list below the activities that you would enjoy doing as a tourist.

參加旅行團	参加旅行团
拍照(片)	拍照(片)
嚐小吃	尝小吃
買紀念品	买纪念品
上網寫博客	上网写博客
聽導遊講故事	听导游讲故事
想了解少數民族的生活習慣	想了解少数民族的生活习惯

b. Combine the activities you have selected above with 肯定, 經常/经常, 有時候/有时候, or 從來不/从来不. By doing so, tell a partner what kind of tourist you are. You can start by saying…

我旅行的時候/我旅行的时候…

G. Writing Practice

Based on the text, compile a daily itinerary of Zhang Tianming and his friends' trips starting from when they first depart Nanjing or Beijing.

第一天
第二天
…

Pinyin Text

Xīn xuéqī kāishǐ qián, Zhāng Tiānmíng, Lìshā hé Kē Lín, Xuěméi yìqǐ qù Yúnnán lǚyóu. Tāmen yuē hǎo xīngqīwǔ wǎnshang fēnbié cóng Nánjīng hé Běijīng chūfā, xīngqītiān zài Kūnmíng jiàn miàn. Cóng xīngqī yī kāishǐ, tāmen zài Yúnnán lǚyóu le yí ge xīngqī.

   Zhōngguó de huǒchē, dǎoyóu hé Yúnnán měilì de fēngjǐng, dōu gěi Tiānmíng liú xia hěn shēn de yìnxiàng.

   Zhāng Tiānmíng měitiān xiě bókè, ràng péngyou men fēnxiǎng zìjǐ de kuàilè.

   Qù Yúnnán zhī qián, wǒmen zài wǎng shang bàomíng cānjiā le yí ge lǚxíngtuán. Tuán fèi bāokuò❶ jiāotōng, lǚguǎn, sān cān, hé jǐngdiǎn ménpiào.

   Wǒmen shì zuò huǒchē qù de Yúnnán, wèile néng gēn bié de lǚkè liànxí shuō Zhōngwén, wǒmen mǎi le yìngwò❷ piào, yīnwèi yìngwò chēxiāng měi ge "fángjiān" dōu méiyǒu mén, róngyì zhǎo rén liáo tiānr. Wǒ zài shàng pù, shàng pù bǐ xià pù hé zhōng pù ānjìng yì diǎn, wǎnshang kěyǐ shuì ge hǎo jiào. Chuáng shang yǒu tǎnzi hé zhěntou, hěn gānjìng.

   Wǒ yě qù ruǎnwò chēxiāng kàn le kan. Nàli měi ge xiǎo fángjiān li yǒu liǎng ge shàng pù, liǎng ge xià pù, chuáng bǐjiào ruǎn yě bǐjiào dà, fángjiān de mén kěyǐ guān shang. Wǒmen méiyǒu mǎi ruǎnwò piào, hái yīnwèi pà bié rén shuì jiào dǎ hūlu. Nǐ xiǎng xiang, zài zhème xiǎo de fángjiān li, guān shang mén, rúguǒ yǒu rén bùtíng de dǎ hūlu, nǐ hái néng shuì de zháo jiào❸ ma?

   Zhè shì cānchē. Wǒmen zài cānchē shang chī le yí dùn fàn, nàli de fàn, wǒ juéde yòu guì yòu nánchī, bùrú❶ mǎi héfàn❹ huòzhě fāngbiàn miàn❺.

   Wǒ hé Lìshā zài Kūnmíng xià chē hòu, děng le liǎng ge duō xiǎoshí, Xuěméi hé Kē Lín tāmen de huǒchē cái dào. Wǒmen yí jiàn miàn, dàjiā jiù gāoxìng de yōngbào qi lai, suīrán cái fēnbié jǐ tiān, kěshì hǎoxiàng hǎo jiǔ bú jiàn le. Wǒmen yìqǐ zǒu chu huǒchē zhàn, kàn dào dǎoyóu zhèng jǔ zhe páizi zhǎo wǒmen, páizi shang xiě de shì wǒmen sì ge rén de míngzi. Wǒmen de dǎoyóu shuō huà hěn yōumò, cháng dòu de dàjiā hā hā dà xiào. Búguò yǒushí❻ tā shuō de huà wǒmen sān ge rén dōu tīng bu dǒng, Xuěméi zhǐhǎo gěi wǒmen dāng fānyì.

   Dǎoyóu jièshào shuō Yúnnán shì yí ge shěng, zài Zhōngguó de xīnán bù, shěnghuì shì Kūnmíng. Yúnnán zìrán fēngjǐng hěn měi, yǒu shān yǒu shuǐ, zhèli zhù zhe hěn duō shǎoshù mínzú. Lái Yúnnán lǚyóu, kěyǐ qīnyǎn kàn kan bù tóng mínzú de jiànzhù, fúzhuāng, yǐnshí, liǎojiě gè ge mínzú de fēngsú xíguàn.

Dì yī tiān wǒmen yóulǎn le Shílín. Zhè shì yì zhāng Shílín de zhàopiàn. Shílín yǒu hěn duō yánsè hěn shēn de shítou, yuǎn kàn jiù xiàng shùlín yíyàng. Shítou de yàngzi qiān qí bǎi guài②. Wǒmen zài Shílín li yìbiān zǒu, yìbiān tīng dǎoyóu jiǎng nà xiē shítou de gùshi, fēicháng yǒu yìsi. Shílín gěi wǒmen liú xia le hěn shēn de yìnxiàng.

Zhè shì Dàlǐ sān tǎ, jiànzhù hěn gǔlǎo, hěn yǒumíng. Dàlǐ chéng li yǒu hěn duō mài jìniànpǐn de shāngdiàn, dǎoyóu bǎ wǒmen dài dào nàr, xīwàng dàjiā duō mǎi dōngxi. Xuěméi hé Lìshā hěn gāoxìng, mǎi le bù shǎo jìniànpǐn, ér wǒ gēn Kē Lín shòu bu liǎo, jiù bàoyuàn shuō tài làngfèi shíjiān le. Xià cì nǐmen dào Zhōngguó lǚyóu zhǎo lǚxíngtuán, yídìng yào xiān wèn qīngchu, qiānwàn bié zhǎo yǒu "gòuwù" de tuán. Nǐmen kěyǐ zìzhùyóu❼, nàyàng jiù zìyóu duō le.

Dì sān tiān, dào le yǒumíng de Lìjiāng gǔchéng❽, wǒmen fēicháng xǐhuan zhèli. Zhè ge gǔchéng bú dà, cóng dōngbian zǒu dào xībian búguò yì liǎng ge xiǎoshí. Zuì tèbié de shì yǒu yì tiáo fēicháng gānjìng de xiǎo hé③ cóng chéng zhōngjiān liú guo. Xiǎo hé liǎng biān yǒu hěn duō shāngdiàn, cháguǎn, xiǎo fànguǎn. Nà tiān wǎnshang, wǒmen zài yí ge hěn yǒu Yúnnán tèsè de cháguǎn li hē chá, kàn zhe wài bian de xiǎo hé, mén páng de hóng dēnglong, hái yǒu lái lái wǎng wǎng de yóukè, dōu bù xiǎng huí lǚguǎn qù shuì jiào le.

Zài Lìjiāng, wǒmen zhù le liǎng tiān jiātíng lǚguǎn. Fángjiān suīrán hěn xiǎo, dànshì hěn gānjìng, yě néng shàng wǎng. Fángdōng hái gěi wǒmen zuò le xiē jiācháng cài, là là de, wèidao hěn búcuò.

Yúnnán gè ge dìfang de fēngjǐng bù yíyàng, hái yǒu hěn duō hǎowán de dìfang. Wǒmen míng tiān yào qù yóulǎn dà xuěshān. Wǒ guò jǐ tiān huì bǎ pāi hǎo de zhàopiàn fàng zài bókè shang.

English Text

Before the new semester started, Zhang Tianming, Lisa, Ke Lin, and Xuemei went on a trip to Yunnan. They agreed to leave separately from Nanjing and Beijing on Friday evening and meet up in Kunming on Sunday. From [the following] Monday they toured Yunnan for a week.

China's trains, tour guides, and Yunnan's beautiful scenery all made a deep impression on Tianming.

Zhang Tianming updated his blog every day to share his pleasant experience with his friends.

Before we went to Yunnan, we signed up online to join a tour group. The fees for the tour group included transportation, hotels, three meals [a day], and admission tickets to the scenic spots.

We went to Yunnan by train. In order to practice speaking Chinese with the other passengers, we bought tickets for a hard sleeper because the "rooms" of the hard sleeper cars don't have doors, so it's easier to find people to chat with. I had the upper bunk. The upper bunk was quieter than the middle and lower bunks, so I could get a good night's sleep. On the bunk there was a blanket and a pillow. They were very clean.

I also went to the soft sleeper car to have a look. There each compartment had two upper bunks and two lower bunks. The bunks were softer and also bigger, and the doors could be closed. The other reason we didn't buy tickets for a soft sleeper was that we were afraid the others in our compartment would snore. Just think, in such a small compartment with the doors closed, if someone snored non-stop, would you be able to sleep?

This is the dining car. We ate in the dining car once. I thought the food was both expensive and terrible-tasting. It's better to get a box lunch or instant noodles.

After Lisa and I got off the train in Kunming, we waited for more than two hours for Xuemei and Ke Lin's train to arrive. When we saw one another, we happily hugged. Although we had been apart for only a few days, it seemed like we hadn't seen one another for a long time. We walked out of the train station together and saw our tour guide holding a sign looking for us. Our names were written on the sign. Our tour guide was very humorous, making us laugh all the time, but sometimes we three didn't understand him. Xuemei had to be our interpreter.

Our tour guide told us that Yunnan is a province in southwestern China. The provincial capital is Kunming. The natural landscape of Yunnan is very beautiful, with mountains and rivers. Many minority groups also live here. If you take a trip to Yunnan, you can see firsthand the architecture, costumes, food and drinks of the different ethnic groups and understand the customs of each ethnic group.

On the first day we visited the Stone Forest. This is a picture of the Stone Forest. There are many deep-colored rocks in the Stone Forest which, when viewed from a distance, look like a forest of trees. The appearances of the rocks are all different and bizarre. We walked around in the Stone Forest and listened to the guide tell stories about the rocks. They were very interesting. The Stone Forest made a deep impression on us.

These are the Three Pagodas of Dali. The buildings are very ancient and very famous. There are many stores that sell souvenirs in Dali. The guide took us there and hoped that we would buy lots of things. Xuemei and Lisa were very glad and bought many souvenirs, but Ke Lin and I couldn't stand it and complained that it was a waste of time. Next time when you are in China looking for a tour group, you must ask questions first to make sure that you don't join a "shopping" tour group. Or perhaps you can travel on your own. That way you'll be much freer.

On the third day we arrived in the famous old town of Lijiang. We really like it here. This old town is not very large, and it takes only a couple of hours to walk from the east to the west side. The most unusual thing [about the old town] is a very clean small river running through the city. The two sides of the river are lined with many stores, teahouses, and small restaurants. That night we drank tea in a distinctly Yunnanese teahouse while looking at the river, the red lanterns beside the doors, and the comings and goings of the tourists. We almost didn't want to go back to the hotel to sleep.

In Lijiang we stayed in a family-run hotel for two days. The rooms were small, but they were very clean, and we could also access the internet. The landlord made us some home-style dishes that were spicy and very tasty.

Each region of Yunnan has a different landscape, and there are also many fun places. Tomorrow we will visit the big snow mountain. In a few days I'll post my photos on this blog.

SELF-ASSESSMENT

How well can you do these things? Check (✔) the boxes to evaluate your progress and see which tasks you may need to practice more.

I can	Very Well	OK	A Little
Itemize the expenses of joining a group tour	☐	☐	☐
Give a brief description of a Chinese sleeper car	☐	☐	☐
Describe some natural objects such as mountains, rivers, trees and rocks	☐	☐	☐
Discuss some of the things that tourists may expect to see or experience at a tourist site	☐	☐	☐

第十四課
生活與
健康

第十四课
生活与
健康

14

 LEARNING OBJECTIVES

In this lesson, you will learn to use Chinese to

1. Talk about your exercise routine;

2. Outline some healthy eating habits;

3. Describe habits that could make you age prematurely or harm your health.

RELATE AND GET READY

In your own culture/community—

• Do many people exercise in the morning in parks?

• Do people go to the gym to exercise?

• Are people conscientious about health and fitness?

• Are many people concerned about their weight?

Before You Study

Check the statements that apply to you.

☐ 1. I exercise regularly.

☐ 2. I exercise in the morning.

When You Study

Listen to the audio recording and scan the text. Ask yourself the following questions before you begin a close reading of the text.

1. Who is Li Wen?

2. Why is Lisa staying with Li Wen?

 麗莎到北京後沒有住留學生公寓，為了更多地了解中國人的
生活，她住進了一個中國家庭。房東夫妻二人都已①退休，女兒
李文在博物館工作，與②父母住在一起。李文很想去美國留學，
所以請麗莎做她的英文家教，這樣麗莎就不必付房租了。由於
麗莎每天都跟李文的父母說中文，所以她的中文也進步得很快。

　　麗莎每天早上都出去散步，在她住的這個社區，在街邊，
在公園，都能看見很多人，特別是老人，在鍛煉身體。他們
有的③站成一個圈，高高興興地跳舞，有的排成隊，慢慢地

☐ 3. I eat three meals a day.
☐ 4. I am careful about what I eat.
☐ 5. I often stay up late.

3. What does Lisa see every morning that impresses her so much?
4. Does Lisa exercise and take good care of her health?
5. What's Lisa's advice to Li Wen?

 丽莎到北京后没有住留学生公寓，为了更多地了解中国人的生活，她住进了一个中国家庭。房东夫妻二人都已①退休，女儿李文在博物馆工作，与②父母住在一起。李文很想去美国留学，所以请丽莎做她的英文家教，这样丽莎就不必付房租了。由于丽莎每天都跟李文的父母说中文，所以她的中文也进步得很快。

丽莎每天早上都出去散步，在她住的这个小区，在街边，在公园，都能看见很多人，特别是老人，在锻炼身体。他们有的③站成一个圈，高高兴兴地跳舞，有的排成队，慢慢地打太極拳。這些早晨鍛鍊❶的人們，成為北京特別的"風景"，使④這個城市顯得非常有活力。

這一天早上麗莎正要出門，李文從房間走出來。

李文：　　麗莎，今天是星期六，怎麼這麼早就起床了？

麗莎：　　我本來想跟叔叔、阿姨去學太極拳，沒想到他們那麼早就出去了。

李文：　　我以為你只喜歡做瑜伽❷，怎麼對太極拳也有興趣？

麗莎：　　太極拳和瑜伽一樣，不但對身體有好處，而且動作很美。

李文：　　麗莎，你看大樹下邊，我爸、我媽正在跟那些退休老人打太極拳呢！你去找他們吧。

麗莎：　　好，一會兒就去。他們打得真棒，好像在表演一樣。我每天早晨出去散步，看見到處都是運動的人。中國人真重視鍛鍊身體啊！

李文：　　對，現在大家都越來越注意身體健康了。哎，麗莎，美國人一般怎麼鍛鍊身體？

麗莎：　　一般是跑步、游泳、打球等等，有些人也去健身房。至於我，除了做瑜伽以外，偶爾也跑步。

李文：　　難怪你的身體這麼健康，身材這麼好。

麗莎：　　我覺得如果想身體健康、身材好，除了多運動以外，還應該注意飲食。

李文：　　你一點兒都不胖，還需要注意飲食嗎？

麗莎：　　注意飲食不等於減肥。我認為只要身體健康就好，胖瘦並不重要。

李文：　　我工作忙，沒時間好好兒吃飯，常常隨便亂吃。你是怎麼注意飲食的呢？

麗莎：　　多喝水，多吃青菜、水果。另外，即使你非常忙，也一定要吃早飯，而且早飯要有營養；午飯要吃飽，因為下午還

LANGUAGE NOTES

❶ 在早晨進行練習或鍛鍊/在早晨进行练习或锻炼 can be shortened to 晨練/晨练.

打太极拳。这些早晨锻炼❶的人们，成为北京特别的"风景"，使④这个城市显得非常有活力。

这一天早上丽莎正要出门，李文从房间走出来。

李文：　丽莎，今天是星期六，怎么这么早就起床了？

丽莎：　我本来想跟叔叔、阿姨去学太极拳，没想到他们那么早就出去了。

李文：　我以为你只喜欢做瑜伽❷，怎么对太极拳也有兴趣？

丽莎：　太极拳和瑜伽一样，不但对身体有好处，而且动作很美。

李文：　丽莎，你看大树下边，我爸、我妈正在跟那些退休老人打太极拳呢！你去找他们吧。

丽莎：　好，一会儿就去。他们打得真棒，好像在表演一样。我每天早晨出去散步，看见到处都是运动的人。中国人真重视锻炼身体啊！

李文：　对，现在大家都越来越注意身体健康了。哎，丽莎，美国人一般怎么锻炼身体？

丽莎：　一般是跑步、游泳、打球等等，有些人也去健身房。至于我，除了做瑜伽以外，偶尔也跑步。

李文：　难怪你的身体这么健康，身材这么好。

丽莎：　我觉得如果想身体健康、身材好，除了多运动以外，还应该注意饮食。

李文：　你一点儿都不胖，还需要注意饮食吗？

丽莎：　注意饮食不等于减肥。我认为只要身体健康就好，胖瘦并不重要。

李文：　我工作忙，没时间好好儿吃饭，常常随便乱吃。你是怎么注意饮食的呢？

丽莎：　多喝水，多吃青菜、水果。另外，即使你非常忙，也一定要吃早饭，而且早饭要有营养；午饭要吃饱，因为下午还

---

❷ 瑜伽 can also be written as 瑜珈.

要學習和工作；晚飯就要少吃一點，不然會越來越胖，因為離上床睡覺的時間太近了。

李文： 我們中國人有一句話：早餐要吃好，午餐要吃飽，晚餐要吃少❸，跟你說的幾乎一樣。

麗莎： 真的？中國人也這樣說？可見是有科學道理的。

李文： 要想身體好，在其他方面也要注意。

麗莎： 你的意思是要有良好的生活習慣，對不對？

李文： 對。不吸煙，不喝酒，早睡早起，最好不要熬夜。別的都沒問題，就是不熬夜我可做不到。我晚上常常得開夜車❹準備考研究生。

麗莎： 那你必須❺儘可能找時間補充睡眠。

李文： 你說得對，我是得注意了，否則我的兩隻眼睛都快變成熊貓❻眼了。

After You Study

Challenge yourself to complete the following tasks in Chinese.

1. Describe the scenes that make Lisa think Beijing is lively and full of energy.
2. Explain the similarity between tai chi and yoga, according to Lisa.

LANGUAGE NOTES

❸ 早餐 is the same as 早飯/早饭. 午餐 is synonymous with 午飯/午饭, and 晚餐 with 晚飯/晚饭.

❹ 開夜車/开夜车 means staying up late to work or study.

要学习和工作；晚饭就要少吃一点，不然会越来越胖，因为离上床睡觉的时间太近了。

李文：　我们中国人有一句话：早餐要吃好，午餐要吃饱，晚餐要吃少❸，跟你说的几乎一样。

丽莎：　真的？中国人也这样说？可见是有科学道理的。

李文：　要想身体好，在其它方面也要注意。

丽莎：　你的意思是要有良好的生活习惯，对不对？

李文：　对。不吸烟，不喝酒，早睡早起，最好不要熬夜。别的都没问题，就是不熬夜我可做不到。我晚上常常得开夜车❹准备考研究生。

丽莎：　那你必须❺尽可能找时间补充睡眠。

李文：　你说得对，我是得注意了，否则我的两只眼睛都快变成熊猫❻眼了。

---

3. List the things that keep Lisa fit and healthy.
4. Explain why Li Wen is not getting enough sleep.

---

❺ The negative of 必須/必须 is often 不必 or 不用.

❻ 熊貓/熊猫 in Taiwan is known as 貓熊/猫熊.

VOCABULARY

1.	與	与	yǔ	conj/prep	and; with [See Grammar 2.]
2.	夫妻		fūqī	n	husband and wife; couple
3.	退休		tuìxiū	v	to retire
4.	博物館	博物馆	bówùguǎn	n	museum
5.	散步		sàn bù	vo	to take a walk; to go for a walk
6.	鍛煉	锻炼	duànliàn	v	to exercise; to work out; to undergo physical training
7.	圈		quān	n/v	circle; to encircle; to mark with a circle
8.	排		pái	v/n/m	to line up; row; line; (measure word for rows)
9.	隊	队	duì	n/m	a row or line of people; column; (measure word for teams and lines)
10.	太極拳	太极拳	tàijíquán	n	tai chi; a form of traditional Chinese shadow boxing
11.	早晨		zǎochén	n	morning; early morning
12.	成為	成为	chéngwéi	v	to become; to turn into
13.	使		shǐ	v	to make; to cause; to have someone do something [See Grammar 4.]
14.	顯得	显得	xiǎnde	v	to appear (to be); to seem
15.	活力		huólì	n	vitality; energy
16.	出門	出门	chū mén	vo	to go out; to leave home
17.	瑜伽		yújiā	n	yoga
18.	動作	动作	dòngzuò	n	movement; action
19.	樹	树	shù	n	tree
20.	表演		biǎoyǎn	v/n	to perform; to act; performance

21.	重視	重視	zhòngshì	v	to attach importance to; to think much of
22.	注意		zhùyì	v/n	to pay attention to; attention
23.	等		děng	p	and so forth; etc.
24.	健身房		jiànshēnfáng	n	fitness center; gym
25.	偶爾	偶尔	ǒu'ěr	adv	occasionally
26.	身材		shēncái	n	stature; figure
27.	等於	等于	děngyú	v	to equal; to be equivalent to; to amount to
28.	減肥	减肥	jiǎn féi	vo	to lose weight
29.	只要		zhǐyào	conj	only if; as long as
30.	隨便	随便	suíbiàn	adj/vo	casual; careless; to do as one pleases
31.	即使		jíshǐ	conj	even if
32.	營養	营养	yíngyǎng	n	nutrition; nourishment
33.	飽	饱	bǎo	adj	full; satiated (after a meal)
34.	可見	可见	kějiàn	conj	it is obvious that; it can be seen that
35.	科學	科学	kēxué	n/adj	science; scientific; rational
36.	方面		fāngmiàn	n	aspect; respect
37.	吸煙	吸烟	xī yān	vo	to smoke a cigarette
38.	熬夜		áo yè	vo	to stay up late or all night; to burn the midnight oil
39.	必須	必须	bìxū	adv	must; have to; be obliged to
40.	補充	补充	bǔchōng	v	to supplement; to replenish
41.	睡眠		shuìmián	n	sleep
42.	否則	否则	fǒuzé	conj	otherwise

| 43. | 隻 | 只 | zhī | m | (measure word for one of certain paired things and some animals) |
| 44. | 熊貓 | 熊猫 | xióngmāo | n | panda |

Proper Noun

| 45. | 李文 | | Lǐ Wén | | (a personal name) |

qiáng strong
強

這家商店賣的禮物與紀念品都做成熊貓的樣子或者有熊貓的照片。
这家商店卖的礼物与纪念品都做成熊猫的样子或者有熊猫的照片。

Enlarged Characters

| 與 | 隊 | 極 | 顯 | 隨 | 養 | 貓 |
| 与 | 队 | 极 | 显 | 随 | 养 | 猫 |

麗莎不住這兒。
丽莎不住这儿。

Culture Highlights

1 In the past, most people in Beijing lived in courtyard houses called 四合院 (sìhéyuàn). Because of the rapid increase in population, many of the traditional residential neighborhoods have been demolished to make way for high-rise apartment buildings. Although some courtyard houses in the city center have been renovated to make them more amenable to modern living, most have been replaced by gated residential subdivisions that often have enticing names.

四合院

小區裏有個公園。
小区里有个公园。

2 Unlike in Western countries, there are still many smokers in China. The Chinese government has begun taking steps to discourage people from smoking.

這些都是不准吸煙的意思。
这些都是不准吸烟的意思。

3 Many Chinese people like to exercise in the morning. City residents, especially the elderly, take exercising very seriously. Morning exercises have become very popular. Older people congregate on street corners or in neighborhood parks. Some practice tai chi or tai chi sword dance. Some practice various kinds of calisthenic exercise. Dances of all types—traditional folk dancing, ballroom dancing, and so on—are also popular.

小區裏給人鍛煉身體的地方
小区里给人锻炼身体的地方

Grammar

1. Disyllabic Words Becoming Monosyllabic

In written Chinese some two-syllable modal verbs, adverbs, conjunctions and so on may appear in monosyllabic form, e.g.,

已經/已经 ➜ 已 (already)

應該/应该 ➜ 應/应 (should)

可以 ➜ 可 (can, may)

因為/因为 ➜ 因 (because)

為了/为了 ➜ 為/为 (for the sake of)

比較/比较 ➜ 較/较 (relatively; rather)

多半 ➜ 多 (most, mostly)

雖然/虽然 ➜ 雖/虽 (although)

但是 ➜ 但 (but, however)

2. Conjunction and Preposition 與/与

與/与 is a conjunction as well as a preposition. It appears in written Chinese.

A: 與/与 is a conjunction in 生活與健康/生活与健康 and is synonymous with 和 and 跟. Here are two more examples: 教師與學生/教师与学生 (teachers and students), 沙漠與河流/沙漠与河流 (deserts and rivers).

B: Like 和 and 跟, 與/与 can serve as a preposition, e.g. 李文與父母住在一起/李文与父母住在一起 (Li Wen lives with her parents), 麗莎與天明一起去雲南旅行/丽莎与天明一起去云南旅行 (Lisa travels to Yunnan with Tianming), 我購物的標準與你們不同/我购物的标准与你们不同 (My shopping criteria are different from yours).

3. 有的…, 有的…

❶   中午，旅行團的人都累了，他們有的躺在椅子上睡覺，有的靠在椅子上休息，都不說話了。

中午，旅行团的人都累了，他们有的躺在椅子上睡觉，有的靠在椅子上休息，都不说话了。

(Around midday, everyone in the tour group was tired. Some lay down on the chairs to take a nap, and some leaned back against the chairs to take a rest. Everybody stopped talking.)

❷   我到公園的時候，看見有的人在散步，有的人排成隊打太極拳，有的人站成圈跳舞。

我到公园的时候，看见有的人在散步，有的人排成队打太极拳，有的人站成圈跳舞。

(When I got to the park, I saw some people taking walks,
some people in rows practicing tai chi, and some people in a circle dancing.)

❸   我進學校的時候，看見孩子們有的在打球，有的在玩游戲，有的坐在地上休息。

我进学校的时候，看见孩子们有的在打球，有的在玩游戏，有的坐在地上休息。

(When I arrived at the school, I saw that some children were playing ball, some were playing games, and some were sitting on the ground taking a break.)

4. 使 and Pivotal Sentences

使 means "to cause" or "to make."

❶   由於房東整天不斷地抱怨這抱怨那，使他很不高興，決定馬上搬家。

由于房东整天不断地抱怨这抱怨那，使他很不高兴，决定马上搬家。

(The landlord's constant complaints made him very unhappy and he decided to move out right away.)

❷ 老師剛才說的話，使我理解了我為什麼考試考得不好。

老师刚才说的话，使我理解了我为什么考试考得不好。

(What the teacher just said made me realize why I didn't do well on the exam.)

This usage of 使 appears in this pattern:

Noun (subject) + 使 + noun (object/subject) + verb…

The noun after 使 acts as the object of 使 as well as the subject of the following verb as in ❷.

老師的話/老师的话 (subject) + 使 + 我 (object/subject) + 理解…

(*The teacher's words* [subject] made *me* [object/subject] realize…)

This kind of sentence is called a pivotal sentence.

Other verbs that can be used in this way include 叫, 讓/让, etc. The 使 in sentences ❶ and ❷ can be replaced with 叫 or 讓/让.

(1a) 由於房東整天不斷地抱怨這抱怨那，讓他很不高興，決定馬上搬家。

由于房东整天不断地抱怨这抱怨那，让他很不高兴，决定马上搬家。

(2a) 老師剛才說的話，叫我理解了我為什麼考試考得不好。

老师刚才说的话，叫我理解了我为什么考试考得不好。

叫 and 讓/让 are colloquial. In comparison, 使 is more literary. Therefore, the examples above differ stylistically. In other words, in spoken language it is more appropriate to use 叫 or 讓/让, whereas it is more appropriate to use 使 in written-style language.

Please also note that 叫 and 讓/让 sometimes express a request or permission, e.g.,

❸ 指導教授叫/讓你去一下。

指导教授叫/让你去一下。

(The advisor asked you to go see him.)

❹ 那兒太危險，媽媽不叫/讓我去。

那儿太危险，妈妈不叫/让我去。

(That place is too dangerous. Mom wouldn't let me go there.)

使 cannot be used in this manner. Therefore, 叫 or 讓/让 in sentences ❸ and ❹ cannot be replaced by 使.

Words & Phrases

A. 顯得/显得 (to appear [to be]; to seem)

顯得/显得 is generally followed by an adjective, which is in turn often qualified by an adverb expressing degree or extent:

❶ 今天天氣很好，樹顯得特別綠，花顯得特別美。
今天天气很好，树显得特别绿，花显得特别美。
(Today's weather is great. The trees look unusually green, and the flowers unusually beautiful.)

❷ 你穿上這件襯衫顯得更漂亮。
你穿上这件衬衫显得更漂亮。
(This shirt makes you look even better.)

❸ 我房間牆的顏色很深，顯得屋子很小。
我房间墙的颜色很深，显得屋子很小。
(The color of the walls in my room is very dark. It makes the room seem very small.)

B. 重視/重视 (to attach importance to; to think much of)

重視/重视 is used mainly as a predicate in a sentence and generally followed by an object. Sometimes 重視/重视 can also be used as an attributive.

❶ 公司很重視我姐夫，又給他加工資了。 [predicate]
公司很重视我姐夫，又给他加工资了。
(The company thinks very highly of my brother-in-law and gave him another raise.)

❷ 我們大學很重視科學研究，我們的教授在研究方面都很
有名。 [predicate]
我们大学很重视科学研究，我们的教授在研究方面都很
有名。
(Our university places a great deal of importance on scientific research. Our professors are all very famous for their research.)

❸ 我爸爸現在最重視的事情是我的學習。[attributive]

我爸爸现在最重视的事情是我的学习。

(What my dad cares the most about now is my studies.)

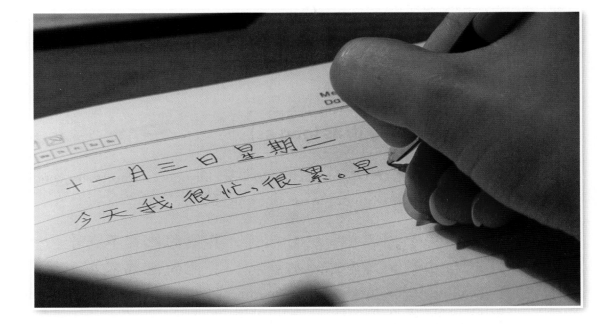

C. 等於/等于 (to equal; to be equivalent to; to amount to)

等於/等于 can mean that two numbers or two things are equal to each other.

❶ 已經一個星期了，你男朋友打電話你一直不接，不等於告訴他
要跟他分手嗎？

已经一个星期了，你男朋友打电话你一直不接，不等于告诉他
要跟他分手吗？

(You haven't taken your boyfriend's phone calls for a week now. Doesn't that amount to telling him you want to break up with him?)

❷ 孩子要什麼就給什麼不等於愛孩子，可能會使孩子變壞。

孩子要什么就给什么不等于爱孩子，可能会使孩子变坏。

(Giving a child whatever he wants isn't the same as loving the child. You might spoil the child instead.)

❸   二加二等於四。

二加二等于四。

(Two plus two equals four.)

❹   十五減九等於六。

十五减九等于六。

(Fifteen minus nine equals six.)

D. 只要…(就)… (only if; as long as)

In the "只要…(就)…" construction, 只要 introduces a necessary condition for the result expressed by the word or phrase following 就.

❶   小林租房子，只要環境好就行，其他的他都不在乎。

小林租房子，只要环境好就行，其他的他都不在乎。

(When Little Lin is looking for an apartment, as long as the environment is good he'll rent it. He doesn't care about anything else.)

❷   只要你好好兒用功學習，你的中文就一定會進步。

只要你好好儿用功学习，你的中文就一定会进步。

(As long as you study diligently, your Chinese will definitely improve.)

❸   很多父母認為，只要孩子平安、健康，就是自己最大的幸福。

很多父母认为，只要孩子平安、健康，就是自己最大的幸福。

(Many parents think that their biggest happiness is the safety and health of their children.)

E. 隨便/随便 (casual; careless; to do as one pleases)

隨便/随便 is an adjective. In this lesson, 隨便/随便 means doing whatever one wants regardless of whether the action or behavior is appropriate or not. It can be a predicate or an adverbial.

❶ A: 明天的歡迎晚會我穿什麼衣服好？
　　明天的欢迎晚会我穿什么衣服好？
　　(What should I wear for tomorrow's welcome party?)

　 B: 隨便。你想穿什麼就穿什麼。[predicate]
　　随便。你想穿什么就穿什么。
　　(Whatever you like.)

❷ 現在是上課時間，你一會兒出去，一會兒進來，
　太隨便了。[predicate]
　現在是上课时间，你一会儿出去，一会儿进来，
　太随便了。
　(It's class time now. You are in and out of the classroom as you please. That's way out of line.)

❸ 上課不能隨便說話，有問題要舉手。[adverbial]
　上课不能随便说话，有问题要举手。
　(You can't speak whenever you feel like it. If you have a question, raise your hand.)

❹ A: 你為什麼問他交沒交女朋友？
　　你为什么问他交没交女朋友？
　　(Why did you ask if he had a girlfriend?)

　 B: 沒什麼，只是隨便問問。[adverbial]
　　没什么，只是随便问问。
　　(No reason. I was just asking a casual question.)

F. 即使 (even if)

In 即使⋯也⋯, 即使 indicates a condition and a concession. The structure 即使⋯ usually presents a hypothetical situation, and the 也⋯ structure indicates a result or conclusion reached despite the previously mentioned hypothetical scenario.

❶   即使熬夜不睡覺，我也要把這篇文章寫完。

即使熬夜不睡觉，我也要把这篇文章写完。

(Even if I [have to] stay up all night, I will finish writing this article.)

❷   我啊！即使不吃東西只喝水，也會胖。

我啊！即使不吃东西只喝水，也会胖。

(For me, even if I didn't eat anything and just drank water, I'd still put on weight.)

❸   他的事業非常成功，但是太忙。即使是感恩節，也在辦公室
工作。

他的事业非常成功，但是太忙。即使是感恩节，也在办公室
工作。

(His career is very successful, but he is too busy. He has to work in the office even on Thanksgiving.)

G. 可見／可见 (it is obvious that; it can be seen that)

可見／可见 is a conjunction. It introduces a conclusion based on a previous statement or scenario.

❶   **A:**   小李，對不起，昨天去健身房鍛煉，我忘了找你了。

小李，对不起，昨天去健身房锻炼，我忘了找你了。

(Little Li, I'm sorry. I went to the gym to work out yesterday, and forgot to ask you to come along.)

B: 可見你不重視我這個朋友。

可见你不重视我这个朋友。

(Obviously, you don't think much of me as a friend.)

A: 不，不，我最近老忘這忘那的。

不，不，我最近老忘这忘那的。

(Oh no, I've been absent-minded recently.)

B: 沒事兒，我只是隨便說說，開玩笑。

没事儿，我只是随便说说，开玩笑。

(It's OK. I didn't really mean it. I was just joking.)

❷ 現在很多人都不吸煙了，可見人們對健康還是重視的。

现在很多人都不吸烟了，可见人们对健康还是重视的。

(Nowadays many people have stopped smoking. You can see that people do care about their health.)

❸ 你申請哪個公司哪個公司要你，可見你很棒。

你申请哪个公司哪个公司要你，可见你很棒。

(Every company you applied to wanted to hire you. Obviously, you are outstanding.)

H. 否則/否则 (otherwise)

否則/否则 is synonymous with 要不然, but is more literary in flavor. It generally occurs at the beginning of the second clause of a compound sentence:

❶ 麗莎說，旅行的時候一定要多帶幾件衣服，否則會很不方便。

丽莎说，旅行的时候一定要多带几件衣服，否则会很不方便。

(Lisa says that when you travel [you must] be sure to pack a lot of clothes; otherwise it'll be very inconvenient.)

❷ 過年的時候你一定要給爺爺奶奶打電話拜年，否則他們會不高興的。

过年的时候你一定要给爷爷奶奶打电话拜年，否则他们会不高兴的。

(You must call Grandpa and Grandma on New Year; otherwise they won't be very happy.)

❸   發燒得趕快去看醫生，否則小病變成大病就糟糕了。

发烧得赶快去看医生，否则小病变成大病就糟糕了。

(If you have a fever, you'd better see a doctor as soon as possible, or a small ailment will turn into a serious medical condition.)

Language Practice

A. The Domino Effect

Based on each of the scenarios below, use 使 to express the idea that one thing sets another thing in motion.

EXAMPLE:

reading Chinese news online every day → his Chinese is getting better and better

→   每天上網看中文新聞，   每天上网看中文新闻，
　　　使他的中文越來越好。   使他的中文越来越好。

1. staying at a bed-and-breakfast every night → he saved a lot of money

2. practicing tai chi every morning → he is getting healthier

3. staying up late often → her eyes have almost become like a panda's

4. her dog is getting fatter and fatter → she is very worried

B. How's Your Math?

Work with a partner to do the following math problems in Chinese.

EXAMPLE: 135 + 40 = ?

→ A: 一百三十五加四十等於多少？ A: 一百三十五加四十等于多少？
  B: 一百三十五加四十等於   B: 一百三十五加四十等于
    一百七十五。   一百七十五。

1. 76 + 36 = ? **2.** 308 + 699 = ?
3. 1122 − 34 = ? **4.** 253 − 148 = ?

C. Are You Accommodating?

a. As an accommodating host, what would you say to make your guest feel at ease?

EXAMPLE:

Guest: 你叫我給你寫幾個漢字？ Guest: 你叫我给你写几个汉字？
    寫什麼？   写什么？
→ Host: 隨便寫。   Host: 随便写。

1. Guest: 我把地圖還給您。 **1.** Guest: 我把地图还给您。
      放哪兒？   放哪儿？

  Host: Host:

2. Guest: 你這兒這麼多雜誌， **2.** Guest: 你这儿这么多杂志，
      我能不能拿一本？   我能不能拿一本？

  Host: Host:

3. Guest: 電視裏有足球賽， **3.** Guest: 电视里有足球赛，
      籃球賽，你想看什麼   篮球赛，你想看什么
      比賽？   比赛？

  Host:

b. You are the kind of easygoing person who will go along with whatever comes your way, and you think that people should do whatever they like.

EXAMPLE: What would you like for dinner?

→ A: 今天晚餐想吃點兒什麼？   A: 今天晚餐想吃点儿什么？

   B: 隨便，你做什麼就吃什麼。   B: 随便，你做什么就吃什么。

1. Which outfit should I wear for tonight's party?

2. Which color should we choose for the walls in the living room?

3. Where should we spend our Thanksgiving holiday?

4. Which tour group should we sign up for?

D. It's Obvious That...

Work with a partner. First state the given scenario, and then draw an inference from that description by using 可見/可见.

EXAMPLE:

他不回你的電話、電郵、短信，   他不回你的电话、电邮、短信，
可見他不想跟你交朋友。   可见他不想跟你交朋友。

1. 張天明從早到晚玩電腦遊戲，   **1.** 张天明从早到晚玩电脑游戏，
   常常忘了吃飯、睡覺，   常常忘了吃饭、睡觉，
   _____   _____

2. 張天明買衣服只看牌子，   **2.** 张天明买衣服只看牌子，
   從來不管價錢，   从来不管价钱，
   _____   _____

3. 麗莎在餐館點菜，   **3.** 丽莎在餐馆点菜，
   老是點青菜、豆腐，   老是点青菜、豆腐，
   _____   _____

4. 柯林和雪梅兩個人在一起   **4.** 柯林和雪梅两个人在一起
   無論做什麼都是有説有笑的…   无论做什么都是有说有笑的…
   _____   _____

E. Giving Your Advice

Warn your friend of the likely negative consequences if he or she doesn't do the following things.

EXAMPLE:　復習　　　　　　　　　　　复习

→　你得復習，否則考試考得不好。你得复习，否则考试考得不好。

1. 鍛煉
2. 注意飲食
3. 早睡早起

1. 锻炼
2. 注意饮食
3. 早睡早起

F. To Exercise or Not to Exercise

a. With a partner, take turns answering the following questions concerning your workout routine. If you don't work out at all, explain why.

1. 你平常鍛煉身體嗎？
2. 你平常怎麼鍛煉身體？
3. 你多長時間鍛煉一次？
4. 你每次鍛煉多長時間？
5. 你覺得鍛煉身體有什麼好處？

1. 你平常锻炼身体吗？
2. 你平常怎么锻炼身体？
3. 你多长时间锻炼一次？
4. 你每次锻炼多长时间？
5. 你觉得锻炼身体有什么好处？

b. Connect your answers into to a coherent paragraph, and tell your class about your exercise routine.

G. It's Good for Your Body!

a. What would a doctor, a dietitian, or a personal trainer advise you to do to stay healthy, fit, and young? Write their advice on the following chart.

多 _____   少 _____   別 _____

_____

b. In addition to the above, what other advice can you think of?

_____

買菜的時候買什麼？
买菜的时候买什么？

H. Writing Practice

Fill in the blanks with the proper words and phrases from below and from the text of this lesson.

除了	以外	最好	要	還/还	另外

一個人要想身體好，就應該重視鍛煉身體，＿＿＿＿鍛煉身體＿＿＿＿，＿＿＿＿要注意飲食，＿＿＿＿多喝水，多吃青菜水果；早餐＿＿＿＿，午餐＿＿＿＿，晚餐＿＿＿＿。＿＿＿＿，還要有良好的生活習慣，不＿＿＿＿，不＿＿＿＿，早睡早起，＿＿＿＿不熬夜。

一个人要想身体好，就应该重视锻炼身体，＿＿＿＿锻炼身体＿＿＿＿，＿＿＿＿要注意饮食，＿＿＿＿多喝水，多吃青菜水果；早餐＿＿＿＿，午餐＿＿＿＿，晚餐＿＿＿＿。＿＿＿＿，还要有良好的生活习惯，不＿＿＿＿，不＿＿＿＿，早睡早起，＿＿＿＿不熬夜。

Pinyin Text

Lìshā dào Běijīng hòu méiyǒu zhù liúxuéshēng gōngyù, wèile gèng duō de liǎojiě Zhōngguó rén de shēnghuó, tā zhù jìn le yí ge Zhōngguó jiātíng. Fángdōng fūqī èr rén dōu yǐ① tuì xiū, nǚ'ér Lǐ Wén zài bówùguǎn gōngzuò, yǔ② fùmǔ zhù zài yìqǐ. Lǐ Wén hěn xiǎng qù Měiguó liú xué, suǒyǐ qǐng Lìshā zuò tā de Yīngwén jiājiào, zhèyàng Lìshā jiù búbì fù fángzū le. Yóuyú Lìshā měi tiān dōu gēn Lǐ Wén de fùmǔ shuō Zhōngwén, suǒyǐ tā de Zhōngwén yě jìnbù de hěn kuài.

Lìshā měi tiān zǎoshang dōu chū qu sàn bù, zài tā zhù de zhè ge xiǎoqū, zài jiē biān, zài gōngyuán, dōu néng kàn jiàn hěn duō rén, tèbié shì lǎorén, zài duànliàn shēntǐ. Tāmen yǒude③ zhàn chéng yí ge quān gāo gāo xìng xìng de tiào wǔ, yǒude pái chéng duì, màn mān de dǎ tàijíquán. Zhè xiē zǎochen duànliàn❶ de rénmen, chéngwéi Běijīng tèbié de "fēngjǐng", shǐ④ zhè ge chéngshì xiǎnde fēicháng yǒu huólì.

Zhè yì tiān zǎoshang Lìshā zhèng yào chū mén, Lǐ Wén cóng fángjiān zǒu chu lai.

Lǐ Wén:	Lìshā, jīntiān shì xīngqīliù, zěnme zhème zǎo jiù qǐ chuáng le?
Lìshā:	Wǒ běnlái xiǎng gēn shūshu, āyí qù xué tàijíquán, méi xiǎng dào tāmen nàme zǎo jiù chū qu le.
Lǐ Wén:	Wǒ yǐwéi nǐ zhǐ xǐhuan zuò yújiā❷, zěnme duì tàijíquán yě yǒu xìngqù?
Lìshā:	Tàijíquán hé yújiā yíyàng, búdàn duì shēntǐ yǒu hǎochu, érqiě dòngzuò hěn měi.
Lǐ Wén:	Lìshā, nǐ kàn dà shù xià bian, wǒ bà, wǒ mā zhèngzài gēn nà xiē tuì xiū lǎorén dǎ tàijíquán ne! Nǐ qù zhǎo tāmen ba.
Lìshā:	Hǎo, yí huìr jiù qù. Tāmen dǎ de zhēn bàng, hǎoxiàng zài biǎoyǎn yíyàng. Wǒ měitiān zǎochen chū qu sàn bù, kàn jiàn dàochù dōu shì yùndòng de rén. Zhōngguó rén zhēn zhòngshì duànliàn shēntǐ a!
Lǐ Wén:	Duì, xiànzài dàjiā dōu yuè lái yuè zhùyì shēntǐ jiànkāng le. Āi, Lìshā, Měiguó rén yìbān zěnme duànliàn shēntǐ?
Lìshā:	Yībān shì pǎo bù, yóu yǒng, dǎ qiú děng děng, yǒu xiē rén yě qù jiànshēnfáng. Zhìyú wǒ, chúle zuò yújiā yǐwài, ǒu'ěr yě pǎo bù.
Lǐ Wén:	Nánguài nǐ de shēntǐ zhème jiànkāng, shēncái zhème hǎo.
Lìshā:	Wǒ juéde rúguǒ xiǎng shēntǐ jiànkāng, shēncái hǎo, chúle duō yùndòng yǐwài, hái yīnggāi zhùyì yǐnshí.
Lǐ Wén:	Nǐ yì diǎnr dōu bú pàng, hái xūyào zhùyì yǐnshí ma?

Lìshā: Zhùyì yǐnshí bù děngyú jiǎn féi. Wǒ rènwéi zhǐyào shēntǐ jiànkāng jiù hǎo, pàng shòu bìng bú zhòngyào.

Lǐ Wén: Wǒ gōngzuò máng, méi shíjiān hǎo hāor chī fàn, chángcháng suíbiàn luàn chī. Nǐ shì zěnme zhùyì yǐnshí de ne?

Lìshā: Duō hē shuǐ, duō chī qīngcài, shuǐguǒ. Lìngwài, jíshǐ nǐ fēicháng máng, yě yídìng yào chī zǎofàn, érqiě zǎofàn yào yǒu yíngyǎng; wǔfàn yào chī bǎo, yīnwèi xiàwǔ hái yào xuéxí hé gōngzuò; wǎnfàn jiù yào shǎo chī yì diǎn, bùrán huì yuè lái yuè pàng, yīnwèi lí shàng chuáng shuì jiào de shíjiān tài jìn le.

Lǐ Wén: Wǒmen Zhōngguó rén yǒu yí jù huà: Zǎocān yào chī hǎo, wǔcān yào chī bǎo, wǎncān yào chī shǎo❸, gēn nǐ shuō de jīhū yíyàng.

Lìshā: Zhēn de? Zhōngguó rén yě zhème shuō? Kějiàn shì yǒu kēxué dàoli de.

Lǐ Wén: Yào xiǎng shēntǐ hǎo, zài qítā fāngmiàn yě yào zhùyì.

Lìshā: Nǐ de yìsi shì yào yǒu liánghǎo de shēnghuó xíguàn, duì bu duì?

Lǐ Wén: Duì. Bù xī yān, bù hē jiǔ, zǎo shuì zǎo qǐ, zuìhǎo bú yào áo yè. Bié de dōu méi wèntí, jiù shì bù áo yè wǒ kě zuò bú dào. Wǒ wǎnshang chángcháng děi kāi yèchē❹ zhǔnbèi kǎo yánjiūshēng.

Lìshā: Nà nǐ bìxū❺ jǐn kěnéng zhǎo shíjiān bǔchōng shuìmián.

Lǐ Wén: Nǐ shuō de duì, wǒ shì děi zhùyì le, fǒuzé wǒ de liǎng zhī yǎnjing dōu kuài biàn chéng xióngmāo❻ yǎn le.

English Text

After Lisa arrived in Beijing, she didn't stay in the international students' dorm. To learn more about the lives of the Chinese people, she moved in with a Chinese family. The landlord and his wife are both retired. Their daughter Li Wen works at a museum and lives with her parents. Li Wen would very much like to go to America to study, so she asked Lisa to be her English tutor. This way Lisa won't have to pay rent. Because Lisa speaks Chinese with Li Wen's parents every day, her Chinese has improved a lot.

Every morning Lisa goes out for a walk. In the residential area where she lives, on the street corners and in the parks you can see many people, especially older people, exercising. Some of them stand in circles and have a good time dancing. Some form rows and slowly practice tai chi. These people who exercise every morning have become a special part of the Beijing "landscape" and make the city seem full of vitality.

This morning Lisa is about to go out when Li Wen comes out from her room.

Li Wen: Lisa, today is Saturday. How come you are up so early?

Lisa: I thought I'd like to learn tai chi with Uncle and Auntie. I didn't expect them to go out so early.

Li Wen: I thought you only liked to do yoga. How come you are interested in tai chi, too?

Lisa: Tai chi and yoga are alike. Not only are they good for you, the movements are also very beautiful.

Li Wen: Lisa, look, under the big trees my mom and dad are practicing tai chi with those retirees. Go look for them.

Lisa: OK. I'll leave in a moment. They are so great; they look as if they were performing. Every morning I go out for a walk and see people exercising everywhere. Chinese people really take exercising very seriously.

Li Wen: That's right. Nowadays people pay more and more attention to health. Lisa, how do Americans usually exercise?

Lisa: Generally, they jog, swim, play ball, and so on. Some people also go to the gym. As for me, besides doing yoga, I occasionally jog, too.

Li Wen: No wonder you are so healthy and have such a good figure.

Lisa: I think if you want to be healthy and have a good figure, besides getting plenty of exercise, you also have to pay attention to your diet.

Li Wen: You don't have one ounce of fat on you. Do you still need to pay attention to your diet?

Lisa: Paying attention to your diet is not the same as losing weight. I think as long as you are healthy then you're fine. Weight isn't so important.

Li Wen: I'm busy with work and don't have time to eat well. I often just eat whatever I can find. How do you pay attention to your diet?

Lisa: I drink lots of water and eat lots of vegetables and fruit. Besides, even if you are very busy, you must have breakfast, and it must be nutritious. Have a big lunch because you have to study and work in the afternoon. Have a small dinner. Otherwise you'll put on more and more weight, because it's too close to bedtime.

Li Wen: We Chinese have a saying, "Eat a good breakfast, a big lunch, and a small dinner," which says more or less the same thing.

Lisa: Really? The Chinese say the same thing? Then obviously, there's a scientific basis to it.

Li Wen: If you want to be healthy, you have to pay attention to other areas, too.

Lisa: You mean you have to have a good lifestyle, right?

Li Wen: Right. Don't smoke, don't drink. Go to bed early and get up early. It's best not to stay up late. I can do them all except for not staying up late. I often have to burn the midnight oil to prepare for the graduate admissions exam.

Lisa: Then you must find time to make up for your sleep deficit as much as possible.

Li Wen: You're right. I do have to pay attention, or my two eyes will soon turn into panda eyes.

SELF-ASSESSMENT

How well can you do these things? Check (✓) the boxes to evaluate your progress and see which areas you may need to practice more.

I can	Very Well	OK	A Little
Talk about my exercise routine	☐	☐	☐
Outline healthy eating habits	☐	☐	☐
Describe lifestyle habits that could make me age prematurely or harm my health	☐	☐	☐

第十五課　第十五課
男女平等　男女平等

 LEARNING OBJECTIVES

In this lesson, you will learn to use Chinese to

1. Talk about how couples treat each other as equals;
2. Discuss gender equality in the workplace;
3. Summarize briefly the changes in Chinese women's social status in the twentieth century;
4. Report the score and results of a sports game.

RELATE AND GET READY

In your own culture/community—

- Do men and women both do chores at home?
- Do people tease men who are overly deferential to their wives?
- Do male and female athletes receive equal pay in professional sports?

Before You Study

Check the statements that apply to you.

☐ 1. I know couples that share household responsibilities.

When You Study

Listen to the audio recording and scan the text. Ask yourself the following questions before you begin a close reading of the text.

☐ 1. Historically speaking, were men and women treated as equals in China?

☐ 2. What were the two different stages in the evolution of Chinese women's social status since 1950?

在歷史上，中國是一個重男輕女的社會，婦女的家庭地位和社會地位都比男人低得多。1950年以後，情況逐漸❶發生了變化。特別是在城市裏，女孩子和男孩子一樣有受教育和參加工作的機會，婦女的社會地位也有了很大的提高。

但是改革開放以來，在某①些企業和事業單位❷，又出現了男女不平等的現象。比如，找工作的時候，婦女常常比男人更

LANGUAGE NOTES

❶ 逐漸/逐渐 means the same thing as 漸漸/渐渐 except that 漸漸/渐渐 is more colloquial.

❷ 企業單位/企业单位 refers to work units that are engaged in economic activities such as production, transportation, and trade. Typical 企業單位/企业单位 include factories, mines, railroad enterprises,

☐ 2. I have witnessed unequal treatment between the two genders.

☐ 3. I have encountered unfair treatment at school or in the workplace because of my gender.

☐ 3. Does Xuemei's uncle share household chores with his wife?

☐ 4. Is Xuemei's uncle's wife a fan of the Chinese men's soccer team?

☐ 5. Does the Chinese men's soccer team have a winning record?

 在历史上，中国是一个重男轻女的社会，妇女的家庭地位和社会地位都比男人低得多。1950年以后，情况逐渐❶发生了变化。特别是在城市里，女孩子和男孩子一样有受教育和参加工作的机会，妇女的社会地位也有了很大的提高。

但是改革开放以来，在某①些企业和事业单位❷，又出现了男女不平等的现象。比如，找工作的时候，妇女常常比男人更

and companies. 事業單位/事业单位, on the other hand, refers to units that are financed not by their own economic activities but through government funding, such as schools and hospitals.

困難；一些工廠和公司還沒有做到男女同工同酬。當然，也有一些女性，無論在工作上還是收入上，都超過一般男人。不過她們在女性中畢竟②只是少數。

現在在一般中國家庭中，很多夫妻都是互相體貼、互相照顧，所以，家庭可能是現在中國社會男女最平等的地方。拿林雪梅的舅舅來說吧，他是個大球迷，只有在看電視裏的足球賽的時候才表現出一點兒"大男子主義"，什麼家務都不做。可是比賽一結束，他就忙著幫舅媽做飯、洗碗，又成了一位"模範丈夫"。

雪梅：	舅舅，今天怎麼您洗碗呀？
舅舅：	哈哈，因為我洗碗洗得比你舅媽乾淨啊。
雪梅：	我來洗吧！我洗碗也是洗得很乾淨的③。
舅媽：	別、別、別，你們從雲南旅遊回來，就忙著找工作、面試，還没休息過來④呢。再說，你舅舅呀，昨天晚上看球看到夜裏一點，今天還不得好好表現表現？
柯林：	舅舅，您是不是得了那種病，叫什麼"氣管炎"？
舅舅：	柯林，你的中文水平真不錯，連這個都知道。不過不是"氣管炎"，而是"妻管嚴"❸。"妻"是"妻子"的"妻"。
柯林：	對、對、對，"氣管炎"是一種病。
舅舅：	你小心，"妻管嚴"可比"氣管炎"屬害多了。你將來千萬可別得這種病。
雪梅：	舅舅，看您說的。對了，昨天晚上是什麼比賽啊？
舅舅：	男子足球賽，北京隊對上海隊。
舅媽：	那有什麼好看的？我最討厭那些男足隊員了，平常驕傲得不得了，可是比賽的時候老輸球。所以，我只看中國女足，她們比男足棒多了。

LANGUAGE NOTES

❸ 妻管嚴/妻管严, which literally means "the wife strictly controls [the husband]," is a facetious phrase coined to sound like 氣管炎/气管炎 (tracheitis). Sometimes people say someone has 氣管炎/气管炎

困难；一些工厂和公司还没有做到男女同工同酬。当然，也有一些女性，无论在工作上还是收入上，都超过一般男人。不过她们在女性中毕竟②只是少数。

现在在一般中国家庭中，很多夫妻都是互相体贴、互相照顾，所以，家庭可能是现在中国社会男女最平等的地方。拿林雪梅的舅舅来说吧，他是个大球迷，只有在看电视里的足球赛的时候才表现出一点儿"大男子主义"，什么家务都不做。可是比赛一结束，他就忙着帮舅妈做饭、洗碗，又成了一位"模范丈夫"。

雪梅：	舅舅，今天怎么您洗碗呀？
舅舅：	哈哈，因为我洗碗洗得比你舅妈干净啊。
雪梅：	我来洗吧！我洗碗也是洗得很干净的③。
舅妈：	别、别、别，你们从云南旅游回来，就忙着找工作、面试，还没休息过来④呢。再说，你舅舅呀，昨天晚上看球看到夜里一点，今天还不得好好表现表现？
柯林：	舅舅，您是不是得了那种病，叫什么"气管炎"？
舅舅：	柯林，你的中文水平真不错，连这个都知道。不过不是"气管炎"，而是"妻管严"❸。"妻"是"妻子"的"妻"。
柯林：	对、对、对，"气管炎"是一种病。
舅舅：	你小心，"妻管严"可比"气管炎"厉害多了。你将来千万可别得这种病。
雪梅：	舅舅，看您说的。对了，昨天晚上是什么比赛啊？
舅舅：	男子足球赛，北京队对上海队。
舅妈：	那有什么好看的？我最讨厌那些男足队员了，平常骄傲得不得了，可是比赛的时候老输球。所以，我只看中国女足，她们比男足棒多了。

---

when they mean that he has a case of 妻管嚴/妻管严 (being henpecked). Some would argue that this expression is itself an example of sexism.

雪梅： 不錯，女足是比男足成績好，可是我聽説女足隊員掙的錢
不到男足的十分之一❹，真不公平。

柯林： 別忘了，他們的收入是由市場經濟來決定的。美國職業女
籃隊員的薪水跟職業男籃比，也少多了。

舅舅： 哎，別老説中國男足輸球了。我剛看到網上的消息説，中
國男足昨天贏了世界冠軍隊。

舅媽： 我不相信，網上亂説吧？

舅舅： 好像是真的。網上説，這次中國男足踢得不錯，比分一直
是0比0。比賽結束前一分鐘，中國男足才踢進一球，以
1比0贏了比賽。

柯林： 沒想到，真的沒想到，太棒了！那這個世界冠軍隊是巴西
隊還是意大利隊？

舅舅： 中國乒乓球女隊。

大家： 啊？

舅媽： 肯定是什麼人在開男足的玩笑！

舅舅： 哈哈哈⋯

After You Study

Challenge yourself to complete the following tasks in Chinese.

1. Recap what has happened to women in China since the Reform and Opening-Up policy was implemented.

2. Recap the joking explanations by Xuemei's uncle and aunt of why her uncle is doing the dishes.

LANGUAGE NOTES

❹ 十分之一 means 1/10, literally "one [part] out of ten."

雪梅： 不错，女足是比男足成绩好，可是我听说女足队员挣的钱不到男足的十分之一❹，真不公平。

柯林： 别忘了，他们的收入是由市场经济来决定的。美国职业女篮队员的薪水跟职业男篮比，也少多了。

舅舅： 哎，别老说中国男足输球了。我刚看到网上的消息说，中国男足昨天赢了世界冠军队。

舅妈： 我不相信，网上乱说吧？

舅舅： 好像是真的。网上说，这次中国男足踢得不错，比分一直是0比0。比赛结束前一分钟，中国男足才踢进一球，以1比0赢了比赛。

柯林： 没想到，真的没想到，太棒了！那这个世界冠军队是巴西队还是意大利队？

舅舅： 中国乒乓球女队。

大家： 啊？

舅妈： 肯定是什么人在开男足的玩笑！

舅舅： 哈哈哈…

3. Explain why Xuemei's aunt is not fond of the Chinese men's soccer team.

4. Summarize what Xuemei finds unfair about Chinese soccer players' pay levels.

5. Recap Xuemei's uncle's report of the match between the Chinese men's soccer team and the world champion team.

VOCABULARY

1.	平等		píngděng	adj/n	equal; equality
2.	重男 輕女	重男 轻女	zhòng nán qīng nǚ		to regard males as superior to females; to privilege men over women
3.	婦女	妇女	fùnǚ	n	women
4.	地位		dìwèi	n	position; status
5.	以來	以来	yǐlái	t	since
6.	情況	情况	qíngkuàng	n	situation; condition; circumstances
7.	逐漸	逐渐	zhújiàn	adv	gradually; little by little
8.	機會	机会	jīhuì	n	opportunity
9.	改革 開放	改革 开放	gǎigé kāifàng		to reform and open up; Reform and Opening-Up
10.	某		mǒu	pr	certain; some; an indefinite person or thing [See Grammar 1.]
11.	企業	企业	qǐyè	n	enterprise; business; company; firm
12.	單位	单位	dānwèi	n	unit
13.	出現	出现	chūxiàn	v	to appear; to arise; to emerge
14.	現象	现象	xiànxiàng	n	phenomenon; appearance
15.	困難	困难	kùnnan	n/adj	difficulty; difficult
16.	工廠	工厂	gōngchǎng	n	factory
17.	同工 同酬		tóng gōng tóng chóu		equal pay for equal work
18.	女性		nǚxìng	n	female gender; woman
19.	超過	超过	chāoguò	v	to surpass; to exceed

20.	畢竟	毕竟	bìjìng	adv	after all; all in all; in the final analysis; when all is said and done [See Grammar 2.]
21.	互相		hùxiāng	adv	mutually; each other; reciprocally
22.	體貼	体贴	tǐtiē	v	to care for; to be considerate of (someone)
23.	表現	表现	biǎoxiàn	v/n	to display; to manifest; performance; manifestation
24.	大男子主義	大男子主义	dà nánzǐ zhǔyì		male chauvinism
25.	家務	家务	jiāwù	n	household chores; household duties
26.	模範	模范	mófàn	adj/n	exemplary; model; fine example
27.	丈夫		zhàngfu	n	husband
28.	氣管炎	气管炎	qìguǎnyán	n	tracheitis
29.	妻管嚴	妻管严	qī guǎn yán		wife controls (her husband) strictly
30.	妻子		qīzi	n	wife
31.	得病		dé bìng	vo	to fall ill; to contract a disease
32.	男子		nánzǐ	n	man; male
33.	討厭	讨厌	tǎoyàn	v/adj	to dislike; to loathe; disgusting; disagreeable
34.	隊員	队员	duìyuán	n	team member
35.	驕傲	骄傲	jiāo'ào	adj/n	proud; arrogant; full of oneself; pride
36.	不得了		bù déliǎo		extremely; exceedingly; couldn't be more
37.	輸	输	shū	v	to lose; to be defeated

38.	成績	成绩	chéngjì	n	performance; achievement; result; score; grade
39.	公平		gōngpíng	adj	fair; just; impartial; equitable
40.	由		yóu	prep	by
41.	市場	市场	shìchǎng	n	market
42.	職業	职业	zhíyè	n	occupation; profession; vocation
43.	薪水	薪水	xīnshuǐ	n	salary; pay; wages
44.	消息		xiāoxi	n	news; message; information
45.	贏	赢	yíng	v	to win
46.	冠軍	冠军	guànjūn	n	champion; first place in a competition
47.	相信		xiāngxìn	v	to believe; to trust
48.	比分		bǐfēn	n	score
49.	乒乓球		pīngpāngqiú	n	Ping-Pong; table tennis

Proper Nouns

50.	巴西		Bāxī		Brazil
51.	意大利		Yìdàlì		Italy

Enlarged Characters

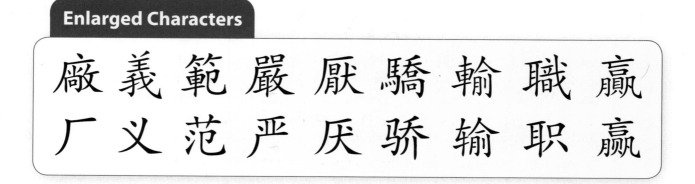

廠 義 範 嚴 厭 驕 輸 職 贏
厂 义 范 严 厌 骄 输 职 赢

Culture Highlights

❶ From the 1950s to the late 1970s, China used to be a planned economy, 計劃經濟/计划经济, under which national economic plans were made by the central government and implemented by all the enterprises. Throughout the years of economic reform in recent decades, China has gradually evolved into a market economy, 市場經濟/市场经济, which the Chinese government calls a "socialist market economy." The Chinese Reform and Opening-Up known as 改革開放/改革开放 started in 1978. Since then, tens of millions of people have been lifted out of poverty.

❷ Traditional Chinese culture heavily favored men over women. Even today, in the countryside the desire to have boys remains very strong. This preference for boys has resulted in a gender imbalance in the country's population.

❸ In some sports, such as volleyball, soccer, long-distance running, and swimming, female Chinese athletes have consistently done better than their male counterparts.

❹ 男人, 女人, 男子, 女子, 男性, 女性, 男生, 女生, 婦女/妇女: These words for men and women are used in different stylistic contexts. 男人 and 女人 can refer to unfamiliar or indefinite people: 房間裏有幾個男人/房间里有几个男人 (There are several men in the room), 一個女人的笑聲/一个女人的笑声 (the sound of a woman laughing). However, it sounds disrespectful and impolite to use these to refer to a definite person, especially an acquaintance. For instance, 那個男人是你的男朋友嗎？/那个男人是你的男朋友吗？ (Is that man your boyfriend?) It sounds better to say: 那個男的是你的男朋友嗎？/那个男的是你的男朋友吗？ 男的 and 女的 are more neutral. When 男人 and 女人 are used as collective nouns, there is no question of being impolite: 男人的問題和女人不同/男人的问题和女人不同。 (Men and women have different issues.) 男子 and 女子 are often used to refer to gender-specific categories or institutions such as names of competitive sports, e.g., 男子100米 (men's hundred-meter dash), 女子跳高 (women's high jump), 女子時裝/女子时装 (women's fashion), 女子學院/女子学院 (women's college), etc. 男性 and 女性 are usually used as collective nouns and are more polite than 男人 and 女人. 男生 and 女生 literally refer to male and female students. However, in Taiwan they often mean men and women in general. This usage has also caught on among some young people in mainland China. The word 婦女/妇女 often has social and political connotations, e.g., 婦女節/妇女节 (Women's Day), 婦女運動/妇女运动 (women's movement), etc. There isn't a corresponding term for men.

❺ The words 丈夫 and 妻子 (husband and wife) refer to partners in a marriage. They occur mainly in legal contexts such as on official forms. Sometimes, one can also refer to a spouse as 我丈夫 (my husband) or 他妻子 (his wife). However, these terms are rarely used among friends and acquaintances. After 1949, most people in mainland China called their spouses 愛人/爱人. However, since the 1980s, the word has gradually lost currency. However, on formal occasions, particularly among educated people, 愛人/爱人 is still quite common. In Taiwan, however, 愛人/爱人 means "lover." During the Republican era before 1949, 先生 and 太太 were the default terms for husband and wife. After 1949, people in mainland China stopped using them completely because the words were considered "feudal" or "bourgeois." They have been revived in recent years. However, they are still not common in mainland China, particularly among the working classes. 老公 (lǎogōng) and 老婆 (lǎopó) are informal terms that have become trendy among some young people. They can be used to refer to one's marriage partner or to address him or her directly. In northern China, many young men call their wives 媳婦/媳妇 (xífu). Older people call their spouses 老伴兒/老伴儿. As has been noted, these usages can differ somewhat among Chinese speakers of different regions, ages, and socioeconomic groups.

Grammar

1. Pronoun 某

某 is a pronoun referring to a person or object that is indefinite either because the referent is unclear or because the speaker does not wish to name it.

❶ 我們班某個同學最近常常不來上課，這樣下去恐怕學習會有大問題。

我们班某个同学最近常常不来上课，这样下去恐怕学习会有大问题。

(A certain student in our class has been skipping classes lately. If he continues like this, he'll have a big problem academically.)

❷ 我昨天去某個男生宿舍看了看，太亂了。

我昨天去某个男生宿舍看了看，太乱了。

(Yesterday I went to a certain male students' dorm. It was too messy.)

2. Adverb 畢竟/毕竟

This adverb means "everything else having been considered." The speaker is basing his or her conclusion on all the factors including extenuating circumstances. The point of the statement is to elucidate or emphasize a fact or underlying reason, so the word is similar in meaning to the English expressions "after all" and "when all is said and done."

❶ 他畢竟才學了幾個星期的瑜伽，有些動作還做得不好。

他毕竟才学了几个星期的瑜伽，有些动作还做得不好。

(After all, he's only been taking yoga lessons for a few weeks. He still can't master some of the movements.)

❷ 張太太畢竟剛搬進小區，對附近的環境還不太熟悉。

张太太毕竟刚搬进小区，对附近的环境还不太熟悉。

(After all, Mrs. Zhang has just moved to this residential community. She's not familiar with the surroundings yet.)

到底 can also be used in this way. In the above sentences, 畢竟/毕竟 can be replaced with 到底.

(1a) 他到底才學了幾個星期的瑜伽，有些動作還做得不好。

他到底才学了几个星期的瑜伽，有些动作还做得不好。

(2a) 張太太到底剛搬進小區，對附近的環境還不太熟悉。

张太太到底刚搬进小区，对附近的环境还不太熟悉。

到底 can also be used to make further inquiries. 畢竟/毕竟 cannot. Therefore, in the following sentences 到底 and 畢竟/毕竟 are not interchangeable:

❸ 　你到底去不去哈爾濱看冰燈？

你到底去不去哈尔滨看冰灯？

(Are you going to Harbin to see the ice lanterns or not?)

❹ **A:** 你昨天晚上到底幾點睡的覺？你看你的眼睛都快變成熊貓眼了。

你昨天晚上到底几点睡的觉？你看你的眼睛都快变成熊猫眼了。

(What time did you go to bed last night after all? Look at the dark circles under your eyes.) [lit. Your eyes are turning into panda eyes.]

B: 我昨天熬夜準備期末考，早晨五點才睡。

我昨天熬夜准备期末考，早晨五点才睡。

(I stayed up all night to prepare for the final exam, and didn't go to bed until five o'clock this morning.)

3. 是…的 to Affirm a Statement

是…的 makes a statement sound stronger. Let's take a look at this sentence:

我是昨天來的。

我是昨天来的。

(I arrived yesterday.)

We have come across this construction in Level 1. When a verb such as 來/来 in the example above denotes a completed action that has already taken place, 是 is used to introduce the time (e.g., 昨天 in the example), place, or manner of the action. The construction highlights the focal point of the sentence. 是 can be omitted, but 的 is required. However, in this lesson, 是…的 functions differently.

❶   我洗碗也是洗得很乾淨的。

       我洗碗也是洗得很干净的。

       (I also do a good job washing dishes.)

是…的 here is to affirm the statement and to assure the listener of its truth.

❷   別擔心，醫生說你父親的身體健康情況是(很)不錯的。

       别担心，医生说你父亲的身体健康情况是(很)不错的。

       (Don't worry. The doctor says that your father's health is [quite] good.)

❸   我相信住在校内是很安全的。

       (I believe it is very safe to live on campus.)

❹   只知道減肥，不注意飲食與睡眠，也不鍛煉，對你是沒有好處的。

       只知道减肥，不注意饮食与睡眠，也不锻炼，对你是没有好处的。

       (Focusing only on losing weight while ignoring your diet and sleep and not exercising won't do you any good.)

       [有好處/有好处 is acting as an adjective.]

❺   我們是很重視学生的健康的。

       我们是很重视学生的健康的。

       (We do take students' health very seriously.)

是…的 can be removed from these sentences. However, the tone of voice will be weaker.

(2a) 別擔心，醫生說你父親的身體健康情況不錯。

       别担心，医生说你父亲的身体健康情况不错。

(3a) 我相信住在校内很安全。

(4a) 只知道減肥，不注意飲食與睡眠，也不鍛煉，對你沒有好處。

只知道减肥，不注意饮食与睡眠，也不锻炼，对你没有好处。

(5a) 我們很重視學生的健康。

我们很重视学生的健康。

The words that can be used with 是···的 in this way are adjectives, as in ❶, ❷, ❸, and ❹. They often take 很, as they tend to do when serving as predicates.

However, verbs can also be used in this 是···的 construction. They have to either follow a modal verb as in ❻ and ❼, have a potential complement as in ❽, or be mental verbs that can be modified by 很, as in ❺. Generally, verbs alone cannot be inserted into the construction; see (6a), (7a), and (8a).

❻ 他是會丟三拉四的。

他是会丢三拉四的。

(He will be a scatterbrain.)

❼ 小張這個人是不會忘這忘那的。

小张这个人是不会忘这忘那的。

(Little Zhang is not someone who is careless and forgetful.)

❽ 你的電腦是找得到的。

你的电脑是找得到的。

(Your computer can be found.)

(6a) *他是丟三拉四的。

(7a) *小張這個人是不忘這忘那的。

*小张这个人是不忘这忘那的。

(8a) *你的電腦是找到的。

*你的电脑是找到的。

4. Complement 過來/过来

As a complement, 過來/过来 can express a resultative meaning: a return to a normal active state.

❶   這幾天他睡得太少了，昨天睡得不錯，都九點了，還沒醒(xǐng)過來呢。

這几天他睡得太少了，昨天睡得不错，都九点了，还没醒(xǐng)过来呢。

(He has been sleeping too little in the last few days. Last night he slept pretty well; it's already nine o'clock, and he still hasn't woken up.)

❷   他病得很厲害，醫生費了好大力氣才把他救(jiù)过来。

他病得很厉害，医生费了好大力气才把他救(jiù)过来。

(He was seriously ill. The doctor barely managed to save him [from the brink of death].)

❸   老師給他講了好幾次，他才明白過來。

老师给他讲了好几次，他才明白过来。

(The teacher explained several times; only then did he get it.)

The opposite of 過來/过来 is 過去/过去. Here are some examples of 過去/过去 as a complement: 死過去了/死过去了 (passed away), 睡過去了/睡过去了 (fell asleep), 暈過去了/晕过去了 (yūn) (lost consciousness).

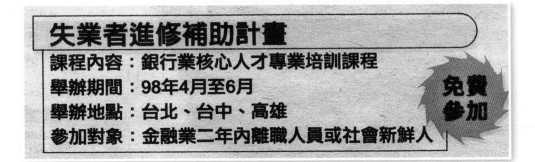

男女都可參加嗎？
男女都可参加吗？

Words & Phrases

A. 逐漸/逐渐 (gradually; little by little)

逐漸/逐渐 is an adverb.

❶ 春天了，天氣逐漸暖和了。

春天了，天气逐渐暖和了。

(It's spring, and the weather has gradually begun to warm up.)

❷ 我開始有點兒討厭我的同屋，後來對他逐漸了解了，也逐漸喜歡他了。

我开始有点儿讨厌我的同屋，后来对他逐渐了解了，也逐渐喜欢他了。

(I didn't like my roommate all that much at first, but later I got to know him more and more and began to like him more and more.)

❸ 柯林到北京一兩個月了，對這個城市逐漸不再感覺陌生了。

柯林到北京一两个月了，对这个城市逐渐不再感觉陌生了。

(Ke Lin has been in Beijing for a couple of months now. He is slowly beginning to feel more and more at home.)

B. ⋯以來/以来 (since)

"⋯以來/以来" means "from a certain point in the past up till now."

❶ 年初以來，已經下了好幾次雪了。

年初以来，已经下了好几次雪了。

(Since the beginning of the year, it has already snowed several times.)

❷ 麗莎自從住在李文家以來，已經逐漸習慣中國人的生活了。

丽莎自从住在李文家以来，已经逐渐习惯中国人的生活了。

(Ever since Lisa started living at Li Wen's place, she's gradually been getting used to the lifestyles of Chinese people.)

❸　改革開放以來，中國的經濟發生了很大的變化。

改革开放以来，中国的经济发生了很大的变化。

(Since the beginning of the Reform and Opening-Up period, China's economy has gone through a great deal of changes.)

C. 拿⋯來說/拿⋯来说 (take...for example)

拿⋯來說/拿⋯来说 is used to cite examples:

❶　我們小區退休的老人都很喜歡運動，拿我爺爺來說吧，就天天鍛煉，一天不鍛煉，就覺得不舒服。

我们小区退休的老人都很喜欢运动，拿我爷爷来说吧，就天天锻炼，一天不锻炼，就觉得不舒服。

(All the retirees in our residential subdivision love to exercise. My grandfather, for example, exercises every day. If he doesn't exercise even for a day, he doesn't feel well.)

❷　1990年以來，中國的變化很大，拿北京來說吧，老北京的樣子幾乎看不出來了。

1990年以来，中国的变化很大，拿北京来说吧，老北京的样子几乎看不出来了。

(Since 1990, China's transformation has been tremendous. Take Beijing for example, you almost can't see the old Beijing anymore.)

D. 表現/表现 (to show; to display; to manifest; performance; manifestation)

表現/表现 is a verb. It is often followed by 出 or 出來/出来 as a complement.

❶　看見我的遊戲機，弟弟表現出極大的興趣。

看见我的游戏机，弟弟表现出极大的兴趣。

(Upon seeing my video game system, my younger brother showed a great deal of interest.)

❷ 等一會兒看見律師，你雖然很緊張，但是也不要表現出來。

等一会儿看见律师，你虽然很紧张，但是也不要表现出来。

(When you meet the lawyer in a moment, although you'll be very nervous, don't show it.)

❸ 比賽贏球，千萬不要表現出驕傲的樣子來。

比赛赢球，千万不要表现出骄傲的样子来。

(When winning a ballgame, never, ever act superior to others.)

表現／表现 can also be a noun.

❹ 他見到你有什麼表現？生氣還是高興？

他见到你有什么表现？生气还是高兴？

(How did he seem [lit. what body language did he reveal] when he saw you? Was he angry or happy?)

E. 看你說的／看你说的 (listen to yourself)

看你說的／看你说的 expresses disagreement and sometimes connotes blame or reproach. However, when responding to a compliment or an expression of gratitude, 看你說的／看你说的 indicates modesty.

❶ **A:** 你整天丟三拉四，忘這忘那，哪個公司哪個工廠敢要你啊？

你整天丢三拉四，忘这忘那，哪个公司哪个工厂敢要你啊？

(You're absentminded and careless. What company or factory would dare to hire you?)

B: 看你說的，沒有那麼嚴重。

看你说的，没有那么严重。

(You're exaggerating. It's not that serious.)

❷ **A:** 你太重要了，這次如果你不跟我們一起來旅遊，我們可能什麼都聽不懂，那還不如不來。

你太重要了，这次如果你不跟我们一起来旅游，我们可能什么都听不懂，那还不如不来。

(You're too important. If you hadn't come with us on this trip, very likely we wouldn't have understood anything we heard and we might as well have not come.)

B: 看你説的，還有導遊呢！
看你说的，还有导游呢！

(You're exaggerating. There's still the tour guide!)

F. 不得了 (extremely; exceedingly)

The expression 不得了 indicates a very high degree.

❶ 他是在這個城市長大的，對這兒熟悉得不得了。
他是在这个城市长大的，对这儿熟悉得不得了。

(He grew up in this city, and nobody knows more about this place than he does.)

❷ 那個人討厭得不得了，別跟他説話。
那个人讨厌得不得了，别跟他说话。

(That guy is an out-and-out nuisance. Don't talk to him.)

❸ 大家聽到球隊贏了冠軍的消息，都高興得不得了。
大家听到球队赢了冠军的消息，都高兴得不得了。

(Upon hearing the news that the team had won the championship, everyone was carried away with joy.)

G. 由 (by)

由 is a preposition. Its function is to introduce the agent performing an action. The agent is indicated by a noun or a pronoun.

❶ 他的學習時間由你安排，我不擔心。
他的学习时间由你安排，我不担心。

(His study hours are set by you. [That's why] I don't have to worry.)

❷ 學什麼專業由我自己選擇，我父母不管。
学什么专业由我自己选择，我父母不管。

(It's up to me to choose my major. My parents don't interfere.)

❸ 我的學費完全由父母負擔。
我的学费完全由父母负担。

(My tuition is taken care of by my parents.)

Language Practice

A. Think About It, After All

Based on each of the scenarios, create a mini-dialogue using 畢竟/毕竟.

EXAMPLE:

Your father is disappointed that you can't read an article in Chinese, and you defend yourself by saying that you have only studied Chinese for two years.

→ **A:** 你怎麼連一篇中文文章都看不懂啊？

B: 我畢竟只學了兩年中文。

A: 你怎么连一篇中文文章都看不懂啊？

B: 我毕竟只学了两年中文。

1. You and your friend are watching a Ping-Pong game on TV. He is amazed at how good the players are, and you remind him that the two players are respectively this year's and last year's champions.

→

2. Your guest is praising the lavish feast you have prepared. You reply by saying that it is, after all, Chinese New Year's Eve.

→

3. Your tour guide asks you to move on to the next scenic site instead of taking a break. You complain by saying you've walked for so long, you're hungry and tired, and need to take a break.

→

B. Delegating Responsibilities

You are planning a party, and you want to put your friends in charge of different tasks.

Things to do:

找音樂	找音乐
請客人	请客人
買飲料	买饮料
準備遊戲	准备游戏
搬桌子、椅子	搬桌子、椅子
晚會後整理房間	晚会后整理房间

EXAMPLE:

→　天明，音樂由你(來)找。　　　　　天明，音乐由你(来)找。

1. Classmate #1

2. Classmate #2

3. Classmate #3

4. Classmate #4

5. Classmate #5

C. Do You Know Any Model Couples?

Discuss with a partner if you know any couples that share the following household responsibilities with each other. Describe how they split the responsibilities.

買菜/买菜	做飯/做饭	洗碗
洗衣服	打掃屋子/打扫屋子	教育孩子

D. My Ideal Spouse

In addition to a willingness to share household chores, what other qualities are you looking for in your future spouse? For instance, a cheerful personality, being considerate, being caring, the ability to earn a good income, having a similar educational background, similar interests, a good sense of humor, etc.?

a. List your future spouse's ideal qualities here:

1. _____

2. _____

3. _____

4. _____

5. _____

b. Describe your ideal mate. You may start by saying

我的丈夫/妻子除了能幫我做家務以外，還必須⋯

我的丈夫/妻子除了能帮我做家务以外，还必须⋯

一對模範夫妻
一对模范夫妻

E. My Ideal Workplace

Make a presentation on your ideal workplace. Would your dream job be in a company or a factory, or another setting? You may also want to mention that it should be a place where people trust each other and care for each other, where nobody dislikes you, where you get good pay, where men and women get equal pay for equal work, etc.

1. _____

2. _____

3. _____

4. _____

5. _____

6. _____

F. How Has Women's Social Status Changed?

a. Give a brief summary of the important changes that took place in terms of women's social status in twentieth-century China.

→

Historically speaking	After 1950	After the Reform and Opening-Up
_____	_____	_____
_____	_____	_____
_____		_____

b. Ask yourself if there have been similar changes in women's social status in your own society. What were the historical turning points, and what has been achieved since then? Try to focus on women's situations in the family and workplace. You may use English for proper nouns.

1. _____

2. _____

3. _____

4. _____

5. _____

G. Such a Fan!

Are you the kind of sports fan who knows the rules and regulations of the game inside and out? Do you follow the sports news religiously? Do you always know which teams are playing and who is winning?

a. Here is your opportunity to describe your favorite team sport ball game in Chinese and share your enthusiasm with sports fans in China.

1. 我是＿＿球的球迷。
2. 一個球隊有＿＿個隊員。
3. 一場球賽打＿＿分鐘。
4. 去年的冠軍隊是＿＿隊。
5. 昨天有一場球賽，是＿＿隊對＿＿隊，比分是＿比＿。＿＿隊贏了，＿＿隊輸了。

1. 我是＿＿球的球迷。
2. 一个球队有＿＿个队员。
3. 一场球赛打＿＿分钟。
4. 去年的冠军队是＿＿队。
5. 昨天有一场球赛，是＿＿队对＿＿队，比分是＿比＿。＿＿队赢了，＿＿队输了。

b. Connect the sentences above to give a simple report on the sport you love best. Feel free to supplement it with information such as how addicted you are to the games, your favorite and least favorite players, which players have an attitude problem, etc.

Pinyin Text

Zài lìshǐ shang, Zhōngguó shì yí ge zhòng nán qīng nǚ de shèhuì, fùnǚ de jiātíng dìwèi hé shèhuì dìwèi dōu bǐ nánrén dī de duō. 1950 nián yǐhòu, qíngkuàng zhújiàn❶ fāshēng le biànhuà. Tèbié shì zài chéngshì li, nǚ háizi hé nán háizi yíyàng yǒu shòu jiàoyù hé cānjiā gōngzuò de jīhuì, fùnǚ de shèhuì dìwèi yě yǒu le hěn dà de tígāo.

Dànshì gǎigé kāifàng yǐlái①, zài mǒu① xiē qǐyè hé shìyè dānwèi❷, yòu chūxiàn le nánnǚ bù píngděng de xiànxiàng. Bǐrú, zhǎo gōngzuò de shíhou, fùnǚ chángcháng bǐ nánrén gèng kùnnan; yìxiē gōngchǎng hé gōngsī hái méiyǒu zuò dào nánnǚ tóng gōng tóng chóu. Dāngrán, yě yǒu yì xiē nǚxìng, wúlùn zài gōngzuò shang háishi shōurù shang, dōu chāoguò yìbān nánrén. Búguò tāmen zài nǚxìng zhōng bìjìng② zhǐ shì shǎoshù.

Xiànzài zài yìbān Zhōngguó jiātíng zhōng, hěn duō fūqī dōu shì hùxiāng tǐtiē, hùxiāng zhàogù, suǒyǐ, jiātíng kěnéng shì xiànzài Zhōngguó shèhuì nánnǚ zuì píngděng de dìfang. Ná Lín Xuěméi de jiùjiu lái shuō ba, tā shì ge dà qiúmí, zhǐ yǒu zài kàn diànshì li de zúqiú sài de shíhou cái biǎoxiàn chū yì diǎnr "dà nánzǐ zhǔyì", shénme jiāwù dōu bú zuò. Kěshì bǐsài yì jiéshù, tā jiù máng zhe bāng jiùmā zuò fàn, xǐ wǎn, yòu chéng le yí wèi "mófàn zhàngfu".

Xuěméi: Jiùjiu, jīntiān zěnme nín xǐ wǎn ya?

Jiùjiu: Hā ha, yīnwèi wǒ xǐ wǎn xǐ de bǐ nǐ jiùmā gānjìng a.

Xuěméi: Wǒ lái xǐ ba! Wǒ xǐ wǎn yě shì xǐ de hěn gānjìng de③.

Jiùmā: Bié, bié, bié, nǐmen cóng Yúnnán lǚyóu huí lai, jiù máng zhe zhǎo gōngzuò, miànshì, hái méi xiūxi guo lai④ ne. Zàishuō, nǐ jiùjiu ya, zuótiān wǎnshang kàn qiú kàn dào yèli yì diǎn, jīntiān hái bù děi hǎo hāo biǎoxian biǎoxian?

Kē Lín: Jiùjiu, nín shì bu shì dé le nèi zhǒng bìng, jiào shénme "qìguǎnyán"?

Jiùjiu: Kē Lín, nǐ de Zhōngwén shuǐpíng zhēn búcuò, lián zhè ge dōu zhīdào. Búguò bú shì "qìguǎnyán", érshì "qī guǎn yán"❸. "Qī" shì "qīzi" de "qī".

Kē Lín: Duì, duì, duì, "qìguǎnyán" shì yì zhǒng bìng.

Jiùjiu: Nǐ xiǎoxīn, "qī guǎn yán" kě bǐ "qìguǎnyán" lìhai duō le. Nǐ jiānglái qiānwàn kě bié dé zhè zhǒng bìng.

Xuěméi: Jiùjiu, kàn nín shuō de. Duì le, zuótiān wǎnshang shì shénme bǐsài a?

Jiùjiu: Nánzǐ zúqiú sài, Běijīng duì duì Shànghǎi duì.

Jiùmā: Nà yǒu shénme hǎokàn de? Wǒ zuì tǎoyàn nà xiē nán zú duìyuán le, píngcháng jiāo'ào de bù déliǎo, kěshì bǐsài de shíhou lǎo shū qiú. Suǒyǐ, wǒ zhǐ kàn Zhōngguó nǚ zú, tāmen bǐ nán zú bàng duō le.

Xuěméi: Búcuò, nǚ zú shì bǐ nán zú chéngjì hǎo, kěshì wǒ tīngshuō nǚ zú duìyuán zhèng de qián bú dào nán zú de shí fēn zhī yī[4], zhēn bù gōngpíng.

Kē Lín: Bié wàng le, tāmen de shōurù shì yóu shìchǎng jīngjì lái juédìng de. Měiguó zhíyè nǚ lán duìyuán de xīnshuǐ gēn zhíyè nán lán bǐ, yě shǎo duō le.

Jiùjiu: Āi, bié lǎo shuō Zhōngguó nán zú shū qiú le. Wǒ gāng kàn dào wǎng shang de xiāoxi shuō, Zhōngguó nán zú zuótiān yíng le shìjiè guànjūn duì.

Jiùmā: Wǒ bù xiāngxìn, wǎng shang luàn shuō ba?

Jiùjiu: Hǎoxiàng shì zhēn de. Wǎng shang shuō, zhè cì Zhōngguó nán zú tī de búcuò, bǐfēn yìzhí shì 0 bǐ 0. Bǐsài jiéshù qián yì fēnzhōng, Zhōngguó nán zú cái tī jìn yì qiú, yǐ 1 bǐ 0 yíng le bǐsài.

Kē Lín: Méi xiǎng dào, zhēn de méi xiǎng dào, tài bàng le! Nà zhè ge shìjiè guànjūn duì shì Bāxī duì háishi Yìdàlì duì?

Jiùjiu: Zhōngguó pīngpāngqiú nǚ duì.

Dàjiā: Á?

Jiùmā: Kěndìng shì shénme rén zài kāi nán zú de wánxiào!

Jiùjiu: Hā hā hā…

English Text

Historically, China was a society that favored men over women. Women's status in the family and in society was much lower than that of men. After 1950 the situation changed gradually. Especially in the cities, girls and boys had equal access to education and employment. Women's social status also improved substantially.

However, since the Reform and Opening-Up [started], in certain for-profit and nonprofit enterprises, the phenomenon of gender inequity has resurfaced. For example, when looking for work, women tend to have more difficulty than men. Some factories and companies haven't implemented equal pay for equal work. Of course, there are some women who have surpassed men in terms not only of work achievement but also income, but in the final analysis their number among women is still few and far between.

Nowadays, in Chinese households, many couples are considerate of and attentive to each other. Therefore, within the family is perhaps where men and women are most equal in Chinese society. Take Xuemei's uncle for example—he is a big soccer fan. The only time he shows a bit of "male chauvinism" is when there is a soccer game on TV, when he won't do any housework. However, as soon as the game is over, he will be busy helping [Xuemei's] aunt cook and wash dishes, and he'll turn into a "model husband" again.

Xuemei:	Uncle, how come you are doing the dishes today?
Uncle:	Ha ha, because I wash the dishes cleaner than your aunt.
Xuemei:	Come, let me wash the dishes. I do a great job washing dishes too.
Aunt:	No, no. You just got back from Yunnan and you've been busy looking for work and having job interviews. You haven't had a chance to rest and recover yet. Besides, last night your uncle watched a ball game until one o'clock. Today he'd better be on his best behavior, hadn't he?
Ke Lin:	Uncle, have you caught that disease, what do you call it? "Qìguǎnyán" (tracheitis)?
Uncle:	Ke Lin, your Chinese is really good. You even know about this. But it's not "tracheitis." Rather it's "qī guǎn yán" (being henpecked). "Qī" as in "qīzi" (wife).
Ke Lin:	Right, right. "Qìguǎnyán" is a medical disease.
Uncle:	You'd better be careful. "Qī guǎn yán" is much more serious than "qìguǎnyán." You'd better not catch this disease.
Xuemei:	Uncle, listen to you. Oh right, what game was on last night?
Uncle:	Men's soccer, Beijing vs. Shanghai.
Aunt:	Men's soccer, what's there to watch? I really detest those men's soccer players. They are so arrogant. But come game time, they always lose. That's why I only watch the Chinese women's soccer team. They are so much better than the men's soccer team.
Xuemei:	That's right. Women's soccer *is* better than men's soccer, but I hear that women soccer players make less than one tenth of what men make. How unfair.
Ke Lin:	Don't forget, their income is determined by the market economy. The American women's professional basketball teams' salaries are also much lower than the men's teams' salaries.
Uncle:	Hey, don't keep saying that the Chinese men's soccer team lost again. I just saw a news story on the internet. Yesterday the Chinese men's soccer team defeated the world champions.
Aunt:	I don't believe it. That must be a made-up internet story.
Uncle:	It seems it's true. According to the internet story, this time the Chinese men's soccer team played quite well. The score was 0 to 0 until one minute before the game ended when the Chinese men's team scored a goal and won 1 to 0.
Ke Lin:	Who knew! I would have never guessed it. That's fantastic! Then was their opponent the Brazilian team or the Italian team?

Uncle: The Chinese women's Ping-Pong team.

Everyone: Huh?

Aunt: Someone must have been making fun of the men's soccer team.

Uncle: Ha ha ha...

SELF-ASSESSMENT

How well can you do these things? Check (✔) the boxes to evaluate your progress and see which areas you may need to practice more.

I can	Very Well	OK	A Little
Talk about how couples can treat each other as equals	☐	☐	☐
Discuss gender equality in the workplace	☐	☐	☐
Summarize briefly the changes in Chinese women's social status in the twentieth century	☐	☐	☐
Report the score and result of a sports game	☐	☐	☐

Let's Review! (Lessons 11-15)

I. Chinese Character Crossword Puzzles

You have learned many vocabulary items in Lessons 1–15. You may have noticed that some words and phrases share the same characters. Let's see whether you can recall these characters. The common character is positioned in the center of the cluster of rings. The block arrows indicate which way you should read the words. Work with a partner and see how many association rings you can complete. Of course, you may add more rings if you can think of additional words and phrases sharing the same characters, or you may create your own clusters of rings.

EXAMPLE:

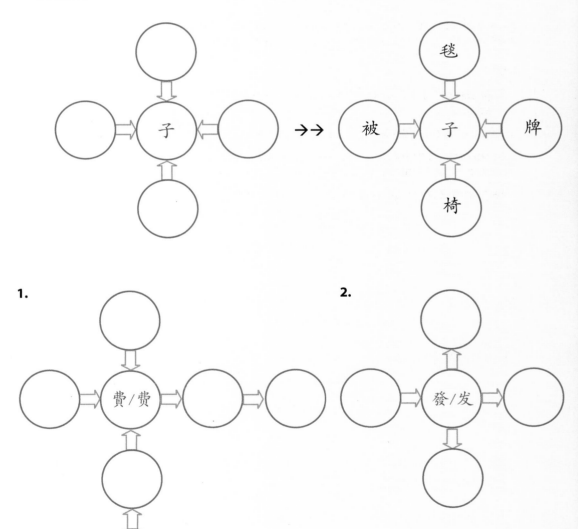

3.

4.

5.

6.

7.

8.

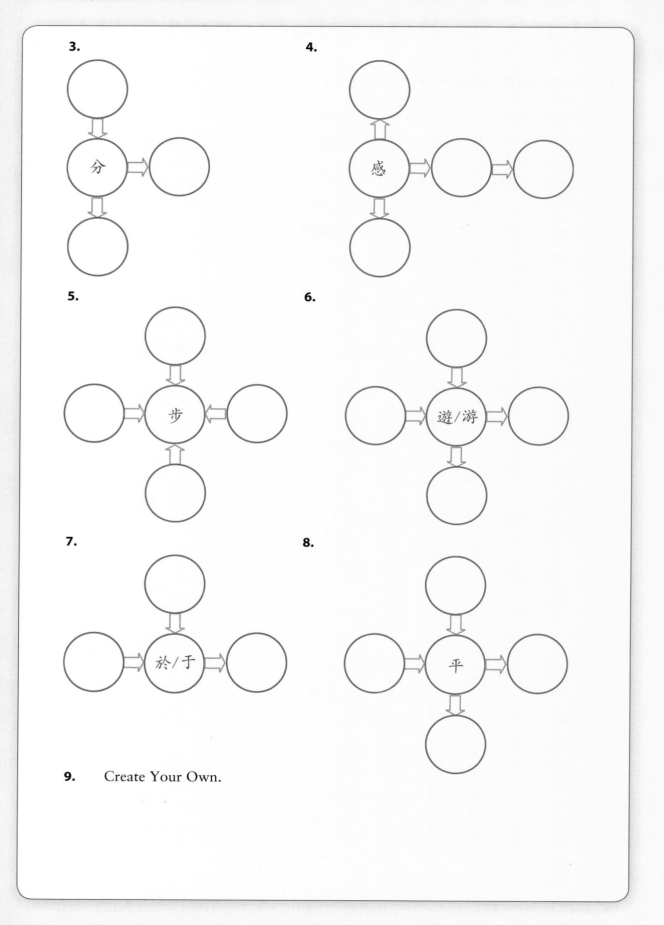

9. Create Your Own.

II. Matching Words

A. Draw a line connecting the verb with its proper object.

1. 鍛煉/锻炼	睡眠
2. 取得	快樂/快乐
3. 出現/出现	比賽/比赛
4. 保留	身體/身体
5. 分享	變化/变化
6. 補充/补充	特色
7. 參加/参加	成績/成绩
8. 發生/发生	現象/现象

B. Draw a line connecting the noun with the adjective that can best describe it.

1. 事業/事业	美
2. 氣氛/气氛	深
3. 工作	高
4. 風景/风景	成功
5. 印象	熱鬧/热闹
6. 地位	順利/顺利

III. Put Your Thoughts into Words

A. Brainstorm with a partner and ask each other what words or phrases you can use when you want to

1. describe the festivities during Chinese New Year

foods	activities	atmosphere
_____	_____	_____
_____	_____	_____
_____	_____	_____
_____	_____	_____

2. plan a trip or join a tour group

people

_____

_____

_____

_____

expenses

_____

_____

_____

_____

attractions

_____

_____

_____

_____

activities

_____

_____

_____

_____

3. talk about the changes in a city

Past

sights

_____

_____

_____

_____

sounds

_____

_____

_____

_____

Present

sights

_____

_____

_____

_____

sounds

_____

_____

_____

_____

4. offer your advice and share ways to stay healthy and fit

eating habits	other ways
_____	_____
_____	_____
_____	_____
_____	_____

5. describe a model couple that are nice to each other or a model company that is fair to its employees

couple	company
_____	_____
_____	_____
_____	_____
_____	_____

B. Work with a couple of classmates to group the following words/phrases according to their meanings and usages. Feel free to add other words/phrases to the list.

儘可能/尽可能	可見/可见	否則/否则	
只要…就…	即使…也…	的確	不如
要不是	看來/看来	竟(然)	等(等)
不管	包括	沒有…那麼/那么	
畢竟/毕竟	是…的		

1. When you wish to offer encouragement: _____

2. When you wish to include or cite examples: _____

3. When you wish to warn or deter: _____

4. When you wish to infer from what's occurred: _____

5. When you wish to express your surprise: _____

6. When you wish to point out the obvious: _____

7. When you wish to assure someone or affirm something: _____

8. When you wish to compare: _____

9. Others: _____

IV. Presentation

With a partner, give a brief presentation on one of these topics: Chinese festivals, travel in China, modernization of Chinese cities, morning exercises in a Chinese city, or gender issues in Chinese society.

Preparation: Discuss with your partner

a. which topic you will select, and why;

b. what aspects of the topic you want to focus on;

c. what words or phrases from III A should be used in your presentation;

d. what information should be presented first, next, and last;

e. what transitions may be needed between parts of the presentation;

f. what linking devices should be used to connect your sentences;

g. what words or phrases from III B can be useful in presenting your point of view.

It may be a good idea to jot down sentences that you wish to say, then number them in the order you think they should be presented, and finally consider how to organize your sentences in a coherent paragraph. Then make your presentation to the class.

V. How Well Can You Speak?

Reorganize the following sentences to compose a well-connected paragraph praising Mr. Wang's devotion to his wife. Pay attention to time expressions, location expressions, and pronouns.

1. 不管妻子要他做什麼，他都儘可能做到
2. 從公園回來，他就買菜、整理房間，做家務
3. 王先生自己有什麼看法呢？
4. 王先生對太太很體貼
5. 你呢？你相信嗎？
6. 有人覺得他在家裏的地位太低，是"妻管嚴"
7. 要不是親眼看到，很多人並不相信王先生對太太那麼好
8. 他認為夫妻本來就應該互相照顧
9. 一天三頓都是他做飯，他洗碗，他從來都不抱怨
10. 每天早晨陪太太去公園散步
11. 有人覺得他愛太太，尊重太太，的確是個模範丈夫
12. 妻子的健康、快樂就是他最大的幸福

1. 不管妻子要他做什么，他都尽可能做到
2. 从公园回来，他就买菜、整理房间，做家务
3. 王先生自己有什么看法呢？
4. 王先生对太太很体贴
5. 你呢？你相信吗？
6. 有人觉得他在家里的地位太低，是"妻管严"
7. 要不是亲眼看到，很多人并不相信王先生对太太那么好
8. 他认为夫妻本来就应该互相照顾
9. 一天三顿都是他做饭，他洗碗，他从来都不抱怨
10. 每天早晨陪太太去公园散步
11. 有人觉得他爱太太，尊重太太，的确是个模范丈夫
12. 妻子的健康、快乐就是他最大的幸福

第十六課　　第十六课

環境保護　　环境保护
與節約能源　与节约能源

 LEARNING OBJECTIVES

In this lesson, you will learn to use Chinese to

1. Describe a scene in which people are busily engaged in all kinds of activities;
2. Talk about indicators of a clean environment;
3. List some green energy sources;
4. Give examples of practices that are environmentally friendly.

RELATE AND GET READY

In your own culture/community—

- How has pollution affected your immediate environment?
- In what ways do you see green power being put to use in your community?
- How have people changed their behavior to consume less energy?

Before You Study

Check the statements that apply to you.

☐ 1. I take public transportation whenever I can.

☐ 2. I turn off the lights when I am the last one to leave a room.

When You Study

Listen to the audio recording and scan the text. Ask yourself the following questions before you begin a close reading of the text.

1. Why do Zhang Tianming and his friends go on an outing?

張天明他們四個人來北京已經兩三個月了，天氣也逐漸暖和了。他們每天上課的上課①，找工作的找工作，半個月沒見面了，更沒有機會接近大自然❶。今天是星期六，大家都想輕鬆輕鬆②，天明建議去爬山，麗莎和雪梅不反對，柯林也覺得這個建議不錯，他說正好他的新朋友馬克也想去。

LANGUAGE NOTES

❶ 大自然 means "Mother Nature."

3. I recycle.

4. I bring my own bag when grocery shopping.

5. I don't use disposable utensils.

2. How do they plan to get to their destination?

3. What do they see and feel that inspires them to talk about protecting the environment?

4. What do they volunteer to do?

张天明他们四个人来北京已经两三个月了，天气也逐渐暖和了。他们每天上课的上课①，找工作的找工作，半个月没见面了，更没有机会接近大自然❶。今天是星期六，大家都想轻松轻松②，天明建议去爬山，丽莎和雪梅不反对，柯林也觉得这个建议不错，他说正好他的新朋友马克也想去。

可是怎麼去呢？坐出租車吧，太貴，而且也沒意思；坐公交車❷吧❸，人太多，太擠。柯林想出了一個主意，騎自行車！大家馬上就同意了，覺得騎自行車又能鍛煉身體，又省錢，而且有益於❹環境保護。

他們早上很早就出發了。騎了很長的一段路以後，有點熱，也有點累，就下了車，一邊推著車，一邊聊了起來。

★　★　★

張天明：　這兒的空氣真新鮮！

麗莎：　　對，比城裏好多了。到處都是綠色，看起來❸真舒服！

柯林：　　哎呀，渴死了，…你們看，一瓶水都喝完了！這兒有回收垃圾筒嗎？空瓶子不能隨便亂扔。

雪梅：　　對，我們應該注意環保❹，回收垃圾筒就在樹下邊。

麗莎：　　我好久沒買瓶裝水了。我們班有的同學建議，為了保護綠色的地球，自己帶水喝，不買瓶裝水。

雪梅：　　這個建議不錯。哎，你們看，那邊房子上有些亮亮的東西，是什麼？

柯林：　　是利用太陽能發電吧？我在美國也見過。

雪梅：　　利用太陽能，太好了！

馬克：　　要是自行車也能利用太陽能發電，那多酷啊！

雪梅：　　現在世界上很多國家都在鬧❺能源危機，太陽能可是取之不盡❻的啊！

柯林：　　別忘了，風能也是取之不盡的。

雪梅：　　如果全世界都利用太陽能和風能，那能節約多少石油和煤啊！而且…

另外四人：環保！哈哈…

LANGUAGE NOTES

❷ 公 is short for 公共, and 交 is short for 交通.

❸ The 起來/起来 in (看)起來/起来 is similar to (住)起來/起来 in usage. See Words & Phrases A in Lesson 11.

❹ 環保/环保 is short for 環境保護/环境保护. Similarly, 北京大學/北京大学 can be shortened to 北大, and 室內溫度 to 室溫.

可是怎么去呢？坐出租车吧，太贵，而且也没意思；坐公交车❷吧③，人太多，太挤。柯林想出了一个主意，骑自行车！大家马上就同意了，觉得骑自行车又能锻炼身体，又省钱，而且有益于④环境保护。

他们早上很早就出发了。骑了很长的一段路以后，有点热，也有点累，就下了车，一边推着车，一边聊了起来。

★　★　★

张天明：　这儿的空气真新鲜！

丽莎：　对，比城里好多了。到处都是绿色，看起来③真舒服！

柯林：　哎呀，渴死了，…你们看，一瓶水都喝完了！这儿有回收垃圾筒吗？空瓶子不能随便乱扔。

雪梅：　对，我们应该注意环保④，回收垃圾筒就在树下边。

丽莎：　我好久没买瓶装水了。我们班有的同学建议，为了保护绿色的地球，自己带水喝，不买瓶装水。

雪梅：　这个建议不错。哎，你们看，那边房子上有些亮亮的东西，是什么？

柯林：　是利用太阳能发电吧？我在美国也见过。

雪梅：　利用太阳能，太好了！

马克：　要是自行车也能利用太阳能发电，那多酷啊！

雪梅：　现在世界上很多国家都在闹❺能源危机，太阳能可是取之不尽❻的啊！

柯林：　别忘了，风能也是取之不尽的。

雪梅：　如果全世界都利用太阳能和风能，那能节约多少石油和煤啊！而且…

另外四人：　环保！哈哈…

---

❺ 鬧/闹 is a verb here. Its object usually denotes something unpleasant, e.g., 鬧病/闹病 (to fall ill), 鬧彆扭/闹别扭 (to be at odds with someone), 鬧脾氣/闹脾气 (nào píqi, to throw a tantrum), 鬧矛盾/闹矛盾 (nào máodùn, to have a conflict).

❻ In 取之不盡/取之不尽, 取 means 拿 (to take). 之 is a pronoun indicating what it is that one is taking. 盡/尽 means 完 (to finish). Therefore, 取之不盡/取之不尽 means 拿不完 (inexhaustible) or very bountiful.

麗莎： 我聽說中國政府規定辦公室和公共場所，冬天暖氣溫度不能高於⑤攝氏❼20度，夏天空調不能低於26度。

柯林： 這個規定我舉雙手贊成。你們還記得嗎，我們美國學校的教室，冬天穿襯衫還出汗，夏天穿毛衣還冷得不得了。

雪梅： 可不是嗎，太浪費了。

麗莎： 我聽說現在不少人去餐廳吃飯自帶餐具，不用一次性❽的。

張天明： 這個做法非常好。拿一次性筷子來說吧，每年要砍多少樹啊？

馬克： 除了上餐館自帶筷子，買東西也得自己帶包了。

麗莎： 對，現在中國超市❾不給塑料袋，要自己買，所以很多人都自己帶包，這樣一年不知道能減少多少白色污染！

雪梅： 還有汽車，不但要用很多能源，而且還對空氣造成嚴重污染。

柯林： 大家都應該像我們這樣，少開車，多騎車、多走路，又環保節能❿、又有益於健康。哈哈…

張天明： 對，地球是我們的家，我們應該好好保護它！

雪梅： 我們應該從小地方做起，比如隨手關燈，節約用水。還要讓大家知道，如果再繼續浪費能源，繼續污染環境，後果會不堪設想。

另外四人： 好！同意！

麗莎： 哎，你們看，說著說著⑥，都到了山下了。咱們開始爬山吧，看誰先到山上！加油！

After You Study

Challenge yourself to complete the following tasks in Chinese.

1. List three ways mentioned by the characters in the dialogue to produce less garbage.
2. List the forms of green energy mentioned in the dialogue.

LANGUAGE NOTES

❼ Fahrenheit is 華氏/华氏 (Huáshì).

❽ 一次性 in this lesson refers to things that are discarded after being used only once, i.e., "disposable" objects.

丽莎：　我听说中国政府规定办公室和公共场所，冬天暖气温度不能高于⑤摄氏❼20度，夏天空调不能低于26度。

柯林：　这个规定我举双手赞成。你们还记得吗，我们美国学校的教室，冬天穿衬衫还出汗，夏天穿毛衣还冷得不得了。

雪梅：　可不是吗，太浪费了。

丽莎：　我听说现在不少人去餐厅吃饭自带餐具，不用一次性❽的。

张天明：这个做法非常好。拿一次性筷子来说吧，每年要砍多少树啊？

马克：　除了上餐馆自带筷子，买东西也得自己带包了。

丽莎：　对，现在中国超市❾不给塑料袋，要自己买，所以很多人都自己带包，这样一年不知道能减少多少白色污染！

雪梅：　还有汽车，不但要用很多能源，而且还对空气造成严重污染。

柯林：　大家都应该像我们这样，少开车，多骑车、多走路，又环保节能❿、又有益于健康。哈哈…

张天明：对，地球是我们的家，我们应该好好保护它！

雪梅：　我们应该从小地方做起，比如随手关灯，节约用水。还要让大家知道，如果再继续浪费能源，继续污染环境，后果会不堪设想。

另外四人：好！同意！

丽莎：　哎，你们看，说着说着⑥，都到了山下了。咱们开始爬山吧，看谁先到山上！加油！

---

3. Give at least three examples of additional things that the group thinks each individual can do to protect the earth.

---

❾ 超市 is short for 超級市場/超级市场.

❿ As in 太陽能/太阳能 and 風能/风能, the 能 in 節能/节能 is short for 能源. 節能/节能 is short for 節約能源/节约能源.

The pole was made by factories

VOCABULARY

1.	保護　保护	bǎohù	v	to protect; to safeguard
2.	節約　节约	jiéyuē	v	to economize; to save; to conserve
3.	能源	néngyuán	n	energy; energy source
4.	爬山	pá shān	vo	to hike in the mountains; to climb mountains
5.	有益	yǒuyì	adj	beneficial; useful [See Grammar 4.]
6.	於　　于	yú	prep	towards; in; on; at; (indicating comparison) [See Grammar 4 and Grammar 5.]
7.	段	duàn	m	(measure word for section, segment, or part)
8.	推	tuī	v	to push; to shove
9.	空氣　空气	kōngqì	n	air; atmosphere
10.	回收	huíshōu	v	to recycle
11.	筒	tǒng	n	thick tube-shaped object
12.	扔	rēng	v	to throw; to toss; to throw away
13.	瓶裝水　瓶装水	píngzhuāng shuǐ		bottled water
14.	地球	dìqiú	n	the earth; the globe
15.	亮	liàng	adj	bright; light
16.	太陽　太阳	tàiyáng	n	sun
17.	太陽能　太阳能	tàiyángnéng	n	solar energy; solar power
18.	利用	lìyòng	v	to use; to utilize; to take advantage of; to exploit
19.	發電　发电	fā diàn	vo	to generate electricity

廚余 compost
chú yú

20.	國家	国家	guójiā	n	country; nation
21.	鬧	闹	nào	v/adj	to suffer from; to be troubled by; to make a noise; noisy
22.	危機	危机	wēijī	n	crisis
23.	取之不盡	取之不尽	qǔ zhī bú jìn		(of resources) inexhaustible
24.	風	风	fēng	n	wind
25.	全		quán	adj/adv	entire; whole; complete; completely
26.	石油		shíyóu	n	petroleum; oil
27.	煤		méi	n	coal
28.	規定	规定	guīdìng	v/n	to regulate; to specify; rules and regulations; provisions
29.	公共場所	公共场所	gōnggòng chǎngsuǒ		public place
30.	暖氣	暖气	nuǎnqì	n	heating
31.	溫度		wēndù	n	temperature
32.	度		dù	m	(measure word for degree of temperature, heat, hardness, humidity, etc.)
33.	贊成	赞成	zànchéng	v	to approve
34.	出汗		chū hàn	vo	to sweat
35.	餐具		cānjù	n	eating utensils; tableware
36.	一次性		yícìxìng	adj	one-time
37.	筷子		kuàizi	n	chopsticks
38.	砍		kǎn	v	to cut; to chop

39.	超市		chāoshì	n	supermarket
40.	塑料袋		sùliào dài		plastic bag
41.	减少	减少	jiǎnshǎo	v	to reduce; to decrease; to lessen
42.	污染		wūrǎn	v/n	to pollute; to contaminate; pollution; contamination
43.	造成		zào chéng	vc	to cause; to give rise to
44.	随手	随手	suíshǒu	adv	without extra effort or motion; conveniently
45.	後果	后果	hòuguǒ	n	consequence; fallout; aftermath
46.	不堪設想	不堪设想	bùkān shèxiǎng		(of consequences) too ghastly to contemplate; unimaginable; extremely bad or dangerous
47.	加油		jiā yóu	vo	to make an extra effort; to work harder; to refuel

Proper Nouns

48.	馬克	马克	Mǎkè		Mark
49.	攝氏	摄氏	Shèshì		Celsius; centigrade

Enlarged Characters

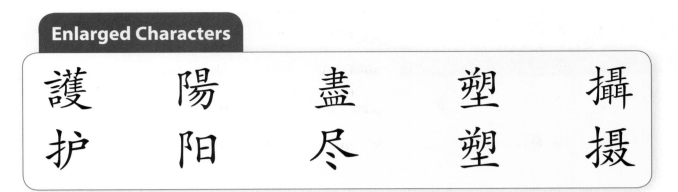

| 護 | 陽 | 盡 | 塑 | 攝 |
| 护 | 阳 | 尽 | 塑 | 摄 |

塑膠(jiāo)袋就是塑料袋，免洗餐具就是一次性餐具。
塑胶(jiāo)袋就是塑料袋，免洗餐具就是一次性餐具。

Culture Highlights

 Starting in June 2008, the Chinese government banned the production, sale, and use of "super-thin" (less than 0.025mm) plastic shopping bags. Supermarkets and shopping centers could no longer give away free plastic bags. Instead, shoppers would have to purchase them or bring their own shopping bags.

❷ Although coal remains the largest source of energy in China as well as a major source of air pollution, China is investing heavily in green power, particularly solar and wind power. China is already a major exporter of solar panels and is on course to become the world's largest market for wind turbines.

❸ In June 2007, China's State Council or cabinet issued an administrative decree stipulating that except for hospitals and facilities with special needs, no public buildings or private enterprises should set the thermostat for air conditioning below twenty-six degrees Celsius.

Grammar

---

1. V1的V1, V2的V2

上課的/上课的 in 上課的上課/上课的上课 (or 找工作的 in 找工作的找工作) is equivalent to a noun. This kind of structure means, "Some people are taking classes; some are looking for jobs." The implication is that everyone is doing something; no one is idle.

❶ 下班了，人們回家的回家，約朋友吃飯的約朋友吃飯，辦公室很快就没有人了。

下班了，人们回家的回家，约朋友吃饭的约朋友吃饭，办公室很快就没有人了。

(After work, some went home, and some made plans to eat out with friends. The office was soon empty [of people].)

❷ 運動場上學生們踢球的踢球，跑步的跑步，非常有活力。

运动场上学生们踢球的踢球，跑步的跑步，非常有活力。

(On the athletic fields, some students are playing soccer and some are jogging. [The atmosphere is] full of vitality.)

❸ 硬臥車廂裏旅客聊天兒的聊天兒，唱歌的唱歌，熱鬧極了。

硬卧车厢里旅客聊天儿的聊天儿，唱歌的唱歌，热闹极了。

(Among the travelers in the hard-berth sleeper car, some are chatting and some are singing. It's extremely boisterous.)

2. Adjectives That Can Be Reduplicated Like Verbs

[handwritten: repeat adj 地 verb]

輕鬆/轻松 is an adjective. Its reduplicated form is AABB 輕輕鬆鬆/轻轻松松. This form of reduplication has a heightening effect:

❶ 這次考試不難，她輕輕鬆鬆地就考了100分。

这次考试不难，她轻轻松松地就考了100分。

(This time the exam wasn't difficult. She easily scored a 100.)

[輕輕鬆鬆/轻轻松松=很輕鬆/很轻松]

輕鬆/轻松 can also be reduplicated in the ABAB form like a verb, as in this lesson. The meaning is causative:

❷ 今天是星期六，大家都想輕鬆輕鬆。

今天是星期六，大家都想轻松轻松。

(Today is Saturday. Everyone wants to relax a little.)

[輕鬆輕鬆/轻松轻松=make one 輕鬆/轻松 or relaxed]

輕鬆輕鬆/轻松轻松 in the above example means "to have some fun or do whatever to make one feel more relaxed."

❸ 快來！來涼快涼快吧。

快来！来凉快凉快吧。

(Come here quickly to cool down.)

[涼快涼快/凉快凉快=make oneself cool]

❹ 爺爺今年過八十歲生日，我們應該好好兒地熱鬧熱鬧。

爷爷今年过八十岁生日，我们应该好好儿地热闹热闹。

(This year is Grandpa's eightieth birthday. We should have a big celebration and have a great time.)

[熱鬧熱鬧/热闹热闹=to make the celebration a lively festive occasion]

This kind of reduplication is sometimes preceded by the verb 使, 讓/让 or 叫:

❺ 你把這個好消息告訴他，使/讓/叫他高興高興。

你把这个好消息告诉他，使/让/叫他高兴高兴。

(Tell him the good news to cheer him up.)

[使/讓/叫他高興高興/使/让/叫他高兴高兴= to make him happy]

ABAB — verb for a bit
AABB — adverb, emphasize verb

3. …吧, …吧

This construction, usually found in spoken Chinese, suggests two alternatives. It is used to indicate that the speaker is in a dilemma and unable to make a decision.

❶　可是怎麼去呢？坐出租車吧，太貴，而且也沒意思；坐公交車吧，人太多，太擠。

可是怎么去呢？坐出租车吧，太贵，而且也没意思；坐公交车吧，人太多，太挤。

(But how should we get there? Taking a cab is too expensive and kind of boring, too. And the bus is too crowded.)

❷　我的車舊了，最近老有問題。買新的吧，沒有錢，不買新的吧，舊車又不可靠，真難辦。

我的车旧了，最近老有问题。买新的吧，没有钱，不买新的吧，旧车又不可靠，真难办。

(My car is old, and lately it's been having many problems. I could buy a new one, but I don't have the money. I could keep the old one, but it's not reliable. I don't know what to do.)

❸　**A:**　你說住在城裏好，還是住在城外好？

你说住在城里好，还是住在城外好？

(Do you think it's better to live in town or outside of town?)

B:　很難說。住在城裏吧，上、下班，購物都很方便，可是空氣不太好；住在城外吧，環境好，空氣新鮮，但做什麼都不太方便。

很难说。住在城里吧，上、下班，购物都很方便，可是空气不太好；住在城外吧，环境好，空气新鲜，但做什么都不太方便。

(It's hard to say. If you live in town, commuting and go shopping are convenient, but the air quality is not so good. If you live in the suburbs, the environment is good and the air is fresh, but everything is quite inconvenient.)

❹   他女朋友的妹妹明天過生日，有個生日晚會。他想，去吧，沒
     有錢買禮物；不去吧，又怕女朋友生氣。怎麼辦呢？

他女朋友的妹妹明天过生日，有个生日晚会。他想，去吧，没
有钱买礼物；不去吧，又怕女朋友生气。怎么办呢？

(His girlfriend's younger sister is having a birthday party tomorrow. He thinks if he
goes, he won't have the money to buy a present; but if he doesn't go, he's afraid that his
girlfriend will be angry. What should he do?)

---

4. (有益)於/(有益)于   ~~~~~~ noun

The preposition 於/于 is generally used in written language. It is often used after a verb.
於/于 has many meanings. In 有益於/有益于, 於/于 means 對/对 (to). 有益
於/有益于 means 對…有好處/对…有好处 (good/beneficial for/to...).

❶   大家覺得騎自行車又能鍛煉身體，又省錢，而且有益於
     環境保護。

大家觉得骑自行车又能锻炼身体，又省钱，而且有益于
环境保护。

(Everybody feels that biking is good exercise and saves money. Furthermore, it helps
to protect the environment.)

❷   多聽錄音，有益於中文學習。

多听录音，有益于中文学习。

(Listening to recordings more helps [you] learn Chinese.)

❸   多聽別人意見，有益於與人相處。

多听别人意见，有益于与人相处。

(Listening to others more helps [you] get along with people.)

❹   體育運動有益於身體健康。

体育运动有益于身体健康。

(Sports are beneficial to your health.)

5. Adj + 於/于

Used after an adjective, 於/于 means 比. 高於/高于 is synonymous with 比…高. Likewise 低於/低于 means 比…低.

(1a) 今天的氣温低於昨天。

今天的气温低于昨天。

(1b) 今天的氣温比昨天低。

今天的气温比昨天低。

(Today's temperature is lower than yesterday's.)

More examples:

(2a) 四大於三。

四大于三。

(2b) 四比三大。

(Four is larger than three.)

(3a) 那個國家水甚至貴於油。

那个国家水甚至贵于油。

(3b) 那個國家的水甚至比油貴。

那个国家的水甚至比油贵。

(In that country water is even more expensive than oil.)

6. V著V著/V着V着

"V著V著/V着V着…" must be followed by a verbal phrase. It signifies that while the action denoted in the phrase "V著V著…/V着V着…" is going on, a second action happens as an unintended result or by surprise. There is often a 就 before the second verb.

❶ 哎，你們看，說著說著，都到了山下了。

哎，你们看，说着说着，都到了山下了。

(Hey, look! We were so busy talking that we didn't realize we'd arrived at the foot of the mountain.)

❷   媽媽走了以後，那個孩子哭著哭著就睡著了。

妈妈走了以后，那个孩子哭着哭着就睡着了。

(After his mother left, the child cried and cried and fell asleep.)

❸   我第一次來這個城市，開車出去，開著開著就迷路了。

我第一次来这个城市，开车出去，开着开着就迷路了。

(The first time I came to this city, I was driving around and got lost.)

❹   弟弟躺在床上想下午剛看的電影，想著想著笑了起來。

弟弟躺在床上想下午刚看的电影，想着想着笑了起来。

(Lying in bed and thinking about the movie he had just seen this afternoon, my younger brother burst out laughing.)

Words & Phrases

> **A. 想起(來)/想起(来) (to recall) vs. 想出(來)/想出(来) (to come up with)**

想起來/想起来 means to recall something that has been forgotten. 想出來/想出来 means to come up with a new way, method, name, etc.

❶   這個人我十年前見過，他叫什麼名字我想不起來了。

这个人我十年前见过，他叫什么名字我想不起来了。

(I met this person ten years ago. I can't think of his name.)

❷ **A:** 你知道小區健身房在哪兒嗎？

你知道小区健身房在哪儿吗？

(Do you know where the community gym is?)

   B: 我去過，可是忘了⋯我想起來了，就在老人活動中心旁邊。

我去过，可是忘了⋯我想起来了，就在老人活动中心旁边。

(I've been there, but I've forgotten... I remember now. It's next to the Senior Citizens' Activity Center.)

❸   **A:**   你的孩子快出生了，叫什麼名字，你想出來了嗎？
         你的孩子快出生了，叫什么名字，你想出来了吗？
         (Your child will be born soon. Have you come up with a name yet?)

       B: 我們給孩子想出來一個很好聽的名字。
         我们给孩子想出来一个很好听的名字
         (Yes, we've come up with a very nice-sounding name for the child.)

❹   這件事雖然很麻煩，但是他想來想去，還是想出來一個解決的
       辦法。
       这件事虽然很麻烦，但是他想来想去，还是想出来一个解决的
       办法。
       (Although this problem is very complicated, he dwelled on it for a long time and came
       up with a way to solve it.)

B.環境保護/环境保护 (environmental protection)

When a two-syllable abstract verb and a two-syllable abstract noun are combined to form a
four-character phrase in formal speech and writing, the noun usually comes before the verb.
This is especially true when the phrase functions as the subject, object or attributive in a
sentence

❶   能源管理是大問題   [能源管理 as a subject]
       能源管理是大问题   [能源管理 as a subject]
       (Energy management is a big problem.)

❷   …有益於環境保護   [環境保護 as an object]
       …有益于环境保护   [环境保护 as an object]
       (…beneficial for environmental protection)

❸   注意垃圾回收工作   [垃圾回收 as an attributive]
       (Pay attention to the work on garbage recycling.)

C. 可不是嗎/可不是吗 (Isn't that so? How true!)

可不是嗎/可不是吗 indicates agreement with the other speaker. It is used in spoken Chinese.

❶ A: 聽説雪梅的舅舅和舅媽感情特別好。
　　听说雪梅的舅舅和舅妈感情特别好。
　　(I hear that Xuemei's uncle and aunt love each other very much.)

　　B: 可不是嗎，他們從來没吵過架。
　　　可不是吗，他们从来没吵过架。
　　　(That's very true. They've never quarreled with each other.)

❷ A: 最近能源危機越來越嚴重。
　　最近能源危机越来越严重。
　　(The energy crisis has been getting even worse recently.)

　　B: 可不是嗎？我們每個人都應該儘可能節約能源。從小地方做起，比如隨手關燈，節約用水，少開車等等。
　　　可不是吗？我们每个人都应该尽可能节约能源。从小地方做起，比如随手关灯，节约用水，少开车等等。
　　　(How true! We should all do our best to save energy, starting with small things like turning off the lights behind us, conserving water, driving less, and so on.)

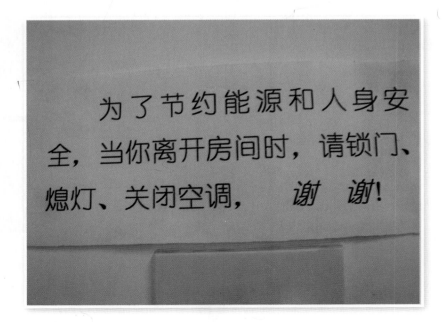

D. 造成 (to cause; to give rise to)

造成 is a verb. The object of 造成 is usually a two-syllable noun denoting an undesirable or unfavorable result.

❶ 汽車要用很多能源，而且還對空氣造成嚴重污染。

汽车要用很多能源，而且还对空气造成严重污染。

(Automobiles consume a lot of energy and cause severe pollution to the atmosphere.)

❷ 他的政治學教授這個學期上課經常遲到，造成很壞的影響。

他的政治学教授这个学期上课经常迟到，造成很坏的影响。

(His political science professor has frequently been late to class this semester, which has had a very negative impact.)

❸ 壞影響已經造成了，你只能好好表現，讓大家慢慢忘了吧。

坏影响已经造成了，你只能好好表现，让大家慢慢忘了吧。

(The damage has already been done. All you can do is be on your best behavior and let everyone slowly forget about it.)

E. 從⋯做起/从⋯做起 (to start with)

從⋯做起/从⋯做起 means "to start with." 起 means "to begin."

❶ (節約)大家應該從小地方做起。

(节约)大家应该从小地方做起。

(Conservation) begins with our doing small things.

❷ 保護環境應該從節約能源做起。

保护环境应该从节约能源做起。

(Protecting the environment should start with the conservation of energy.)

❸ 男女平等應該從日常生活、從每個家庭做起。

男女平等应该从日常生活、从每个家庭做起。

(Equality between men and women should begin with everyday life and every family.)

> ## F. 不堪設想/不堪设想 ([of consequences] too ghastly to contemplate; unimaginable; extremely bad or dangerous)

不堪設想/不堪设想 is a set expression meaning that a situation is extremely, unimaginably bad.

❶   如果再繼續浪費能源，繼續污染環境，後果會不堪設想。

如果再继续浪费能源，继续污染环境，后果会不堪设想。

(If we continue to waste energy and pollute the environment, the consequences will be unimaginable.)

❷   已經三個月沒下雨了，再不下，後果會不堪設想。

已经三个月没下雨了，再不下，后果会不堪设想。

(It's been three months since the last time it rained. If it doesn't rain soon, I can't imagine what will happen.)

❸   你再整天玩電腦，不學習，這樣下去，前途(qiántú)不堪設想。

你再整天玩电脑，不学习，这样下去，前途(qiántú)不堪设想。

(If you keep on playing with computers instead of studying, I can't imagine what your future will be like.)

Language Practice

A. A Busy Scene

Work with a partner to describe what people are doing in the given locations.

EXAMPLE: hospital

→　醫院裏，看病的看病，　　　医院里，看病的看病，
　　拿藥的拿藥。　　　　　　　拿药的拿药。

1. train station

2. shopping center

3. gym

4. park

B. Which Is Better? Tough to Say

Work in pairs. Based on the topics given, one of you should seek advice from the other, who in turn replies by expressing an inability to decide between two equally viable options, using "⋯吧，⋯吧."

EXAMPLE:

旅行		旅行	
a.參加旅行團	**b.**自助遊	**a.**参加旅行团	**b.**自助游

→ A: 你覺得出去旅行，參加旅行團好還是自助遊好？

B: 參加旅行團吧，由導遊安排管理，不必擔心，但沒有那麼自由；自助遊吧，很自由，但什麼都由自己安排，有點麻煩。哪個好，很難說，要看自己的情況。

A: 你觉得出去旅行，参加旅行团好还是自助游好？

B: 参加旅行团吧，由导游安排管理，不必担心，但没有那么自由；自助游吧，很自由，但什么都由自己安排，有点麻烦。哪个好，很难说，要看自己的情况。

1. 大一新生
a.住校內   **b.**住校外
→

1. 大一新生
a.住校内   **b.**住校外

2. 大學畢業以後
a.工作   **b.**念研究生
→

2. 大学毕业以后
a.工作   **b.**念研究生

3. 查資料
a.上網查   **b.**去圖書館查
→

3. 查资料
a.上网查   **b.**去图书馆查

4. 過春節
a.待在家裏   **b.**出去旅遊
→

4. 过春节
a.待在家里   **b.**出去旅游

C. Paradise on Earth

Let's create a Shangri-La in the twenty-first century.

a. Connect each object with the adjective that fits it best.

1. 山　　　　　　　　　　　　　美
2. 樹/树　　　　　　　　　　　新鲜/新鲜
3. 河水　　　　　　　　　　　　少
4. 風景/风景　　　　　　　　　安靜/安静
5. 地　　　　　　　　　　　　　高
6. 人和車/车　　　　　　　　　乾淨/干净
7. 空氣/空气　　　　　　　　　大
8. 環境/环境　　　　　　　　　綠/绿

b. Describe that ideal place.

我希望這個地方…	我希望这个地方…

D. Energy Sources

a. Work with a partner to list various energy sources.

傳統能源/传统能源

1. _____

2. _____

3. _____

綠色能源/绿色能源

1. _____

2. _____

3. _____

b. Tell your partner what green energy sources can generate electricity.

→ 我們能利用___#1, #2, #3___發電。   我们能利用___#1, #2, #3___发电。

1. _____

2. _____

3. _____

1. _____

2. _____

3. _____

c. Discuss advantages and disadvantages for using each of the energy sources.

E. Do Your Part to Reduce Pollution

a. Work with a partner to list the ways that people can reduce pollution.

空氣污染/空气污染

1._____

2._____

3._____

水污染

1._____

2._____

3._____

白色污染

1._____

2._____

3._____

b. Give a presentation to the class based on your list.

我們認為_____
可以減少空氣污染；

_____

可以減少水污染；

_____

可以減少白色污染。

我们认为_____
可以减少空气污染；

_____

可以减少水污染；

_____

可以减少白色污染。

F. Become a Conservation Advocate

With the help of the pictures provided, work with a partner to prepare a brief oral presentation promoting conservation in daily life. You want to encourage people to start with small things. Feel free to add other ways to help conserve resources.

節約能源，從小地方做起：　　　节约能源，从小地方做起：

1.

2.

3.

4.

5.

6.

Pinyin Text

Zhāng Tiānmíng tāmen sì ge rén lái Běijīng yǐjīng liǎng sān ge yuè le, tiānqì yě zhújiàn nuǎnhuo le. Tāmen měi tiān shàng kè de shàng kè①, zhǎo gōngzuò de zhǎo gōngzuò, bàn ge yuè méi jiàn miàn le, gèng méiyǒu jīhuì jiējìn dà zìrán❶. Jīntiān shì xīngqīliù, dàjiā dōu xiǎng qīngsong qīngsong②, Tiānmíng jiànyì qù pá shān, Lìshā hé Xuěméi bù fǎnduì, Kē Lín yě juéde zhè ge jiànyì búcuò, tā shuō zhènghǎo tā de xīn péngyou Mǎkè yě xiǎng qù.

　　Kěshì zěnme qù ne? Zuò chūzūchē ba, tài guì, érqiě yě méi yìsi; Zuò gōngjiāochē❷ ba③, rén tài duō, tài jǐ. Kē Lín xiǎng chu le yí ge zhúyi, qí zìxíngchē! Dàjiā mǎshàng jiù tóngyì le, juéde qí zìxíngchē yòu néng duànliàn shēntǐ, yòu shěng qián, érqiě yǒuyì yú④ huánjìng bǎohù.

　　Tāmen zǎoshang hěn zǎo jiù chūfā le. Qí le hěn cháng de yí duàn lù yǐhòu, yǒu diǎn rè, yě yǒu diǎn lèi, jiù xià le chē, yìbiān tuī zhe chē, yìbiān liáo le qi lai.

Zhāng Tiānmíng:	Zhèr de kōngqì zhēn xīnxian!
Lìshā:	Duì, bǐ chéng li hǎo duō le. Dàochù dōu shì lǜsè, kàn qi lai❸ zhēn shūfu!
Kē Lín:	Āiyā, kě sǐ le,... Nǐmen kàn, yì píng shuǐ dōu hē wán le! Zhèr yǒu huíshōu lājī tǒng ma? Kōng píngzi bù néng suíbiàn luàn rēng.
Xuěméi:	Duì, wǒmen yīnggāi zhùyì huánbǎo④. Huíshōu lājī tǒng jiù zài shù xiàbian.
Lìshā:	Wǒ hǎo jiǔ méi mǎi píngzhuāng shuǐ le. Wǒmen bān yǒude tóngxué jiànyì, wèile bǎohù lǜsè de dìqiú, zìjǐ dài shuǐ hē, bù mǎi píngzhuāng shuǐ.
Xuěméi:	Zhè ge jiànyì búcuò. Āi, nǐmen kàn, nà bian fángzi shang yǒu xiē liàng liàng de dōngxi, shì shénme?
Kē Lín:	Shì lìyòng tàiyángnéng fā diàn ba? Wǒ zài Měiguó yě jiàn guo.
Xuěméi:	Lìyòng tàiyángnéng, tài hǎo le!
Mǎkè:	Yàoshi zìxíngchē yě néng lìyòng tàiyángnéng fādiàn, nà duō kù a!
Xuěméi:	Xiànzài shìjiè shang hěn duō guójiā dōu zài nào❺ néngyuán wēijī, tàiyángnéng kě shì qǔ zhī bú jìn❻ de a!
Kē Lín:	Bié wàng le, fēngnéng yě shì qǔ zhī bú jìn de.

Xuěméi:　　　　Rúguǒ quán shìjiè dōu lìyòng tàiyángnéng hé fēngnéng, nà néng jiéyuē duōshao shíyóu hé méi a! Érqiě…

Lìngwài sì rén:　Huánbǎo! Hā hā…

Lìshā:　　　　Wǒ tīngshuō Zhōngguó zhèngfǔ guīdìng bàngōngshì hé gōnggòng chǎngsuǒ, dōngtiān nuǎnqì wēndù bù néng gāo yú⑤ Shèshì❼ 20 dù, xiàtiān kōngtiáo bù néng dī yú 26 dù.

Kē Lín:　　　　Zhè ge guīdìng wǒ jǔ shuāng shǒu zànchéng. Nǐmen hái jìde ma, wǒmen Měiguó xuéxiào de jiàoshì, dōngtiān chuān chènshān hái chū hàn, xiàtiān chuān máoyī hái lěng de bù déliǎo.

Xuěméi:　　　　Kě bu shì ma, tài làngfèi le.

Lìshā:　　　　Wǒ tīngshuō xiànzài bù shǎo rén qù cāntīng chī fàn zì dài cānjù, bú yòng yícìxìng❽ de.

Zhāng Tiānmíng:　Zhè ge zuòfǎ fēicháng hǎo. Ná yícìxìng kuàizi lái shuō ba, měi nián yào kǎn duōshao shù a?

Mǎkè:　　　　Chúle shàng cānguǎn zì dài kuàizi, mǎi dōngxi yě děi zìjǐ dài bāo le.

Lìshā:　　　　Duì, xiànzài Zhōngguó chāoshì❾ bù gěi sùliào dài, yào zìjǐ mǎi, suǒyǐ hěn duō rén dōu zìjǐ dài bāo, zhèyàng yì nián bù zhīdào néng jiǎnshǎo duōshao báisè wūrǎn!

Xuěméi:　　　　Hái yǒu qìchē, búdàn yào yòng hěn duō néngyuán, érqiě hái duì kōngqì zàochéng yánzhòng wūrǎn.

Kē Lín:　　　　Dàjiā dōu yīnggāi xiàng wǒmen zhèyang, shǎo kāi chē, duō qí chē, duō zǒu lù, yòu huánbǎo jiénéng❿, yòu yǒuyì yú jiànkāng. Hā hā…

Zhāng Tiānmíng:　Duì, dìqiú shì wǒmen de jiā, wǒmen yīnggāi hǎo hǎo bǎohù tā!

Xuěméi:　　　　Wǒmen yīnggāi cóng xiǎo dìfāng zuò qǐ, bǐrú suíshǒu guān dēng, jiéyuē yòng shuǐ. Hái yào ràng dàjiā zhīdào, rúguǒ zài jìxù làngfèi néngyuán, jìxù wūrǎn huánjìng, hòuguǒ huì bù kān shè xiǎng.

Lìngwài sì rén:　Hǎo! Tóngyì!

Lìshā:　　　　Āi, nǐmen kàn, shuō zhe shuō zhe⑥, dōu dào le shān xia le. Zánmen kāishǐ pá shān ba, kàn shéi xiān dào shān shang! Jiā yóu!

English Text

Zhang Tianming and his three friends have been in Beijing for two or three months now. The weather has also started to gradually warm up. Every day they are busy either with classes or with job-hunting. They haven't seen one another for half a month now, nor have they had a chance to be near nature. Today is Saturday, and everybody wants to relax a little. Tianming suggests they go mountain climbing. Lisa and Xuemei don't object, and Ke Lin feels that it is not a bad idea, either. He says that his new friend Mark would like to go, too.

But how should they get there? Taking a cab would be too expensive, and boring, too. Public transportation is too full of people, too crowded. Ke Lin comes up with an idea—biking! Everyone agrees at once. They all feel that biking is not only good exercise but also saves money. On top of that, it would be good for protecting the environment.

They set out very early in the morning. After riding a long way, they feel a little hot and a little tired, too, so they get off their bikes. They push their bikes and chat at the same time.

Zhang Tianming: The air here is really fresh!

Lisa: That's right. It's so much better than in the city. It's green everywhere. It looks so relaxing.

Ke Lin: Oh my, I'm dying of thirst.... Look, I've finished a whole bottle of water. Are there any recycling bins here? We're not supposed to litter.

Xuemei: Right. We should do our part to protect the environment. There's a recycling bin under the tree.

Lisa: I haven't bought any bottled water in a long time. Some of my classmates suggested that to protect the earth we should bring [our own] water instead of buying bottled water.

Xuemei: That's not a bad suggestion. Oh look, those houses over there have shiny things on top of them. What are those?

Ke Lin: They are to use solar power to generate electricity, I think. I've seen them in the U.S., too.

Xuemei: How great it is to use solar energy!

Mark: If bikes could also use solar energy to generate electricity, how cool would that be!

Xuemei: Today many countries in the world are having an energy crisis, but solar energy is inexhaustible.

Ke Lin:	Don't forget that wind power, too, is inexhaustible.
Xuemei:	If the whole world could use solar and wind energy, think of how much that would save on petroleum and coal! And....
The other four:	And it would protect the environment! Haha....
Lisa:	I hear that the Chinese government stipulates that offices and other public spaces shouldn't set the heaters above 20 degrees Celsius in winter or set the air conditioning below 26 degrees Celsius in summer.
Ke Lin:	I raise both of my hands to support this stipulation. Do you remember? In the U. S. in winter, in the classroom you'd be sweating wearing just a shirt and in summer you'd still feel very cold wearing a sweater.
Xuemei:	I couldn't agree more. It's too wasteful.
Lisa:	I hear that nowadays many people bring their own utensils to restaurants instead of using disposable ones.
Zhang Tianming:	That's a great idea. Take disposable chopsticks, for example. Every year, how many trees get cut down [to make them]?
Mark:	Besides bringing our own chopsticks, we have to bring our own bags when we go shopping.
Lisa:	That's correct. Nowadays Chinese supermarkets don't give away plastic bags. You have to buy your own. That's why many people bring their own bags. Think of how much white pollution can be reduced every year this way!
Xuemei:	Then there are cars, which not only consume lots of energy, but also cause serious air pollution.
Ke Lin:	Everybody should be like us, drive less, bike more and walk more. It'd be better for the environment and better for our health, too. Haha...
Zhang Tianming:	That's right. The earth is our home. We should protect it well!
Xuemei:	We should start small. For example, we should turn off the lights [whenever we don't need them] and conserve water. We should also let everyone know that if we continue wasting energy and polluting the environment, the consequences would be unimaginable.
The other four:	OK. Agreed!
Lisa:	Look, we got so caught up in talking that we didn't realize we've come to the foot of the mountain already. Let's start climbing. Let's see who gets to the top of the mountain first! Come on, let's go!

SELF-ASSESSMENT

How well can you do these things? Check (✔) the boxes to evaluate your progress and see which tasks you may need to practice more.

I can	Very Well	OK	A Little
Describe a scene in which people are busily engaged in all kinds of activities	☐	☐	☐
Describe some of the features of a clean environment	☐	☐	☐
Name commonly known green energy sources	☐	☐	☐
Give examples of practices that are friendly to the environment	☐	☐	☐

第十七課
理財與
投資

第十七课
理财与
投资

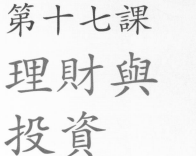

 LEARNING OBJECTIVES

In this lesson, you will learn to use Chinese to

1. Describe if you're a saver or a spender;
2. Identify ways to invest money;
3. Talk about ways to purchase a big-ticket item;
4. Describe your spending habits;
5. Describe in basic terms the ups and downs of the stock market.

RELATE AND GET READY

In your own culture/community—

- Do many people save?
- Do many people invest in the stock market or the housing market?
- Do people get a mortgage or pay cash when purchasing a house?

Before You Study

Check the statements that apply to you.

- [ ] 1. I have a savings account.
- [ ] 2. I spend most or all of the money I earn.

When You Study

Listen to the audio recording and scan the text. Ask yourself the following questions before you begin a close reading of the text.

1. In general, do you think Chinese people are savers or spenders?

中國改革開放以前，一般人收入不高，沒有剩餘的錢，所以沒有投資理財的問題。可是現在不一樣了，很多人收入增加了，而且中國老百姓一向^①省吃儉用，所以很多家庭在銀行都有存款。錢存在銀行，安全是安全，但利息太少，錢增加得太慢。於是很多人開始考慮用別的方式投資理財了。

3. I think investing in the stock market is risky.

4. I hope to buy a house after I graduate from college.

2. Why do many Chinese people start to look into ways to invest their money?

3. What does Tianming's cousin want Tianming's aunt to do?

4. Does Tianming's aunt follow her son's advice?

 中国改革开放以前，一般人收入不高，没有剩余的钱，所以没有投资理财的问题。可是现在不一样了，很多人收入增加了，而且中国老百姓一向①省吃俭用，所以很多家庭在银行都有存款。钱存在银行，安全是安全，但利息太少，钱增加得太慢。于是很多人开始考虑用别的方式投资理财了。

最近一些年，中國的房價❶漲得很快，買房子成為一些人投資的選擇。也有人看見別人"炒股"❷，賺錢好像很容易，於是也炒起股來。還有一些人更願意把錢花在子女教育上，他們覺得讓子女受到最好的教育，將來事業成功、生活幸福，才是最好的投資。

當然也有人認為有錢就應該消費享受，有人甚至說"錢只有花了才是自己的。"在他們看來，把②錢省下來投資，不如舒舒服服地享受生活。

張天明平常不大考慮投資理財的事，今天他表哥跟他在網上聊了半天這個問題，才引起他的思考。他剛剛下綫，麗莎就走了進來。

★　★　★

麗莎：　　天明，又上網聊天兒了？

張天明：　對，是表哥找我聊天兒。姑媽跟表哥鬧起矛盾來了，表哥好像有點兒鬱悶。

麗莎：　　為什麼？

張天明：　說來話長。姑媽退休前省吃儉用存了一筆錢，要留給孫子孫女上大學用。

麗莎：　　表哥還沒結婚呢！這錢看來得存二十年啊。

張天明：　可不是，表哥也這樣說。後來姑媽想出了一個花錢的主意。

麗莎：　　什麼主意？

張天明：　表哥不是明年要結婚嗎？姑媽要給表哥的未婚妻買一輛新車，算是結婚禮物。

麗莎：　　姑媽真好。

張天明：　可是表哥他們不同意買車。他們倆上班的地方很近，合用一輛車就行了。他們勸姑媽買房子，說姑媽辛苦了幾十年，應該住一套大一些的房子，舒舒服服地享受退休生活。

LANGUAGE NOTES

❶ 房價/房价 is short for 房子的價格/房子的价格 (housing price).

最近一些年，中国的房价❶涨得很快，买房子成为一些人投资的选择。也有人看见别人"炒股"❷，赚钱好像很容易，于是也炒起股来。还有一些人更愿意把钱花在子女教育上，他们觉得让子女受到最好的教育，将来事业成功、生活幸福，才是最好的投资。

当然也有人认为有钱就应该消费享受，有人甚至说"钱只有花了才是自己的。"在他们看来，把②钱省下来投资，不如舒舒服服地享受生活。

张天明平常不大考虑投资理财的事，今天他表哥跟他在网上聊了半天这个问题，才引起他的思考。他刚刚下线，丽莎就走了进来。

★　★　★

丽莎：　　天明，又上网聊天儿了？

张天明：　对，是表哥找我聊天儿。姑妈跟表哥闹起矛盾来了，表哥好像有点儿郁闷。

丽莎：　　为什么？

张天明：　说来话长。姑妈退休前省吃俭用存了一笔钱，要留给孙子孙女上大学用。

丽莎：　　表哥还没结婚呢！这钱看来得存二十年啊。

张天明：　可不是，表哥也这样说。后来姑妈想出了一个花钱的主意。

丽莎：　　什么主意？

张天明：　表哥不是明年要结婚吗？姑妈要给表哥的未婚妻买一辆新车，算是结婚礼物。

丽莎：　　姑妈真好。

张天明：　可是表哥他们不同意买车。他们俩上班的地方很近，合用一辆车就行了。他们劝姑妈买房子，说姑妈辛苦了几十年，应该住一套大一些的房子，舒舒服服地享受退休生活。

---

❷ 股 is 股票 (stock or share). 炒股 is slang meaning "to flip stocks" or "to speculate in stocks."

麗莎：　　他們說得太對了！再說，買房子也是一種不錯的投資啊。

張天明：　可是姑媽說她的錢不夠買一套房子。我表哥說他可以為姑媽貸款，還給姑媽講了一個美國老太太❸和一個中國老太太的故事。

麗莎：　　這個故事我以前也聽說過。說的是，一個中國老太太攢了三十年錢，到了老年才買上一套房子，住了進去。而一個美國老太太，三十年前就貸款買房子住進去了。比一比，哪個老太太更會生活？

張天明：　對，表哥就用這個故事說服❹了姑媽，姑媽終於同意買房子了。

麗莎：　　好啊，問題算是解決了。

張天明：　事情還沒完，你聽我接著說啊。兩個星期前，他們看中了一套三室一廳兩衛的房子，本來後天就要去簽購房合同了，沒想到姑媽的想法突然變了。

麗莎：　　看中了另外一套房子了？

張天明：　不是。姑媽退休以後常跟以前在一起工作的老姐妹們打打❸麻將，聊聊天兒。前幾天姑媽聽說有幾個人這兩年炒股賺了不少錢，就變主意了，不想買房子了。

麗莎：　　難道她想投資股市❺？

張天明：　可不是嗎？

麗莎：　　可是姑媽不知道炒股有風險嗎？跟李文父母一起打太極拳的一位老先生，把房子抵押給銀行，然後把錢全買了股票，沒想到股市一直跌，不到三個月，賠了一半。

張天明：　買房子是不是就沒有風險呢？

麗莎：　　房價太高的時候買房子，當然有風險。

張天明：　看來投資真不是一件簡單的事，不知道姑媽最後會怎麼決定。

LANGUAGE NOTES

❸ 老太太 means an elderly lady. However, it is rarely used as a form of direct address. We can say 老太太, 老爺子/老爷子 to refer to older relatives in our immediate family. In China, respect for the elderly is still an important traditional value. The word 老 carries no stigma. The term 老師/老师,

丽莎：　　他们说得太对了！再说，买房子也是一种不错的投资啊。

张天明：　可是姑妈说她的钱不够买一套房子。我表哥说他可以为姑妈贷款，还给姑妈讲了一个美国老太太❸和一个中国老太太的故事。

丽莎：　　这个故事我以前也听说过。说的是，一个中国老太太攒了三十年钱，到了老年才买上一套房子，住了进去。而一个美国老太太，三十年前就贷款买房子住进去了。比一比，哪个老太太更会生活？

张天明：　对，表哥就用这个故事说服❹了姑妈，姑妈终于同意买房子了。

丽莎：　　好啊，问题算是解决了。

张天明：　事情还没完，你听我接着说啊。两个星期前，他们看中了一套三室一厅两卫的房子，本来后天就要去签购房合同了，没想到姑妈的想法突然变了。

丽莎：　　看中了另外一套房子了？

张天明：　不是。姑妈退休以后常跟以前在一起工作的老姐妹们打打③麻将，聊聊天儿。前几天姑妈听说有几个人这两年炒股赚了不少钱，就变主意了，不想买房子了。

丽莎：　　难道她想投资股市❺？

张天明：　可不是吗？

丽莎：　　可是姑妈不知道炒股有风险吗？跟李文父母一起打太极拳的一位老先生，把房子抵押给银行，然后把钱全买了股票，没想到股市一直跌，不到三个月，赔了一半。

张天明：　买房子是不是就没有风险呢？

丽莎：　　房价太高的时候买房子，当然有风险。

张天明：　看来投资真不是一件简单的事，不知道姑妈最后会怎么决定。

---

for instance, is widely used to refer to not just one's teachers but also to anyone accomplished in some discipline or field.

❹ 說服/说服 is pronounced "shuìfú" in Taiwan.

❺ 股市 is short for 股票市場/股票市场 (stock market).

After You Study

Challenge yourself to complete the following tasks in Chinese.

1. Recap the story of the two elderly women told by Tianming's cousin.

2. In chronological order, list Tianming's aunt's ideas for what to do with her money.

帳　號 A/C											户　名 NAME
	拾億	億	仟萬	佰萬	拾萬	萬	仟	佰	拾	元	
台幣金額 (小寫)AMT											
次交票據 總金額											
外　匯	原幣別：☐美金USD　　☐歐元EUR　　☐日幣JPY　　☐港幣HKD ☐其他 _____ 外幣金額(小寫) _____										

一張銀行存款單
一张银行存款单

3. Among the investment options mentioned in the text, pick the one that you think is most appropriate for you.

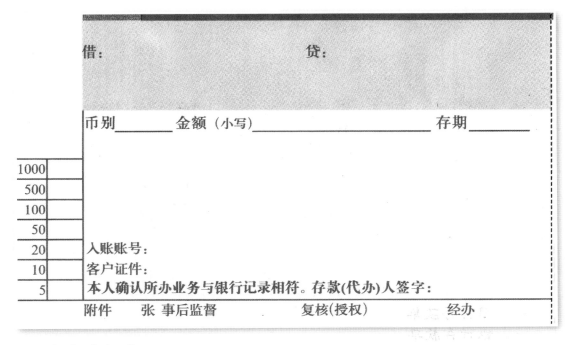

借:	贷:

币别＿＿＿＿＿金额（小写）＿＿＿＿＿＿＿＿＿＿＿＿＿存期＿＿＿＿＿＿

1000	
500	
100	
50	
20	入账账号：
10	客户证件：
5	本人确认所办业务与银行记录相符。存款(代办)人签字：

附件　　张 事后监督　　　　　复核(授权)　　　　经办

一張銀行存款單
一张银行存款单

VOCABULARY

1.	理財	理财	lǐcái	vo	to manage money
2.	投資	投资	tóuzī	v/n	to invest (money); (financial) investment
3.	剩餘	剩余	shèngyú	v/n	to be left over; surplus
4.	利息		lìxī	n	interest
5.	增加		zēngjiā	v	to increase; to add
6.	一向		yíxiàng	adv	all along; the whole time; constantly [See Grammar 1.]
7.	省吃儉用	省吃俭用	shěng chī jiǎn yòng		to be frugal (with food and other living expenses)
8.	存款		cúnkuǎn	n	bank savings
9.	方式		fāngshì	n	way; method
10.	漲	涨	zhǎng	v	(of water, prices, etc.) to rise; to surge; to go up
11.	炒		chǎo	v	to stir-fry; to sauté; to speculate (for profit)
12.	消費	消费	xiāofèi	v	to consume
13.	享受		xiǎngshòu	v/n	to enjoy; enjoyment; pleasure
14.	引起		yǐnqǐ	v	to give rise to; to lead to
15.	思考		sīkǎo	v/n	to think deeply; to ponder over; contemplation; cogitation
16.	矛盾		máodùn	n/adj	contradiction; contradictory; conflicting
17.	鬱悶	郁闷	yùmèn	adj	gloomy; depressed

18.	筆	笔	bǐ	m	(measure word for sums of money)
19.	孫子	孙子	sūnzi	n	son's son; grandson
20.	孫女	孙女	sūnnü	n	son's daughter; granddaughter
21.	未婚妻		wèihūnqī	n	fiancée
22.	算		suàn	v	to count as; to be considered as
23.	合		hé	v	to combine; to join
24.	勸	劝	quàn	v	to persuade; to advise; to urge
25.	辛苦		xīnkǔ	adj/v	hard; strenuous; toilsome; laborious; to work hard; to go to trouble
26.	老太太		lǎotàitai	n	elderly lady
27.	攢	攒	zǎn	v	to accumulate; to hoard; to save; to scrape together
28.	老年		lǎonián	n	old age
29.	說服	说服	shuōfú	v	to persuade; to convince
30.	終於	终于	zhōngyú	adv	at last; in the end; finally; eventually
31.	接著	接着	jiēzhe	v	to follow; to continue
32.	中		zhòng	v	to fit exactly; to hit
33.	簽	签	qiān	v	to sign; to autograph
34.	合同		hétong	n	agreement; contract
35.	想法		xiǎngfǎ	n	idea; opinion
36.	突然		tūrán	adj	sudden; unexpected
37.	姐妹		jiěmèi	n	sisters; female friends or co-workers who share a sister-like bond
38.	麻將	麻将	májiàng	n	mahjong
39.	股市		gǔshì	n	stock market

40.	風險	风险	fēngxiǎn	n	risk; danger; hazard
41.	抵押		dǐyā	v	to mortgage
42.	股票		gǔpiào	n	stock; share
43.	跌		diē	v	to fall
44.	賠	赔	péi	v	to lose (money, etc.); to suffer a loss in a deal

Enlarged Characters

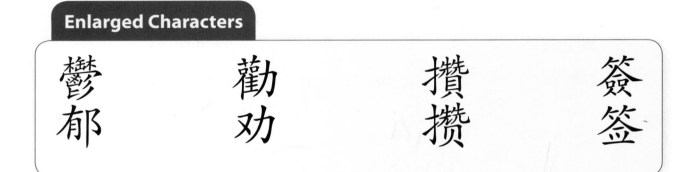

鬱   勸   攢   簽
郁   劝   攒   签

信用有循环
理财又享受

先消费,后还款,
更有最长50天免息
期,让您理财更灵活,
消费更便利。

這是一個銀行的信用卡廣告。
这是一个银行的信用卡广告。

Culture Highlights

1 The Chinese national savings rate is close to fifty percent, which is the highest among the world's major economies. The average family puts away approximately a third of its income in savings.

2 Before the early 1990s housing was allocated to city residents by the Chinese government. Rent was minimal. Most people have since purchased their rentals at very inexpensive prices. This kind of subsidized housing was so-called welfare housing. However, it is no longer available.

Currently, the housing stock in China consists of "low-rent housing" (廉租房), "economical, practical housing" (經濟適用房/经济适用房) sold below market rates to low-income people, and "commercial housing" (商品房). No matter what the housing type, the state owns the land. Land use rights have a term of seventy years.

As of 2009, there is no residential housing tax in China.

3 There are two stock exchanges in mainland China, the Shanghai Stock Exchange and the Shenzhen Stock Exchange, each with its own stock index. Hong Kong also has an important stock exchange, as does Taiwan.

Grammar

> ## 1. 一向 vs. 一直

一向 means persisting from the past to the present.

❶   中國老百姓一向省吃儉用。

中国老百姓一向省吃俭用。

(Ordinary Chinese people have always been thrifty.)

❷   我一向不喜歡上網看新聞、查資料，因為我的眼睛不太好。

我一向不喜欢上网看新闻、查资料，因为我的眼睛不太好。

(I have never liked going online for reading news or looking up information because of my poor eyesight.)

❸   小張的爸爸一向不會理財，所以總也買不起房子。

小张的爸爸一向不会理财，所以总也买不起房子。

(Little Zhang's dad has never been good at managing money. That's why he hasn't been able to afford to buy a house.)

一直 denotes a continuous action or constant, unchanging state within a time frame.

❹   昨天晚上他一直打電話，我給他打了好幾次電話，都打不進去。

昨天晚上他一直打电话，我给他打了好几次电话，都打不进去。

(Last night he was on the phone for a long time. I called him several times but couldn't get through.)

❺   上大學的時候他們一直是同屋，感情很好。

上大学的时候他们一直是同屋，感情很好。

(Throughout college they were roommates. They were very close.)

❻   他去年一直想投資買股票，但他太太不贊成。

他去年一直想投资买股票，但他太太不赞成。

(He was constantly thinking of investing in stocks last year, but his wife didn't agree.)

❼　老王炒股，賠了很多錢，大家一直勸他別太難過。

　　老王炒股，赔了很多钱，大家一直劝他别太难过。

(Old Wang lost a lot of money on the stock market. Everyone has constantly been trying to comfort him.)

2. Summary of the 把 Construction (I)

If we want to describe what someone has done to something, and if that something is known to the listener, it is best to use the 把 construction.

❶　把你在雲南買的紀念品給我們看看。

　　把你在云南买的纪念品给我们看看。

(Show us the souvenirs that you got in Yunnan.)

❷　**A:**　你新買的枕頭和被子呢？怎麼不用？

　　　　你新买的枕头和被子呢？怎么不用？

(What happened to the pillows and comforters that you just bought? Why aren't you using them?)

　　B:　我把它們送給我表哥了，算是給他和他未婚妻的結婚禮物。

　　　　我把它们送给我表哥了，算是给他和他未婚妻的结婚礼物。

(I gave them to my cousin and his fiancée as a wedding gift.)

❸　房間裏空氣太不好了，把窗戶打開吧。

　　房间里空气太不好了，把窗户打开吧。

(The air in the room isn't very good. Why don't you open the windows?)

The 把 structure consists of:

Subject + 把 + noun + verb + other element (complement, 了, reduplicated verb, etc.)

把 is a preposition. In a typical 把 sentence, the noun after 把 is not only the object of 把, but also the object of the verb. In ❶, 紀念品/纪念品 is also the object of 看. In ❷, 它們/它们 is also the object of 送. In ❸, 窗戶 is also the object of 開/开.

Please pay attention to the following when using the 把 structure:

A. The object of 把 must be known or at least recognizable to the listener. If you suddenly say to someone:

❹   你把雜誌給我。
        你把杂志给我。
        (Give me the magazine.)

That person may be confused if the magazine was not mentioned or defined previously, and ask

        什麼雜誌/哪本雜誌?
        什么杂志/哪本杂志?
        (What magazine/which magazine?)

But if you say:

❺   剛才我把一本雜誌丟了。
        刚才我把一本杂志丢了。
        (I just lost a magazine.)

The listener will understand that you lost a magazine, not a computer or something else.

B. There is usually a complement indicating result, a 了, or some other element after the verb. This is because there is usually an impact on the object as a result of someone's action, e.g., 開/开 in ❸. Here are some examples:

❻   大風把花吹下來了。
        大风把花吹下来了。
        (The gusty wind blew that flower to the ground.)

❼   昨天的剩菜把我的肚子吃壞了。
        昨天的剩菜把我的肚子吃坏了。
        (Yesterday's leftovers gave me stomach trouble.)

❽   請把這封信拿給老師。
        请把这封信拿给老师。
        (Please give this letter to the teacher.)
        [Your giving will cause the letter to be in the teacher's possession.]

⑨ 媽媽擔心我會把信用卡丟了。

妈妈担心我会把信用卡丢了。

(My mother worries I'll lose my credit card.)

[了 here also conveys result, namely, loss.]

The verb in a 把 sentence can also appear in reduplicated form, e.g.

⑩ 請你把剛買回來的月餅給我嚐嚐。

请你把刚买回来的月饼给我尝尝。

(Please let me try the moon cakes that you've just bought.)

⑪ 他把那個合同看了看，又放下了。

他把那个合同看了看，又放下了。

(He took a look at the contract and put it down.)

To sum up, when using the 把 construction, be sure to include a complement or some other element after the verb. See Lesson 20 for more on the 把 construction.

3. Reduplication of Verbs

We have studied the reduplication of verbs to make the tone of the sentence milder, e.g.,

❶ 請你談談應該怎樣理財。

请你谈谈应该怎样理财。

(Can you please talk about how to manage money?)

❷ 你看看這本書，寫的是環境保護方面的事情，寫得非常好。

你看看这本书，写的是环境保护方面的事情，写得非常好。

(Take a look at this book. It's about environmental protection, and it's very well written.)

The above are both imperative sentences. The actions are yet to happen. In this lesson, the reduplicated verbs are not time-specific. Rather, they indicate actions that occur frequently.

❸ 姑媽退休以後常跟以前在一起工作的老姐妹們打打麻將，聊聊
天兒。

姑妈退休以后常跟以前在一起工作的老姐妹们打打麻将，聊聊
天儿。

(Since she retired, [Tianming's] aunt often plays mahjong and chats with her old
co-workers.)

This kind of reduplication usually occurs in pairs or threes and often suggests a sense of
leisure and casualness.

❹ **A:** 你週末做什麼？

你周末做什么？

(What do you do on weekends?)

B: 要麼上網聊聊天，要麼打打球，一般不學習。

要么上网聊聊天，要么打打球，一般不学习。

(I either chat online [with friends] or play ball for a bit. I don't usually study.)

❺ 老人們每天早晨跳跳舞，打打拳，散散步，挺高興。

老人们每天早晨跳跳舞，打打拳，散散步，挺高兴。

(Every morning the elderly people have a pleasant time dancing, practicing tai chi, or
walking. They are quite happy.)

Words & Phrases

> ### A. 引起 (to give rise to; to lead to)

The verb 引起 usually takes as objects nouns such as 注意, 思考, 重視/重视, 反
對/反对, 討論/讨论, 興趣/兴趣, or 危機/危机.

❶ 孩子的教育問題還沒有引起這兩個父母的注意。

孩子的教育问题还没有引起这两个父母的注意。

(The issue of their children's education has not attracted these two parents' attention.)

❷ 環保問題已經引起各個國家的重視。

環保问题已经引起各个国家的重视。

(The issue of environmental protection has drawn much attention in different countries.)

❸ 小王的建議引起同學們的反對。

小王的建议引起同学们的反对。

(Little Wang's proposal met with objections from other students.)

B. 算(是) (to count as; to be considered as)

The basic meaning of 算 is "to count." In this lesson 算 means "to count as," or "can be taken as." 是 is optional.

❶ 姑媽要給表哥的未婚妻買一輛新車，算是結婚禮物。

姑妈要给表哥的未婚妻买一辆新车，算是结婚礼物。

([Tianming's] aunt wanted to buy a new car for [Tianming's] cousin's fiancée as a wedding gift.)

❷ 這錢算我借給你的，你什麼時候還給我都行。

这钱算我借给你的，你什么时候还给我都行。

(Take this money as a loan from me. You can return it whenever.)

❸ 這個孩子算是他的兒子吧。

这个孩子算是他的儿子吧。

(This child could be considered his son, I guess.)

算是 sometimes means more or less the same as 是, as in ❶—The car *is* a wedding gift—and ❷— The money *can* be considered a loan. However, sometimes 算是 is not the same as 是. In ❸, "this child" is definitely not his biological son, but "is considered" his son.

C. 合 (to combine; to join)

合 means two or more people together:

❶ 他們倆上班的地方很近，合用一輛車就行了。

他们俩上班的地方很近，合用一辆车就行了。

(Their workplaces are close to one another. They can share a car.)

❷ 麗莎打算跟雪梅合租一套房子。

丽莎打算跟雪梅合租一套房子。

(Lisa plans to rent a house with Xuemei.)

❸ 我跟指導教授合寫了一本書。

我跟指导教授合写了一本书。

(I co-wrote a book with my advisor.)

More examples: 合唱一個歌/合唱一个歌 (to sing a song in chorus), 合開一家飯館/合开一家饭馆 (to open a restaurant with a partner).

D. 終於/终于 (at last; in the end; finally; eventually)

終於/终于 means the materialization of a certain, usually positive, result after long waiting and numerous changes.

❶ 表哥就用這個故事說服了姑媽，姑媽終於同意買房子了。

表哥就用这个故事说服了姑妈，姑妈终于同意买房子了。

([Tianming's] cousin used this story to persuade [Tianming's] aunt. Aunt finally agreed to buy a place.)

❷ 林先生林太太辛辛苦苦地工作了二十多年，現在兩個人退休了，終於可以輕鬆輕鬆，享受退休生活。

林先生林太太辛辛苦苦地工作了二十多年，现在两个人退休了，终于可以轻松轻松，享受退休生活。

(Mr. and Mrs. Lin worked hard for over twenty years. Now they are retired, and they can finally relax and enjoy their lives.)

❸   期末考終於考完了，我可以好好玩幾天了。

期末考终于考完了，我可以好好玩几天了。

(The final exams were finally over. I could have some fun for a few days.)

E. 接著/接着 (to follow; to continue)

接著/接着 means "to continue doing something", as in ❶ and ❷, or "to go on to do something," as in ❸.

❶   事情還沒完，你聽我接著説啊。

事情还没完，你听我接着说啊。

(It's not over yet. Let me continue with the story.)

❷   吃完了炒菜，後邊還有餃子，咱們接著吃。

吃完了炒菜，后边还有饺子，咱们接着吃。

(There will be dumplings after the stir-fries. Let's continue to eat.)

❸   麗莎先打了一遍太極拳，接著又做瑜伽，覺得很舒服。

丽莎先打了一遍太极拳，接着又做瑜伽，觉得很舒服。

(Lisa practiced a tai chi sequence and continued with yoga. She felt very good [afterwards].)

F. 突然 (sudden; unexpected)

突然 is an adjective. It can be used as an adverbial, a predicate, or a complement following 得.

❶   沒想到姑媽的想法突然變了。 [adverbial]

没想到姑妈的想法突然变了。

(Who would have imagined Aunt would suddenly change her mind.)

❷   剛才天氣很好，可是突然下起雨來。 [adverbial]

刚才天气很好，可是突然下起雨来。

(The weather was fine just now, but all of a sudden it started to rain.)

❸ 這件事很突然，我一點準備也沒有。[predicate]

这件事很突然，我一点准备也没有。

(This thing was too sudden. I wasn't prepared for it at all.)

❹ 他病得太突然了，我根本沒想到。[complement]

(He became ill without warning. I had had no idea whatsoever.)

Language Practice

A. Happy-Go-Lucky

Li Zhe has earned enough credits for graduation and is currently waiting for word about an internship opportunity, so he has been taking it easy and relaxing these past few weeks. Based on the pictures, describe Li Zhe's daily activities by using reduplicated verbs.

EXAMPLE: Early Morning:

→ 每天早晨李哲要麼打打籃球，要麼打打太極拳。　每天早晨李哲要么打打籃球，要么打打太极拳。

1. Morning:

2. Afternoon:

3. After dinner:

B. Think of It This Way!

Suppose you have an old friend who is in a financially difficult situation. You want to help him/her out with some money but he/she refuses to take it. Try to press your old friend into accepting the money by using 算 or 算是.

EXAMPLE: a loan from me

→　　這點錢算是我借給你的。　这点钱算是我借给你的。

1. Thanksgiving gift

2. Chinese New Year gift

3. my investment in you

C. Sunny or Gloomy

Some people's moods are determined by the weather. For instance,

只要天氣好，出太陽，就很高興。　只要天气好，出太阳，就很高兴。
只要天氣不好，下雨，就很鬱悶。　只要天气不好，下雨，就很郁闷。

Some people's moods are set by the ups and downs of the stock market:

_____

_____

Some people's moods are set by the appreciation and depreciation of the value of their house:

_____

_____

D. Save Up, Give Up, or Something Else?

a. Ask a partner what big-ticket item he or she would like to purchase. Is it a refrigerator, a TV, a laptop, a car, or a house?

b. Ask him or her how he or she plans to pay for it. Is he or she going to save up for it, use bank savings, get a loan, ask his or her parents to lend him or her money, ask his or her parents for money as a gift, get a part-time job to pay for it, or give up?

你打算怎麼買？   你打算怎么买？

_____

_____

_____

_____

_____

_____

還是不打算買了？   还是不打算买了？

c. Can you offer your partner any advice?

我覺得你應該   我觉得你应该

E. Best Ways to Invest

a. Brainstorm with a partner and list ways to invest money.

_____

_____

_____

_____

b. Discuss with your partner the profitability and risk factors of the methods above. Rank them with #1 being the most profitable and least risky.

c. Present your conclusion to the class:

我們認為＿＿＿＿＿＿＿是最好的
投資方式，不但安全，風險低，
而且錢增加得很快。

我们认为＿＿＿＿＿＿＿是最好的
投资方式，不但安全，风险低，
而且钱增加得很快。

d. Comment on the other items on your list in terms of their relative profitability and risk.

F. Are You a Spender or a Saver?

a. Sort the words/phrases given into the following two groups to characterize a "spender" and a "saver":

整天叫外賣　　　　　整天叫外卖
經常亂買東西　　　　经常乱买东西
把錢存在銀行裏　　　把钱存在银行里
省吃儉用　　　　　　省吃俭用
借錢炒股　　　　　　借钱炒股
投資買房　　　　　　投资买房
享受生活　　　　　　享受生活
貸款買車　　　　　　贷款买车

Spender

＿＿＿＿＿＿＿＿＿＿＿

＿＿＿＿＿＿＿＿＿＿＿

＿＿＿＿＿＿＿＿＿＿＿

＿＿＿＿＿＿＿＿＿＿＿

Saver

＿＿＿＿＿＿＿＿＿＿＿

＿＿＿＿＿＿＿＿＿＿＿

＿＿＿＿＿＿＿＿＿＿＿

＿＿＿＿＿＿＿＿＿＿＿

b. Compare your lists with a partner's and discuss how your lists are the same or different.

c. Ask your partner to explain if he or she considers himself or herself a spender or a saver.

G. Be a Financial Consultant

Role play: Imagine you're a financial consultant, and your partner is a person seeking advice. You are looking at your partner's monthly income and spending, and trying to offer advice on how he or she can cut expenses and put the money in the bank or the stock market.

a. List income: salary, allowance, scholarship, etc.

收入 _____

_____

_____

_____

b. List expenditures: rent, groceries, utilities, car loan, cell phone, internet, books, restaurant take-out, etc.

支出 (zhīchū) _____

_____

_____

_____

_____

_____

_____

_____

c. Look at the two lists, and advise your partner on where he or she can cut expenses to put money into a savings account or invest it in the stock market.

你可以少/不＿＿＿＿＿＿，
把省下的錢存到銀行裏。
or
你可以少/不＿＿＿＿＿＿，
把省下的錢投資股市。

你可以少/不＿＿＿＿＿＿，
把省下的钱存到银行里。
or
你可以少/不＿＿＿＿＿＿，
把省下的钱投资股市。

Pinyin Text

Zhōngguó gǎigé kāifàng yǐqián, yìbān rén shōurù bù gāo, méiyǒu shèngyú de qián, suǒyǐ méiyǒu tóuzī lǐcái de wèntí. Kěshì xiànzài bù yíyàng le, hěn duō rén shōurù zēngjiā le, érqiě Zhōngguó lǎobǎixìng yíxiàng ① shěng chī jiǎn yòng, suǒyǐ hěn duō jiātíng zài yínháng dōu yǒu cúnkuǎn. Qián cún zài yínháng, ānquán shì ānquán, dàn lìxī tài shǎo, qián zēngjiā de tài màn. Yúshì hěn duō rén kāishǐ kǎolǜ yòng bié de fāngshì tóuzī lǐcái le.

Zuìjìn yì xiē nián, Zhōngguó de fáng jià ❶ zhǎng de hěn kuài, mǎi fángzi chéngwéi yì xiē rén tóuzī de xuǎnzé. Yě yǒu rén kàn jiàn biérén "chǎo gǔ" ❷, zhuàn qián hǎoxiàng hěn róngyì, yúshì yě chǎo qi gǔ lai. Hái yǒu yì xiē rén gèng yuànyi bǎ qián huā zài zǐnǚ jiàoyù shang, tāmen juéde ràng zǐnǚ shòu dào zuì hǎo de jiàoyù, jiānglái shìyè chénggōng, shēnghuó xìngfú, cái shì zuì hǎo de tóuzī.

Dāngrán yě yǒu rén rènwéi yǒu qián jiù yīnggāi xiāofèi xiǎngshòu, yǒu rén shènzhì shuō "qián zhǐyǒu huā le cái shì zìjǐ de." Zài tāmen kàn lai, bǎ ② qián shěng xia lai tóuzī, bùrú shū shu fú fú de xiǎngshòu shēnghuó.

Zhāng Tiānmíng píngcháng bú dà kǎolǜ tóuzī lǐcái de shì, jīntiān tā biǎogē gēn tā zài wǎng shang liáo le bàntiān zhè ge wèntí, cái yǐnqǐ tā de sīkǎo. Tā gānggāng xià xiàn, Lìshā jiù zǒu le jin lai.

Lìshā:	Tiānmíng, yòu shàng wǎng liáo tiānr le?
Zhāng Tiānmíng:	Duì, shì biǎogē zhǎo wǒ liáo tiānr. Gūmā gēn biǎogē nào qi máodùn lai le, biǎogē hǎoxiàng yǒu diǎnr yùmèn.
Lìshā:	Wèishénme?
Zhāng Tiānmíng:	Shuō lái huà cháng. Gūmā tuìxiū qián shěng chī jiǎn yòng cún le yì bǐ qián, yào liú gěi sūnzi sūnnǚ shàng dàxué yòng.
Lìshā:	Biǎogē hái méi jié hūn ne! Zhè qián kàn lai děi cún èrshí nián a.
Zhāng Tiānmíng:	Kě bu shì, biǎogē yě zhèyàng shuō. Hòulái gūmā xiǎng chu le yí ge huā qián de zhúyi.
Lìshā:	Shénme zhúyi?
Zhāng Tiānmíng:	Biǎogē bú shì míngnián yào jié hūn ma? Gūmā yào gěi biǎogē de wèihūnqī mǎi yí liàng xīn chē, suàn shì jié hūn lǐwù.
Lìshā:	Gūmā zhēn hǎo.
Zhāng Tiānmíng:	Kěshì biǎogē tāmen bù tóngyì mǎi chē. Tāmen liǎ shàng bān de dìfāng hěn jìn, hé yòng yí liàng chē jiù xíng le. Tāmen quàn gūmā

	mǎi fángzi, shuō gūmā xīnkǔ le jǐ shí nián, yīnggāi zhù yí tào dà yì xiē de fángzi, shū shu fú fú de xiǎngshòu tuìxiū shēnghuó.
Lìshā:	Tāmen shuō de tài duì le! Zàishuō, mǎi fángzi yě shì yì zhǒng búcuò de tóuzī a.
Zhāng Tiānmíng:	Kěshì gūmā shuō tā de qián bú gòu mǎi yí tào fángzi. Wǒ biǎogē shuō tā kěyǐ wèi gūmā dài kuǎn, hái gěi gūmā jiǎng le yí ge Měiguó lǎotàitai❸ hé yí ge Zhōngguó lǎotàitai de gùshi.
Lìshā:	Zhè ge gùshi wǒ yǐqián yě tīngshuō guo. Shuō de shì, yí ge Zhōngguó lǎotàitai zǎn le sānshí nián qián, dào le lǎonián cái mǎi shang yí tào fángzi, zhù le jin qu. Ér yí ge Měiguó lǎotàitai, sān shí nián qián jiù dài kuǎn mǎi fángzi zhù jin qu le. Bǐ yì bǐ, nǎ ge lǎotàitai gèng huì shēnghuó?
Zhāng Tiānmíng:	Duì, biǎogē jiù yòng zhè ge gùshi shuōfú❹ le gūmā, gūmā zhōngyú tóngyì mǎi fángzi le.
Lìshā:	Hǎo a, wèntí suàn shì jiějué le.
Zhāng Tiānmíng:	Shìqing hái méi wán, nǐ tīng wǒ jiēzhe shuō a. Liǎng ge xīngqī qián, tāmen kàn zhòng le yí tào sān shì yì tīng liǎng wèi de fángzi, běnlái hòutiān jiù yào qù qiān gòu fáng hétong le, méi xiǎng dào gūmā de xiǎngfǎ tūrán biàn le.
Lìshā:	Kàn zhòng le lìngwài yí tào fángzi le?
Zhāng Tiānmíng:	Bú shì. Gūmā tuìxiū yǐhòu cháng gēn yǐqián zài yìqǐ gōngzuò de lǎo jiěmèi men dǎ da❸ májiàng, liáo liao tiānr. Qián jǐ tiān gūmā tīngshuō yǒu jǐ ge rén zhè liǎng nián chǎo gǔ zhuàn le bù shǎo qián, jiù biàn zhúyì le, bù xiǎng mǎi fángzi le.
Lìshā:	Nándào tā xiǎng tóuzī gǔshì❺?
Zhāng Tiānmíng:	Kě bu shì ma?
Lìshā:	Kěshì gūmā bù zhīdào chǎo gǔ yǒu fēngxiǎn ma? Gēn Lǐ Wén fùmǔ yìqǐ dǎ tàijíquán de yí wèi lǎoxiānsheng, bǎ fángzi dǐyā gěi yínháng, ránhòu bǎ qián quán mǎi le gǔpiào, méi xiǎng dào gǔshì yìzhí diē, bú dào sān ge yuè, péi le yí bàn.
Zhāng Tiānmíng:	Mǎi fángzi shì bú shì jiù méiyǒu fēngxiǎn ne?
Lìshā:	Fáng jià tài gāo de shíhou mǎi fángzi, dāngrán yǒu fēngxiǎn.
Zhāng Tiānmíng:	Kàn lai tóuzī zhēn bú shì yí jiàn jiǎndān de shì, bù zhīdào gūmā zuìhòu huì zěnme juédìng.

English Text

Before China's Reform and Opening-Up, the income of average people was not very high, and [most people] didn't have any spare money, so there was no question of investment and money management. However, it is different now. Many people's incomes have gone up. Besides, ordinary Chinese people have always been frugal, and that is why many families have savings in the bank. Depositing money in the bank may be safe, but the interest is minimal, and the money accumulates too slowly. So many people have started considering other ways to invest and manage their money.

In recent years China's housing prices have risen rapidly. Buying real estate has become an investment choice for some people. There are also people who see others "flipping stocks," seemingly having an easy time making money, so they begin to flip stocks, too. There are still others who prefer to spend their money on their children's education. They feel that letting their children receive the best education [possible so that they] will have a successful career and a happy life in the future is the best investment.

Of course, there are also people who think that money is to be spent and enjoyed. Some go so far as to say that "money is not yours until you've spent it." In their view, rather than saving money to invest it's far better to live in comfort.

Zhang Tianming ordinarily doesn't give much thought to investment and money management. Today his cousin chatted with him on the internet about this question for a long time, and only then did he start to think about it. He had just logged off when Lisa came in.

Lisa:	Tianming, you were chatting online again?
Zhang Tianming:	Yes, it was my cousin. He wanted to chat with me. My aunt and cousin started to clash with each other. My cousin seemed a little depressed.
Lisa:	Why [did they clash with each other]?
Zhang Tianming:	It's a long story. Before retiring, my aunt scraped and saved some money and planned to leave it for her future grandson or granddaughter's college education.
Lisa:	Your cousin isn't even married yet! Seems the money will have to stay in the bank for twenty years.
Zhang Tianming:	Exactly. That's what my cousin said. Then my aunt came up with an idea to spend the money.
Lisa:	What idea?
Zhang Tianming:	[You know how] my cousin is getting married next year, right? My aunt wanted to buy my cousin's fiancée a new car as a wedding gift.
Lisa:	That's really kind of your aunt.

Zhang Tianming:　But my cousin and his fiancée wouldn't agree to her buying a car. Their work-places were so close to each other that they could share a car. They urged my aunt to buy an apartment. They said that my aunt had worked hard for years. She should live in a bigger apartment and enjoy her retired life in comfort.

Lisa:　They were right! Besides, buying an apartment is not a bad investment.

Zhang Tianming:　But my aunt said that she didn't have enough money to buy an apartment. My cousin said that he could take out a loan for her. He also told my aunt a story about an elderly American lady and an elderly Chinese lady.

Lisa:　I've also heard the story before. It is about an old Chinese lady who saved for thirty years. It wasn't until she was very old that she bought an apartment and moved in. However, the old American lady took out a loan and bought a house and moved in thirty years earlier. If you compare them, which old lady knows how to live better?

Zhang Tianming:　That's right. My cousin used this story to persuade my aunt to finally buy an apartment.

Lisa:　That's great. Problem solved.

Zhang Tianming:　That wasn't the end of it. Listen to what happened next [lit. Listen to me tell the rest of it]. Two weeks ago they had zeroed in on an apartment with three bedrooms, a living room and two bathrooms. Originally, they were going to sign the purchase agreement the day after tomorrow. Who could have imagined it? My aunt suddenly changed her mind.

Lisa:　Did she have her eyes on another apartment?

Zhang Tianmng:　No. Since she retired, my aunt often gets together with her old friends from work to play mahjong and chat. A few days ago my aunt heard that some of them had made quite a bit of money flipping stocks. So she changed her mind, and doesn't want to buy the apartment anymore.

Lisa:　Are you saying she wants to invest in the stock market?

Zhang Tianming:　Exactly.

Lisa:　But doesn't your aunt know that flipping stocks is risky? An old gentleman who practices tai chi with Li Wen's parents mortgaged his house to the bank and used all of the money to buy stocks. But who would have imagined that the stock market would keep falling. Within three months he lost half [of the money].

Zhang Tianming:　Is buying an apartment risk-free?

Lisa:　Buying an apartment when housing prices are too high naturally is risky.

Zhang Tianming:　It seems that investment isn't a simple matter. I don't know in the end what my aunt will decide to do.

SELF-ASSESSMENT

How well can you do these things? Check (✔) the boxes to evaluate your progress and see which tasks you may need to practice more.

I can	Very Well	OK	A Little
Talk about my philosophy on spending and saving	☐	☐	☐
Mention some common ways of investing money	☐	☐	☐
Discuss if the stock market is risky or profitable	☐	☐	☐
Say how I would pay for a big-ticket item	☐	☐	☐
Describe how I balance my money	☐	☐	☐

第十八課　第十八课

中國歷史　中国历史

 LEARNING OBJECTIVES

In this lesson, you will learn to use Chinese to

1. Name some of the most important dynasties in Chinese history;
2. Describe briefly the historical significance of some major Chinese dynasties;
3. Talk in basic terms about some of China's important historical figures.

 RELATE AND GET READY

In your own culture/community—

- Is there a history museum?
- Are people familiar with the events that led to the founding of their country?
- Do people know any great inventions their country has given to the world?

Before You Study

Check the statements that apply to you.

☐ 1. I like to visit museums.

☐ 2. I am interested in Chinese history.

When You Study

Listen to the audio recording and scan the text. Ask yourself the following questions before you begin a close reading of the text.

☐ 1. Why does Lisa want Li Wen to give her a tour of the museum?

 麗莎這個學期除了中文課以外還選了一門中國歷史課。中國是
世界文明古國之一^①，有文字記載的歷史就有四千多年。為了對
中國歷史有更多的了解，她請李文帶她去中國國家博物館參觀。
張天明和柯林對中國歷史也有興趣，聽說麗莎要參觀博物館，也
要跟她們一起去。李文很高興地答應了。

3. I've heard of Confucius.
4. I can name a couple of Chinese dynasties.
5. I've heard of Sun Yat-sen.

2. Does Li Wen plan to take Lisa and her friends to every part of the museum?
3. What are the dynasties that the tour covers?

丽莎这个学期除了中文课以外还选了一门中国历史课。中国是世界文明古国之一①，有文字记载的历史就有四千多年。为了对中国历史有更多的了解，她请李文带她去中国国家博物馆参观。张天明和柯林对中国历史也有兴趣，听说丽莎要参观博物馆，也要跟她们一起去。李文很高兴地答应了。

中國國家博物館很大，中國歷史雖然只是其中^②的一部分，可是也不是幾個小時就能參觀完的。李文建議今天只看幾個朝代，以後再慢慢參觀。麗莎他們覺得這個建議很好。

李文：　你們都是學生，我先給你們介紹中國歷史上最重要的一位教育家。你們知道是誰嗎？

麗莎：　是孔子吧？

李文：　對。孔子是中國歷史上最偉大的教育家和思想家，到現在對中國教育還有很大的影響。

張天明：我們學校還有孔子學院呢。

李文：　是嗎？聽說世界各國已經建立了幾百個孔子學院了。

柯林：　我的一件T恤衫上有孔子的一句話：“有朋自遠方來，不亦樂乎❶。”

麗莎：　我在中文課上也學過這句話。

★　★　★

孔子的塑像

李文：　現在我們來到秦朝的展廳。秦始皇是中國的第一個皇帝。

麗莎：　我在歷史課上學到，秦始皇對統一中國有很大的貢獻。

李文：　對，他還統一了文字。

柯林：　還讓老百姓修長城。

李文：　秦始皇做的事都對嗎？

張天明：他殺了幾百個讀書人，燒了很多古書，是嗎？

麗莎：　他還讓千千萬萬的人給他修宮殿、修墳墓。

LANGUAGE NOTES

❶ This saying is from *The Analects*. It means, "Having friends from afar—isn't that also a great joy?"
[朋=朋友; 自=從/从; 亦=也; 樂/乐=快樂/快乐]

　　中国国家博物馆很大，中国历史虽然只是其中②的一部分，可是也不是几个小时就能参观完的。李文建议今天只看几个朝代，以后再慢慢参观。丽莎他们觉得这个建议很好。

李文：　你们都是学生，我先给你们介绍中国历史上最重要的一位教育家。你们知道是谁吗？

丽莎：　是孔子吧？

李文：　对。孔子是中国历史上最伟大的教育家和思想家，到现在对中国教育还有很大的影响。

张天明：我们学校还有孔子学院呢。

李文：　是吗？听说世界各国已经建立了几百个孔子学院了。

柯林：　我的一件T恤衫上有孔子的一句话："有朋自远方来，不亦乐乎❶。"

丽莎：　我在中文课上也学过这句话。

★　★　★

李文：　现在我们来到秦朝的展厅。秦始皇是中国的第一个皇帝。

丽莎：　我在历史课上学到，秦始皇对统一中国有很大的贡献。

李文：　对，他还统一了文字。

秦始皇的畫像/秦始皇的画像

柯林：　还让老百姓修长城。

李文：　秦始皇做的事都对吗？

张天明：他杀了几百个读书人，烧了很多古书，是吗？

丽莎：　他还让千千万万的人给他修宫殿、修坟墓。

李文：　你們說得都很對。你們看，這就是秦始皇的兵馬俑，他死了以後還讓千千萬萬的"兵馬"保護他。

兵馬俑/兵马俑

★　★　★

李文：　秦朝時間不長，下一個重要的朝代是漢朝。漢朝在秦朝的基礎上，使統一的中國在政治、經濟各個方面都有很大的發展。漢族❷這個稱呼就是從漢朝開始的。

麗莎：　"絲綢之路"❸也跟漢朝有關係吧?

李文：　對，跟西方進行貿易是從漢朝開始的。

絲綢之路/丝绸之路

★　★　★

張天明：你們看，我們來到唐朝了。我爸爸常跟我說中國唐詩最有名。

李文：　對，唐朝出現了很多大詩人。你學過誰的詩?

張天明：我學過李白的詩。

LANGUAGE NOTES

❷ 漢族/汉族 is 漢民族/汉民族, the Han ethnic group.

李文： 你们说得都很对。你们看，这就是秦始皇的兵马俑，他死了以后还让千千万万的"兵马"保护他。

★ ★ ★

李文： 秦朝时间不长，下一个重要的朝代是汉朝。汉朝在秦朝的基础上，使统一的中国在政治、经济各个方面都有很大的发展。汉族❷这个称呼就是从汉朝开始的。

丽莎： "丝绸之路"❸也跟汉朝有关系吧？

李文： 对，跟西方进行贸易是从汉朝开始的。

兵馬俑/兵马俑

李白的畫像/李白的画像

★ ★ ★

张天明： 你们看，我们来到唐朝了。我爸爸常跟我说中国唐诗最有名。

李文： 对，唐朝出现了很多大诗人。你学过谁的诗？

张天明： 我学过李白的诗。

❸ 絲綢之路/丝绸之路 is the Silk Road.

李文： 李白是唐朝最有名的詩人之一。還有，那時④由於唐朝經濟、文化非常發達，很多外國留學生來留學。

柯林： 跟我們一樣。

★　★　★

李文： 你們知道嗎，在歷史上，中國科學技術曾經是很先進的。

麗莎： 你是説四大發明嗎？

張天明： 我知道，是造紙、火藥、指南針、活字印刷。

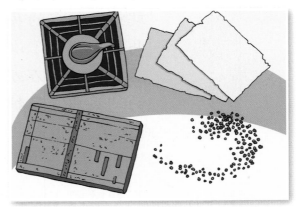

四大發明/四大发明

李文： 對，造紙、火藥發明得較早。活字印刷是宋朝發明的，指南針也在宋朝發展到了很高的水平。

★　★　★

李文： 我們現在來到中國最後一個朝代：清朝。

柯林： 為什麼是最後一個？

麗莎： 因為孫中山領導革命⑤，建立了中華民國，再也没有皇帝了。

張天明： 我們真不簡單，一兩個小時就走過了幾千年。

麗莎： 我好像聽到一個聲音。

李文： 什麼聲音？

麗莎： 歷史的腳步聲。

張天明： 我也聽到了一個聲音。

麗莎： 你要説肚子叫的…

張天明： 對了。

李文： 你們在説什麼呀？

After You Study

Challenge yourself to complete the following tasks in Chinese.

1. Say a few sentences about why Confucius is important.
2. List a few things that the First Emperor of the Qin Dynasty did.

LANGUAGE NOTES

④ 那時/那时 is short for 那個時候/那个时候 (at that time).

李文：　　李白是唐朝最有名的诗人之一。还有，那时❹由于唐朝经济、文化非常发达，很多外国留学生来留学。

柯林：　　跟我们一样。

★　★　★

李文：　　你们知道吗，在历史上，中国科学技术曾经是很先进的。

丽莎：　　你是说四大发明吗？

张天明：　我知道，是造纸、火药、指南针、活字印刷。

李文：　　对，造纸、火药发明得较早。活字印刷是宋朝发明的，指南针也在宋朝发展到了很高的水平。

★　★　★

李文：　　我们现在来到中国最后一个朝代：清朝。

柯林：　　为什么是最后一个？

丽莎：　　因为孙中山领导革命❺，建立了中华民国，再也没有皇帝了。

张天明：　我们真不简单，一两个小时就走过了几千年。

丽莎：　　我好像听到一个声音。

李文：　　什么声音？

丽莎：　　历史的脚步声。

张天明：　我也听到了一个声音。

丽莎：　　你要说肚子叫的…

张天明：　对了。

李文：　　你们在说什么呀？

孙中山的塑像/孙中山的塑像

3. Name the dynasty that is famous for its poetry.

4. Name the technologies that the Song Dynasty contributed.

5. Say a few sentences about why Sun Yat-sen is important.

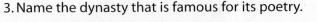

❺ It was the Revolution of 1911 or 辛亥革命 (Xīnhài Gémìng, the Xinhai Revolution).

VOCABULARY

1.	文明		wénmíng	n/adj	civilization; civilized
2.	文字		wénzì	n	characters; written form of a language
3.	記載	记载	jìzǎi	v/n	to put down in writing; to record; record; account
4.	參觀	参观	cānguān	v	to visit; to look around
5.	其中		qízhōng		among which/whom; in which/whom; of which/whom [See Grammar 2.]
6.	部分		bùfen	n	portion; part
7.	朝代		cháodài	n	dynasty
8.	偉大	伟大	wěidà	adj	great; outstanding; magnificent
9.	思想		sīxiǎng	n	thinking; ideology; thoughts
10.	學院	学院	xuéyuàn	n	college; academy; institute
11.	建立		jiànlì	v	to build; to establish
12.	展廳	展厅	zhǎntīng	n	exhibition hall; gallery
13.	皇帝		huángdì	n	emperor
14.	統一	统一	tǒngyī	v/adj	to unify; to unite; unified; centralized
15.	貢獻	贡献	gòngxiàn	v/n	to contribute; to devote; contribution
16.	修		xiū	v	to build; to repair; to mend; to fix
17.	殺	杀	shā	v	to kill
18.	燒	烧	shāo	v	to burn; to set fire to; to cook
19.	千千萬萬	千千万万	qiān qiān wàn wàn		thousands upon thousands
20.	宮殿	宫殿	gōngdiàn	n	palace

21.	墳墓	坟墓	fénmù	n	grave; tomb
22.	兵馬俑	兵马俑	bīngmǎyǒng	n	terracotta warriors and horses
23.	基礎	基础	jīchǔ	n	foundation; basis
24.	發展	发展	fāzhǎn	v	to develop
25.	稱呼	称呼	chēnghu	n/v	term of address; to address as
26.	絲綢	丝绸	sīchóu	n	silk; silk fabric
27.	關係	关系	guānxì	n	relation; relationship; connection
28.	進行	进行	jìnxíng	v	to carry on; to carry out; to conduct
29.	貿易	贸易	màoyì	n	trade
30.	詩	诗	shī	n	poetry; poem
31.	詩人	诗人	shīrén	n	poet
32.	發達	发达	fādá	adj/v	developed; flourishing; to develop
33.	技術	技术	jìshù	n	technology; technique
34.	曾經	曾经	céngjīng	adv	once; at some time in the past
35.	先進	先进	xiānjìn	adj	advanced
36.	發明	发明	fāmíng	n/v	invention; to invent
37.	造紙	造纸	zào zhǐ	vo	to make paper
38.	火藥	火药	huǒyào	n	gunpowder
39.	指南針	指南针	zhǐnánzhēn	n	compass
40.	活字印刷		huózì yìnshuā		moveable-type printing; letterpress printing
41.	領導	领导	lǐngdǎo	v/n	to lead; to exercise leadership; leadership; leader
42.	革命		gémìng	n	revolution

Proper Nouns

43.	孔子		Kǒngzǐ	Confucius
44.	秦朝		Qíncháo	Qin Dynasty
45.	秦始皇		Qínshǐhuáng	First Emperor of the Qin Dynasty
46.	漢朝	汉朝	Hàncháo	Han Dynasty
47.	西方		Xīfāng	the West
48.	唐朝		Tángcháo	Tang Dynasty
49.	李白		Lǐ Bái	Li Bai; Li Po (701–762 CE)
50.	宋朝		Sòngcháo	Song Dynasty
51.	清朝		Qīngcháo	Qing Dynasty
52.	孫中山	孙中山	Sūn Zhōngshān	Sun Yat-sen
53.	中華 民國	中华 民国	Zhōnghuá Mínguó	Republic of China

Enlarged Characters

載 觀 偉 獻 燒 墳 礎
载 观 伟 献 烧 坟 础

Culture Highlights

❶ Born in the place known today as Qufu 曲阜, Shandong 山東／山东 Province, Confucius (551–479 BCE) was a thinker, educator, and the founder of the Confucian school of philosophy of the late Spring and Autumn period (770–476 BCE). Although Confucius wanted to play an active role in politics, his bureaucratic career was thwarted because of his political views. He taught many disciples, and his thinking had a long-lasting impact on later generations.

In today's Qufu, Shandong, one can find the residence of the Kong clan 孔府, the Confucian Temple 孔廟／孔庙, and the cemetery of the Kong clan known as 孔林 (forest of the memorial steles of the Kong clan). All three monuments are on the UNESCO World Heritage roster.

❷ *The Analects* 論語／论语 (Lúnyǔ) is a classic in the Confucian canon. Compiled by several generations of students of Confucius, it is a collection of the master's words and deeds. Much of *The Analects* is in dialogue form and reflects Confucius' political, ethical, moral and pedagogical principles. The most widely circulated version of *The Analects* is divided into twenty chapters. While the language of *The Analects* is simple and concise, many of the views expressed in the work are still regarded as profound truths.

A statue of Confucius in Quzhou, Zhejiang Province.

牆上的圖，上面是孔廟，下面是孔林。
墙上的图，上面是孔庙，下面是孔林。

曲阜孔廟一景。
曲阜孔庙一景。

3 The ancient trade route extending from China to the eastern rim of the Mediterranean was named after silk, which along with porcelain was a major luxury export item throughout much of China's history. In 138 BCE, Emperor Wu of the Han Dynasty sent Zhang Qian and an entourage of about a hundred people westward on a diplomatic mission. En route, he was captured and detained for eleven years by the nomadic people known as Xiongnu. Zhang Qian managed to escape and return to the Han capital, Chang'an (長安/长安). He reported what he had seen in Central Asian countries and suggested that the Han empire should have friendly relationships with them.

In 119 BCE, Emperor Wu sent Zhang Qian on a second mission to Central Asia. Zhang Qian and his delegation visited many Central Asian countries, which later reciprocated with trade and diplomatic missions. Contact between the Han empire and Central Asia became increasingly frequent.

In 73 CE, the East Han envoy Ban Chao went to Central Asia and re-mained there for thirty years. He greatly strengthened the relations between Central Asia and the Han empire. Ban Chao sent a diplomat to the Persian Gulf, then part of the Roman empire. In 166, an envoy visited Luoyang, capital of the Eastern Han. Chinese historians view this visit as the first direct contact between Europe and China.

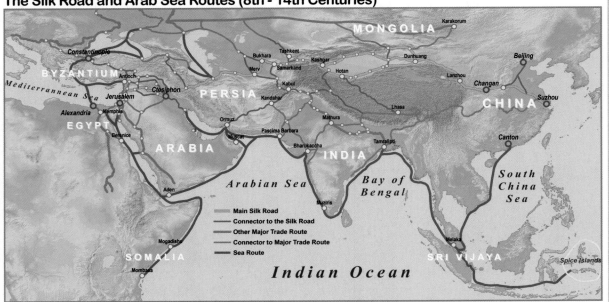

The Silk Road and Arab Sea Routes (8th - 14th Centuries)

Source: Data adapted from Rob Harris   Cartography: Jean-Paul Rodrigue, Dept. of Global Studies & Geography, Hofstra University

Silk and other goods traveled along the trade route from China to the Middle East and Europe, hence the name Silk Road. Later on, sea routes were also involved in Silk Road trading.

❹ Sun Yat-sen was born in Xiangshan 香山, Guangdong 廣東/广东 Province on November 12, 1866. His original name was Sun Wen, 孫文/孙文. Yat-sen 逸仙 (Yìxiān in Mandarin) is the Cantonese pronunciation of

his sobriquet or style name. While in exile in Japan, he adopted the alias 中山樵 (Zhōngshānqiáo). That's why he is most widely known as 孫中山/孙中山 (Sūn Zhōngshān) in China. He led the revolution of 1911, which overthrew the Qing empire. Because Sun Yat-sen founded the Republic of China and became the first interim president, he is revered as the father of the Chinese Republic. Sun Yat-sen died of cancer on March 12, 1925.

❺ The 1911 Revolution ended two thousand years of dynastic rule in Chinese history. 1911 was the year of Xinhai, 辛亥, according to the Chinese heavenly stem, 天干 (tiāngān), and earthly branch, 地支 (dìzhī) calendar system. That is the reason the revolution is known as 辛亥革命 in Chinese. Ten heavenly stems (甲 jiǎ, 乙 yǐ, 丙 bǐng, 丁 dīng, 戊 wù, 己 jǐ, 庚 gēng, 辛 xīn, 壬 rén, 癸 guǐ) and twelve earthly branches (子 zǐ, 丑 chǒu, 寅 yín, 卯 mǎo, 辰 chén, 巳 sì, 午 wǔ, 未 wèi, 申 shēn, 酉 yǒu, 戌 xū, 亥 hài) are combined to form a sixty-year calendar cycle.

❻ Paper, printing, gunpowder, and the compass are known as China's Four Great Inventions, 四大發明/四大发明.

❼ The First Emperor's awe-inspiring terracotta army consists of individual warriors and horses that were created and fired in parts and then joined afterward.

8 A Brief Chronology of Chinese Dynasties

Major dynasties are in red.

Xia Dynasty 夏 Xià		2100 – 1600 BCE	Jin Dynasty 晉 Jìn	Western Jin Dynasty 西晉 Xī Jìn	265 – 317 CE
Shang Dynasty 商 Shāng		1600 – 1046 BCE		Eastern Jin Dynasty 東晉 Dōng Jìn	317 – 420 CE
Zhou Dynasty 周 Zhōu	Western Zhou Dynasty 西周 Xī Zhōu	1046 – 771 BCE	Northern and Southern Dynasties 南北朝 Nánběi Cháo		420 – 589 CE
	Eastern Zhou Dynasty 東周／东周 Dōng Zhōu	770 – 256 BCE	Sui Dynasty 隋 Suí		581 – 618 CE
	Eastern Zhou Dynasty traditionally divided into		Tang Dynasty 唐 Táng		618 – 907 CE
	Spring and Autumn Period 春秋 Chūnqiū	770 – 476 BCE	Five Dynasties 五代 Wǔdài		907 – 960 CE
	Warring States 戰國／战国 Zhànguó	475 – 221 BCE	Song Dynasty 宋 Sòng	Northern Song Dynasty 北宋 Běi Sòng	960 – 1127 CE
Qin Dynasty 秦 Qín		221 – 206 BCE		Southern Song Dynasty 南宋 Nán Sòng	1127 – 1279 CE
Han Dynasty 漢／汉 Hàn	Western Han Dynasty 西漢／西汉 Xī Hàn	206 BCE – 25 CE	Jin Dynasty 金 Jīn		1115 – 1234 CE
	Eastern Han Dynasty 東漢／东汉 Dōng Hàn	25 – 220 CE	Yuan Dynasty 元 Yuán		1271 – 1368 CE
Three Kingdoms 三國／三国 Sānguó		220 – 280 CE	Ming Dynasty 明 Míng		1368 – 1644 CE
			Qing Dynasty 清 Qīng		1644 – 1911 CE

Grammar

1. 之一

之 is a structural particle inherited from Classical Chinese. It is used in a way similar to 的, which is more common in modern Chinese. 之一 means "one of."

❶ 中國是世界文明古國之一。

中国是世界文明古国之一。

(China is one of the world's ancient civilizations.)

❷ 我認為買賣股票是最有風險的投資方式之一。

我认为买卖股票是最有风险的投资方式之一。

(I think that buying stocks is one of the riskiest forms of investment.)

❸ 上海是中國最有活力的城市之一。

上海是中国最有活力的城市之一。

(Shanghai is one of the most dynamic cities in China.)

之一 must be preceded by a phrase denoting scope, such as 世界文明古國/世界文明古国 (world's ancient civilizations), 最有風險的投資方式/最有风险的投资方式 (riskiest forms of investment), 最有活力的城市 (most dynamic cities) in the examples.

2. 其中

其 is a pronoun meaning 那 or 那些. 其中 means "among them."

❶ 中國國家博物館很大，中國歷史雖然只是其中的一部分，可是也不是幾個小時就能參觀完的。

中国国家博物馆很大，中国历史虽然只是其中的一部分，可是也不是几个小时就能参观完的。

(The National Museum of China is very large. Although Chinese history takes up only a portion of the museum, it is still impossible to see all the exhibits within a few hours.)

❷ 我去過中國很多省旅遊，其中我對雲南和四川的印象最深。

我去过中国很多省旅游，其中我对云南和四川的印象最深。

(Of all the provinces I've been to in China as a tourist, Yunnan and Sichuan impress me the most.)

❸ 上個學期我選了三門課，其中金融課最難。

上个学期我选了三门课，其中金融课最难。

(Last semester I took three courses. Among them, Finance was the hardest.)

When using 其中, there must be an antecedent to 其 to make it clear to what 其 refers, such as 中國國家博物館／中国国家博物馆 (the National Museum of China), 很多省 (many provinces), and 三門課／三门课 (three courses) in the examples above.

這也是個博物館。

这也是个博物馆。

Words & Phrases

[handwritten: study tour] *[handwritten: scenic more fun, relaxing]*

> ## A. 參觀/参观 (to visit; to look around) vs. 遊覽/游览 (to go sightseeing; to tour; excursion)

遊/游 means "to roam about"; 覽/览 means "to view." 遊覽/游览 is to go on a sightseeing trip. The destination is usually a scenic spot or a historical site. 參觀/参观 is often a study tour, e.g., 參觀學校/参观学校 (to visit a school), 參觀博物館/参观博物馆 (to visit a museum), 參觀工廠/参观工厂 (to visit a factory), and so on.

❶ 昨天我們參觀了一個建築公司，他們給我們介紹他們正在蓋的大廈。

昨天我们参观了一个建筑公司，他们给我们介绍他们正在盖的大厦。

(Yesterday we visited a construction company, and they briefed us on the high-rise they were building.)

❷ 我想參觀附近那個科學研究單位，不知道讓不讓參觀。

我想参观附近那个科学研究单位，不知道让不让参观。

(I'd like to visit that scientific research institute nearby. I don't know if they allow [people to] visit.)

❸ 我去中國一定要遊覽長城。

我去中国一定要游览长城。

(If I go to China, I'll definitely tour the Great Wall.)

❹ 寒假我去中國西北高原遊覽，拍了很多照片。

寒假我去中国西北高原游览，拍了很多照片。

(During the winter break I toured China's northwest plateau region and took many photographs.)

服務台	語音導覽	多媒體放映室	洗手間	護理站
售票處	物品寄存處	兒童學藝中心	無障礙洗手間	咖啡廳

禁止吸煙

禁止飲食

禁止拍照錄影

關閉行動電話

禁止寵物入內

保持肅靜

參觀博物館時會看到這些
参观博物馆时会看到这些

B. 千千萬萬／千千万万 (thousands upon thousands)

千千萬萬／千千万万 is a set expression suggesting an enormous number.

❶ 他還讓千千萬萬人給他修宮殿、修墳墓。
他还让千千万万人给他修宮殿、修坟墓。
(He also made tens of thousands of people build palaces and a tomb for him.)

❷ 在海裏我看見千千萬萬條魚在游來游去。
在海里我看见千千万万条鱼在游来游去。
(In the sea I saw tens of thousands of fish swimming here and there.)

❸ 為了蓋房子，為了造紙，全世界每年要砍千千萬萬的樹。
为了盖房子，为了造纸，全世界每年要砍千千万万的树。
(For housing construction and papermaking, thousands upon thousands of trees are cut down around the world every year.)

在這裏，可以修什麼？
在这里，可以修什么？

C. 在…基礎上/在…基础上 (on the basis of...; based on ...)

In the middle of this expression can be a noun or a complex verb phrase:

❶ 我認為婚姻(hūnyīn)應該建立在愛情的基礎上。
我认为婚姻(hūnyīn)应该建立在爱情的基础上。
(I think that marriage should be built on the basis of love.)

❷ 在經濟不斷發展的基礎上，老百姓的生活水平提高了。
在经济不断发展的基础上，老百姓的生活水平提高了。
(On account of a constantly developing economy, ordinary people's lives are becoming better.)

❸ 這兩個人在互相了解的基礎上，逐漸成為了好朋友。
这两个人在互相了解的基础上，逐渐成为了好朋友。
(These two people gradually became good friends based on mutual understanding.)

D. 在⋯方面 (in terms of; in the area of)

❶ 在學習方面，他幫助我，在生活方面我幫助他。
在学习方面，他帮助我，在生活方面我帮助他。
(He helps me with my studies. I help him with matters of daily life.)

❷ 在找工作方面，他的經驗很多，你可以聽聽他的意見。
在找工作方面，他的经验很多，你可以听听他的意见。
(When it comes to looking for a job, he is much more experienced. You can listen to his opinions.)

❸ 他在各個方面的表現都很好。
他在各个方面的表现都很好。
(His performance in many different areas is outstanding.)

E. 跟⋯有關(係)/跟⋯有关(系) (related to; having to do with)

跟⋯有關(係)/跟⋯有关(系) can act as a predicate or an attributive:

❶ 節約能源跟每一個工廠都有關係，你不能不重視。[predicate]
节约能源跟每一个工厂都有关系，你不能不重视。
(Energy conservation applies to every factory. You cannot dismiss it.)

❷ 最近跟環保有關(係)的新聞特別多。[attributive]
最近跟环保有关(系)的新闻特别多。
(There has been much news related to environmental protection recently.)

When the construction is used as an attributive, 係/系 is often omitted, especially in written Chinese. However, when 沒有關係/没有关系 occurs at the end of a sentence as a predicate, 係/系 cannot be omitted.

❸ 比賽的事跟我沒有關係，我走了。[predicate]
比赛的事跟我没有关系，我走了。
(The game has nothing to do with me. I'm leaving.)

❹　對不起，跟投資理財有關的事情，我完全不懂。[attributive]

對不起，跟投资理财有关的事情，我完全不懂。

(Sorry, I know nothing about investment or financial management.)

F. 再也没/不 (no more; not anymore)

再也没/不 carries a strong feeling of negation.

❶　建立了中華民國，再也没有皇帝了。

建立了中华民国，再也没有皇帝了。

(After the founding of the Republic of China, there were no more emperors.)

❷　他跟我老是抱怨這，抱怨那，我再也不想見他了。

他跟我老是抱怨这，抱怨那，我再也不想见他了。

(He's always complaining to me about this or that. I don't want to see him ever again.)

❸　這個城市非常重視環保，現在買東西都得自己帶包，商店再也不給免費的塑料袋了。

这个城市非常重视环保，现在买东西都得自己带包，商店再也不给免费的塑料袋了。

(People attach a lot of importance to environmental protection in this city. Now you have to bring your own bags for shopping, and the stores no longer provide free plastic shopping bags.)

Language Practice

A. One of Them

Let's talk about China's significance in the world.

EXAMPLE   China   old civilizations

→   中國是世界文明古國之一。   中国是世界文明古国之一。

1. Beijing   biggest cities

2. Yangtze River   longest rivers

3. papermaking   most important inventions

4. the First Emperor of the Qin Dynasty   most famous emperors

B. Take Your Pick

Work with a partner, and discuss your favorite tourist spot, most famous political leader, most important historical figure, and most famous poet.

EXAMPLE   cities   most impressive

→   A: 你去過那麼多城市，   A: 你去过那么多城市，
        哪個城市給你的印象最深?   哪个城市给你的印象最深?
     B: 我去過很多城市，   B: 我去过很多的城市，
        其中紐約給我的印象最深。   其中纽约给我的印象最深。

1. tourist sites   favorite

2. political leaders   most famous

3. historical figures   most influential

4. poets   most famous

C. Getting the Facts Straight

a. Work with a partner to connect with a line the name of the dynasty and the historical fact that dynasty is often associated with.

絲綢之路/丝绸之路	秦朝
四大發明/四大发明	唐朝
文字統一/文字统一	清朝
外國人去中國留學/外国人去中国留学	宋朝
歷史上最後一個皇帝/历史上最后一个皇帝	漢朝/汉朝

b. Take turns with your partner to quiz each other about the facts that you have worked on above.

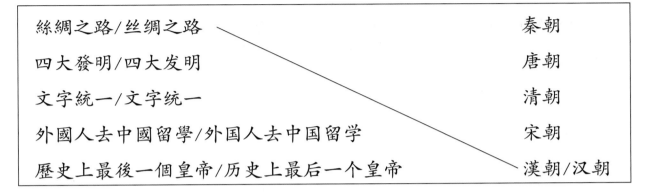

EXAMPLE: 絲綢之路   丝绸之路

➔　**A:** 絲綢之路跟哪個朝代有關係？　**A:** 丝绸之路跟哪个朝代有关系？

　B: 絲綢之路跟漢朝有關係。　**B:** 丝绸之路跟汉朝有关系。

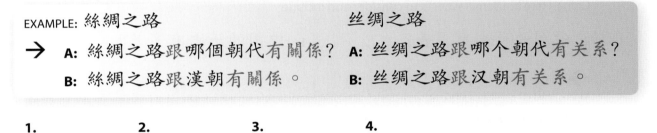

1.　　　　　**2.**　　　　　**3.**　　　　　**4.**

D. Never Again

People often claim that they won't repeat the same mistake. Based on the information given, take turns with a partner, and practice how to say that in Chinese.

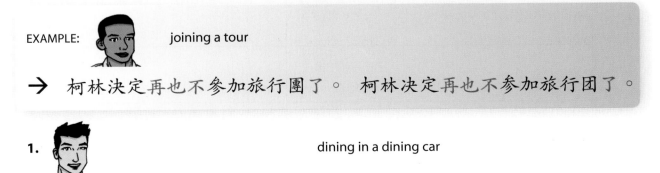

EXAMPLE:　　　　　joining a tour

➔　柯林決定再也不參加旅行團了。　柯林决定再也不参加旅行团了。

1.　　　　　　　　　dining in a dining car

2. staying up late

3. watching men's soccer

4. drinking bottled water

5. using disposable chopsticks

E. Chinese History 101

Work with a partner to prepare an outline for someone who is just starting to learn some basic facts about China. Here are some aspects to consider and include:

1. 中國的歷史有多長？

→

1. 中国的历史有多长？

2. 中國歷史上有那麼多朝代，
   哪些朝代比較重要，
   比較有影響？

→

2. 中国历史上有那么多朝代，
   哪些朝代比较重要，
   比较有影响？

3. 寫出那些朝代名，
   並説説它們為什麼重要。

3. 写出那些朝代名，
   并说说它们为什么重要。

朝代名	歷史重要性/历史重要性

F. Know Your Own Country

a. Work with a partner to name some of the great historical figures in your country. The names do not have to be in Chinese.

1. 教育家：　　　　＿＿＿＿＿＿＿＿＿＿＿＿＿＿＿＿＿

2. 畫家/画家：　　　＿＿＿＿＿＿＿＿＿＿＿＿＿＿＿＿＿

3. 哲學家/哲学家：　＿＿＿＿＿＿＿＿＿＿＿＿＿＿＿＿＿

b. Report to the class by saying:

我們認為(name of the person)是我國
歷史上最偉大的＿＿＿家之一。

我们认为(name of the person)是我国
历史上最伟大的＿＿＿家之一。

c. Work with your partner to name some of your country's inventions and their inventors. The inventors' names do not have to be in Chinese.

發明/发明　　　　　發明人/发明人

1.

2.

3.

…

d. Report to the class by saying

我們國家發明了＿＿＿＿＿＿，
是 (name of the inventor) 發明的。

我们国家发明了＿＿＿＿＿＿，
是 (name of the inventor) 发明的。

G. Be a Biographer

a. Ask a partner what should be included when writing a biography of a famous historical figure. Jot down the information here:

1. _____

2. _____

3. _____

4. _____

5. _____

6. _____

b. You are going to write a simple biography of Confucius or Sun Yat-sen. Here's a checklist to help you organize. The notes you have made above will also help you gather information. (BCE: 公元前) (to pass away: 去世)

1. 他是哪一年出生的？
2. 他是在哪一省出生的？
3. 他是哪一年去世的？
4. 他是中國歷史上偉大的 _____家。
5. 他對中國歷史/社會有什麼 貢獻/影響？

1. 他是哪一年出生的？
2. 他是在哪一省出生的？
3. 他是哪一年去世的？
4. 他是中国历史上伟大的 _____家。
5. 他对中国历史/社会有什么 贡献/影响？

c. Use the sentences above and the information brainstormed from your discussion with your partner to compose a short biography of Confucius or Sun Yat-sen.

Pinyin Text

Lìshā zhè ge xuéqī chúle Zhōngwén kè yǐwài hái xuǎn le yì mén Zhōngguó lìshǐ kè. Zhōngguó shì shìjiè wénmíng gǔguó zhī yī①, yǒu wénzì jìzǎi de lìshǐ jiù yǒu sì qiān duō nián. Wèile duì Zhōngguó lìshǐ yǒu gèng duō de liǎojiě, tā qǐng Lǐ Wén dài tā qù Zhōngguó Guójiā Bówùguǎn cānguān. Zhāng Tiānmíng hé Kē Lín duì Zhōngguó lìshǐ yě yǒu xìngqù, tīngshuō Lìshā yào cānguān bówùguǎn, yě yào gēn tāmen yìqǐ qù. Lǐ Wén hěn gāoxìng de dāying le.

Zhōngguó Guójiā Bówùguǎn hěn dà, Zhōngguó lìshǐ suīrán zhǐ shì qízhōng② de yí bùfen, kěshì yě bú shì jǐ ge xiǎoshí jiù néng cānguān wán de. Lǐ Wén jiànyì jīntiān zhǐ kàn jǐ ge cháodài, yǐhòu zài màn mān cānguān. Lìshā tāmen juéde zhè ge jiànyì hěn hǎo.

Lǐ Wén: Nǐmen dōu shì xuésheng, wǒ xiān gěi nǐmen jièshào Zhōngguó lìshǐ shang zuì zhòngyào de yí wèi jiàoyùjiā. Nǐmen zhīdao shì shéi ma?

Lìshā: Shì Kǒngzǐ ba?

Lǐwén: Duì. Kǒngzǐ shì Zhōngguó lìshǐ shang zuì wěidà de jiàoyùjiā hé sīxiǎngjiā, dào xiànzài duì Zhōngguó jiàoyù hái yǒu hěn dà de yǐngxiǎng.

Zhāng Tiānmíng: Wǒmen xuéxiào hái yǒu Kǒngzǐ Xuéyuàn ne.

Lǐ Wén: Shì ma? Tīngshuō shìjiè gè guó yǐjīng jiànlì le jǐ bǎi ge Kǒngzǐ Xuéyuàn le.

Kē Lín: Wǒ de yí jiàn tīxùshān shang yǒu Kǒngzǐ de yí jù huà: "Yǒu péng zì yuǎnfāng lái, bú yì lè hū❶."

Lìshā: Wǒ zài Zhōngwén kè shang yě xué guo zhè jù huà.

* * *

Lǐ Wén: Xiànzài wǒmen lái dào Qíncháo de zhǎntīng. Qínshǐhuáng shì Zhōngguó de dì yī ge huángdì.

Lìshā: Wǒ zài lìshǐ kè shang xué dào, Qínshǐhuáng duì tǒngyī Zhōngguó yǒu hěn dà de gòngxiàn.

Lǐ Wén: Duì, tā hái tǒngyī le wénzì.

Kē Lín: Hái ràng lǎobǎixìng xiū Chángchéng.

Lǐ Wén: Qínshǐhuáng zuò de shì dōu duì ma?

Zhāng Tiānmíng: Tā shā le jǐ bǎi ge dúshū rén, shāo le hěn duō gǔ shū, shì ma?

Lìshā: Tā hái ràng qiān qiān wàn wàn de rén gěi tā xiū gōngdiàn, xiū fénmù.

Lǐ Wén: Nǐmen shuō de dōu hěn duì. Nǐmen kàn, zhè jiù shì Qínshǐhuáng de bīngmǎyǒng, tā sǐ le yǐhòu hái ràng qiān qiān wàn wàn de "bīng mǎ" bǎohù tā.

    * * *

Lǐ Wén: Qíncháo shíjiān bù cháng, xià yí ge zhòngyào de cháodài shì Hàncháo. Hàncháo zài Qíncháo de jīchǔ shang, shǐ tǒngyī de Zhōngguó zài zhèngzhì, jīngjì gè ge fāngmiàn dōu yǒu hěn dà de fāzhǎn. Hànzú❷ zhè ge chēnghu jiù shì cóng Hàncháo kāishǐ de.

Lìshā: "Sīchóu zhī lù"❸ yě gēn Hàncháo yǒu guānxi ba?

Lǐ Wén: Duì, gēn Xīfāng jìnxíng màoyì shì cóng Hàncháo kāishǐ de.

    * * *

Zhāng Tiānmíng: Nǐmen kàn, wǒmen lái dào Tángcháo le. Wǒ bàba cháng gēn wǒ shuō Zhōngguó Táng shī zuì yǒumíng.

Lǐ Wén: Duì, Tángcháo chūxiàn le hěn duō dà shīrén. Nǐ xué guo shéi de shī?

Zhāng Tiānmíng: Wǒ xué guo Lǐ Bái de shī.

Lǐ Wén: Lǐ Bái shì Tángcháo zuì yǒumíng de shīrén zhī yī. Háiyǒu, nà shí❹ yóuyú Tángcháo jīngjì, wénhuà fēicháng fādá, hěn duō wàiguó liúxuéshēng lái liúxué.

Kē Lín: Gēn wǒmen yíyàng.

    * * *

Lǐ Wén: Nǐmen zhīdào ma, zài lìshǐ shang, Zhōngguó kēxué jìshù céngjīng shì hěn xiānjìn de.

Lìshā: Nǐ shì shuō sì dà fāmíng ma?

Zhāng Tiānmíng: Wǒ zhīdào, shì zào zhǐ, huǒyào, zhǐnánzhēn, huózì yìnshuā.

Lǐ Wén: Duì, zào zhǐ, huǒyào fāmíng de jiào zǎo. Huózì yìnshuā shì Sòngcháo fāmíng de, zhǐnánzhēn yě zài Sòngcháo fāzhǎn dào le hěn gāo de shuǐpíng.

    * * *

Lǐ Wén: Wǒmen xiànzài lái dào Zhōngguó zuìhòu yí ge cháodài—Qīngcháo.

Kē Lín: Wèishénme shì zuìhòu yí ge?

Lìshā: Yīnwèi Sūn Zhōngshān lǐngdǎo gémìng❺, jiànlì le Zhōnghuá Mínguó, zài yě méi yǒu huángdì le.

Zhāng Tiānmíng: Wǒmen zhēn bù jiǎndān, yì liǎng ge xiǎoshí jiù zǒu guo le jǐ qiān nián.

Lìshā: Wǒ hǎoxiàng tīng dào yí ge shēngyīn.

Lǐ Wén: Shénme shēngyīn?

Lìshā: Lìshǐ de jiǎobù shēng.

Zhāng Tiānmíng: Wǒ yě tīng dào le yí ge shēngyīn.

Lìshā: Nǐ yào shuō dùzi jiào de …

Zhāng Tiānmíng: Duì le.

Lǐwén: Nǐmen zài shuō shénme ya?

English Text

This semester, besides Chinese, Lisa is also taking an elective course in Chinese history. China is one of the world's ancient civilizations, with a recorded history of more than four thousand years. In order to know more about Chinese history, she asks Li Wen to take her to the National Museum of China for a visit. Zhang Tianming and Ke Lin are also interested in Chinese history. When they hear that Lisa is going to visit the museum, they want to go with them. Li Wen very happily agrees.

The National Museum of China is very big. Even though Chinese history is only one part of it, to see it all would take more than a few hours. Li Wen suggests that they concentrate on just a few dynasties today. They could visit the museum again later at a more leisurely pace. Lisa and her friends think that that is an excellent suggestion.

Li Wen: You are all students. I'll first tell you about the most important educator in Chinese history. Do you know who he is?

Lisa: Is it Confucius?

Li Wen: Correct. Confucius was the greatest educator and thinker in Chinese history. Even today he has a great impact on Chinese education.

Tianming: Our school has a Confucius Institute.

Li Wen: Is that right? I hear several hundred Confucius Institutes have been established all over the world.

Ke Lin: My T-shirt has a saying by Confucius on it: "Having friends from afar—isn't that a great joy?"

Lisa: I learned that saying in my Chinese class.

* * *

Li Wen:	We are now in the Qin Dynasty gallery. The First Emperor of the Qin Dynasty was the first emperor of China.
Lisa:	I learned in my history class that the First Emperor made a great contribution to the unification of China.
Li Wen:	Correct. He also unified the script.
Ke Lin:	And he made the people build the Great Wall.
Li Wen:	Was everything he did right?
Tianming:	He killed several hundred scholars and burned many classics. Is that right?
Lisa:	And he made tens of thousands of people build palaces and a tomb for him.
Li Wen:	You are all correct. Look, these are the First Emperor's terracotta warriors. Even in death, he made tens of thousands of warriors protect him.

* * *

Li Wen:	The Qin Dynasty didn't last long. The next important dynasty is the Han Dynasty. On the foundation of the Qin Dynasty, the Han enabled a united China to make great strides politically and economically. The term "Han" [for the Han ethnicity] originated with the Han Dynasty.
Lisa:	The Silk Road also has to do with the Han Dynasty, right?
Li Wen:	Right. Trade with the West started in the Han Dynasty.

* * *

Tianming:	Look, we've come to the Tang [gallery]. My dad often says that Chinese Tang poetry is very famous.
Li Wen:	Correct. Many great poets emerged during the Tang Dynasty. Whose poems have you studied?
Tianming:	I've studied Li Bai's poems.
Li Wen:	Li Bai is one of the most famous poets from the Tang Dynasty. Also, at that time, because of the Tang Dynasty's flourishing economy and culture, many international students came [to China] to study.
Ke Lin:	Just like us.

* * *

Li Wen:	Did you know [something]? Historically, China's science and technology was quite advanced.
Lisa:	Are you talking about the Four Great Inventions?

Tianming: I know. They are paper, gunpowder, the compass, and movable-type printing.

Li Wen: Yes, paper and gunpowder were invented early. Movable-type printing was invented during the Song Dynasty. The compass also reached a sophisticated level of development during the Song.

* * *

Li Wen: We've now come to China's last dynasty, the Qing Dynasty.

Ke Lin: Why was it the last dynasty?

Lisa: Because Sun Yat-sen led the Revolution of 1911. With the establishment of the Republic of China, there were no more emperors.

Tianming: We covered several thousand years of history in a couple of hours. That's no small feat.

Lisa: I seem to be hearing a sound.

Li Wen: What sound?

Lisa: The sound of history marching.

Tianming: I'm also hearing a sound.

Lisa: You mean the sound of your stomach…

Tianming: Correct.

Li Wen: What are you talking about?

SELF-ASSESSMENT

How well can you do these things? Check (✔) the boxes to evaluate your progress and see which areas you may need to practice more.

I can	Very Well	OK	A Little
Name some of the most important dynasties in Chinese history	☐	☐	☐
Say a few sentences about a major dynasty and its importance in Chinese history	☐	☐	☐
Give a brief introduction of a historic figure in China	☐	☐	☐

第十九课

面試

第十九课

面试

19

 LEARNING OBJECTIVES

In this lesson, you will learn to use Chinese to

1. Say one or two sentences to describe signs of nervousness;
2. Explain in basic terms why China has been able to attract talent and foreign companies;
3. Describe in basic terms your time management methods;
4. Congratulate someone on his or her accomplishments.

 RELATE AND GET READY

In your own culture/community—

- Are there many returnees from overseas with foreign college degrees?
- How extensive is the interviewing process for entry-level positions?
- What are some typical questions you'd expect to be asked during a job interview?

Before You Study

Check the statements that apply to you.

☐ 1. I have studied abroad.

☐ 2. I have interviewed for a job.

When You Study

Listen to the audio recording and scan the text. Ask yourself the following questions before you begin a close reading of the text.

1. What is the Chinese term for people like Xuemei who have returned to China to work after receiving their degrees overseas?

 21世紀初以來，中國的經濟有了很大的發展，不少跨國公司紛紛進入中國。這些大公司吸引了世界各地不少的人材，包括一些在西方國家學有所成的中國留學生。他們從海外歸來，因此被叫做“海歸”。有的人還開玩笑地把他們叫做“海龜”❶。今天中

LANGUAGE NOTES

❶ 海龜/海龟 or "sea turtle" is another facetious pun. It is pronounced exactly the same as 海歸/海归 (returnee from overseas, typically someone highly educated or qualified.)

☐ 3. I am willing to work for a company in a foreign country.
☐ 4. I think people should dress formally for interviews.
☐ 5. I think people should be candid about their weaknesses during job interviews.

2. Is the interviewer friendly toward Xuemei?
3. Is Xuemei confident about her performance during the interview?

 21世纪初以来，中国的经济有了很大的发展，不少跨国公司纷纷进入中国。这些大公司吸引了世界各地不少的人材，包括一些在西方国家学有所成的中国留学生。他们从海外归来，因此被叫做"海归"。有的人还开玩笑地把他们叫做"海龟"❶。今天中國經濟的高速發展，給了這些"海龜"們一片新的海洋。林雪梅現在就成了這片海洋中的一隻新"海龜"。

雪梅回到中國以後不久，就開始上網查資料、找工作。她去過幾家公司實習，但是都不太滿意。昨天有一家她非常喜歡的大公司叫她今天上午去面試。面試以後，剛回到家裏就接到麗莎的電話。

麗莎：	哎，"海龜"小姐，今天的面試怎麼樣？
雪梅：	哈，開始有些緊張，出了好多汗，套裝的上衣都快濕了。
麗莎：	啊，套裝？我還以為你會穿旗袍去面試呢。
雪梅：	我是去跨國公司面試，申請的是國際銷售部經理，不是去參加晚會❷。
麗莎：	哈哈，我是跟你開玩笑。不過你又①不是第一次面試，幹嗎那麼緊張？
雪梅：	給我面試的是他們公司的總經理，挺嚴肅的，第一句話就是："你是不是在美國找不到工作才回中國來的？"
麗莎：	這個總經理可真的挺嚇人的！難怪你緊張。
雪梅：	我越緊張就越②解釋不清楚。後來我突然想出了一個主意，什麼也不說了，從包裏拿出兩張紙，放到他前面。他一看，臉上馬上陰轉多雲了❸。
麗莎：	什麼紙？我也去買兩張準備著。
雪梅：	是加州的兩家公司五月寄給我的錄用通知。總經理看了接著問："既然③你在美國公司找到了工作，為什麼還要回中國工作呢？"
麗莎：	這個問題不難回答，你的男朋友在中國留學嘛！
雪梅：	我要是這樣說，他很可能會以為我在中國找工作，只是短期打算。好在這個時候我已經不緊張了。於是我就從中國經濟發展，談到他們公司的產品，再談產品的銷售，然後

LANGUAGE NOTES

❷ 晚會/晚会 refers to an evening party, rather than an evening meeting.

国经济的高速发展，给了这些"海龟"们一片新的海洋。林雪梅现在就成了这片海洋中的一只新"海龟"。

　　雪梅回到中国以后不久，就开始上网查资料、找工作。她去过几家公司实习，但是都不太满意。昨天有一家她非常喜欢的大公司叫她今天上午去面试。面试以后，刚回到家里就接到丽莎的电话。

丽莎：	哎，"海龟"小姐，今天的面试怎么样？
雪梅：	哈，开始有些紧张，出了好多汗，套装的上衣都快湿了。
丽莎：	啊，套装？我还以为你会穿旗袍去面试呢。
雪梅：	我是去跨国公司面试，申请的是国际销售部经理，不是去参加晚会❷。
丽莎：	哈哈，我是跟你开玩笑。不过你又①不是第一次面试，干吗那么紧张？
雪梅：	给我面试的是他们公司的总经理，挺严肃的，第一句话就是："你是不是在美国找不到工作才回中国来的？"
丽莎：	这个总经理可真的挺吓人的！难怪你紧张。
雪梅：	我越紧张就越②解释不清楚。后来我突然想出了一个主意，什么也不说了，从包里拿出两张纸，放到他前面。他一看，脸上马上阴转多云了❸。
丽莎：	什么纸？我也去买两张准备着。
雪梅：	是加州的两家公司五月寄给我的录用通知。总经理看了接着问："既然③你在美国公司找到了工作，为什么还要回中国工作呢？"
丽莎：	这个问题不难回答，你的男朋友在中国留学嘛！
雪梅：	我要是这样说，他很可能会以为我在中国找工作，只是短期打算。好在这个时候我已经不紧张了。于是我就从中国经济发展，谈到他们公司的产品，再谈产品的销售，然后

---

❸ 陰轉多雲/阴转多云 means "from overcast to partly cloudy." It is a phrase borrowed from weather forecasts often jokingly used to describe a slight improvement in someone's mood as reflected by a change in his or her facial expression.

解釋為什麼希望去他們公司工作。總經理聽著聽著，臉上終於多雲轉晴了[4]。

麗莎：　面試結束了？

雪梅：　還沒呢！這時候總經理突然笑著問："你覺得你自己最大的缺點是什麼？"

麗莎：　哈，我覺得，你最大的缺點就是愛吃零食。

雪梅：　那他不是要把我看成小女孩了？

麗莎：　那你是怎麼回答的？

雪梅：　我說，一個優秀的管理人材，應該能科學地安排自己的時間，善於工作的人往往也是善於休息的人，我在這方面還很不夠。實習的時候，我工作一有壓力就熬夜加班。所以，不太會休息可能是我最大的缺點。

麗莎：　雪梅，你到底是在說自己的缺點還是優點啊？

雪梅：　我接著又說：只要我們能把缺點變成優點，缺點就沒那麼可怕了。說到這兒，總經理站起來，一邊跟我握手，一邊笑著說，他相信我的能力，讓我等他們的好消息。

麗莎：　太棒了！恭喜你，林經理！

After You Study

Challenge yourself to complete the following tasks in Chinese.

1. Talk about Xuemei's attire for the interview.
2. List the three questions that the interviewer asked Xuemei.

LANGUAGE NOTES

[4] 多雲轉晴/多云转晴, another weather phrase meaning "from partly cloudy to sunny," is used to describe a brightening up of someone's facial expression.

解释为什么希望去他们公司工作。总经理听着听着，脸上终于多云转晴了 ❹。

丽莎：　面试结束了？

雪梅：　还没呢！这时候总经理突然笑着问："你觉得你自己最大的缺点是什么？"

丽莎：　哈，我觉得，你最大的缺点就是爱吃零食。

雪梅：　那他不是要把我看成小女孩了？

丽莎：　那你是怎么回答的？

雪梅：　我说，一个优秀的管理人材，应该能科学地安排自己的时间，善于工作的人往往也是善于休息的人，我在这方面还很不够。实习的时候，我工作一有压力就熬夜加班。所以，不太会休息可能是我最大的缺点。

丽莎：　雪梅，你到底是在说自己的缺点还是优点啊？

雪梅：　我接着又说：只要我们能把缺点变成优点，缺点就没那么可怕了。说到这儿，总经理站起来，一边跟我握手，一边笑着说，他相信我的能力，让我等他们的好消息。

丽莎：　太棒了！恭喜你，林经理！

3. Explain whether the interviewer was pleased with Xuemei's answers.
4. Retell what Xuemei thinks her weakness is.

VOCABULARY

1.	世紀	世纪	shìjì	n	century
2.	跨國	跨国	kuàguó	adj	transnational; multinational
3.	紛紛	纷纷	fēnfēn	adv	one after another; in succession
4.	進入	进入	jìnrù	v	to enter; to get into
5.	吸引		xīyǐn	v	to attract; to draw; to fascinate
6.	學有所成	学有所成	xué yǒu suǒ chéng		to have achieved academic success
7.	海外		hǎiwài	n	overseas; abroad
8.	歸來	归来	guīlái	v	to return; to come back
9.	因此		yīncǐ	conj	so; therefore; for this reason; consequently
10.	叫做		jiào zuò	vc	to be called; to be known as
11.	海龜	海龟	hǎiguī	n	sea turtle
12.	海洋		hǎiyáng	n	seas and oceans; the ocean
13.	滿意	满意	mǎnyì	v	to be satisfied; to be pleased
14.	套裝	套装	tàozhuāng	n	suit; a set of matching outer garments
15.	上衣		shàngyī	n	upper outer garment; jacket
16.	濕	湿	shī	adj	wet
17.	旗袍		qípáo	n	chi-pao; mandarin gown
18.	銷售	销售	xiāoshòu	v	to sell; to market
19.	經理	经理	jīnglǐ	n	manager
20.	幹嗎	干吗	gànmá	qpr	why; why on earth; whatever for
21.	總	总	zǒng	adj	general; chief
22.	嚴肅	严肃	yánsù	adj	stern; serious

23.	嚇人	吓人	xiàrén	adj	scary; frightening
24.	解釋	解释	jiěshì	v	to explain
25.	陰	阴	yīn	adj	overcast; hidden from the sun
26.	轉	转	zhuǎn	v	to turn; to shift; to change
27.	雲	云	yún	n	cloud
28.	寄		jì	v	to mail
29.	錄用	录用	lùyòng	v	to take someone on staff; to employ
30.	通知		tōngzhī	n/v	notice; to notify; to inform
31.	既然		jìrán	conj	since; as; now that [See Grammar 3.]
32.	回答		huídá	v	to reply; to answer
33.	短期		duǎnqī	n	short term
34.	好在		hǎozài	adv	fortunately; luckily
35.	產品	产品	chǎnpǐn	n	product; merchandise
36.	晴		qíng	adj	sunny
37.	缺點	缺点	quēdiǎn	n	shortcoming; defect; weakness
38.	零食		língshí	n	snacks; nibbles
39.	優秀	优秀	yōuxiù	adj	outstanding; excellent
40.	善於	善于	shànyú		be good at; be adept in
41.	往往		wǎngwǎng	adv	more often than not
42.	加班		jiā bān	vo	to work overtime; to work extra shifts
43.	優點	优点	yōudiǎn	n	merit; strong point; advantage
44.	可怕		kěpà	adj	awful; terrible; fearful
45.	握手		wò shǒu	vo	to shake hands; to clasp hands
46.	能力		nénglì	n	ability; capacity; competence

Enlarged Characters

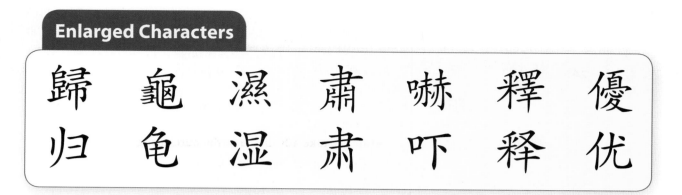

歸	龜	濕	肅	嚇	釋	優
归	龟	湿	肃	吓	释	优

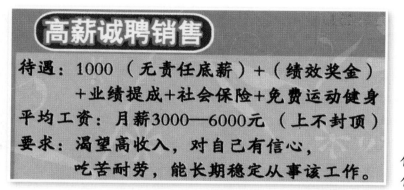

高薪诚聘销售

待遇：1000（无责任底薪）+（绩效奖金）
　　　+业绩提成+社会保险+免费运动健身
平均工资：月薪3000—6000元（上不封顶）
要求：渴望高收入，对自己有信心，
　　　吃苦耐劳，能长期稳定从事该工作。

你對這份銷售工作有興趣嗎？
你对这份销售工作有兴趣吗？

Culture Highlights

❶ Many of the world's largest and best-known multinational companies have set up shop in China in recent years hoping to take advantage of the purchasing power of the country's burgeoning middle class. Starbucks and most of the fast-food franchises have become familiar sights to Chinese urbanites. Retailers such as Carrefour, Walmart, and Ikea have also found success in China. This is a significant change from the beginning of the century, when China was known mainly as "the world's factory" while its tantalizing market potential remained elusive. Meanwhile, China continues to be a manufacturing powerhouse. Many Fortune 500 companies such as GM, Ford, Volkswagen, Motorola, Nokia, Siemens, Exxon Mobil, Sony, and Toyota, to name a few, have joint ventures or solely owned subsidiaries in China.

❷ 旗 means "banner." The Manchus, who founded China's last dynasty, were colloquially known as 旗人 (bannermen) because they were divided into eight banners or administrative divisions symbolized by different colored banners. 袍 is a loose, usually unwaisted, gown. 旗袍, however, refers to the type of modified Manchu women's dress (with a Mandarin collar) that became popular in the early part of the twentieth century. In fact, it almost became the national dress for many Chinese women. Some women still like to wear it on very formal or ceremonial occasions. Some restaurants have their hostesses dressed in 旗袍 to welcome guests. See also Culture Highlights 3 in Level 1 Part 1, Lesson 9.

她在餐館工作。
她在餐馆工作。

❸ According to Chinese government sources, from 1978 to 2004 more than 700,000 Chinese students studied abroad. About 170,000 of them have returned to China. With the help of seed money from the government, many of the returnees from overseas 海歸/海归 have opened businesses in China and become successful entrepreneurs. Most of the university presidents, doctoral advisors, and high-ranking scientists in China have studied abroad.

Grammar

1. Adverb 又

又 can be used in a negative sentence or a rhetorical question to add emphasis.

❶　你又不是第一次面試，幹嗎那麼緊張？

　　你又不是第一次面试，干吗那么紧张？

(That was not your first interview. How come you were that nervous?)

❷　**A:**　你怎麼現在來找他幫忙？他忙得連吃飯的時間都沒有。

　　　　你怎么现在来找他帮忙？他忙得连吃饭的时间都没有。

(How come you are looking for him to help you now? He is so busy that he doesn't even have time to eat.)

　　B:　又沒有人告訴我他忙，我怎麼知道？

　　　　又没有人告诉我他忙，我怎么知道？

([But] nobody told me that he was busy. How would I have known?)

❸　**A:**　麻煩你在購屋貸款合同上簽個字。

　　　　麻烦你在购屋贷款合同上签个字。

(May I ask you to sign the contract for the purchase of the house, please?]

　　B:　這套房子我又沒決定買，幹嗎簽字？

　　　　这套房子我又没决定买，干吗签字？

(I haven't even made up my mind to buy this house. Why should I sign?)

2. 越···, 越···

"越 A, 越 B" means that B changes in accordance with A, or "the more A, the more B."

❶　我越緊張就越解釋不清楚。

　　我越紧张就越解释不清楚。

(The more nervous I got, the more incoherent I was with my explanation.)

❷　他很着急，車越開越快。

　　他很着急，车越开越快。

(He was in a big rush. He [His car] began to drive faster and faster.)

❸　明天你儘可能早點來，越早越好。

　　明天你尽可能早点来，越早越好。

(Tomorrow, come as early as you can. The earlier, the better.)

這個旅行社廣告吸引你嗎？

这个旅行社广告吸引你吗？

3. Conjunction 既然

既然 is used in the first clause of a compound sentence. It restates a known scenario, reason, or premise. The main clause presents the logical conclusion deriving from the condition outlined in the first clause.

❶　既然你在美國公司找到了工作，為什麼還要回中國工作呢？

　　既然你在美国公司找到了工作，为什么还要回中国工作呢？

(Since you got a job with an American company, why did you still want to come back to work in China?)

[The speaker knows that the other person found a job at an American company.]

❷　**A:**　老師，本來今天下午我應該去你的辦公室談我這個學期的表現，可是我病了。

　　　　老师，本来今天下午我应该去你的办公室谈我这个学期的表现，可是我病了。

(Teacher, originally I was supposed to go to your office to discuss my performance this semester, but I got sick.)

　　B:　既然你病了，就換個時間吧。

　　　　既然你病了，就换个时间吧。

(Since you are sick, let's find another time.)

❸ **A:** 昨天我們看的那套公寓，聽說已經賣了。

昨天我们看的那套公寓，听说已经卖了。

(I heard that the apartment we saw yesterday has already been sold.)

B: 既然那套賣了，那麼我們再看看別的房子吧。

既然那套卖了，那么我们再看看别的房子吧。

(Since that apartment was sold, then let's look at some other ones.)

Note that although 既然 also indicates a reason, it must have already been known or stated. It cannot be replaced by 因為/因为.

Words & Phrases

A. 叫做 (to be called; to be known as)

叫做 is a "verb + complement" construction. It occurs mainly in formal speech.

❶ 他們從海外歸來，因此被叫做"海歸"。

他们从海外归来，因此被叫做"海归"。

(They are returnees from overseas. That's why they are called "repatriates.")

❷ 我們把一年級的學生叫做"新生"。

我们把一年级的学生叫做"新生"。

(We call first-year students "freshmen.")

❸ Peanut 在中國南方有的地方叫做"土豆"，北方叫做"花生"。

Peanut 在中国南方有的地方叫做"土豆"，北方叫做"花生"。

(In China, peanuts are called 土豆 in some places in the south and 花生 in the north.)

B. 好在 (fortunately; luckily)

好在 points out something in someone's favor in an otherwise unfavorable situation.

❶   好在這個時候我已經不緊張了。
好在这个时候我已经不紧张了。
(Luckily, by that time I was no longer nervous.)

❷   **A:**   哎呀，我的錄取通知拉在房間了。
哎呀，我的录取通知拉在房间了。
(Shoot, I left my acceptance letter in the room.)

   B: 快回去取吧，好在我們走得不遠。
快回去取吧，好在我们走得不远。
(Go back and get it. Fortunately, we haven't gone very far.)

❸   今天老師突然説要考漢字，好在我這幾天練習寫漢字了，要不然一定考得很糟糕。
今天老师突然说要考汉字，好在我这几天练习写汉字了，要不然一定考得很糟糕。
(Today the teacher suddenly announced that there was going to be a test on Chinese characters. Luckily, I had been practicing writing characters. Otherwise I would have definitely flunked the test.)

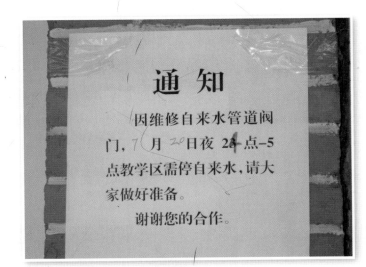

這不是錄用通知，這是停水通知。
这不是录用通知，这是停水通知。

C. 善於/善于 (be good at; be adept in)

善於/善于 means "to excel in something."

❶ 善於工作的人往往也是善於休息的人。
善于工作的人往往也是善于休息的人。
(People who know how to work often also know how to rest.)

❷ 這個人在大家面前很善於表現自己的優點。
这个人在大家面前很善于表现自己的优点。
(This person is good at showing off his strong points to everyone.)

❸ 很多退休的老人不善於理財投資。
很多退休的老人不善于理财投资。
(Many retired people are not good at financial planning and investing.)

D. 往往 (more often than not) vs. 常常 (often)

往往 is an adverb indicating that a certain action is likely to occur under certain circumstances.

❶ 週末我往往跟家人在一起，很少去公司加班。
周末我往往跟家人在一起，很少去公司加班。
(On weekends, more often than not I am with my family. I rarely put in extra time at the company.)

❷ 在跨國貿易公司工作的人，往往必須跟不同國家的人打交道。
在跨国贸易公司工作的人，往往必须跟不同国家的人打交道。
(Those who work at a multinational company often have to deal with people from different countries.)

❸ 這個健身房中午往往一個客人也沒有，我想不是太貴，就是管理得不好。
这个健身房中午往往一个客人也没有，我想不是太贵，就是管理得不好。
(This gym is often completely empty at midday. I think it's either because it is too expensive or because it is ill-managed.)

往往 is used in reference to hitherto predictable circumstances, whereas 常常 simply refers to repeated actions which do not follow any predictable pattern. 常常 can refer to future events. 往往 cannot.

❹ 請你以後常常來我們工廠參觀。

请你以后常常来我们工厂参观。

(Please come to visit our factory often.)

*請你以後往往來我們工廠參觀。

*请你以后往往来我们工厂参观。

When the sentence is about a habitual action or behavior that is not bound to a specific time, only 常常 can be used.

❺ 爺爺奶奶很重視鍛煉身體，常常去公園打太極拳。

爷爷奶奶很重视锻炼身体，常常去公园打太极拳。

(Grandpa and Grandma take exercising seriously. They often go to the park to do tai chi.)

Language Practice

A. Who Do You Think I Am?

Suppose someone asks you a question, but you are not in a position to answer that question (#1–#5) or to complete the requested action (#6–#8). Be sure to use 又 in your reply, and make clear that the response is rather strong by using 幹嗎/干吗.

EXAMPLE:　**A:** 我們星期幾有中文考試？　　**A:** 我们星期几有中文考试？

→　　　**B:** 你問我幹嗎？我又不是中文老師。　　**B:** 你问我干吗？我又不是中文老师。

1. A: 肚子疼吃這種藥有用嗎？　　**A:** 肚子疼吃这种药有用吗？

→

2. A: 你覺得那家跨國公司
會不會錄用小李？

→

A: 你觉得那家跨国公司
会不会录用小李？

3. A: 那家服裝店什麼時候打折？

→

A: 那家服装店什么时候打折？

4. A: 做糖醋魚放這麼多鹽夠不夠？

→

A: 做糖醋鱼放这么多盐够不够？

5. A: 現在炒股，會賺錢還是賠錢？

→

A: 现在炒股，会赚钱还是赔钱？

B. More and More

Use the pattern "越 A, 越 B" to express the idea "the more A, the more B."

EXAMPLE: 李文忙   李文睡不好覺   李文忙   李文睡不好觉
→   李文越忙越睡不好覺。   李文越忙越睡不好觉。

1. 麗莎學太極拳
麗莎喜歡太極拳

→

1. 丽莎学太极拳
丽莎喜欢太极拳

2. 總經理聽雪梅説話
總經理覺得雪梅是個人材

→

2. 总经理听雪梅说话
总经理觉得雪梅是个人材

3. 柯林開車開得快
雪梅緊張

→

3. 柯林开车开得快
雪梅紧张

4. 王爺爺不鍛煉身体
   王爺爺容易生病

   →

4. 王爷爷不锻炼身体
   王爷爷容易生病

5. 丈夫不體貼妻子
   妻子生氣

   →

5. 丈夫不体贴妻子
   妻子生气

C. If That's the Case...

Suppose your friend is always busy, messy, late, and forgetful. But you remain his friend by being accommodating and willing to reschedule your dates.

EXAMPLE: Occasion: playing mahjong   Excuse: working extra shift
            Suggestion: finding another person

→ A: 對不起，我今天晚上   A: 对不起，我今天晚上
      得加班，不能跟你打麻將了。   得加班，不能跟你打麻將了。
   B: 既然你得加班，我就找   B: 既然你得加班，我就找
      別人吧。   別人吧。

1. Occasion: hosting a birthday party   Excuse: room being a mess
   Suggestion: coming to your house

2. Occasion: traveling to Harbin to see the ice lanterns   Excuse: having a cold
   Suggestion: going next year

3. Occasion: going hiking in the mountains   Excuse: feet hurt
   Suggestion: taking him to see the doctor

4. Occasion: going to see a ball game   Excuse: forgot the tickets at home
   Suggestion: going to his place to get the tickets together

D. Thank Goodness!

Suppose you were in a potentially disadvantageous or even disastrous situation. What would be the best thing that could happen? Based on the clues given, state how lucky you were.

EXAMPLE: teacher gave a pop quiz today   I reviewed last night.

→ 老師今天突然給我們考試，
好在我昨天晚上復習了。

老师今天突然给我们考试，
好在我昨天晚上复习了。

1. The stock market dropped 100 points today.   I no longer flip stocks.

2. The air conditioner broke last night.   It's only 27 degrees Celsius today.

3. The cost of electricity is skyrocketing.   My house is powered by solar power.

4. The energy crisis is getting more and   Wind power is inexhaustible.
more serious.

5. There were too many dynasties and emperors   I'm not a Chinese history major.
in Chinese history.

E. If I Were the Boss...

When hiring, the boss needs to know who has the expertise to be good at the job. If you were forming a new company, whom would you hire?

EXAMPLE: marketing department

→ 我們必須錄用善於
銷售的人材。

我们必须录用善于
销售的人材。

1. management level

2. research department

3. conservation department

4. financial planning department

這可能是雪梅的辦公室。
这可能是雪梅的办公室。

F. Nerve-Racking Interview

For first-time job seekers, interviewing can be a nerve-racking experience. Take turns with a partner and practice describing how nervous a first-time interviewee could be.

EXAMPLE: receiving the interview notice on the phone   was startled

→ 接到面試電話通知時，
   我緊張得嚇了一跳。

   接到面试电话通知时，
   我紧张得吓了一跳。

1. leaving for your interview   left the car key at home

2. meeting the company's manager   forgot to shake her hand

3. answering the first question   couldn't speak

4. answering the second question   couldn't explain clearly

5. sitting in the manager's office   was sweating a lot

6. before the interview ended   forgot to ask when you would hear from the company

7. saying goodbye to the manager   forgot to shake her hand again

G. How Well Do You Know Them?

After following the adventures of Zhang Tianming and his friends for more than six months, do you know them well?

a. Discuss with a partner and list the strengths and weaknesses of Zhang Tianming and each of his friends.

	優點/优点	缺點/缺点
Another character of your choice		

b. Based on the list, present your comments to the class. You can start by saying…

我們認為 (name of the character) 的
優點是…缺點是…

我们认为 (name of the character) 的
优点是…缺点是…

c. How are your strengths and weaknesses similar to or different from those of any of the characters? Please share them with your class.

我跟 (name of the character) (不)一樣，
我的優點是…缺點是…

我跟 (name of the character) (不)一样，
我的优点是…缺点是…

H. I'm So Happy for You

In addition to 太好了, 太棒了, 我真為你高興/我真为你高兴, 恭喜 is another good word to show people how happy you are for their good news or accomplishments.

Take turns and practice the following with your partner:

EXAMPLE:　passed the college entrance exam

→　　太棒了，恭喜你考上大學。　　太棒了，恭喜你考上大学。

1. passed the graduate school entrance exam

2. bought a new house

3. won the competition

4. won first prize

5. aced the interview and got the job

I. To Go or Not to Go to China?

What attracts people and companies to go to China and what doesn't?

a. Connect the noun with its predicate to form possible reasons why people would or would not like to go to China.

中國吸引人的地方⋯   中国吸引人的地方⋯

衣食住行	美
經濟發展/经济发展	越來越先進/越来越先进
消費人口/消费人口	便宜
科學技術/科学技术	好
教育基礎/教育基础	多
旅遊景點的風景/旅游景点的风景	快
Add your own:	
_____	

中國不吸引人的地方⋯   中国不吸引人的地方⋯

空氣污染/空气污染	吵
交通	大
環境/环境	嚴重/严重
投資風險/投资风险	擠/挤
Add your own:	
_____	

b. Discuss with a partner if you would go to China based on the desirable and undesirable aspects listed above.

c. Discuss with your partner if a transnational company should open a branch office in China.

Pinyin Text

21 shìjì chū yǐlái, Zhōngguó de jīngjì yǒu le hěn dà de fāzhǎn, bù shǎo kuàguó gōngsī fēnfēn jìn rù Zhōngguó. Zhè xiē dà gōngsī xīyǐn le shìjiè gè dì bù shǎo de réncái, bāokuò yì xiē zài Xīfāng guójiā xué yǒu suǒ chéng de Zhōngguó liúxuéshēng. Tāmen cóng hǎiwài guīlái, yīncǐ bèi jiào zuò "hǎiguī". Yǒude rén hái kāi wánxiào de bǎ tāmen jiào zuò "hǎiguī"❶. Jīntiān Zhōngguó jīngjì de gāosù fāzhǎn, gěi le zhè xiē "hǎiguī" men yí piàn xīn de hǎiyáng. Lín Xuěméi xiànzài jiù chéng le zhè piàn hǎiyáng zhōng de yì zhī xīn "hǎiguī".

   Xuěméi huí dào Zhōngguó yǐhòu bù jiǔ, jiù kāishǐ shàng wǎng chá zīliào, zhǎo gōngzuò. Tā qù guo jǐ jiā gōngsī shíxí, dànshì dōu bú tài mǎnyì. Zuótiān yǒu yì jiā tā fēicháng xǐhuan de dà gōngsī jiào tā jīntiān shàngwǔ qù miànshì. Miànshì yǐhòu, gāng huí dào jiā li jiù jiē dào Lìshā de diànhuà.

                 *   *   *

Lìshā: Āi, "hǎiguī" xiǎojie, jīntiān de miànshì zěnmeyàng?

Xuěméi: Hā, kāishǐ yǒu xiē jǐnzhāng, chū le hǎo duō hàn, tàozhuāng de shàngyī dōu kuài shī le.

Lìshā: Á, tàozhuāng? Wǒ hái yǐwéi nǐ huì chuān qípáo qù miànshì ne.

Xuěméi: Wǒ shì qù kuàguó gōngsī miànshì, shēnqǐng de shì guójì xiāoshòu bù jīnglǐ, bú shì qù cānjiā wǎnhuì.

Lìshā: Hā hā, wǒ shì gēn nǐ kāi wánxiào. Búguò nǐ yòu① bú shì dì yī cì miànshì, gànmá nàme jǐnzhāng?

Xuěméi: Gěi wǒ miànshì de shì tāmen gōngsī de zǒng jīnglǐ, tǐng yánsù de, dì yī jù huà jiù shì: "Nǐ shì bú shì zài Měiguó zhǎo bú dào gōngzuò cái huí Zhōngguó lái de?"

Lìshā: Zhè ge zǒng jīnglǐ kě zhēn de tǐng xiàrén de! Nánguài nǐ jǐnzhāng.

Xuěméi: Wǒ yuè jǐnzhāng jiù yuè② jiěshì bù qīngchu. Hòulái wǒ tūrán xiǎng chū le yí ge zhúyi, shénme yě bù shuō le, cóng bāo li ná chu liǎng zhāng zhǐ, fàng dào tā qiánmian. Tā yí kàn, liǎn shang mǎshàng yīn zhuǎn duō yún le❷.

Lìshā: Shénme zhǐ? Wǒ yě qù mǎi liǎng zhāng zhǔnbèi zhe.

Xuěméi: Shì Jiāzhōu de liǎng jiā gōngsī wǔyuè jì gěi wǒ de lùyòng tōngzhī. Zǒng jīnglǐ kàn le jiēzhe wèn: "Jìrán③ nǐ zài Měiguó gōngsī zhǎo dào le gōngzuò, wèishénme hái yào huí Zhōngguó gōngzuò ne?"

Lìshā: Zhè ge wèntí bù nán huídá, nǐ de nán péngyou zài Zhōngguó liú xué ma!

第二十課
外國人
在中國

第二十课
外国人
在中国

20

◆ LEARNING OBJECTIVES

In this lesson, you will learn to use Chinese to

1. Welcome a visitor from afar at a welcoming party;
2. Bid someone farewell at a farewell party;
3. Pay homage to old-timers when joining a new community;
4. Describe the ease or difficulty of adjusting to life in a different country.

◆ RELATE AND GET READY

In your own culture/community—

• How do people welcome visitors from afar?
• How do people send off friends who are leaving?
• Is it culturally appropriate for people to ask about each other's professions when they meet for the first time?

Before You Study

Check the statements that apply to you.

- [ ] 1. I have hosted a welcoming party.
- [ ] 2. I have hosted a farewell party.

When You Study

Listen to the audio recording and scan the text. Ask yourself the following questions before you begin a close reading of the text.

1. Why are Xuemei and Ke Lin throwing a party?
2. Why is Li Zhe in Beijing?

 雪梅面試後，那家公司通知她下週開始上班。雪梅和柯林都很高興，他們決定請朋友們到雪梅住的地方來聚會，慶祝一下。

張天明的好朋友李哲也來到中國了，他接受了天明的建議，到一家跨國公司來實習。結果，慶祝晚會也成了為李哲接風的晚會。

張天明和麗莎學期結束後很快就要回美國了。所以這次聚會也成了給他們餞行的晚會。

來的客人除了天明、麗莎、李哲外，還有李文和馬克。

3. I have lived or worked in a foreign country.
4. I have asked for advice from experienced people when starting a new job.

3. Why is Xuemei so happy that Li Zhe is in Beijing?

4. Is Mark content with his life in China?

5. What's the general sentiment shared by Li Zhe's friends about whether it's possible to adjust to life in another culture?

 雪梅面试后，那家公司通知她下周开始上班。雪梅和柯林都很高兴，他们决定请朋友们到雪梅住的地方来聚会，庆祝一下。

张天明的好朋友李哲也来到中国了，他接受了天明的建议，到一家跨国公司来实习。结果，庆祝晚会也成了为李哲接风的晚会。

张天明和丽莎学期结束后很快就要回美国了。所以这次聚会也成了给他们饯行的晚会。

来的客人除了天明、丽莎、李哲外，还有李文和马克。

柯林去超市買了很多飲料、零食和水果^①。雪梅準備了一個火鍋，還從附近的一家餐館叫了外賣❶。

★ ★ ★

柯林： 今天我們大家聚在一起，是為了給李哲接風，給天明和麗莎餞行，也慶祝雪梅找到工作。

雪梅： 對，大家不要客氣，好好吃，好好玩。

馬克： 雪梅，恭喜你找到了好工作。什麼時候上班？

雪梅： 下個星期一，星期五就要到歐洲出差，推銷太陽能熱水器。

馬克： 太陽能熱水器？太好了！最近跟環保和節能有關係的綠色產品市場上都賣得很火❷。

張天明： 哎，馬克，李文，你們過來，我來介紹一下，這是我們在美國的校友，李哲，剛從美國來。

李文、馬克： 歡迎來北京。

李哲： 大家好！請多關照❸。

雪梅： 李哲，你來北京哪家公司實習？

李哲： 我已經告訴天明了，就是你要去的那個公司。他沒把這個消息告訴你^②？那天面試你的是我哥哥的好朋友。

雪梅： 真的？那咱們不就是同事了嗎？太好了，以後咱們可以互相幫助，互相照顧。

李哲： 所以我說請多關照嘛。

雪梅： 還不知道誰關照誰呢。

李哲： 馬克，你來中國多長時間了？

馬克： 六年了。

麗莎： 馬克，你在中國都做什麼工作？

LANGUAGE NOTES

❶ 叫外賣/叫外卖 means "to order takeout." We can also say 叫車/叫车 (to hail a cab) and 叫菜/叫菜 (to order a dish). 叫 literally means "to shout."

❷ 火 can describe a brisk, flourishing business.

柯林去超市买了很多饮料、零食和水果①。雪梅准备了一个火锅，还从附近的一家餐馆叫了外卖❶。

★　★　★

柯林：	今天我们大家聚在一起，是为了给李哲接风，给天明和丽莎饯行，也庆祝雪梅找到工作。
雪梅：	对，大家不要客气，好好吃，好好玩。
马克：	雪梅，恭喜你找到了好工作。什么时候上班？
雪梅：	下个星期一，星期五就要到欧洲出差，推销太阳能热水器。
马克：	太阳能热水器？太好了！最近跟环保和节能有关系的绿色产品市场上都卖得很火❷。
张天明：	哎，马克，李文，你们过来，我来介绍一下，这是我们在美国的校友，李哲，刚从美国来。
李文、马克：	欢迎来北京。
李哲：	大家好！请多关照❸。
雪梅：	李哲，你来北京哪家公司实习？
李哲：	我已经告诉天明了，就是你要去的那个公司。他没把这个消息告诉你②？那天面试你的是我哥哥的好朋友。
雪梅：	真的？那咱们不就是同事了吗？太好了，以后咱们可以互相帮助，互相照顾。
李哲：	所以我说请多关照嘛。
雪梅：	还不知道谁关照谁呢。
李哲：	马克，你来中国多长时间了？
马克：	六年了。
丽莎：	马克，你在中国都做什么工作？

---

❸請多關照/请多关照 is a formulaic saying. 請多關照/请多关照 literally means something like "please be liberal with your help and consideration." It is often said when introducing oneself to new colleagues for the first time. It is meant to convey modesty.

馬克：	我是個 "自由" 職業者❹，當過英文家教，演過電視劇，還拍過廣告，有時候也搞點兒翻譯。
李文：	我說怎麼有點兒面熟呢，我看過你演的電視劇。你演得很不錯。
馬克：	不過是三流演員而已，不值一提❺。
麗莎：	看來你的工作機會很多，很忙啊。
馬克：	不一定，有的時候很忙，有的時候沒事做。說白了❻，實際上是工作有點兒不穩定。不過沒關係，生活沒問題。在這兒，我生活得很快樂，交了很多中國朋友。
柯林：	難怪你的中文這麼好。
雪梅：	李哲，你哥哥的朋友真不簡單啊，這麼年輕就當上總經理了。
李哲：	聽說他不僅懂銷售，也是個優秀的管理人材。在他的領導下，公司越辦越好。
李文：	現在在中國的外國人越來越多，你們在中國生活習慣嗎？
麗莎：	你說呢？我在你們家，每天跟你父母打太極拳，吃他們做的又好吃、又健康的飯菜，都不想回去了。
天明：	我更沒問題了。
柯林：	你還寫博客嗎？
天明：	當然。在這裏，我每天都會看到、聽到新鮮的事，永遠也寫不完。
馬克：	我就不用說了，不然❼怎麼會住這麼久呢？我覺得自己已經融入這個社會了。
李哲：	我本來還怕自己適應不了這兒的生活。聽了你們的話，我放心多了。
李文：	現在外國人來中國發展，中國人到國外學習、工作，大家的聯繫多了，關係近了，世界變小了。

LANGUAGE NOTES

❹ 自由職業者/自由职业者 refers to members of the "liberal professions" 自由職業/自由职业. This term, meaning occupations that emphasize special professional qualifications and individual responsibility, e.g., medicine and law, was introduced from the West. Mark is joking here, putting the stress on 自由, meaning that he is a "free lancer."

马克：　我是个"自由"职业者❹，当过英文家教，演过电视剧，还拍过广告，有时候也搞点儿翻译。

李文：　我说怎么有点儿面熟呢，我看过你演的电视剧。你演得很不错。

马克：　不过是三流演员*而已*，不值一提❺。

丽莎：　看来你的工作机会很多，很忙啊。

马克：　不一定，有的时候很忙，有的时候没事做。说白了❻，实际上是工作有点儿不稳定。不过没关系，生活没问题。在这儿，我生活得很快乐，交了很多中国朋友。

柯林：　难怪你的中文这么好。

雪梅：　李哲，你哥哥的朋友真不简单啊，这么年轻就当上总经理了。

李哲：　听说他不仅懂销售，也是个优秀的管理人材。在他的领导下，公司越办越好。

李文：　现在在中国的外国人越来越多，你们在中国生活习惯吗？

丽莎：　你说呢？我在你们家，每天跟你父母打太极拳，吃他们做的又好吃、又健康的饭菜，都不想回去了。

天明：　我更没问题了。

柯林：　你还写博客吗？

天明：　当然。在这里，我每天都会看到、听到新鲜的事，永远也写不完。

马克：　我就不用说了，不然❼怎么会住这么久呢？我觉得自己已经融入这个社会了。

李哲：　我本来还怕自己适应不了这儿的生活。听了你们的话，我放心多了。

李文：　现在外国人来中国发展，中国人到国外学习、工作，大家的联系多了，关系近了，世界变小了。

---

❺ In 不值一提, 值 means 值得 (worth). 不值一提 means "not worth mentioning."
❻ 説白了/说白了 to speak frankly. 白 means "plain, unadorned."
❼ 不然 is short for 要不然.

雪梅：　　　李文說得真好。朋友們，來，大家舉起杯來，為我們的友
　　　　　　誼乾杯！

張天明：　　為你們在中國事業成功乾杯！

柯林：　　　祝天明和麗莎一路平安！

麗莎：　　　祝大家身體健康！

眾人：　　　乾杯！

After You Study

Challenge yourself to complete the following tasks in Chinese.

1. List the items prepared by Xuemei and Ke Lin for the party.

2. Explain why Xuemei and Li Zhe are impressed with the general manager of Xuemei's new company.

雪梅：　　　李文说得真好。朋友们，来，大家举起杯来，为我们的友谊干杯！

张天明：　　为你们在中国事业成功干杯！

柯林：　　　祝天明和丽莎一路平安！

丽莎：　　　祝大家身体健康！

众人：　　　干杯！

---

3. Recap what Mark has done for a living in China.

4. Paraphrase Li Wen's comments on the increasing contacts between the Chinese and foreigners.

VOCABULARY

1. 週	周	zhōu	n	week
2. 聚會	聚会	jùhuì	v/n	to get together; to congregate; party; get-together; social gathering
3. 慶祝	庆祝	qìngzhù	v	to celebrate
4. 接受		jiēshòu	v	to accept; to take on; to undertake
5. 接風	接风	jiēfēng	v	to give a welcome dinner for a visitor from afar
6. 餞行	饯行	jiànxíng	v	to give a farewell dinner
7. 客人		kèren	n	guest; visitor
8. 火鍋	火锅	huǒguō	n	hotpot
9. 聚		jù	v	to gather; to get together; to congregate
10. 出差		chū chāi	vo	to be away on official business or on a business trip
11. 推銷	推销	tuīxiāo	v	to market; to promote the sale (of goods/merchandise)
12. 熱水器	热水器	rèshuǐqì	n	water heater
13. 火		huǒ	adj/n	thriving; flourishing; fire; flame
14. 校友		xiàoyǒu	n	schoolfellow; alumni
15. 關照	关照	guānzhào	v	to take care of; to look after
16. 同事		tóngshì	n	colleague; co-worker
17. 者		zhě		-er; -ist
18. 電視劇	电视剧	diànshìjù	n	TV drama; TV series
19. 搞		gǎo	v	to do; to carry on; to be engaged in

20.	面熟		miànshú	adj	familiar-looking
21.	流		liú		class; level; rank; category
22.	演員	演员	yǎnyuán	n	actor; actress; performer
23.	而已		éryǐ	p	and no more
24.	值（得）		zhí (de)	v	worthy; worthwhile
25.	穩定	稳定	wěndìng	adj/v	stable; steady; to stabilize; to be steady
26.	年輕	年轻	niánqīng	adj	young
27.	不僅	不仅	bùjǐn	conj	not only
28.	永遠	永远	yǒngyuǎn	adv	always; forever
29.	放心		fàng xīn	vo	to feel relieved; to be at ease
30.	國外	国外	guówài	n	overseas; abroad
31.	聯繫	联系	liánxì	v/n	to contact; to get in touch; connection; relation
32.	友誼	友谊	yǒuyì	n	friendship; companionship; fellowship
33.	眾人	众人	zhòngrén	n	everybody; the crowd

Proper Noun

| 34. | 歐洲 | 欧洲 | Ōuzhōu | | Europe |

Enlarged Characters

慶 餞 鍋 劇 穩 僅 聯 繫 眾 歐
庆 饯 锅 剧 稳 仅 联 系 众 欧

火鍋裏有青菜、豆腐。
火锅里有青菜、豆腐。

Culture Highlights

❶ Most foreign nationals living in China are students, especially those studying Chinese language, medicine, literature, history or art. There are also some students studying natural sciences and engineering. Other long-term foreign residents have opened businesses in China or work at foreign-owned companies. Still others work as foreign language teachers, tutors, translators or models and actors. A few have become household names because of their hosting gigs on TV. It is estimated that the number of foreigners living in China exceeds one and a half million.

❷ Food plays an important role in Chinese culture. Every special occasion is celebrated with an elaborate meal. "To welcome a friend or family member from afar" is called 接風/接风 (to welcome a wind-bitten [traveler or guest]) or 洗塵/洗尘 (xǐchén) (to wash off the dust [with wine]). Before a friend or relative leaves on a long journey, he or she is invited to a farewell dinner party. This ritual is called 餞行/饯行 (to prepare a feast to see off a friend).

這是一家餐館的廣告。你會跟朋友在那兒聚會嗎?
这是一家餐馆的广告。你会跟朋友在那儿聚会吗?

Grammar

1. Word Order in Chinese

A. Basic Sentence Structure

The basic Chinese sentence structure can be outlined as follows:

Subject/Agent—(Adverbial)—Verb—(Complement)—(Object/Recipient of the Action)

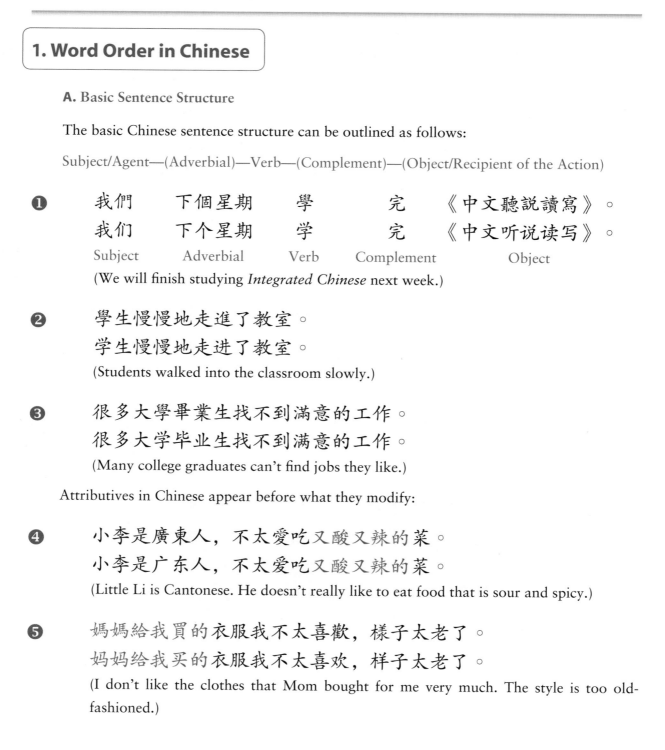

❶ 我們　　下個星期　　學　　完　　《中文聽説讀寫》。
　　我们　　下个星期　　学　　完　　《中文听说读写》。
　　Subject　　Adverbial　　Verb　　Complement　　　　Object
　　(We will finish studying *Integrated Chinese* next week.)

❷ 學生慢慢地走進了教室。
　　学生慢慢地走进了教室。
　　(Students walked into the classroom slowly.)

❸ 很多大學畢業生找不到滿意的工作。
　　很多大学毕业生找不到满意的工作。
　　(Many college graduates can't find jobs they like.)

Attributives in Chinese appear before what they modify:

❹ 小李是廣東人，不太愛吃又酸又辣的菜。
　　小李是广东人，不太爱吃又酸又辣的菜。
　　(Little Li is Cantonese. He doesn't really like to eat food that is sour and spicy.)

❺ 媽媽給我買的衣服我不太喜歡，樣子太老了。
　　妈妈给我买的衣服我不太喜欢，样子太老了。
　　(I don't like the clothes that Mom bought for me very much. The style is too old-fashioned.)

B. Under certain circumstances, Chinese word order can vary:

a. Topic-comment

When something has already been mentioned or understood, it becomes known information. The known information appears at the beginning of a sentence as a topic:

6 面試你的那個人　　　　　我　　　　　認識。
　　　面试你的那个人　　　　　我　　　　　认识。
　　　Recipient of the Action　　Agent　　　　Verb
　　　Topic_____　　_____Comment_____
　　　(The person who interviewed you—I know [him/her].)

7 (我們公司已經決定錄用你了,) 錄用通知　　你　　收到了嗎?
　　　(我们公司已经决定录用你了,) 录用通知　　你　　收到了吗?
　　　　　　　　　　　　　Recipient of the Action　Agent　Verb+Complement
　　　　　　　　　　　　　　　　Topic_____　_____Comment_____
　　　(Our company has decided to hire you. The offer letter—have you received it?)

b. The 把 Structure

When an action has to do with something that is already known by both the speaker and the listener, one can use the 把 sentence. A 把 sentence doesn't follow the basic sentence order.

8 請你把那個炒菜鍋　　　給　　　　我。
　　　请你把那个炒菜锅　　　给　　　　我。
　　　　Direct Object　　　　Verb　　Indirect Object
　　　(Please give that wok to me.)

9 **A:** 我的自行車呢?
　　　　　我的自行车呢?
　　　　　(Where's my bike?)

　　　　B: 你妹妹把它騎走了。
　　　　　　你妹妹把它骑走了。
　　　　　　(Your younger sister took it.)

c. The 被 Structure

In a 被 sentence, the object/recipient of the action is placed in the beginning of the sentence.

⑩
　店裏的太陽能熱水器　　都　被　人　買走了。
　店里的太阳能热水器　　都　被　人　买走了。
　Recipient of the Action　　　　　　Agent　Verb+Complement

(All the solar water heaters in the store were sold out.)

C. Chinese word order can also be affected by other cognitive or organizational principles.

a. General before specific:

⑪
　中國上海靜安區南京西路288號
　中国上海静安区南京西路288号

(China—Shanghai—Jing'an District—West Nanjing Road—No. 288, the exact opposite of addresses in English)

⑫
　2011年9月27號上午8點30分
　2011年9月27号上午8点30分

(Year 2011—September 27th —a.m.—8:30)

b. Arranging actions according to their time of occurrence:

Chinese sentences also usually follow the chronological principle. Whatever happens first is stated first. For example,

⑬
　我常常在圖書館學習。
　我常常在图书馆学习。

[Actions are stated in order of their occurrence: being in the library, and then studying. In English, one would say "I often study in the library."]

⑭
　表哥明天會開車到機場來接我們。
　表哥明天会开车到机场来接我们。

[Actions are mentioned in order of their occurrence: driving, arriving at the airport, picking us up, whereas in English one might say, "My cousin will come to the airport to pick us up by car tomorrow."]

⓯　我在房間用電腦寫文章。

　　我在房间用电脑写文章。

[Actions are stated in order of their occurrence: being in the room, turning on the computer, and then writing the article. In English, one may say "I was writing an article on my computer in my room."]

2. Summary of the 把 Construction (II)

When the object in a sentence is specific or known to both the speaker and the listener and the agent of the action also explicitly mentioned, the 把 is required under the following circumstances:

A. There is an indirect object in the sentence:

❶　你　　　　把　　　這張照片　　　送給　　　我　　　　吧。

　　你　　　　把　　　这张照片　　　送给　　　我　　　　吧。

　　Subject/Agent　　　　Direct Object (Known)　　　　Indirect Object

(Will you please give this photo to me?)

*你送這張照片給我吧

*你送这张照片给我吧。

B. There is a phrase indicating the location of the object after the action has been executed:

❷　他把筷子和方便麵放在了桌子上。

　　他把筷子和方便面放在了桌子上。

(He put the chopsticks and instant noodles on the table.)

*他放了筷子和方便麵在桌子上。

*他放了筷子和方便面在桌子上。

C. The verb is followed by the complement 成:

❸　考試的時候，我不小心把"天"字寫成了"夫"字。

　　考试的时候，我不小心把"天"字写成了"夫"字。

(I was careless and wrote 天 incorrectly as 夫 on the exam.)

[My writing resulted in a wrong character.]

❹   他把宿舍房間變成了一個垃圾場。

他把宿舍房间变成了一个垃圾场。

(He turned the dorm room into a trash dump.)

*他變宿舍房間成了一個垃圾場。

*他变宿舍房间成了一个垃圾场。

Sentences with the 把 construction need a subject, that is to say, agent that is responsible for the action. See the sentences above. Under certain circumstances, the subject can be absent if it is clearly understood:

❺   (你)把門關上。

(你)把门关上。

(Close the door.)

Examples ❻ and ❼ below are without a subject. Therefore, they don't need the 把 construction:

❻   鑰匙   丟了。

钥匙   丢了。

Topic   Comment

(The key was lost.)

[This is a topic-comment sentence. The focus is on what happened to the key rather than who lost it.]

❼   這個紅包給你，那個紅包給小王。

这个红包给你，那个红包给小王。

(This red envelope is for you. That red envelope is for Little Wang.)

In 把 sentences, negative adverbs must be placed before 把:

❽   哎呀，糟糕，我没把你要的地圖帶來。

哎呀，糟糕，我没把你要的地图带来。

(Shoot, I forgot to bring the map that you wanted.)

*…我把你要的地圖沒帶來。

*…我把你要的地图没带来。

❾   你老是丟三拉四的，要是不把護照放在我這裏，過兩天肯定找
不到。

你老是丢三拉四的，要是不把护照放在我这里，过两天肯定找
不到。

(You are such a scatterbrain. If you don't leave your passport with me, you won't be
able to find it in a couple of days.)

*…要是把護照不放在我這裏…

*…要是把护照不放在我这里…

Please also remember that potential complements cannot be used in 把 sentences:

*我把購房合同找不到了。

*我把购房合同找不到了。

*舅舅説舅媽把碗洗不乾淨。

*舅舅说舅妈把碗洗不干净。

把 sentences are one of the most complex structures in Chinese grammar. The application
of the 把 construction also has to do with the larger linguistic context and other factors. But
as you practice recognizing and using them, you'll soon catch on to their nuances.

Words & Phrases

A. 接受 (to accept; to take on; to undertake)

接受 can be followed by an abstract noun such as 建議/建议 (suggestion), 意見/意见 (opinion), 領導/领导 (leadership), 好意 (goodwill), 批評/批评 (pīpíng, criticism), or a concrete noun or pronoun: 禮物/礼物 (gift), 他 (him).

❶ 張天明的好朋友李哲也来到中國了，他接受了天明的建議，到一家跨國公司來實習。

張天明的好朋友李哲也来到中国了，他接受了天明的建议，到一家跨国公司来实习。

(Zhang Tianming's good friend Li Zhe has also arrived in China. He had accepted Tianming's suggestion to intern at a multinational company.)

❷ 國際銷售部經理不願意接受總經理的領導。

国际销售部经理不愿意接受总经理的领导。

(The manager of the International Sales Department is unwilling to accept the general manager's leadership.)

❸ 我不能接受你這麼貴的禮物。

我不能接受你这么贵的礼物。

(I can't accept such an expensive gift from you.)

B. 而已 (and no more)

而已 occurs at the end of a descriptive statement in order to downplay the statement or the importance of the matter. Another phrase that can be used in place of 而已 is 罷了/罢了 (bà le).

❶ 不過是三流演員而已，不值一提。

不过是三流演员而已，不值一提。

(I'm just a third-rate actor and no more, not worth mentioning at all.)

❷ 我只是開玩笑而已，你不必生氣。

我只是开玩笑而已，你不必生气。

(I was just teasing. You don't need to get angry.)

❸ 這件套裝質量不錯，才200塊而已，買了吧。

这件套装质量不错，才200块而已，买了吧。

(The suit is very good quality, and it's only ¥200. Why don't you buy it?)

❹ 這不過是一次小考而已，又不是期末考，你不用太難過。

这不过是一次小考而已，又不是期末考，你不用太难过。

(This is just a small quiz. It's not the final exam. There's no need to feel depressed.)

C. 在…下 (under)

在…下 expresses conditions and appears before the verb or subject of a sentence.

❶ 在他的領導下，公司越辦越好，我哥哥還買了他們公司很多股票呢。

在他的领导下，公司越办越好，我哥哥还买了他们公司很多股票呢。

(Under his leadership the company is becoming better and better managed. My older brother has even bought a lot of the company's stock.)

❷ 在大家的幫助下，事情很快地做完了。

在大家的帮助下，事情很快地做完了。

(With everyone's help, the task was quickly completed.)

❸ 雖然小明的中文基礎不太好，可是在老師的指導下，成績提高得很快。

虽然小明的中文基础不太好，可是在老师的指导下，成绩提高得很快。

(Although the foundation of Xiao Ming's Chinese isn't very good, with the teacher's guidance, his grade quickly improved.)

D. 你説呢？/ 你说呢？(What do you say?; What do you think?)

你説呢？/ 你说呢？ can be used to elicit an opinion, for example:

❶   我這筆錢應該存在銀行，還是炒股？老王，你説呢？
我这笔钱应该存在银行，还是炒股？老王，你说呢？
(Should I deposit this money in the bank or use it for stock speculation? What do you say, Old Wang?)

❷   李文：現在中國的外國人越來越多，你們在中國生活習慣嗎？
李文：现在中国的外国人越来越多，你们在中国生活习惯吗？
(Nowadays there are more and more foreigners in China. Are you used to living in China?)

麗莎：你説呢？(我當然習慣)
丽莎：你说呢？(我当然习惯)
(Lisa: What do you think? [Of course, I am.])

❸   妻子：今天是什麼日子，你怎麼做了這麼多菜？
妻子：今天是什么日子，你怎么做了这么多菜？
(Wife: What day is it today? How come you made so much food?)

丈夫：你説呢？
丈夫：你说呢？
(Husband: What do you think?)

妻子：噢，我想起來了，今天是我的生日！謝謝你！
妻子：噢，我想起来了，今天是我的生日！谢谢你！
(Wife: Oh, I remember now. Today's my birthday. Thank you!)

Language Practice

A. Planning a Party

Imagine you're orchestrating a huge wedding party in Shanghai, and you need to tell your assistants what they need to do and where things should go. To make sure they understand your Chinese, you're jotting down the possible instructions that you need to say in Chinese.

1. Open the windows, please.
2. Place the cake and the flowers on the table.
3. Move those chairs out of the room.
4. Move the piano into the room.
5. Don't paste the 囍 character upside down.
6. Tidy up the kitchen.
7. Turn off the lights before you go home.
8. Don't forget to give me back the key to the room.

Other useful sentences…

B. It's No Big Deal

When you want to downplay the seriousness or importance of a situation, 而已 is a good word to use. Based on the clues given, practice with a partner.

EXAMPLE:	doing yoga beautifully	one year
	A: 你做瑜伽做得真棒，肯定學了很長時間吧？	A: 你做瑜伽做得真棒，肯定学了很长时间吧？
	B: 看你說的，我只學了一年而已。	B: 看你说的，我只学了一年而已。

1. selling water heaters like hotcakes   twenty units
2. winning the championship   class champion
3. losing a lot of money from investing in the stock market   two hundred
4. building a tall building   ten stories high

C. It's Party Time!

Imagine there's an exchange student from China in your class who is going back to China at the end of this semester. You and your classmates are throwing a party to bid farewell to her. Work with your classmates and

a. Name the guest of honor and decide the date, time, and location of the party. Use the information to create an invitation card.

為 (name of the guest of honor)   为 (name of the guest of honor)

_____的聚會   _____的聚会

時間/时间：

地點/地点：

b. Brainstorm fun activities for the party.

_____

_____

_____

_____

_____

c. Write a shopping list to prepare for the party based on the activities listed above.

	吃的	喝的	用的	玩的
Classmate #1				
Classmate #2				
Classmate #3				
Classmate #4				
Classmate #5				

...

d. Compose an email message to notify your class of what and whom the party is for, where and when it will take place, and who will be responsible for bringing what to the party. Don't forget to attach the invitation card you have made.

D. Being a Newcomer

When meeting new colleagues or friends for the first time, in addition to stating your name and saying how happy you are to meet them, you probably need to request their help and advice as you get acquainted with your surroundings.

EXAMPLE: school

→   我剛到學校來工作，對什麼都　　　我刚到学校来工作，对什么都
　　　不熟悉/很陌生，請多關照。　　　不熟悉/很陌生，请多关照。

1. company

2. factory

3. this city

4. this country

E. What to Say?

When welcoming new friends or saying goodbye to old friends, what formal expressions would you say to mark the occasion?

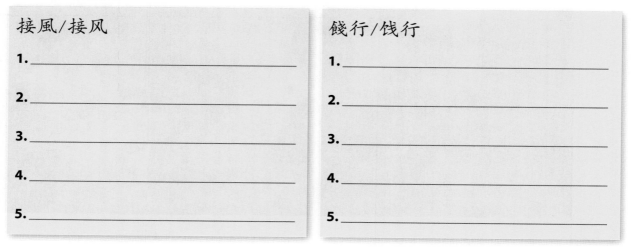

接風/接风

1. _____

2. _____

3. _____

4. _____

5. _____

餞行/饯行

1. _____

2. _____

3. _____

4. _____

5. _____

F. Foreigners in China

As Li Wen says, there are more and more foreigners working and studying in China. List some of their activities here.

 學習中文/学习中文，＿＿＿＿＿＿＿＿＿＿＿＿＿＿＿

 ＿＿＿＿＿＿＿＿＿＿＿＿＿＿＿＿＿＿＿＿

 ＿＿＿＿＿＿＿＿＿＿＿＿＿＿＿＿＿＿＿＿

 當家教/当家教，＿＿＿＿＿，＿＿＿＿＿，＿＿＿＿

Circle the things above that you might do when you go to China. Based on your own situation, use either "不是…就是…", "要麼…要麼…/要么…要么…" or "不僅…而且…/不仅…而且…"in your report to class.

我將來去中國…   我将来去中国…

Pinyin Text

Xuěméi miànshì hòu, nà jiā gōngsī tōngzhī tā xià zhōu kāishǐ shàng bān. Xuěméi hé Kē Lín dōu hěn gāoxìng, tāmen juédìng qǐng péngyou men dào Xuěméi zhù de dìfang lái jùhuì, qìngzhù yí xià.

Zhāng Tiānmíng de hǎo péngyou Lǐ Zhé yě lái dào Zhōngguó le, tā jiēshòu le Tiānmíng de jiànyì, dào yì jiā kuàguó gōngsī lái shíxí. Jiéguǒ, qìngzhù wǎnhuì yě chéng le wèi Lǐ Zhé jiēfēng de wǎnhuì.

Zhāng Tiānmíng hé Lìshā xuéqī jiéshù hòu hěn kuài jiù yào huí Měiguó le. Suǒyǐ zhè cì jùhuì yě chéng le gěi tāmen jiànxíng de wǎnhuì.

Lái de kèrén chúle Tiānmíng, Lìshā, Lǐ Zhé wài, hái yǒu Lǐ Wén hé Mǎkè.

Kē Lín qù chāoshì mǎi le hěn duō yǐnliào, língshí hé shuǐguǒ①. Xuěméi zhǔnbèi le yí ge huǒguō, hái cóng fùjìn de yì jiā cānguǎn jiào le wàimài❶.

Kē Lín:	Jīntiān wǒmen dàjiā jù zài yìqǐ, shì wèile gěi Lǐ Zhé jiēfēng, gěi Tiānmíng hé Lìshā jiànxíng, yě qìngzhù Xuěméi zhǎo dào gōngzuò.
Xuěméi:	Duì, dàjiā bú yào kèqi, hǎo hāo chī, hǎo hāo wán.
Mǎkè:	Xuěméi, gōngxǐ nǐ zhǎo dào le hǎo gōngzuò. Shénme shíhou shàng bān?
Xuěméi:	Xià gè xīngqīyī, xīngqīwǔ jiù yào dào Ōuzhōu chū chāi, tuīxiāo tàiyáng néng rèshuǐqì.
Mǎkè:	Tàiyángnéng rèshuǐqì? Tài hǎo le! Zuìjìn gēn huánbǎo hé jiénéng yǒu guānxi de lǜsè chǎnpǐn shìchǎng shang dōu mài de hěn huǒ❷.
Zhāng Tiānmíng:	Āi, Mǎkè, Lǐ Wén, nǐmen guò lai, wǒ lái jièshào yí xià, zhè shì wǒmen zài Měiguó de xiàoyǒu, Lǐ Zhé, gāng cóng Měiguó lái.
Lǐ Wén, Mǎkè:	Huānyíng lái Běijīng.
Lǐ Zhé:	Dàjiā hǎo! Qǐng duō guānzhào❸.
Xuěméi:	Lǐ Zhé, nǐ lái Běijīng nǎ jiā gōngsī shíxí?
Lǐ Zhé:	Wǒ yǐjīng gàosu Tiānmíng le, jiù shì nǐ yào qù de nà ge gōngsī. Tā méi bǎ zhè ge xiāoxi gàosu nǐ?② Nà tiān miànshì nǐ de shì wǒ gēge de hǎo péngyou.
Xuěméi:	Zhēn de? Nà zánmen bú jiù shì tóngshì le ma? Tài hǎo le, yǐhòu zánmen kěyǐ hùxiāng bāngzhù, hùxiāng zhàogù.
Lǐ Zhé:	Suǒyǐ wǒ shuō qǐng duō guānzhào ma.
Xuěméi:	Hái bù zhīdào shéi guānzhào shéi ne.

Lǐ Zhé:	Mǎkè, nǐ lái Zhōngguó duō cháng shíjiān le?
Mǎkè:	Liù nián le.
Lìshā:	Mǎkè, nǐ zài Zhōngguó dōu zuò shénme gōngzuò?
Mǎkè:	Wǒ shì ge "zìyóu" zhíyè zhě❹, dāng guo Yīngwén jiājiào, yǎn guo diànshìjù, hái pāi guo guǎnggào, yǒu shíhou yě gǎo diǎnr fānyì.
Lǐ Wén:	Wǒ shuō zěnme yǒu diǎnr miànshú ne, wǒ kàn guo nǐ yǎn de diànshìjù. Nǐ yǎn de hěn búcuò.
Mǎkè:	Búguò shì sān liú yǎnyuán éryǐ, bù zhí yì tí❺.
Lìshā:	Kàn lai nǐ de gōngzuò jīhuì hěn duō, hěn máng a.
Mǎkè:	Bù yídìng, yǒude shíhou hěn máng, yǒude shíhou méi shì zuò. Shuō bái le❻, shíjìshang shì gōngzuò yǒu diǎnr bù wěndìng. Búguò méi guānxi, shēnghuó méi wèntí. Zài zhèr, wǒ shēnghuó de hěn kuàilè, jiāo le hěn duō Zhōngguó péngyou.
Kē Lín:	Nánguài nǐ de Zhōngwén zhème hǎo.
Xuěméi:	Lǐ Zhé, nǐ gēge de péngyou zhēn bù jiǎndān a, zhème niánqīng jiù dāng shang zǒng jīnglǐ le.
Lǐ Zhé:	Tīngshuō tā bùjǐn dǒng xiāoshòu, yě shì ge yōuxiù de guǎnlǐ réncái. Zài tā de lǐngdǎo xià, gōngsī yuè bàn yuè hǎo.
Lǐ Wén:	Xiànzài zài Zhōngguó de wàiguó rén yuè lái yuè duō, nǐmen zài Zhōngguó shēnghuó xíguàn ma?
Lìshā:	Nǐ shuō ne? Wǒ zài nǐmen jiā, měitiān gēn nǐ fùmǔ dǎ tàijíquán, chī tāmen zuò de yòu hàochī, yòu jiànkāng de fàn cài, dōu bù xiǎng huí qu le.
Tiānmíng:	Wǒ gèng méi wèntí le.
Kē Lín:	Nǐ hái xiě bókè ma?
Tiānmíng:	Dāngrán. Zài zhèli, wǒ měi tiān dōu huì kàn dào, tīng dào xīnxian de shì, yǒngyuǎn yě xiě bù wán.
Mǎkè:	Wǒ jiù búyòng shuō le, bùrán❼ zěnme huì zhù zhème jiǔ ne? Wǒ juéde zìjǐ yǐjīng róngrù zhè ge shèhuì le.
Lǐ Zhé:	Wǒ běnlái hái pà zìjǐ shìyìng bù liǎo zhèr de shēnghuó. Tīng le nǐmen de huà, wǒ fàngxīn duō le.
Lǐ Wén:	Xiànzài wàiguó rén lái Zhōngguó fāzhǎn, Zhōngguó rén dào guówài xuéxí, gōngzuò, dàjiā de liánxì duō le, guānxì jìn le, shìjiè biàn xiǎo le.

Xuěméi:	Lǐ Wén shuō de zhēn hǎo. Péngyou men, lái, dàjiā jǔ qǐ bēi lái, wèi wǒmen de yǒuyì gān bēi!
Zhāng Tiānmíng:	Wèi nǐmen zài Zhōngguó shìyè chénggōng gān bēi!
Kē Lín:	Zhù Tiānmíng hé Lìshā yí lù píng'ān!
Lìshā:	Zhù dàjiā shēntǐ jiànkāng!
Zhòngrén:	Gān bēi!

English Text

After Xuemei's interview, the company called her in to report for work next week. Xuemei and Ke Lin are both very happy. They decide to invite their friends for a get-together at Xuemei's place to celebrate.

Zhang Tianming's good friend Li Zhe has also come to China. He accepted Tianming's suggestion to intern at a multinational company. As a result, the celebration party has also become a welcoming party for Li Zhe.

Zhang Tianming and Lisa will soon return to America after the semester is over, so this gathering is also a farewell party for them.

The other guests, besides Tianming, Lisa, and Li Zhe, are Li Wen and Mark.

Ke Lin went to the supermarket and bought a lot of beverages, snacks, and fruit. Xuemei prepared a hotpot and ordered takeout from a nearby restaurant.

Ke Lin:	Today we get together here to welcome Li Zhe and say goodbye to Tianming and Lisa, but also to celebrate Xuemei's finding a job.
Xuemei:	That's right. Don't be shy. Have a lot of food and have fun.
Mark:	Xuemei, congratulations on finding a great job. When do you start working?
Xuemei:	Next Monday. Next Friday I'll be in Europe on a business trip promoting solar water heaters.
Mark:	Solar water heaters? That's excellent! Lately, green products having to do with environmental protection and energy conservation have been selling like hotcakes.
Tianming:	Hi, Mark, Li Wen, come over here. Let me introduce our schoolmate in the United States, Li Zhe, who has just arrived from America.
Li Zhe:	Hello everyone! I [hope I can] count on your help and guidance [since I'm new here].

Li Wen & Mark:	Welcome to Beijing.
Xuemei:	Li Zhe, which company in Beijing will you be interning at?
Li Zhe:	I've told Tianming. It's the same company where you'll be working. He didn't tell you the news. The person who interviewed you the other day was my older brother's good friend.
Xuemei:	Really? Then won't that make us colleagues? That's great! We can help each other out.
Li Zhe:	That's why I said I'll be counting on your help.
Xuemei:	Who knows who'll be helping whom?
Li Zhe:	Mark, how long have you been in China?
Mark:	Six years.
Lisa:	Mark, what jobs have you had in China?
Mark:	I am a freelancer. I've been an English tutor. I've acted in TV dramas and commercials. Sometimes I also do some translating.
Li Wen:	No wonder you looked so familiar to me! I've seen your TV dramas. Your acting was quite good.
Mark:	I was just a third-rate actor, hardly worth mentioning at all.
Lisa:	It seems like there are many opportunities for work for you. You seem to be very busy.
Mark:	Not necessarily. Sometimes I'm very busy. But sometimes I don't have anything to do at all. To be frank, the work is not steady. But it doesn't matter. I can survive without a problem. I'm very happy here. I have made lots of Chinese friends.
Ke Lin:	No wonder your Chinese is so good.
Xuemei:	Li Zhe, your brother's friend is extraordinary, becoming a general manager at such a young age.
Li Zhe:	I hear that he not only understands sales but is also an excellent manager. Under his leadership, the company is getting stronger and stronger.
Li Wen:	Nowadays there are more and more foreign nationals in China. Are you used to life in China?
Lisa:	What do *you* think? I stay at your house. Every morning I practice tai chi with your parents and eat their delicious and healthy food every day. I don't even want to go back.
Tianming:	Even less of a problem for me.
Ke Lin:	Do you still update your blog?

Tianming:	Of course. Here, every day I see and hear something new. I have endless things to write about.
Mark:	It goes without saying for me, or I wouldn't have lived here for so long. I think I've become a part of society here.
Li Zhe:	I was worried that I wouldn't be able to adapt to life here. After listening to you, I feel much more at ease.
Li Wen:	Nowadays foreigners come to China for opportunities. Chinese people go abroad to study and work. We are in more frequent and closer contact with one another. The world is getting smaller.
Xuemei:	Li Wen put it well. Friends, let's raise our glasses and have a toast to our friendship!
Tianming:	To your successful careers in China!
Ke Lin:	To a safe journey for Tianming and Lisa.
Lisa:	To everyone's health!
All:	Cheers!

SELF-ASSESSMENT

How well can you do these things? Check (✔) the boxes to evaluate your progress and see which tasks you may need to practice more.

I can	Very Well	OK	A Little
Welcome a visitor from afar at a welcoming party	☐	☐	☐
Bid someone farewell at a farewell party	☐	☐	☐
Ask for guidance and help when joining a new community	☐	☐	☐

Let's Review! (Lessons 16–20)

I. Chinese Character Crossword Puzzles

You have learned many vocabulary items in Lessons 1–20. You may have noticed that some words and phrases share the same characters. Let's see whether you can recall these characters. The common character is positioned in the center of the cluster of rings. The block arrows indicate which way you should read the words. Work with a partner and see how many association rings you can complete. Of course, you may add more rings if you can think of additional words and phrases sharing the same characters, or you may create your own clusters of rings.

EXAMPLE:

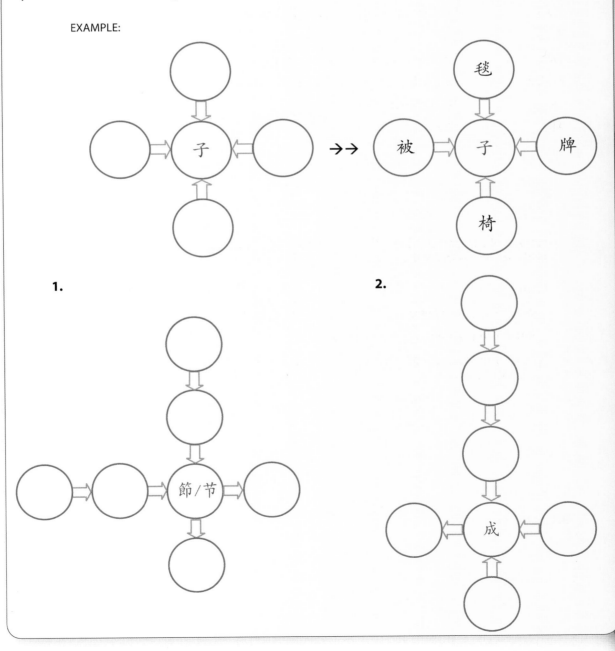

1.

2.

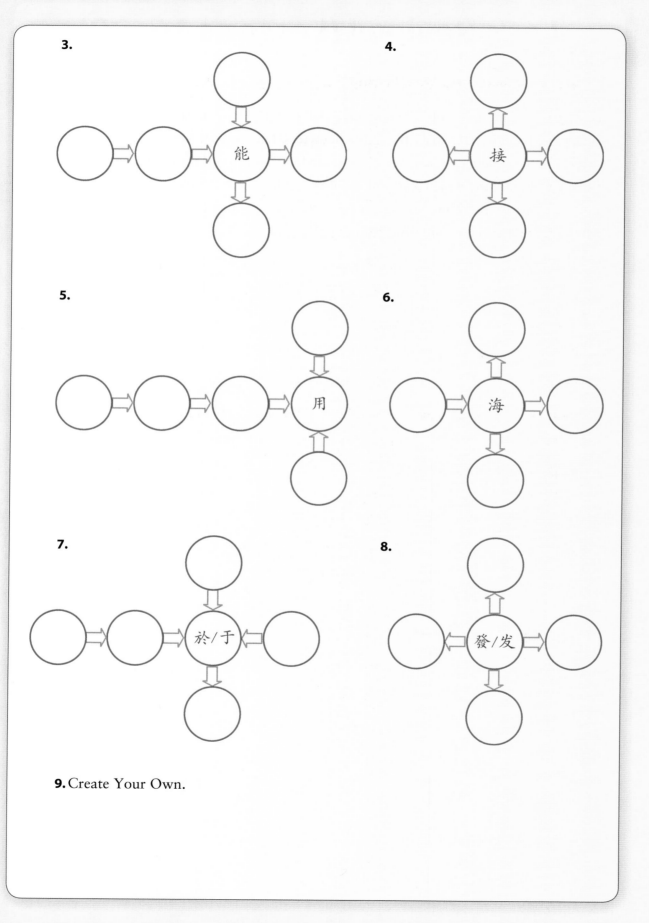

3. 能

4. 接

5. 用

6. 海

7. 於／于

8. 發／发

9. Create Your Own.

II. Matching Words

A. Draw a line connecting the verb with its most appropriate object.

1. 得	矛盾
2. 排	合同
3. 修	病
4. 打	故事
5. 賠/赔	麻將/麻将
6. 蓋/盖	隊/队
7. 鬧/闹	宮殿/宮殿
8. 講/讲	錢/钱
9. 簽/签	房子
10. 抵押	大樓/大楼

B. Draw a line connecting the verb with its most appropriate object.

1. 建立	革命
2. 推銷/推销	思考
3. 領導/领导	方式
4. 進行/进行	產品/产品
5. 造成	國家/国家
6. 享受	經濟/经济
7. 用	建議/建议
8. 引起	污染
9. 接受	生活
10. 發展/发展	貿易/贸易

C. Draw a line connecting the noun with the adjective that can best serve as its predicate.

1.	技術/技术	大
2.	工作	火
3.	心情	鬱悶/郁闷
4.	生活	高
5.	經濟/经济	先進/先进
6.	收入	幸福
7.	餐館/餐馆	穩定/稳定
8.	風險/风险	發達/发达

III. Vocabulary Exercises

Give the opposite of the words listed.

EXAMPLE: 方便⟷<u>麻煩/麻烦</u>

1. 高⟷_____
2. 長/长⟷_____
3. 硬⟷_____
4. 贏/赢⟷_____
5. 老⟷_____
6. 乾/干⟷_____
7. 漲/涨⟷_____
8. 難過/难过⟷_____
9. 增加⟷_____
10. 熟悉⟷_____

IV. In Other Words

A. You've learned many vocabulary items that are actually abbreviations. Give the full phrase or expression for each abbreviation.

EXAMPLE: 古國/古国→<u>古老的國家/古老的国家</u>

1. 古城→

2. 春晚→

3. 環保/环保→

4. 節能/节能→

5. 超市→

6. 房價/房价→

7. 股市→

8. 男足→

9. 海歸/海归→

10. 那時/那时→

B. You've learned several Chinese set phrases and sayings. See if you can explain each of the following in Chinese with the help of your partner.

1. 丟三拉四：

2. 物美價廉/物美价廉：

3. 小兩口吵架不記仇/小两口吵架不记仇：

4. 望子成龍，望女成鳳/望子成龙，望女成凤：

5. 人山人海：

6. 年年有餘/年年有余：

7. 民以食為天/民以食为天：

8. 同工同酬：

9. 妻管嚴/妻管严：

10. 取之不盡/取之不尽：

11. 不堪設想/不堪设想：

12. 省吃儉用/省吃俭用：

13. 有朋自遠方來，不亦樂乎/有朋自远方来，不亦乐乎：

14. 學有所成/学有所成：

V. Put Your Thoughts into Words

A. Brainstorm with a partner and ask each other what words or phrases you can use when you want to

1. advocate for energy conservation

浪費能源/浪费能源	新能源	節約能源/节约能源
_____	_____	_____
_____	_____	_____
_____	_____	_____
_____	_____	_____
_____		

2. do financial planning

怎麼存錢/怎么存钱	怎麼投資/怎么投资
_____	_____
_____	_____
_____	_____
_____	_____

3. briefly talk about one Chinese historical figure and one Chinese dynasty

歷史人物/历史人物	朝代
_____	_____
_____	_____
_____	_____
_____	_____
_____	

4. explain why China attracts foreigners

_____
_____
_____
_____
_____
_____

5. discuss how foreigners adapt to life in China

_____
_____
_____
_____
_____

B. Work with your partner to group the following words/phrases according to their meanings and usages. Feel free to add other words/phrases to the list.

而已　不值一提　終於/终于　其中　跟···有關係/跟···有关系		
因此　既然　　好在　　　你説呢？/你说呢？　又		
之一　在···下　在···方面　···吧···吧　可不是嗎？/可不是吗？		

1. When you wish to cite or refer to examples: _____

2. When you wish to draw a conclusion: _____

3. When you wish to ponder different options: _____

4. When you wish to downplay the importance of something: _____

5. When you wish to express your relief: _____

6. When you wish to point out the relevance of something: _____

7. When you wish to signal your agreement: _____

8. When you wish to point out the obvious: _____

9. When you wish to refer to various aspects of something: _____

VI. Presentation

With a partner, give a brief presentation on one of these topics: your view on energy conservation, your thoughts on the best ways to save or invest money, an aspect of Chinese history, your reasons for going to China, or your expectations of studying or living in China.

Preparation: Discuss with your partner
   a. which topic you will select, and why;
   b. what aspects of the topic you want to focus on;
   c. what words or phrases from IV-A should be used in your presentation;
   d. what should be said first, next, and last;
   e. what transitions may be needed between parts of the presentation;
   f. what linking devices should be used to connect your sentences;
   g. what words or phrases from IV-B can be useful in presenting your point of view.

It may be a good idea to jot down sentences that you wish to say, then number them in the order you think they should be presented, and finally consider how to organize your sentences in a coherent discourse. Then make your presentation to the class.

VII. How Well Can You Speak?

Reorganize the following sentences to compose a well-connected paragraph about Mark's life in China. Pay attention to time expressions, transitional devices, and pronouns.

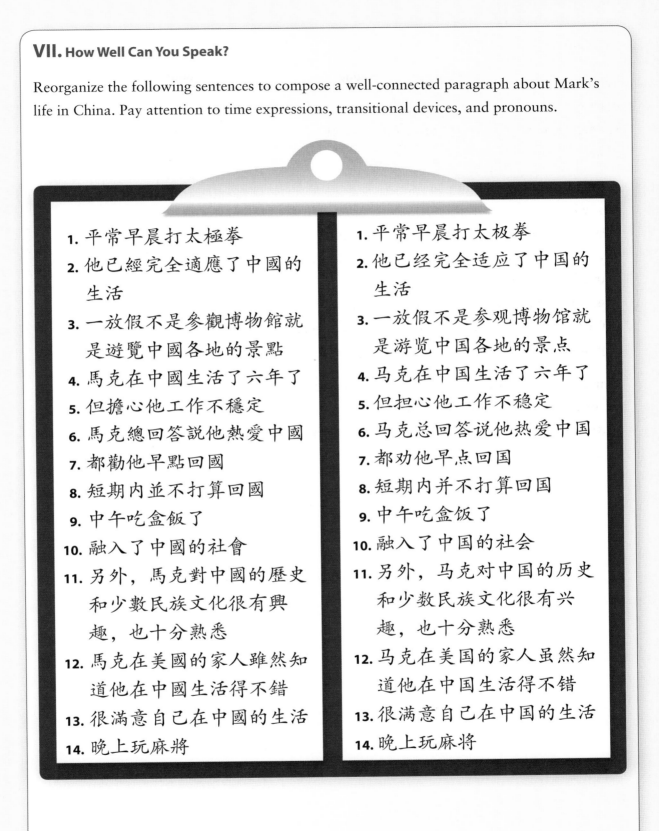

1. 平常早晨打太極拳
2. 他已經完全適應了中國的生活
3. 一放假不是參觀博物館就是遊覽中國各地的景點
4. 馬克在中國生活了六年了
5. 但擔心他工作不穩定
6. 馬克總回答說他熱愛中國
7. 都勸他早點回國
8. 短期內並不打算回國
9. 中午吃盒飯了
10. 融入了中國的社會
11. 另外，馬克對中國的歷史和少數民族文化很有興趣，也十分熟悉
12. 馬克在美國的家人雖然知道他在中國生活得不錯
13. 很滿意自己在中國的生活
14. 晚上玩麻將

1. 平常早晨打太极拳
2. 他已经完全适应了中国的生活
3. 一放假不是参观博物馆就是游览中国各地的景点
4. 马克在中国生活了六年了
5. 但担心他工作不稳定
6. 马克总回答说他热爱中国
7. 都劝他早点回国
8. 短期内并不打算回国
9. 中午吃盒饭了
10. 融入了中国的社会
11. 另外，马克对中国的历史和少数民族文化很有兴趣，也十分熟悉
12. 马克在美国的家人虽然知道他在中国生活得不错
13. 很满意自己在中国的生活
14. 晚上玩麻将

Vocabulary Index (Chinese-English)

The Chinese-English index is alphabetized according to *pinyin*. Words that begin with the same Chinese character are first grouped together. Homonyms appear in the order of their tonal pronunciation (i.e., first tones first, second tones second, third tones third, fourth tones fourth, and neutral tones last). Pinyin in parentheses shows pronunciation of the characters before tone change. Proper nouns are shown in green.

Traditional	Simplified	Pinyin	Part of Speech	English	Lesson
A					
啊		á	interj	eh?; what?	12
哎呀	哎呀	āiyā	interj	(an exclamation to express surprise) gosh; ah	4
愛好	爱好	àihào	n/v	hobby; interest; to love (something)	6
安排		ānpái	v	to arrange	9
安全		ānquán	adj	safe	1
熬夜		áo yè	vo	to stay up late or all night; to burn the midnight oil	14
B					
巴西		Bāxī	pn	Brazil	15
擺	摆	bǎi	v	to put; to place	2
拜年		bài nián	vo	to wish somebody a happy Chinese New Year; to pay a Chinese New Year's call	11
搬家		bān jiā	vo	to move (one's residence)	1
幫忙	帮忙	bāng máng	vo	to help	1
幫助	帮助	bāngzhù	v	to help	7
包括		bāokuò	v	to include; to consist of	13
飽	饱	bǎo	adj	full; satiated (after a meal)	14
保護	保护	bǎohù	v	to protect; to safeguard	16
保留		bǎoliú	v	to remain as before; to retain	12
報名	报名	bào míng	vo	to sign up; to register	13
抱怨		bàoyuàn	v	to complain	9
倍		bèi	m	(measure word for times by which something is multiplied)	10
背景		bèijǐng	n	background	6
被子		bèizi	n	comforter; quilt	2

Traditional	Simplified	Pinyin	Part of Speech	English	Lesson
本來	本来	běnlái	adj/adv	original; originally; at first	11
筆	笔	bǐ	m	(measure word for sums of money)	17
比分		bǐfēn	n	score	15
比較	比较	bǐjiào	adv/v	relatively; comparatively; rather; to compare	1
比如		bǐrú	v	for example	3
畢竟	毕竟	bìjìng	adv	after all; all in all; in the final analysis; when all is said and done	15
畢業	毕业	bì yè	vo	to graduate	5
必須	必须	bìxū	adv	must; have to; be obliged to	14
鞭炮		biānpào	n	firecracker	11
變	变	biàn	v	to change	12
變化	变化	biànhuà	n/v	change; to change	12
標準	标准	biāozhǔn	n/adj	criterion; standard	4
表哥		biǎogē	n	older male cousin of a different surname	12
表現	表现	biǎoxiàn	v/n	to display; to manifest; performance; manifestation	15
表演		biǎoyǎn	v/n	to perform; to act; performance	14
冰燈	冰灯	bīngdēng	n	ice lantern	10
兵馬俑	兵马俑	bīngmǎyǒng	n	terracotta warriors and horses	18
並	并	bìng	adv	actually	9
菠菜	菠菜	bōcài	n	spinach	3
博客		bókè	n	blog	7
博士		bóshì	n	Ph.D.; doctor [academic degree]	9
博物館	博物馆	bówùguǎn	n	museum	14
補充	补充	bǔchōng	v	to supplement; to replenish	14
部		bù		part; section	10
部分		bùfen	n	portion; part	18
不必		(bùbì) búbì	adv	need not; not have to	4
不得了		bù déliǎo		extremely; exceedingly; couldn't be more	15
不斷	不断	(bùduàn) búduàn	adv	continuously	8
不管		bùguǎn	conj	no matter; regardless of	12

Traditional	Simplified	Pinyin	Part of Speech	English	Lesson
不見得	不见得	(bù jiàn de) bú jiàn de		not necessarily	1
不僅	不仅	bùjǐn	conj	not only	20
不堪設想	不堪设想	bùkān shèxiǎng		(of consequences) too ghastly to contemplate; unimaginable; extremely bad or dangerous	16
不如		bùrú	v	not equal to; inferior to; to not measure up to	3
不是… 而是…		(bùshì) búshì… érshì…		it's not...but...	9
不停		bùtíng	adv	continuously; incessantly	6
不同		bù tóng		different; not the same	6
C					
菜單	菜单	càidān	n	menu	3
餐		cān	n	meal	11
餐館兒	餐馆儿	cānguǎnr	n	restaurant	2
餐巾		cānjīn	n	napkin	3
餐具		cānjù	n	eating utensils; tableware	16
參觀	参观	cānguān	v	to visit; to look around	18
參加	参加	cānjiā	v	to participate; to take part; to attend	13
層	层	céng	m	(measure word for stories of a building)	2
曾經	曾经	céngjīng	adv	once; at some time in the past	18
茶館	茶馆	cháguǎn	n	teahouse	13
產品	产品	chǎnpǐn	n	product; merchandise	19
嚐	尝	cháng	v	to taste	12
長	长	cháng	adj	long	1
長江	长江	Cháng Jiāng	pn	the Yangtze River	10
超過	超过	chāoguò	v	to surpass; to exceed	15
超市		chāoshì	n	supermarket	16
朝代		cháodài	n	dynasty	18
炒		chǎo	v	to stir-fry; to sauté; to speculate (for profit)	17
吵架		chǎo jià	vo	to quarrel	6
車廂	车厢	chēxiāng	n	railway carriage	13

Traditional	Simplified	Pinyin	Part of Speech	English	Lesson
稱呼	称呼	chēnghu	n/v	term of address; to address as	18
成功		chénggōng	v/adj	to succeed; successful	11
成績	成绩	chéngjì	n	performance; achievement; result; score; grade	15
成為	成为	chéngwéi	v	to become; to turn into	14
遲到	迟到	chídào	v	to arrive late	7
初		chū		first	11
出版		chūbǎn	v	to publish	7
出差		chū chāi	vo	to be away on official business or on a business trip	20
出發	出发	chūfā	v	to set out; to depart	13
出汗		chū hàn	vo	to sweat	16
出門	出门	chū mén	vo	to go out; to leave home	14
出生		chūshēng	v	to be born	1
出現	出现	chūxiàn	v	to appear; to arise; to emerge	15
除夕		chúxī	n	Chinese New Year's Eve	11
船		chuán	n	boat; ship	10
傳統	传统	chuántǒng	n/adj	tradition; traditional	11
吹		chuī	v	to end a relationship; (lit.) to blow	6
春節	春节	Chūnjié	pn	Spring Festival; Chinese New Year	11
純棉	纯棉	chúnmián	adj	pure cotton; 100 percent cotton	4
從來	从来	cónglái	adv	from past till present; always; at all times	12
存		cún	v	to save up; to deposit	8
存款		cúnkuǎn	n	bank savings	17

D

答應	答应	dāying	v	to agree (to do something); to promise; to answer	6
打呼嚕	打呼噜	dǎ hūlu	vo	to snore	13
打交道		dǎ jiāodào	vo	to deal with	5
大多		dàduō	adv	mostly; for the most part	10
大理		Dàlǐ	pn	Dali	13
大男子主義	大男子主义	dà nánzǐ zhǔyì		male chauvinism	15

Traditional	Simplified	Pinyin	Part of Speech	English	Lesson
大人		dàren	n	adult	8
待		dāi	v	to stay	7
代		dài	v	to replace; to substitute	11
貸款	贷款	dàikuǎn	n/v	loan; to provide a loan	8
單位	单位	dānwèi	n	unit	15
倒		dào	v	to turn upside down; to go backwards	11
到處	到处	dàochù	adv	all around; all over	10
到底		dàodǐ	adv	what on earth; what in the world; in the end	6
道理		dàoli	n	reason; sense	4
道歉		dào qiàn	vo	to apologize	6
得病		dé bìng	vo	to fall ill; to contract a disease	15
燈籠	灯笼	dēnglong	n	lantern	13
等		děng	p	and so forth; etc.	14
等於	等于	děngyú	v	to equal; to be equivalent to; to amount to	14
低		dī	adj	low	8
的確	的确	díquè	adv	indeed	12
抵押		dǐyā	v	to mortgage	17
地道		dìdao	adj	authentic; genuine; pure	2
地理		dìlǐ	n	geography	10
地球		dìqiú	n	the earth; the globe	16
地位		dìwèi	n	position; status	15
地形		dìxíng	n	terrain; topography	10
電視劇	电视剧	diànshìjù	n	TV drama; TV series	20
電影院	电影院	diànyǐngyuàn	n	movie theater	6
跌		diē	v	to fall	17
丟三拉四		diū sān là sì		scatterbrained; forgetful	6
棟	栋	dòng	m	(measure word for buildings)	2
動作	动作	dòngzuò	n	movement; action	14
逗		dòu	v/adj	to tease; to play with; amusing	13
讀書	读书	dú shū	vo	to attend school; to study; to read aloud	8

Traditional	Simplified	Pinyin	Part of Speech	English	Lesson
度		dù	m	(measure word for degree of temperature, heat, hardness, humidity, etc.)	16
端午節	端午节	Duānwǔjié	pn	Dragon Boat Festival	11
短		duǎn	adj	short	10
短期		duǎnqī	n	short term	19
段		duàn	m	(measure word for section, segment, or part)	16
鍛煉	锻炼	duànliàn	v	to exercise; to work out; to undergo physical training	14
隊	队	duì	n/m	a row or line of people; column; (measure word for teams and lines)	14
隊員	队员	duìyuán	n	team member	15
對面	对面	duìmiàn	n	opposite side	12
頓	顿	dùn	m	(measure word for meals)	13

E

Traditional	Simplified	Pinyin	Part of Speech	English	Lesson
而		ér	conj	(conjunction to connect two clauses)	10
而已		éryǐ	p	and no more	20
兒童	儿童	értóng	n	children	9

F

Traditional	Simplified	Pinyin	Part of Speech	English	Lesson
發財	发财	fā cái	vo	to get rich; to make a fortune	11
發達	发达	fādá	adj/v	developed; flourishing; to develop	18
發電	发电	fā diàn	vo	to generate electricity	16
發明	发明	fāmíng	n/v	invention; to invent	18
發生	发生	fāshēng	v	to happen; to occur; to take place	6
發展	发展	fāzhǎn	v	to develop	18
法國	法国	Fǎguó	pn	France	12
番		fān	m	(measure word for rounds; measure word for type or kind)	9
翻譯	翻译	fānyì	v/n	to translate; interpreter; translation	7
反對	反对	fǎnduì	v	to oppose	9
方面		fāngmiàn	n	aspect; respect	14
方式		fāngshì	n	way; method	17

Traditional	Simplified	Pinyin	Part of Speech	English	Lesson
房東	房东	fángdōng	n	landlord or landlady	13
放心		fàng xīn	vo	to feel relieved; to be at ease	20
非…不可		fēi…bù kě		have to; nothing but…would do	4
分別		fēnbié	adv/v	separately; respectively; to part from each other	13
分手		fēn shǒu	vo	to break up; to part company	6
分享		fēnxiǎng	v	to share (joy, happiness, benefit, etc.)	13
紛紛	纷纷	fēnfēn	adv	one after another; in succession	19
墳墓	坟墓	fénmù	n	grave; tomb	18
風	风	fēng	n	wind	16
風景	风景	fēngjǐng	n	scenic landscape; scenery	10
風俗	风俗	fēngsú	n	custom	13
風險	风险	fēngxiǎn	n	risk; danger; hazard	17
否則	否则	fǒuzé	conj	otherwise	14
夫妻		fūqī	n	husband and wife; couple	14
夫子廟	夫子庙	Fūzǐmiào	pn	Temple of Confucius	12
福		fú	n	blessing; good fortune	11
服裝	服装	fúzhuāng	n	clothing; apparel	12
負擔	负担	fùdān	n	burden	8
婦女	妇女	fùnǚ	n	women	15

G

Traditional	Simplified	Pinyin	Part of Speech	English	Lesson
改革開放	改革开放	gǎigé kāifàng		to reform and open up; Reform and Opening-Up	15
蓋	盖	gài	v	to build; to construct	12
乾杯	干杯	gān bēi	vo	to drink a toast; cheers!; bottoms up	11
敢		gǎn	mv	to dare	7
感恩節	感恩节	Gǎn'ēnjié	pn	Thanksgiving	11
感覺	感觉	gǎnjué	n/v	feeling; sense perception; to feel; to perceive	7
感情		gǎnqíng	n	feeling; emotion; affection	11
幹嗎	干吗	gànmá	qpr	why; why on earth; whatever for	19
鋼琴	钢琴	gāngqín	n	piano	9
高原		gāoyuán	n	plateau	10
高中		gāozhōng	n	senior high school	6

Traditional	Simplified	Pinyin	Part of Speech	English	Lesson
搞		gǎo	v	to do; to carry on; to be engaged in	20
革命		gémìng	n	revolution	18
各		gè	pr	each; every	3
根本		gēnběn	adv	at all; simply	6
弓		gōng	n	bow	1
供		gōng	v	to provide; to support financially	8
工廠	工厂	gōngchǎng	n	factory	15
工學院	工学院	gōng xuéyuàn	n	school of engineering	5
工資	工资	gōngzī	n	wages; pay	8
宮殿	宫殿	gōngdiàn	n	palace	18
公共場所	公共场所	gōnggòng chǎngsuǒ		public place	16
公平		gōngpíng	adj	fair; just; impartial; equitable	15
恭喜		gōngxǐ	v	to congratulate	11
貢獻	贡献	gòngxiàn	v/n	to contribute; to devote; contribution	18
購物	购物	gòuwù	v	to shop	4
咕嚕	咕噜	gūlū	ono	rumbling sound	12
姑媽	姑妈	gūmā	n	father's sister	12
古老		gǔlǎo	adj	ancient; old	13
股票		gǔpiào	n	stock; share	17
股市		gǔshì	n	stock market	17
故事		gùshi	n	story; tale	13
掛	挂	guà	v	to hang; to hang up	2
乖		guāi	adj	(of children) obedient; well behaved	8
關	关	guān	v	to close; to turn off	13
關係	关系	guānxì	n	relation; relationship; connection	18
關照	关照	guānzhào	v	to take care of; to look after	20
管		guǎn	v	to control; to manage; to mind; to care about	5
管理學院	管理学院	guǎnlǐ xuéyuàn	n	school of management	5
冠軍	冠军	guànjūn	n	champion; first place in a competition	15
廣東	广东	Guǎngdōng	pn	Guangdong (a Chinese province)	3

Traditional	Simplified	Pinyin	Part of Speech	English	Lesson
廣州	广州	Guǎngzhōu	pn	Guangzhou	10
規定	规定	guīdìng	v/n	to regulate; to specify; rules and regulations; provisions	16
歸來	归来	guīlái	v	to return; to come back	19
櫃子	柜子	guìzi	n	cabinet; cupboard	2
國家	国家	guójiā	n	country; nation	16
國外	国外	guówài	n	overseas; abroad	20
過幾天	过几天	guò jǐ tiān		in a few days	2
過節	过节	guò jié	vo	to celebrate a holiday	10

H

Traditional	Simplified	Pinyin	Part of Speech	English	Lesson
哈		hā	ono	(imitating laughter)	6
哈爾濱	哈尔滨	Hā'ěrbīn	pn	Harbin	10
海		hǎi	n	sea; ocean	10
海龜	海龟	hǎiguī	n	sea turtle	19
海外		hǎiwài	n	overseas; abroad	19
海洋		hǎiyáng	n	seas and oceans; the ocean	19
害		hài	v	to cause trouble; to do harm to	7
漢朝	汉朝	Hàncháo	pn	Han Dynasty	18
好處	好处	hǎochu	n	advantage; benefit	1
好看		hǎokàn	adj	nice-looking; attractive	4
好在		hǎozài	adv	fortunately; luckily	19
河		hé	n	river	13
河流		héliú	n	river	10
合		hé	v	to combine; to join	17
合同		hétong	n	agreement; contract	17
盒飯	盒饭	héfàn	pn	box lunch	13
烘乾機	烘干机	hōnggānjī	n	(clothes) dryer	2
紅包	红包	hóngbāo	n	red envelope containing money to be given as a gift	11
後果	后果	hòuguǒ	n	consequence; fallout; aftermath	16
湖南		Húnán	pn	Hunan (a Chinese province)	3
互相		hùxiāng	adv	mutually; each other; reciprocally	15
畫畫兒	画画儿	huà huàr	vo	to draw; to paint	9
化學	化学	huàxué	n	chemistry	5
環境	环境	huánjìng	n	environment; surroundings	11

Traditional	Simplified	Pinyin	Part of Speech	English	Lesson
皇帝		huángdì	n	emperor	18
黃河		Huáng Hé	pn	the Yellow River	10
回		huí	m	(measure word for frequency of an action)	6
回答		huídá	v	to reply; to answer	19
回收		huíshōu	v	to recycle	16
活力		huólì	n	vitality; energy	14
活字印刷		huózì yìnshuā		moveable-type printing; letterpress printing	18
火		huǒ	adj/n	thriving; flourishing; fire; flame	20
火車	火车	huǒchē	n	train	10
火鍋	火锅	huǒguō	n	hotpot	20
火藥	火药	huǒyào	n	gunpowder	18

J

Traditional	Simplified	Pinyin	Part of Speech	English	Lesson
雞	鸡	jī	n	chicken	3
基礎	基础	jīchǔ	n	foundation; basis	18
幾乎	几乎	jīhū	adv	almost	7
機會	机会	jīhuì	n	opportunity	15
急忙		jímáng	adv	hastily; in a hurry	7
即使		jíshǐ	conj	even if	14
集中		jízhōng	v	to concentrate; to be concentrated	10
擠	挤	jǐ	adj/v	crowded; to push against; to squeeze	10
寄		jì	v	to mail	19
記仇	记仇	jì chóu	vo	to bear a grudge; to harbor resentment	6
記載	记载	jìzǎi	v/n	to put down in writing; to record; record; account	18
紀念品	纪念品	jìniànpǐn	n	souvenir; keepsake; memento	13
既然		jìrán	conj	since; as; now that	19
計時	计时	jì shí	vo	to count time	11
技術	技术	jìshù	n	technology; technique	18
繼續	继续	jìxù	v	to continue; to go on with	11
加		jiā	v	to add	4

Traditional	Simplified	Pinyin	Part of Speech	English	Lesson
加班		jiā bān	vo	to work overtime; to work extra shifts	19
加油		jiā yóu	vo	to make an extra effort; to work harder; to refuel	16
家		jiā	m	(measure word for families and commercial establishments such as restaurants, hotels, shops, companies, etc.)	11
家教		jiājiào	n	tutor	8
家庭		jiātíng	n	family (unit); household	8
家務	家务	jiāwù	n	household chores; household duties	15
家鄉	家乡	jiāxiāng	n	hometown	10
家長	家长	jiāzhǎng	n	parents; guardian of a child	9
價格	价格	jiàgé	n	price	7
價錢	价钱	jiàqian	n	price	4
減肥	减肥	jiǎn féi	vo	to lose weight	14
減輕	减轻	jiǎnqīng	v	to lessen	8
減少	减少	jiǎnshǎo	v	to reduce; to decrease; to lessen	16
建立		jiànlì	v	to build; to establish	18
建議	建议	jiànyì	n/v	suggestion; to suggest	5
建築	建筑	jiànzhù	n/v	architecture; to build	12
健身房		jiànshēnfáng	n	fitness center; gym	14
餞行	饯行	jiànxíng	v	to give a farewell dinner	20
將來	将来	jiānglái		future	5
講	讲	jiǎng	v	to speak; to tell	13
獎學金	奖学金	jiǎngxuéjīn	n	scholarship money	8
交		jiāo	v	to hand over	8
交朋友		jiāo péngyou	vo	to make friends	6
交通		jiāotōng	n	transportation; traffic	13
驕傲	骄傲	jiāo'ào	adj/n	proud; arrogant; full of oneself; pride	15
腳步	脚步	jiǎobù	n	footstep	12
叫		jiào	v	to make (someone do something)	6
叫(菜)	叫(菜)	jiào (cài)	v(o)	to order (food)	3
叫做		jiào zuò	vc	to be called; to be known as	19
教授		jiàoshòu	n	professor	5

Traditional	Simplified	Pinyin	Part of Speech	English	Lesson
教育		jiàoyù	n/v	education; to educate	8
街		jiē	n	street	12
接風	接风	jiēfēng	v	to give a welcome dinner for a visitor from afar	20
接近		jiējìn	v	to be close to	10
接受		jiēshòu	v	to accept; to take on; to undertake	20
接著	接着	jiēzhe	v	to follow; to continue	17
結果	结果	jiéguǒ	conj/n	as a result; result	7
結婚	结婚	jié hūn	vo	to get married; to marry	9
結束	结束	jiéshù	v	to end; to finish	11
節日	节日	jiérì	n	holiday; festival	11
節約	节约	jiéyuē	v	to economize; to save; to conserve	16
解決	解决	jiějué	v	to solve; to resolve	5
解釋	解释	jiěshì	v	to explain	19
姐妹		jiěmèi	n	sisters; female friends or co-workers who share a sister-like bond	17
借		jiè	v	to borrow; to lend	8
芥蘭	芥兰	jièlán	n	Chinese broccoli	3
金融		jīnróng	n	finance; banking	5
儘可能	尽可能	jǐn kěnéng		as much as possible	12
進步	进步	jìnbù	v/adj	to make progress; progressive	11
進入	进入	jìnrù	v	to enter; to get into	19
進行	进行	jìnxíng	v	to carry on; to carry out; to conduct	18
經常	经常	jīngcháng	adv	often; frequently	5
經濟	经济	jīngjì	n	economics; economy	5
經理	经理	jīnglǐ	n	manager	19
經驗	经验	jīngyàn	n/v	experience; to experience	5
景點	景点	jǐngdiǎn	n	scenic spot; tourist spot	10
竟(然)		jìng(rán)	adv	unexpectedly; contrary to one's expectation	12
酒		jiǔ	n	alcohol; liquor	11
舊	旧	jiù	adj	(of things) old	2

Traditional	Simplified	Pinyin	Part of Speech	English	Lesson
舅舅		jiùjiu	n	mother's brother; maternal uncle	11
舅媽	舅妈	jiùmā	n	wife of mother's brother	11
舉	举	jǔ	v	to lift; to raise	11
句		jù	m	(measure word for sentences)	6
聚		jù	v	to gather; to get together; to congregate	20
聚會	聚会	jùhuì	v/n	to get together; to congregate; party; get-together; social gathering	20
決定	决定	juédìng	v/n	to decide; decision	5
K					
卡拉OK		kǎlā–OK (ōukēi)		karaoke	7
開朗	开朗	kāilǎng	adj	extroverted; open and sunny in disposition	6
開玩笑	开玩笑	kāi wánxiào	vo	to crack a joke; to joke around	7
開學	开学	kāi xué	vo	to begin a new semester	1
砍		kǎn	v	to cut; to chop	16
看法		kànfǎ	n	point of view	9
考慮	考虑	kǎolǜ	v	to consider	3
科		kē	n	a branch of academic or vocational study	5
科學	科学	kēxué	n/adj	science; scientific; rational	14
柯林		Kē Lín	pn	Ke Lin (a personal name)	1
可見	可见	kějiàn	conj	it is obvious that; it can be seen that	14
可靠		kěkào	adj	dependable	7
可怕		kěpà	adj	awful; terrible; fearful	19
客人		kèren	n	guest; visitor	20
肯定		kěndìng	adv	definitely	5
空		kōng	adj	empty	2
空調	空调	kōngtiáo	n	air conditioning	2
空氣	空气	kōngqì	n	air; atmosphere	16
恐怕		kǒngpà	adv	I'm afraid that; I think perhaps; probably	2
孔子		Kǒngzǐ	pn	Confucius	18

Traditional	Simplified	Pinyin	Part of Speech	English	Lesson
口水		kǒushuǐ	n	saliva	3
口味		kǒuwèi	n	taste; dietary preference	3
跨國	跨国	kuàguó	adj	transnational; multinational	19
快餐		kuàicān	n	fast food; quick meal	12
筷子		kuàizi	n	chopsticks	16
昆明		Kūnmíng	pn	Kunming (capital of Yunnan Province)	13
困難	困难	kùnnan	n/adj	difficulty; difficult	15

L

Traditional	Simplified	Pinyin	Part of Speech	English	Lesson
垃圾		lājī	n	garbage; trash	7
拉		là	v	to leave (something) behind	1
辣		là	adj	spicy	3
來不及		lái bu jí	vc	not have enough time to do something; too late to do something	12
來往	来往	lái wǎng	v	to come and go; to have dealings with	13
浪費	浪费	làngfèi	v/adj	to waste; to squander; wasteful	11
老百姓		lǎobǎixìng	n	common folk; (ordinary) people	12
老年		lǎonián	n	old age	17
老是		lǎoshì	adv	always	7
老太太		lǎotàitai	n	elderly lady	17
老外		lǎowài	n	foreigner	12
李白		Lǐ Bái	pn	Li Bai; Li Po (701–762CE)	18
李文		Lǐ Wén	pn	Li Wen (a personal name)	14
李哲		Lǐ Zhé	pn	Li Zhe (a personal name)	5
理財	理财	lǐcái	vo	to manage money	17
理解		lǐjiě	v	to understand	9
屬害	厉害	lìhai	adj	terrible; formidable	9
麗江	丽江	Lìjiāng	pn	Lijiang	13
麗莎	丽莎	Lìshā	pn	Lisa (a personal name)	3
歷史	历史	lìshǐ	n	history	5
利息		lìxī	n	interest	17
利用		lìyòng	v	to use; to utilize; to take advantage of; to exploit	16

Traditional	Simplified	Pinyin	Part of Speech	English	Lesson
聯繫	联系	liánxì	v/n	to contact; to get in touch; connection; relation	20
良好		liánghǎo	adj	good	8
亮		liàng	adj	bright; light	16
輛	辆	liàng	m	(measure word for vehicles)	1
了解		liǎojiě	v	to understand; to know about; to be informed	10
林雪梅		Lín Xuěméi	pn	Lin Xuemei (a personal name)	3
零食		língshí	n	snacks; nibbles	19
零用錢	零用钱	língyòngqián	n	allowance; spending money	8
領導	领导	lǐngdǎo	v/n	to lead; to exercise leadership; leadership; leader	18
流		liú	v	to flow	3
流		liú		class; level; rank; category	20
留(下)		liú (xia)	v(c)	to leave behind; to stay behind	13
留學	留学	liú xué	vo	to study abroad	9
留學生	留学生	liúxuéshēng	n	student studying abroad	3
路綫	路线	lùxiàn	n	route; itinerary	10
錄用	录用	lùyòng	v	to take someone on staff; to employ	19
旅客		lǚkè	n	passenger; voyager; traveler	13
旅遊	旅游	lǚyóu	v/n	to travel; travel	10
落伍	落伍	luòwǔ	v	to lag behind; to be outdated	7

M

Traditional	Simplified	Pinyin	Part of Speech	English	Lesson
麻將	麻将	májiàng	n	mahjong	17
馬虎	马虎	mǎhu	adj	careless; perfunctory; mediocre	6
馬克	马克	Mǎkè	pn	Mark	16
馬路	马路	mǎlù	n	road	2
嘛		ma	p	(particle used to emphasize the obvious)	11
滿	满	mǎn	adj	full	9
滿意	满意	mǎnyì	v	to be satisfied; to be pleased	19
矛盾		máodùn	n/adj	contradiction; contradictory; conflicting	17
毛巾		máojīn	n	towel	4
毛衣		máoyī	n	woolen sweater	4

Traditional	Simplified	Pinyin	Part of Speech	English	Lesson
貿易	贸易	màoyì	n	trade	18
煤		méi	n	coal	16
美		měi	adj	beautiful; good	13
美麗	美丽	měilì	adj	beautiful	13
美滿	美满	měimǎn	adj	happy and satisfying	9
門	门	mén	m	(measure word for academic courses)	5
門	门	mén	n	door	2
門口	门口	ménkǒu	n	doorway; entrance	3
門票	门票	ménpiào	n	admission ticket; admission fee	13
迷		mí	n/v	fan; to be infatuated with	6
免費	免费	miǎnfèi	v	to be free of charge	7
麵	面	miàn	n	noodles	13
面積	面积	miànjī	n	area	10
面熟		miànshú	adj	familiar-looking	20
民以食為天	民以食为天	mín yǐ shí wéi tiān		the people think of food as important as heaven	12
民族		mínzú	n	ethnic group; people; nationality	10
名牌(兒)	名牌(儿)	míngpái(r)	n	famous brand; name brand	4
模範	模范	mófàn	adj/n	exemplary; model; fine example	15
末		mò	n	end	12
陌生		mòshēng	adj	unfamiliar; strange; unknown	12
墨西哥		Mòxīgē	pn	Mexico	9
某		mǒu	pr	certain; some; an indefinite person or thing	15

N

Traditional	Simplified	Pinyin	Part of Speech	English	Lesson
難吃	难吃	nánchī	adj	not tasty	8
難道	难道	nándào	adv	Do you mean to say…	4
難怪	难怪	nánguài	adv	no wonder	6
難過	难过	nánguò	adj	sad; hard to bear	12
南京		Nánjīng	pn	Nanjing	10
男子		nánzǐ	n	man; male	15
鬧	闹	nào	v/adj	to suffer from; to be troubled by; to make a noise; noisy	16
鬧彆扭	闹别扭	nào bièniu	vo	to have a small conflict; to be at odds (with someone)	6

Traditional	Simplified	Pinyin	Part of Speech	English	Lesson
嫩		nèn	adj	tender	3
能力		nénglì	n	ability; capacity; competence	19
能源		néngyuán	n	energy; energy source	16
年輕	年轻	niánqīng	adj	young	20
年夜饭	年夜饭	niányèfàn	n	Chinese New Year's Eve dinner	11
牛仔裤	牛仔裤	niúzǎikù	n	jeans	4
農村	农村	nóngcūn	n	countryside; village; rural area	8
農曆	农历	nónglì	n	traditional Chinese lunar calendar; lit. "agricultural calendar"	11
女性		nǚxìng	n	female gender; woman	15
暖氣	暖气	nuǎnqì	n	heating	16

O

Traditional	Simplified	Pinyin	Part of Speech	English	Lesson
噢	噢	ō	interj	oh!	6
歐洲	欧洲	Ōuzhōu	pn	Europe	20
偶爾	偶尔	ǒu'ěr	adv	occasionally	14

P

Traditional	Simplified	Pinyin	Part of Speech	English	Lesson
爬山		pá shān	vo	to hike in the mountains; to climb mountains	16
拍		pāi	v	to take pictures; to shoot film; to clap; to pat	12
排		pái	v/n/m	to line up; row; line; (measure word for rows)	14
牌子		páizi	n	brand	4
陪		péi	v	to accompany	6
賠	赔	péi	v	to lose (money, etc.); to suffer a loss in a deal	17
碰見	碰见	pèng jiàn	vc	to bump into; to run into	5
貧	贫	pín	adj	gabby; glib	4
乒乓球		pīngpāngqiú	n	Ping-Pong; table tennis	15
平等		píngděng	adj/n	equal; equality	15
平原		píngyuán	n	plain	10
瓶裝水	瓶装水	píngzhuāng shuǐ		bottled water	16

Traditional	Simplified	Pinyin	Part of Speech	English	Lesson
Q					
妻管嚴	妻管严	qī guǎn yán		wife controls (her husband) strictly	15
妻子		qīzi	n	wife	15
騎	骑	qí	v	to ride	12
奇怪		qíguài	adj	strange; odd	11
旗袍		qípáo	n	chi-pao; mandarin gown	19
其實	其实	qíshí	adv	actually	5
其他		qítā	pr	other; else	5
其中		qízhōng		among which/whom; in which/whom; of which/whom	18
企業	企业	qǐyè	n	enterprise; business; company; firm	15
氣氛	气氛	qìfēn	n	atmosphere; ambiance	11
氣管炎	气管炎	qìguǎnyán	n	tracheitis	15
簽	签	qiān	v	to sign; to autograph	17
千千萬萬	千千万万	qiān qiān wàn wàn		thousands upon thousands	18
千萬	千万	qiānwàn	adv	by all means; absolutely must	13
欠		qiàn	v	to owe	8
牆	墙	qiáng	n	wall	11
親眼	亲眼	qīnyǎn	adv	(to see) with one's own eyes	13
秦朝		Qíncháo	pn	Qin Dynasty	18
秦始皇		Qínshǐhuáng	pn	First Emperor of the Qin Dynasty	18
清朝		Qīngcháo	pn	Qing Dynasty	18
清淡		qīngdàn	adj	light in flavor	3
清蒸	清蒸	qīngzhēng	v	to steam (food without heavy sauce)	3
輕鬆	轻松	qīngsōng	adj	light; relaxed	5
晴		qíng	adj	sunny	19
情況	情况	qíngkuàng	n	situation; condition; circumstances	15
慶祝	庆祝	qìngzhù	v	to celebrate	20
取得		qǔdé	v	to obtain; to gain; to acquire	8
取之不盡	取之不尽	qǔ zhī bú jìn		(of resources) inexhaustible	16

Traditional	Simplified	Pinyin	Part of Speech	English	Lesson
圈		quān	n/v	circle; to encircle; to mark with a circle	14
全		quán	adj/adv	entire; whole; complete; completely	16
勸	劝	quàn	v	to persuade; to advise; to urge	17
缺點	缺点	quēdiǎn	n	shortcoming; defect; weakness	19
R					
熱鬧	热闹	rènao	adj	(of a place or a scene) lively; buzzing with excitement; bustling with activity	11
熱水器	热水器	rèshuǐqì	n	water heater	20
人材		réncái	n	person of ability, integrity, and talent	9
人口		rénkǒu	n	population	10
人山人海		rén shān rén hǎi		huge crowds of people	10
認為	认为	rènwéi	v	to think; to consider	9
扔		rēng	v	to throw; to toss; to throw away	16
日用品		rìyòngpǐn	n	daily household necessities	2
融入		róngrù	v	to merge into; to meld into	12
軟	软	ruǎn	adj	soft	13
軟件	软件	ruǎnjiàn	n	software	7
S					
散步		sàn bù	vo	to take a walk; to go for a walk	14
嫂子		sǎozi	n	older brother's wife	9
殺	杀	shā	v	to kill	18
沙漠	沙漠	shāmò	n	desert	10
廈	厦	shà		mansion; tall building	12
山		shān	n	mountain; hill	10
善於	善于	shànyú		be good at; be adept in	19
上班		shàng bān	vo	to go to work; to start work; to be on duty	12
上衣		shàngyī	n	upper outer garment; jacket	19
上癮	上瘾	shàng yǐn	vo	to become addicted	7
燒	烧	shāo	v	to burn; to set fire to; to cook	18
少數	少数	shǎoshù	n	small number; few; minority	10

Traditional	Simplified	Pinyin	Part of Speech	English	Lesson
社會	社会	shèhuì	n	society	9
設計	设计	shèjì	v/n	to design; design	9
攝氏	摄氏	Shèshì	pn	Celsius; centigrade	16
深		shēn	adj	profound; deep; dark (color); intimate (of relations or feelings)	13
身材		shēncái	n	stature; figure	14
申請	申请	shēnqǐng	v	to apply (to a school or job)	5
深圳		Shēnzhèn	pn	Shenzhen	10
甚至		shènzhì	adv	even	7
生		shēng	v	to give birth to; to be born	8
生活		shēnghuó	n/v	life; livelihood; to live	1
生氣	生气	shēng qì	vo	to get angry	6
聲音	声音	shēngyīn	n	sound; voice	12
省		shěng	n	province	10
省吃儉用	省吃俭用	shěng chī jiǎn yòng		to be frugal [with food and other living expenses]	17
省會	省会	shěnghuì	n	provincial capital	13
省錢	省钱	shěng qián	vo	to save money; to economize	1
省下來	省下来	shěng xia lai	vc	to save (money, time)	5
剩(下)		shèng (xia)	v(c)	to leave a surplus; to be left (over)	11
剩餘	剩余	shèngyú	v/n	to be left over; surplus	17
濕	湿	shī	adj	wet	19
詩	诗	shī	n	poetry; poem	18
詩人	诗人	shīrén	n	poet	18
時代	时代	shídài	n	era; age	7
時髦	时髦	shímáo	adj	fashionable; stylish	4
十分		shífēn	adv	very	6
實際上	实际上	shíjìshang	adv	in fact; in reality; actually	6
石林		Shílín	pn	The Stone Forest	13
石頭	石头	shítou	n	stone; rock; pebble	13
石油		shíyóu	n	petroleum; oil	16
使		shǐ	v	to make; to cause; to have someone do something	14
市場	市场	shìchǎng	n	market	15
世紀	世纪	shìjì	n	century	19

Traditional	Simplified	Pinyin	Part of Speech	English	Lesson
世界		shìjiè	n	world	5
事情		shìqing	n	thing; matter	8
事業事业		shìyè	n	career; undertaking	9
適合	适合	shìhé	v	to suit	8
適應	适应	shìyìng	v	to adapt; to become accustomed to	1
收入		shōurù	n	income	8
受不了		shòu bu liǎo	vc	cannot take it; unable to bear	5
受到		shòu dào	vc	to receive	8
輸	输	shū	v	to lose; to be defeated	15
書本	书本	shūběn	n	books	9
熟悉		shúxi	v/adj	to know something or someone well; to be familiar with; familiar	12
樹	树	shù	n	tree	14
樹林	树林	shùlín	n	woods; forest	13
數字	数字	shùzì	n	numeral; figure; digit	5
稅		shuì	n	tax	4
睡眠		shuìmián	n	sleep	14
順利	顺利	shùnlì	adj	smooth; successful; without a hitch	11
說不定	说不定	shuōbudìng	adv	perhaps; maybe	6
說服	说服	shuōfú	v	to persuade; to convince	17
碩士	硕士	shuòshì	n	master's degree	9
絲綢	丝绸	sīchóu	n	silk; silk fabric	18
思考		sīkǎo	v/n	to think deeply; to ponder over; contemplation; cogitation	17
思想		sīxiǎng	n	thinking; ideology; thoughts	18
四川		Sìchuān	pn	Sichuan (a Chinese province)	3
四季如春		sìjì rú chūn		spring-like all year around	10
宋朝		Sòngcháo	pn	Song Dynasty	18
塑料袋		sùliào dài		plastic bag	16
算		suàn	v	to count as; to be considered as	17
隨便	随便	suíbiàn	adj/vo	casual; careless; to do as one pleases	14
隨手	随手	suíshǒu	adv	without extra effort or motion; conveniently	16

Traditional	Simplified	Pinyin	Part of Speech	English	Lesson
孫女	孙女	sūnnü	n	son's daughter; granddaughter	17
孫中山	孙中山	Sūn Zhōngshān	pn	Sun Yat-sen	18
孫子	孙子	sūnzi	n	son's son; grandson	17
T					
塔	塔	tǎ	n	tower; pagoda-shaped structure	13
台		tái	m	(measure word for machines)	2
態度	态度	tàidu	n	attitude	6
太極拳	太极拳	tàijíquán	n	tai chi; a form of traditional Chinese shadow boxing	14
太陽	太阳	tàiyáng	n	sun	16
太陽能	太阳能	tàiyángnéng	n	solar energy; solar power	16
談	谈	tán	v	to talk; to discuss	5
毯子		tǎnzi	n	blanket	2
唐朝		Tángcháo	pn	Tang Dynasty	18
討論	讨论	tǎolùn	v	to discuss	5
討厭	讨厌	tǎoyàn	v/adj	to dislike; to loathe; disgusting; disagreeable	15
套裝	套装	tàozhuāng	n	suit; a set of matching outer garments	19
特色		tèsè	n	distinguishing feature or quality; characteristic	12
提		tí	v	to mention; to bring up	6
體貼	体贴	tǐtiē	v	to care for; to be considerate of (someone)	15
T恤衫		tīxùshān	n	t-shirt	4
天津		Tiānjīn	pn	Tianjin	10
條件	条件	tiáojiàn	n	condition; requirement	10
貼	贴	tiē	v	to paste; to glue	11
通知		tōngzhī	n/v	notice; to notify; to inform	19
同工同酬		tóng gōng tóng chóu		equal pay for equal work	15
同事		tóngshì	n	colleague; co-worker	20
同屋		tóngwū	n	roommate	2
同意		tóngyì	v	to agree	4
童年		tóngnián	n	childhood	9

Traditional	Simplified	Pinyin	Part of Speech	English	Lesson
筒		tǒng	n	thick tube-shaped object	16
統一	统一	tǒngyī	v/adj	to unify; to unite; unified; centralized	18
投資	投资	tóuzī	v/n	to invest (money); (financial) investment	17
突然		tūrán	adj	sudden; unexpected	17
團	团	tuán	n	group; organization	13
團圓	团圆	tuányuán	v	to reunite (as a family)	11
推		tuī	v	to push; to shove	16
推銷	推销	tuīxiāo	v	to market; to promote the sale (of goods/merchandise)	20
退休		tuìxiū	v	to retire	14

W

Traditional	Simplified	Pinyin	Part of Speech	English	Lesson
外賣	外卖	wàimài	n	takeout	7
完全		wánquán	adv/adj	completely; fully; complete; whole	9
晚會	晚会	wǎnhuì	n	evening gathering; soiree	11
網絡	网络	wǎngluò	n	network; internet	7
網站	网站	wǎngzhàn	n	website	7
往往		wǎngwǎng	adv	more often than not	19
望女成鳳	望女成凤	wàng nǚ chéng fèng		to hope that one's daughter will become a phoenix; to hope that one's daughter will become successful	9
望子成龍	望子成龙	wàng zǐ chéng lóng		to hope that one's son will become a dragon; to hope that one's son will become successful	9
危機	危机	wēijī	n	crisis	16
偉大	伟大	wěidà	adj	great; outstanding; magnificent	18
緯度	纬度	wěidù	n	latitude	10
味道		wèidao	n	taste; flavor	3
未婚妻		wèihūnqī	n	fiancée	17
衛生紙	卫生纸	wèishēngzhǐ	n	toilet paper	4
溫度		wēndù	n	temperature	16
文具		wénjù	n	stationery; writing supplies	2
文明		wénmíng	n/adj	civilization; civilized	18

Traditional	Simplified	Pinyin	Part of Speech	English	Lesson
文學	文学	wénxué	n	literature	5
文章		wénzhāng	n	essay; article	5
文字		wénzì	n	characters; written form of a language	18
穩定	稳定	wěndìng	adj/v	stable; steady; to stabilize; to be steady	20
臥鋪	卧铺	wòpù	n	sleeping berth or bunk on a train	13
握手		wò shǒu	vo	to shake hands; to clasp hands	19
污染		wūrǎn	v/n	to pollute; to contaminate; pollution; contamination	16
屋子		wūzi	n	room	7
無論	无论	wúlùn	conj	regardless of…; whether it be…	4
物美價廉	物美价廉	wù měi jià lián		attractive goods at inexpensive prices	4

X

Traditional	Simplified	Pinyin	Part of Speech	English	Lesson
西方		Xīfāng	pn	the West	18
吸煙	吸烟	xī yān	vo	to smoke a cigarette	14
吸引		xīyǐn	v	to attract; to draw; to fascinate	19
習慣	习惯	xíguàn	n/v	habit; to be accustomed to	13
洗		xǐ	v	to wash	2
洗衣粉		xǐyīfěn	n	laundry powder	4
洗衣機	洗衣机	xǐyījī	n	washing machine	2
系		xì	n	department (of a college or university)	5
嚇人	吓人	xiàrén	adj	scary; frightening	19
下載	下载	xiàzài	v	to download	7
先進	先进	xiānjìn	adj	advanced	18
鹹	咸	xián	adj	salty	3
嫌		xián	v	to dislike; to mind; to complain of	8
顯得	显得	xiǎnde	v	to appear (to be); to seem	14
現金	现金	xiànjīn	n	cash	4
現象	现象	xiànxiàng	n	phenomenon; appearance	15
香		xiāng	adj	fragrant; pleasant-smelling	3
相處	相处	xiāngchǔ	v	to get along	6
相信		xiāngxìn	v	to believe; to trust	15

Traditional	Simplified	Pinyin	Part of Speech	English	Lesson
想法		xiǎngfǎ	n	idea; opinion	17
想像		xiǎngxiàng	v/n	to imagine; to visualize; imagination	12
享受		xiǎngshòu	v/n	to enjoy; enjoyment; pleasure	17
像		xiàng	v	such as	4
消費	消费	xiāofèi	v	to consume	17
消息		xiāoxi	n	news; message; information	15
銷售	销售	xiāoshòu	v	to sell; to market	19
小吃		xiǎochī	n	small and inexpensive dishes; snacks	12
小區	小区	xiǎoqū	n	residential district; residential complex	11
小學	小学	xiǎoxué	n	elementary school; grade school	9
校內		xiào nèi		on campus	1
校外		xiào wài		off campus	1
校友		xiàoyǒu	n	schoolfellow; alumni	20
心		xīn	n	heart; mind	6
新疆		Xīnjiāng	pn	Xinjiang	10
新生		xīnshēng	n	new student	1
辛苦		xīnkǔ	adj/v	hard; strenuous; toilsome; laborious; to work hard; to go to trouble	17
心情		xīnqíng	n	mood	6
心事		xīnshì	n	something weighing on one's mind	6
薪水	薪水	xīnshuǐ	n	salary; pay; wages	15
新聞	新闻	xīnwén	n	news	7
新鮮	新鲜	xīnxian	adj	fresh	3
幸福		xìngfú	adj/n	happy; happiness	11
性格		xìnggé	n	personality; character	6
熊貓	熊猫	xióngmāo	n	panda	14
修		xiū	v	to build; to repair; to mend; to fix	18
需要		xūyào	v/n	to need; needs	4
選	选	xuǎn	v	to choose	5
選擇	选择	xuǎnzé	n/v	choice; to choose	9
學分	学分	xuéfēn	n	academic credit	5

Traditional	Simplified	Pinyin	Part of Speech	English	Lesson
學位	学位	xuéwèi	n	(academic) degree	5
學有所成	学有所成	xué yǒu suǒ chéng		to have achieved academic success	19
學院	学院	xuéyuàn	n	college; academy; institute	18
Y					
壓力	压力	yālì	n	pressure	8
牙膏		yágāo	n	toothpaste	4
沿海		yánhǎi	n	along the coast	10
研究		yánjiū	v/n	to study; to look into; research	10
研究生		yánjiūshēng	n	graduate student	1
嚴肅	严肃	yánsù	adj	stern; serious	19
嚴重	严重	yánzhòng	adj	serious; grave	7
演唱會	演唱会	yǎnchànghuì	n	vocal concert	6
演員	演员	yǎnyuán	n	actor; actress; performer	20
要不是		yàobúshì	conj	if it were not for; but for	12
要麼…	要么…	yàome…	conj	if it's not…, it's…; either…or…	5
要麼…	要么…	yàome…			
鑰匙	钥匙	yàoshi	n	key	6
一般		(yībān) yìbān	adv	generally	2
一次性		(yīcìxìng) yícìxìng	adj	one-time	16
一帶	一带	(yīdài) yídài	n	the area around a particular place; the neighboring area	10
一乾二淨	一干二净	(yī gān èr jìng) yì gān èr jìng		completely; thoroughly	6
一會兒	一会儿	(yīhuìr) yíhuìr	nm	in a moment; a little while	4
一向		(yīxiàng) yíxiàng	adv	all along; the whole time; constantly	17
衣櫃	衣柜	yīguì	n	wardrobe	2
衣食住行		yī shí zhù xíng		food, clothing, shelter and transportation; basic necessities of life	7
移民		yímín	n/v	immigrant; to immigrate	9
以		yǐ	prep	with	11
以來	以来	yǐlái	t	since	15

Traditional	Simplified	Pinyin	Part of Speech	English	Lesson
意大利		Yìdàlì	pn	Italy	15
意見	意见	yìjiàn	n	opinion	5
意思		yìsi	n	meaning	11
陰	阴	yīn	adj	overcast; hidden from the sun	19
因此		yīncǐ	conj	so; therefore; for this reason; consequently	19
銀行	银行	yínháng	n	bank	8
引起		yǐnqǐ	v	to give rise to; to lead to	17
飲食	饮食	yǐnshí	n	diet; food and drink	13
英語	英语	Yīngyǔ	pn	English language	8
贏	赢	yíng	v	to win	15
營養	营养	yíngyǎng	n	nutrition; nourishment	14
影響	影响	yǐngxiǎng	v/n	to influence; to have an impact; influence	8
硬		yìng	adj	hard	13
擁抱	拥抱	yōngbào	v	to embrace; to hug	13
永遠	永远	yǒngyuǎn	adv	always; forever	20
優點	优点	yōudiǎn	n	merit; strong point; advantage	19
優秀	优秀	yōuxiù	adj	outstanding; excellent	19
幽默		yōumò	adj	humorous	13
由		yóu	prep	by	15
油		yóu	n/adj	oil; oily	3
遊客	游客	yóukè	n	tourist	12
遊覽	游览	yóulǎn	v/n	to go sightseeing; to tour; excursion	13
遊戲	游戏	yóuxì	n	game	7
友誼	友谊	yǒuyì	n	friendship; companionship; fellowship	20
有益		yǒuyì	adj	beneficial; useful	16
有用		yǒuyòng	adj	useful	7
餘	余	yú	v	to surplus; to spare	11
於	于	yú	prep	towards; in; on; at; (indicating comparison)	16
於是	于是	yúshì	conj	so; therefore; thereupon	4
瑜伽		yújiā	n	yoga	14
與	与	yǔ	conj/prep	and; with	14

Traditional	Simplified	Pinyin	Part of Speech	English	Lesson
鬱悶	郁闷	yùmèn	adj	gloomy; depressed	17
原來	原来	yuánlái	adv/adj	as a matter of fact; original; former	6
元宵		yuánxiāo	n	night of the fifteenth of the first lunar month; sweet dumplings made of glutinous rice flour	11
元宵節	元宵节	Yuánxiāojié	pn	Lantern Festival	11
月餅	月饼	yuèbǐng	n	moon cake	11
雲	云	yún	n	cloud	19
雲南	云南	Yúnnán	pn	Yunnan	10

Z

Traditional	Simplified	Pinyin	Part of Speech	English	Lesson
雜誌	杂志	zázhì	n	magazine	7
在乎		zàihu	v	to mind; to care	4
咱們	咱们	zánmen	pr	we; us	4
攢	攢	zǎn	v	to accumulate; to hoard, to save; to scrape together	17
贊成	赞成	zànchéng	v	to approve	16
早晨		zǎochen	n	morning; early morning	14
造成		zào chéng	vc	to cause; to give rise to	16
造紙	造纸	zào zhǐ	vo	to make paper	18
增加		zēngjiā	v	to increase; to add	17
展廳	展厅	zhǎntīng	n	exhibition hall; gallery	18
站		zhàn	n/v	station; stop; to stand	12
張天明	张天明	Zhāng Tiānmíng	pn	Zhang Tianming (a personal name)	1
漲	涨	zhǎng	v	(of water, prices, etc.) to rise; to surge; to go up	17
丈夫		zhàngfu	n	husband	15
哲學	哲学	zhéxué	n	philosophy	5
者		zhě		-er; -ist	20
着急		zháojí	v	to worry	2
真的		zhēn de		really; truly	2
真心		zhēnxīn	n	sincere; wholehearted	6
枕頭	枕头	zhěntou	n	pillow	13
正月		zhēngyuè	n	first month of the lunar year; first moon	11

Traditional	Simplified	Pinyin	Part of Speech	English	Lesson
整天		zhěng tiān		all day long	5
政府		zhèngfǔ	n	government	8
正好		zhènghǎo	adv	coincidentally	3
正式		zhèngshì	adj	formal	7
掙錢	挣钱	zhèng qián	vo	to earn money; to make money	8
隻	只	zhī	m	(measure word for one of certain paired things and some animals)	14
之		zhī	p	(literary counterpart of 的)	13
之間	之间	zhī jiān		between; among	6
知識	知识	zhīshi	n	knowledge	9
知音		zhīyīn	n	someone who truly understands; soulmate	9
值(得)		zhí (de)	v	worthy; worthwhile	20
侄女		zhínǚ	n	brother's daughter	9
職業	职业	zhíyè	n	occupation; profession; vocation	15
指導	指导	zhǐdǎo	v/n	to guide; guidance	5
指南針	指南针	zhǐnánzhēn	n	compass	18
只好		zhǐhǎo	adv	to be forced to; to have no choice but	4
只要		zhǐyào	conj	only if; as long as	14
質量	质量	zhìliàng	n	quality	4
至於	至于	zhìyú	prep	as for; as to	5
中		zhòng	v	to fit exactly; to hit	17
中華民國	中华民国	Zhōnghuá Mínguó	pn	Republic of China	18
中秋節	中秋节	Zhōngqiūjié	pn	Mid-Autumn Festival; Moon Festival	11
終於	终于	zhōngyú	adv	at last; in the end; finally; eventually	17
重男輕女	重男轻女	zhòng nán qīng nǚ		to regard males as superior to females; to privilege men over women	15
重視	重视	zhòngshì	v	to attach importance to; to think much of	14
重要		zhòngyào	adj	important	7
眾人	众人	zhòngrén	n	everybody; the crowd	20
週	周	zhōu	n	week	20

Traditional	Simplified	Pinyin	Part of Speech	English	Lesson
逐漸	逐渐	zhújiàn	adv	gradually; little by little	15
主要		zhǔyào	adj	main; principal	10
主意		(zhǔyi) zhúyi	n	idea	3
注意		zhùyì	v/n	to pay attention to; attention	14
轉	转	zhuǎn	v	to turn; to shift; to change	19
賺錢	赚钱	zhuàn qián	vo	make money	5
資料	资料	zīliào	n	material	7
自然		zìrán	n/adj	nature; natural	10
自行車	自行车	zìxíngchē	n	bicycle	12
自由		zìyóu	adj	free; unconstrained	1
總	总	zǒng	adj	general; chief	19
總	总	zǒng	adv	always	12
總之	总之	zǒngzhī	conj	in short; in brief	7
粽子		zòngzi	n	pyramid-shaped dumplings of glutinous rice wrapped in bamboo or reed leaves	11
尊重		zūnzhòng	v	to respect	9
座		zuò	m	(measure word for buildings and mountains)	12
做法		zuòfǎ	n	way of doing things; course of action	9

Vocabulary Index (English-Chinese)

Proper nouns are shown in green.

English	Traditional	Simplified	Pinyin	Part of Speech	Lesson
A					
ability; capacity; competence	能力		nénglì	n	19
academic credit	學分	学分	xuéfēn	n	5
(academic) degree	學位	学位	xuéwèi	n	5
accept; take on; undertake	接受		jiēshòu	v	20
accompany	陪		péi	v	6
accumulate; hoard, save; scrape together	攢	攒	zǎn	v	17
actor; actress; performer	演員	演员	yǎnyuán	n	20
actually	並	并	bìng	adv	9
actually	其實	其实	qíshí	adv	5
adapt; become accustomed to	適應	适应	shìyìng	v	1
add	加		jiā	v	4
admission ticket; admission fee	門票	门票	ménpiào	n	13
adult	大人		dàren	n	8
advanced	先進	先进	xiānjìn	adj	18
advantage; benefit	好處	好处	hǎochu	n	1
after all; all in all; in the final analysis; when all is said and done	畢竟	毕竟	bìjìng	adv	15
agree	同意		tóngyì	v	4
agree (to do something); promise; to answer	答應	答应	dāying	v	6
agreement; contract	合同		hétong	n	17
air; atmosphere	空氣	空气	kōngqì	n	16
air conditioning	空調	空调	kōngtiáo	n	2
alcohol; liquor	酒		jiǔ	n	11
all along; the whole time; constantly	一向		(yīxiàng) yíxiàng	adv	17
all around; all over	到處	到处	dàochù	adv	10
all day long	整天		zhěng tiān		5

English	Traditional	Simplified	Pinyin	Part of Speech	Lesson
allowance; spending money	零用錢	零用钱	língyòngqián	n	8
almost	幾乎	几乎	jīhū	adv	7
along the coast	沿海		yánhǎi	n	10
always	老是		lǎoshì	adv	7
always	總	总	zǒng	adv	12
always; forever	永遠	永远	yǒngyuǎn	adv	20
among which/whom; in which/whom; of which/whom	其中		qízhōng		18
ancient; old	古老		gǔlǎo	adj	13
and no more	而已		éryǐ	p	20
and so forth; etc.	等		děng	p	14
and; with	與	与	yǔ	conj/ prep	14
apologize	道歉		dào qiàn	vo	6
appear (to be); seem	顯得	显得	xiǎnde	v	14
appear; arise; emerge	出現	出现	chūxiàn	v	15
apply (to a school or job)	申請	申请	shēnqǐng	v	5
approve	贊成	赞成	zànchéng	v	16
architecture; to build	建築	建筑	jiànzhù	n/v	12
area	面積	面积	miànjī	n	10
area around a particular place; the neighboring area	一帶	一带	(yīdài) yídài	n	10
arrange	安排		ānpái	v	9
arrive late	遲到	迟到	chídào	v	7
as a matter of fact; original; former	原來	原来	yuánlái	adv/adj	6
as a result; result	結果	结果	jiéguǒ	conj/n	7
as for; as to	至於	至于	zhìyú	prep	5
as much as possible	儘可能	尽可能	jǐn kěnéng		12
aspect; respect	方面		fāngmiàn	n	14
at all; simply	根本		gēnběn	adv	6
at last; in the end; finally; eventually	終於	终于	zhōngyú	adv	17
atmosphere; ambiance	氣氛	气氛	qìfēn	n	11
attach importance to; think much of	重視	重视	zhòngshì	v	14

English	Traditional	Simplified	Pinyin	Part of Speech	Lesson
attend school; study; read aloud	讀書	读书	dú shū	vo	8
attitude	態度	态度	tàidu	n	6
attract; draw; fascinate	吸引		xīyǐn	v	19
attractive goods at inexpensive prices	物美價廉	物美价廉	wù měi jià lián		4
authentic; genuine; pure	地道		dìdao	adj	2
awful; terrible; fearful	可怕		kěpà	adj	19

B

English	Traditional	Simplified	Pinyin	Part of Speech	Lesson
background	背景		bèijǐng	n	6
bank	銀行	银行	yínháng	n	8
bank savings	存款		cúnkuǎn	n	17
be away on official business or on a business trip	出差		chū chāi	vo	20
be born	出生		chūshēng	v	1
be called; be known as	叫做		jiào zuò	vc	19
be close to	接近		jiējìn	v	10
be forced to; have no choice but	只好		zhǐhǎo	adv	4
be free of charge	免費	免费	miǎnfèi	v	7
be frugal [with food and other living expenses]	省吃儉用	省吃俭用	shěng chī jiǎn yòng		17
be good at; be adept in	善於	善于	shànyú		19
be left over; surplus	剩餘	剩余	shèngyú	v/n	17
be satisfied; be pleased	滿意	满意	mǎnyì	v	19
bear a grudge; harbor resentment	記仇	记仇	jì chóu	vo	6
beautiful	美麗	美丽	měilì	adj	13
beautiful; good	美		měi	adj	13
become addicted	上癮	上瘾	shàng yǐn	vo	7
become; turn into	成為	成为	chéngwéi	v	14
begin a new semester	開學	开学	kāi xué	vo	1
believe; trust	相信		xiāngxìn	v	15
beneficial; useful	有益		yǒuyì	adj	16
between; among	之間	之间	zhī jiān		6
bicycle	自行車	自行车	zìxíngchē	n	12

English	Traditional	Simplified	Pinyin	Part of Speech	Lesson
blanket	毯子		tǎnzi	n	2
blessing; good fortune	福		fú	n	11
blog	博客		bókè	n	7
boat; ship	船		chuán	n	10
books	書本	书本	shūběn	n	9
borrow; lend	借		jiè	v	8
bottled water	瓶裝水	瓶装水	píngzhuāng shuǐ		16
bow	弓		gōng	n	1
box lunch	盒飯	盒饭	héfàn	n	13
branch of academic or vocational study	科		kē	n	5
brand	牌子		páizi	n	4
Brazil	巴西		Bāxī	pn	15
break up; part company	分手		fēn shǒu	vo	6
bright; light	亮		liàng	adj	16
brother's daughter	侄女		zhínǚ	n	9
build; construct	蓋	盖	gài	v	12
build; establish	建立		jiànlì	v	18
build; repair; mend; fix	修		xiū	v	18
bump into; run into	碰見	碰见	pèng jiàn	vc	5
burden	負擔	负担	fùdān	n	8
burn; set fire to; cook	燒	烧	shāo	v	18
by	由		yóu	prep	15
by all means; absolutely must	千萬	千万	qiānwàn	adv	13

C

English	Traditional	Simplified	Pinyin	Part of Speech	Lesson
cabinet; cupboard	櫃子	柜子	guìzi	n	2
cannot take it; unable to bear	受不了		shòu bu liǎo	vc	5
care for; be considerate of (someone)	體貼	体贴	tǐtiē	v	15
career; undertaking	事業	事业	shìyè	n	9
careless; perfunctory; mediocre	馬虎	马虎	mǎhu	adj	6
carry on; carry out; conduct	進行	进行	jìnxíng	v	18
cash	現金	现金	xiànjīn	n	4
casual; careless; to do as one pleases	隨便	随便	suíbiàn	adj/vo	14

English	Traditional	Simplified	Pinyin	Part of Speech	Lesson
cause trouble; do harm to	害		hài	v	7
cause; give rise to	造成		zào chéng	vc	16
celebrate	慶祝	庆祝	qìngzhù	v	20
celebrate a holiday	過節	过节	guò jié	vo	10
Celsius; centigrade	攝氏	摄氏	Shèshì	pn	16
century	世紀	世纪	shìjì	n	19
certain; some; an indefinite person or thing	某		mǒu	pr	15
champion; first place in a competition	冠軍	冠军	guànjūn	n	15
change	變	变	biàn	v	12
change; to change	變化	变化	biànhuà	n/v	12
characters; written form of a language	文字		wénzì	n	18
chemistry	化學	化学	huàxué	n	5
chicken	雞	鸡	jī	n	3
childhood	童年		tóngnián	n	9
children	兒童	儿童	értóng	n	9
Chinese broccoli	芥蘭	芥兰	jièlán	n	3
Chinese New Year's Eve	除夕		chúxī	n	11
Chinese New Year's Eve dinner	年夜飯	年夜饭	niányèfàn	n	11
chi-pao; mandarin gown	旗袍		qípáo	n	19
choice; to choose	選擇	选择	xuǎnzé	n/v	9
choose	選	选	xuǎn	v	5
chopsticks	筷子		kuàizi	n	16
circle; to encircle; to mark with a circle	圈		quān	n/v	14
civilization; civilized	文明		wénmíng	n/adj	18
class; level; rank; category	流		liú		20
close; turn off	關	关	guān	v	13
clothing; apparel	服裝	服装	fúzhuāng	n	12
cloud	雲	云	yún	n	19
coal	煤		méi	n	16
coincidentally	正好		zhènghǎo	adv	3
colleague; co-worker	同事		tóngshì	n	20

English	Traditional	Simplified	Pinyin	Part of Speech	Lesson
college; academy; institute	學院	学院	xuéyuàn	n	18
combine; join	合		hé	v	17
come and go; have dealings with	來往	来往	lái wǎng	v	13
comforter; quilt	被子		bèizi	n	2
common folk; (ordinary) people	老百姓		lǎobǎixìng	n	12
compass	指南針	指南针	zhǐnánzhēn	n	18
complain	抱怨		bàoyuàn	v	9
completely; fully; complete; whole	完全		wánquán	adv/adj	9
completely; thoroughly	一乾二淨	一干二净	(yī gān èr jìng) yì gān èr jìng		6
concentrate; be concentrated	集中		jízhōng	v	10
condition; requirement	條件	条件	tiáojiàn	n	10
Confucius	孔子		Kǒngzǐ	pn	18
congratulate	恭喜		gōngxǐ	v	11
(conjunction to connect two clauses)	而		ér	conj	10
consequence; fallout; aftermath	後果	后果	hòuguǒ	n	16
consider	考慮	考虑	kǎolǜ	v	3
consume	消費	消费	xiāofèi	v	17
contact; get in touch; connection; relation	聯繫	联系	liánxì	v/n	20
continue; go on with	繼續	继续	jìxù	v	11
continuously	不斷	不断	(bùduàn) búduàn	adv	8
continuously; incessantly	不停		bùtíng	adv	6
contradiction; contradictory; conflicting	矛盾		máodùn	n/adj	17
contribute; devote; contribution	貢獻	贡献	gòngxiàn	v/n	18
control; manage; mind; care about	管		guǎn	v	5
count as; be considered as	算		suàn	v	17
count time	計時	计时	jì shí	vo	11
country; nation	國家	国家	guójiā	n	16

English	Traditional	Simplified	Pinyin	Part of Speech	Lesson
countryside; village; rural area	農村	农村	nóngcūn	n	8
crack a joke; joke around	開玩笑	开玩笑	kāi wánxiào	vo	7
crisis	危機	危机	wēijī	n	16
criterion; standard	標準	标准	biāozhǔn	n/adj	4
crowded; to push against; to squeeze	擠	挤	jǐ	adj/v	10
custom	風俗	风俗	fēngsú	n	13
cut; chop	砍		kǎn	v	16

D

English	Traditional	Simplified	Pinyin	Part of Speech	Lesson
daily household necessities	日用品		rìyòngpǐn	n	2
Dali	大理		Dàlǐ	pn	13
dare	敢		gǎn	mv	7
deal with	打交道		dǎ jiāodào	vo	5
decide; decision	決定	决定	juédìng	v/n	5
definitely	肯定		kěndìng	adv	5
department (of a college or university)	系		xì	n	5
dependable	可靠		kěkào	adj	7
desert	沙漠	沙漠	shāmò	n	10
design; design	設計	设计	shèjì	v/n	9
develop	發展	发展	fāzhǎn	v	18
developed; flourishing; develop	發達	发达	fādá	adj/v	18
diet; food and drink	飲食	饮食	yǐnshí	n	13
different; not the same	不同		bù tóng		6
difficulty; difficult	困難	困难	kùnnan	n/adj	15
discuss	討論	讨论	tǎolùn	v	5
dislike; loathe; disgusting; disagreeable	討厭	讨厌	tǎoyàn	v/adj	15
dislike; mind; complain of	嫌		xián	v	8
display; manifest; performance; manifestation	表現	表现	biǎoxiàn	v/n	15
distinguishing feature or quality; characteristic	特色		tèsè	n	12
Do you mean to say...	難道	难道	nándào	adv	4
do; carry on; be engaged in	搞		gǎo	v	20

English	Traditional	Simplified	Pinyin	Part of Speech	Lesson
door	門	门	mén	n	2
doorway; entrance	門口	门口	ménkǒu	n	3
download	下載	下载	xiàzài	v	7
Dragon Boat Festival	端午節	端午节	Duānwǔjié	pn	11
draw; paint	畫畫兒	画画儿	huà huàr	vo	9
drink a toast; cheers!; bottoms up	乾杯	干杯	gān bēi	vo	11
(clothes) dryer	烘乾機	烘干机	hōnggānjī	n	2
dynasty	朝代		cháodài	n	18

E

English	Traditional	Simplified	Pinyin	Part of Speech	Lesson
each; every	各		gè	pr	3
earn money; make money	掙錢	挣钱	zhèng qián	vo	8
earth; globe	地球		dìqiú	n	16
eating utensils; tableware	餐具		cānjù	n	16
economics; economy	經濟	经济	jīngjì	n	5
economize; save; conserve	節約	节约	jiéyuē	v	16
education; to educate	教育		jiàoyù	n/v	8
eh?; what?	啊		á	interj	12
elderly lady	老太太		lǎotàitai	n	17
elementary school; grade school	小學	小学	xiǎoxué	n	9
embrace; hug	擁抱	拥抱	yōngbào	v	13
emperor	皇帝		huángdì	n	18
empty	空		kōng	adj	2
end	末		mò	n	12
end a relationship; (lit.) blow	吹		chuī	v	6
end; finish	結束	结束	jiéshù	v	11
energy; energy source	能源		néngyuán	n	16
English language	英語	英语	Yīngyǔ	pn	8
enjoy; enjoyment; pleasure	享受		xiǎngshòu	v/n	17
enter; get into	進入	进入	jìnrù	v	19
enterprise; business; company; firm	企業	企业	qǐyè	n	15
entire; whole; complete; completely	全		quán	adj/adv	16
environment; surroundings	環境	环境	huánjìng	n	11

English	Traditional	Simplified	Pinyin	Part of Speech	Lesson
equal; be equivalent to; amount to	等於	等于	děngyú	v	14
equal; equality	平等		píngděng	adj/n	15
equal pay for equal work	同工同酬		tóng gōng tong chóu		15
-er; -ist	者		zhě		20
era; age	時代	时代	shídài	n	7
essay; article	文章		wénzhāng	n	5
ethnic group; people; nationality	民族		mínzú	n	10
Europe	歐洲	欧洲	Ōuzhōu	pn	20
even	甚至		shènzhì	adv	7
even if	即使		jíshǐ	conj	14
evening gathering; soiree	晚會	晚会	wǎnhuì	n	11
everybody; the crowd	眾人	众人	zhòngrén	n	20
exemplary; model; fine example	模範	模范	mófàn	adj/n	15
exercise; work out; undergo physical training	鍛煉	锻炼	duànliàn	v	14
exhibition hall; gallery	展廳	展厅	zhǎntīng	n	18
experience; to experience	經驗	经验	jīngyàn	n/v	5
explain	解釋	解释	jiěshì	v	19
extremely; exceedingly; couldn't be more	不得了		bù déliǎo		15
extroverted; open and sunny in disposition	開朗	开朗	kāilǎng	adj	6

F

English	Traditional	Simplified	Pinyin	Part of Speech	Lesson
factory	工廠	工厂	gōngchǎng	n	15
fair; just; impartial; equitable	公平		gōngpíng	adj	15
fall	跌		diē	v	17
fall ill; contract a disease	得病		dé bìng	vo	15
familiar-looking	面熟		miànshú	adj	20
family (unit); household	家庭		jiātíng	n	8
famous brand; name brand	名牌(兒)	名牌(儿)	míngpái(r)	n	4
fan; to be infatuated with	迷		mí	n/v	6
fashionable; stylish	時髦	时髦	shímáo	adj	4

English	Traditional	Simplified	Pinyin	Part of Speech	Lesson
fast food; quick meal	快餐		kuàicān	n	12
father's sister	姑媽	姑妈	gūmā	n	12
feel relieved; be at ease	放心		fàng xīn	vo	20
feeling; emotion; affection	感情		gǎnqíng	n	11
feeling; sense perception; to feel; to perceive	感覺	感觉	gǎnjué	n/v	7
female gender; woman	女性		nǚxìng	n	15
fiancée	未婚妻		wèihūnqī	n	17
finance; banking	金融		jīnróng	n	5
firecracker	鞭炮		biānpào	n	11
first	初		chū		11
First Emperor of the Qin Dynasty	秦始皇		Qínshǐhuáng	pn	18
first month of the lunar year; first moon	正月		zhēngyuè	n	11
fit exactly; hit	中		zhòng	v	17
fitness center; gym	健身房		jiànshēnfáng	n	14
flow	流		liú	v	3
follow; continue	接著	接着	jiēzhe	v	17
food, clothing, shelter and transportation; basic necessities of life	衣食住行		yī shí zhù xíng		7
footstep	腳步	脚步	jiǎobù	n	12
for example	比如		bǐrú	v	3
foreigner	老外		lǎowài	n	12
formal	正式		zhèngshì	adj	7
fortunately; luckily	好在		hǎozài	adv	19
foundation; basis	基礎	基础	jīchǔ	n	18
fragrant; pleasant-smelling	香		xiāng	adj	3
France	法國	法国	Fǎguó	pn	12
free; unconstrained	自由		zìyóu	adj	1
fresh	新鮮	新鲜	xīnxian	adj	3
friendship; companionship; fellowship	友誼	友谊	yǒuyì	n	20
from past till present; always; at all times	從來	从来	cónglái	adv	12
full	滿	满	mǎn	adj	9

English	Traditional	Simplified	Pinyin	Part of Speech	Lesson
full; satiated (after a meal)	飽	饱	bǎo	adj	14
future	將來	将来	jiānglái	n	5

G

English	Traditional	Simplified	Pinyin	Part of Speech	Lesson
gabby; glib	貧	贫	pín	adj	4
game	遊戲	游戏	yóuxì	n	7
garbage; trash	垃圾		lājī	n	7
gather; get together; congregate	聚		jù	v	20
general; chief	總	总	zǒng	adj	19
generally	一般		(yībān) yìbān	adv	2
generate electricity	發電	发电	fā diàn	vo	16
geography	地理		dìlǐ	n	10
get along	相處	相处	xiāngchǔ	v	6
get angry	生氣	生气	shēng qì	vo	6
get married; marry	結婚	结婚	jié hūn	vo	9
get rich; make a fortune	發財	发财	fā cái	vo	11
get together; congregate; party; get-together; social gathering	聚會	聚会	jùhuì	v/n	20
give a farewell dinner	餞行	饯行	jiànxíng	v	20
give a welcome dinner for a visitor from afar	接風	接风	jiēfēng	v	20
give birth to; be born	生		shēng	v	8
give rise to; lead to	引起		yǐnqǐ	v	17
gloomy; depressed	鬱悶	郁闷	yùmèn	adj	17
go out; leave home	出門	出门	chū mén	vo	14
go sightseeing; tour; excursion	遊覽	游览	yóulǎn	v/n	13
go to work; start work; be on duty	上班		shàng bān	vo	12
good	良好		liánghǎo	adj	8
(an exclamation to express surprise) gosh; ah	哎呀	哎呀	āiyā	interj	4
government	政府		zhèngfǔ	n	8
gradually; little by little	逐漸	逐渐	zhújiàn	adv	15
graduate	畢業	毕业	bì yè	vo	5
graduate student	研究生		yánjiūshēng	n	1

English	Traditional	Simplified	Pinyin	Part of Speech	Lesson
grave; tomb	墳墓	坟墓	fénmù	n	18
great; outstanding; magnificent	偉大	伟大	wěidà	adj	18
group; organization	團	团	tuán	n	13
Guangdong (a Chinese province)	廣東	广东	Guǎngdōng	pn	3
Guangzhou	廣州	广州	Guǎngzhōu	pn	10
guest; visitor	客人		kèren	n	20
guide; guidance	指導	指导	zhǐdǎo	v/n	5
gunpowder	火藥	火药	huǒyào	n	18

H

English	Traditional	Simplified	Pinyin	Part of Speech	Lesson
habit; to be accustomed to	習慣	习惯	xíguàn	n/v	13
Han Dynasty	漢朝	汉朝	Hàncháo	pn	18
hand over	交		jiāo	v	8
hang; hang up	掛	挂	guà	v	2
happen; occur; take place	發生	发生	fāshēng	v	6
happy and satisfying	美滿	美满	měimǎn	adj	9
happy; happiness	幸福		xìngfú	adj/n	11
Harbin	哈爾濱	哈尔滨	Hā'ěrbīn	pn	10
hard	硬		yìng	adj	13
hard; strenuous; toilsome; laborious; to work hard; to go to trouble	辛苦		xīnkǔ	adj/v	17
hastily; in a hurry	急忙		jímáng	adv	7
have a small conflict; be at odds (with someone)	鬧彆扭	闹别扭	nào bièniu	vo	6
have achieved academic success	學有所成	学有所成	xué yǒu suǒ chéng		19
have to; nothing but…would do	非⋯不可		fēi…bù kě		4
heart; mind	心		xīn	n	6
heating	暖氣	暖气	nuǎnqì	n	16
help	幫忙	帮忙	bāng máng	vo	1
help	幫助	帮助	bāngzhù	v	7
hike in the mountains; climb mountains	爬山		pá shān	vo	16

English	Traditional	Simplified	Pinyin	Part of Speech	Lesson
history	歷史	历史	lìshǐ	n	5
hobby; interest; to love (something)	愛好	爱好	àihào	n/v	6
holiday; festival	節日	节日	jiérì	n	11
hometown	家鄉	家乡	jiāxiāng	n	10
hope that one's daughter will become a phoenix; hope that one's daughter will become successful	望女成鳳	望女成凤	wàng nǚ chéng fèng		9
hope that one's son will become a dragon; hope that one's son will become successful	望子成龍	望子成龙	wàng zǐ chéng lóng		9
hotpot	火鍋	火锅	huǒguō	n	20
household chores; household duties	家務	家务	jiāwù	n	15
huge crowds of people	人山人海		rén shān rén hǎi		10
humorous	幽默		yōumò	adj	13
Hunan (a Chinese province)	湖南		Húnán	pn	3
husband	丈夫		zhàngfu	n	15
husband and wife; couple	夫妻		fūqī	n	14

I

English	Traditional	Simplified	Pinyin	Part of Speech	Lesson
I'm afraid that; I think perhaps; probably	恐怕		kǒngpà	adv	2
ice lantern	冰燈	冰灯	bīngdēng	n	10
idea	主意		zhúyi	n	3
idea; opinion	想法		xiǎngfǎ	n	17
if it were not for; but for	要不是		yàobúshì	conj	12
if it's not..., it's...; either... or...	要麼… 要麼…	要么… 要么…	yàome...yàome...	conj	5
imagine; visualize; imagination	想像		xiǎngxiàng	v/n	12
(imitating laughter)	哈		hā	ono	6
immigrant; to immigrate	移民		yímín	n/v	9
important	重要		zhòngyào	adj	7
in a few days	過幾天	过几天	guò jǐ tiān		2
in a moment; a little while	一會兒	一会儿	(yīhuìr) yíhuìr	nm	4

English	Traditional	Simplified	Pinyin	Part of Speech	Lesson
in fact; in reality; actually	實際上	实际上	shíjìshang	adv	6
in short; in brief	總之	总之	zǒngzhī	conj	7
include; consist of	包括		bāokuò	v	13
income	收入		shōurù	n	8
increase; add	增加		zēngjiā	v	17
indeed	的確	的确	díquè	adv	12
(of resources) inexhaustible	取之不盡	取之不尽	qǔ zhī bú jìn		16
influence; have an impact; influence	影響	影响	yǐngxiǎng	v/n	8
interest	利息		lìxī	n	17
invention; to invent	發明	发明	fāmíng	n/v	18
invest (money); (financial) investment	投資	投资	tóuzī	v/n	17
it is obvious that; it can be seen that	可見	可见	kějiàn	conj	14
it's not...but...	不是… 而是…		(bùshì) búshì... érshì...		9
Italy	意大利		Yìdàlì	pn	15

J

jeans	牛仔褲	牛仔裤	niúzǎikù	n	4

K

karaoke	卡拉OK		kǎlā–OK (ōukēi)		7
Ke Lin (a personal name)	柯林		Kē Lín	pn	1
key	鑰匙	钥匙	yàoshi	n	6
kill	殺	杀	shā	v	18
know something or someone well; be familiar with; familiar	熟悉		shúxi	v/adj	12
knowledge	知識	知识	zhīshi	n	9
Kunming (capital of Yunnan Province)	昆明		Kūnmíng	pn	13

L

lag behind; be outdated	落伍	落伍	luòwǔ	v	7
landlord or landlady	房東	房东	fángdōng	n	13
lantern	燈籠	灯笼	dēnglong	n	13
Lantern Festival	元宵節	元宵节	Yuánxiāojié	pn	11

English	Traditional	Simplified	Pinyin	Part of Speech	Lesson
latitude	緯度	纬度	wěidù	n	10
laundry powder	洗衣粉		xǐyīfěn	n	4
lead; exercise leadership; leadership; leader	領導	领导	lǐngdǎo	v/n	18
leave (something) behind	拉		là	v	1
leave a surplus; be left (over)	剩(下)		shèng (xia)	v(c)	11
leave behind; stay behind	留(下)		liú (xia)	v(c)	13
lessen	減輕	减轻	jiǎnqīng	v	8
Li Bai; Li Po (701–762CE)	李白		Lǐ Bái	pn	18
Li Wen (a personal name)	李文		Lǐ Wén	pn	14
Li Zhe (a personal name)	李哲		Lǐ Zhé	pn	5
life; livelihood; to live	生活		shēnghuó	n/v	1
lift; raise	舉	举	jǔ	v	11
light in flavor	清淡		qīngdàn	adj	3
light; relaxed	輕鬆	轻松	qīngsōng	adj	5
Lijiang	麗江	丽江	Lìjiāng	pn	13
Lin Xuemei (a personal name)	林雪梅		Lín Xuěméi	pn	3
line up; row; line; (measure word for rows)	排		pái	v/n/m	14
Lisa (a personal name)	麗莎	丽莎	Lìshā	pn	3
(literary counterpart of 的)	之		zhī	p	13
literature	文學	文学	wénxué	n	5
(of a place or a scene) lively; buzzing with excitement; bustling with activity	熱鬧	热闹	rènao	adj	11
loan; to provide a loan	貸款	贷款	dàikuǎn	n/v	8
long	長	长	cháng	adj	1
lose (money, etc.); suffer a loss in a deal	賠	赔	péi	v	17
lose weight	減肥	减肥	jiǎn féi	vo	14
lose; be defeated	輸	输	shū	v	15
low	低		dī	adj	8

M

magazine	雜誌	杂志	zázhì	n	7
mahjong	麻將	麻将	májiàng	n	17
mail	寄		jì	v	19

English	Traditional	Simplified	Pinyin	Part of Speech	Lesson
main; principal	主要		zhǔyào	adj	10
make (someone do something)	叫		jiào	v	6
make an extra effort; work harder; refuel	加油		jiā yóu	vo	16
make friends	交朋友		jiāo péngyou	vo	6
make money	賺錢	赚钱	zhuàn qián	vo	5
make paper	造紙	造纸	zào zhǐ	vo	18
make progress; progressive	進步	进步	jìnbù	v/adj	11
make; to cause; have someone do something	使		shǐ	v	14
male chauvinism	大男子主義	大男子主义	dà nánzǐ zhǔyì		15
man; male	男子		nánzǐ	n	15
manage money	理財	理财	lǐcái	vo	17
manager	經理	经理	jīnglǐ	n	19
mansion; tall building	廈	厦	shà		12
Mark	馬克	马克	Mǎkè	pn	16
market	市場	市场	shìchǎng	n	15
market; promote the sale (of goods/merchandise)	推銷	推销	tuīxiāo	v	20
master's degree	碩士	硕士	shuòshì	n	9
material	資料	资料	zīliào	n	7
meal	餐		cān	n	11
meaning	意思		yìsi	n	11
(measure word for academic courses)	門	门	mén	m	5
(measure word for buildings)	棟	栋	dòng	m	2
(measure word for buildings and mountains)	座		zuò	m	12
(measure word for degree of temperature, heat, hardness, humidity, etc.)	度		dù	m	16
(measure word for families and commercial establishments such as restaurants, hotels, shops, companies, etc.)	家		jiā	m	11

English	Traditional	Simplified	Pinyin	Part of Speech	Lesson
(measure word for frequency of an action)	回		huí	m	6
(measure word for machines)	台		tái	m	2
(measure word for meals)	頓	顿	dùn	m	13
(measure word for one of certain paired things and some animals)	隻	只	zhī	m	14
(measure word for rounds; measure word for type or kind)	番		fān	m	9
(measure word for section, segment, or part)	段		duàn	m	16
(measure word for sentences)	句		jù	m	6
(measure word for stories of a building)	層	层	céng	m	2
(measure word for sums of money)	筆	笔	bǐ	m	17
(measure word for times by which something is multiplied)	倍		bèi	m	10
(measure word for vehicles)	輛	辆	liàng	m	1
mention; bring up	提		tí	v	6
menu	菜單	菜单	càidān	n	3
merge into; meld into	融入		róngrù	v	12
merit; strong point; advantage	優點	优点	yōudiǎn	n	19
Mexico	墨西哥		Mòxīgē	pn	9
Mid-Autumn Festival; Moon Festival	中秋節	中秋节	Zhōngqiūjié	pn	11
mind; care	在乎		zàihu	v	4
mood	心情		xīnqíng	n	6
moon cake	月餅	月饼	yuèbǐng	n	11
more often than not	往往		wǎngwǎng	adv	19
morning; early morning	早晨		zǎochen	n	14
mortgage	抵押		dǐyā	v	17
mostly; for the most part	大多		dàduō	adv	10
mother's brother; maternal uncle	舅舅		jiùjiu	n	11

English	Traditional	Simplified	Pinyin	Part of Speech	Lesson
mountain; hill	山		shān	n	10
move (one's residence)	搬家		bān jiā	vo	1
moveable-type printing; letterpress printing	活字印刷		huózì yìnshuā		18
movement; action	動作	动作	dòngzuò	n	14
movie theater	電影院	电影院	diànyǐngyuàn	n	6
museum	博物館	博物馆	bówùguǎn	n	14
must; have to; be obliged to	必須	必须	bìxū	adv	14
mutually; each other; reciprocally	互相		hùxiāng	adv	15

N

English	Traditional	Simplified	Pinyin	Part of Speech	Lesson
Nanjing	南京		Nánjīng	pn	10
napkin	餐巾		cānjīn	n	3
nature; natural	自然		zìrán	n/adj	10
need; needs	需要		xūyào	v/n	4
need not; not have to	不必		(bùbì) búbì	adv	4
network; internet	網絡	网络	wǎngluò	n	7
new student	新生		xīnshēng	n	1
news	新聞	新闻	xīnwén	n	7
news; message; information	消息		xiāoxi	n	15
nice-looking; attractive	好看		hǎokàn	adj	4
night of the fifteenth of the first lunar month; sweet dumplings made of glutinous rice flour	元宵		yuánxiāo	n	11
no matter; regardless of	不管		bùguǎn	conj	12
no wonder	難怪	难怪	nánguài	adv	6
noodles	麵	面	miàn	n	13
not equal to; inferior to; to not measure up to	不如		bùrú	v	3
not have enough time to do something; too late to do something	來不及		lái bu jí	vc	12
not necessarily	不見得	不见得	(bù jiàn de) bú jiàn de		1
not only	不僅	不仅	bùjǐn	conj	20
not tasty	難吃	难吃	nánchī	adj	8

English	Traditional	Simplified	Pinyin	Part of Speech	Lesson
notice; to notify; to inform	通知		tōngzhī	n/v	19
numeral; figure; digit	數字	数字	shùzì	n	5
nutrition; nourishment	營養	营养	yíngyǎng	n	14

O

English	Traditional	Simplified	Pinyin	Part of Speech	Lesson
(of children) obedient; well behaved	乖		guāi	adj	8
obtain; gain; acquire	取得		qǔdé	v	8
occasionally	偶爾	偶尔	ǒu'ěr	adv	14
occupation; profession; vocation	職業	职业	zhíyè	n	15
off campus	校外		xiào wài		1
often; frequently	經常	经常	jīngcháng	adv	5
oh!	噢	噢	ō	interj	6
oil; oily	油		yóu	n/adj	3
old age	老年		lǎonián	n	17
old (thing)	舊	旧	jiù	adj	2
older brother's wife	嫂子		sǎozi	n	9
older male cousin of a different surname	表哥		biǎogē	n	12
on campus	校內		xiào nèi		1
once; at some time in the past	曾經	曾经	céngjīng	adv	18
one after another; in succession	紛紛	纷纷	fēnfēn	adv	19
one-time	一次性		(yīcìxìng) yícìxìng	adj	16
only if; as long as	只要		zhǐyào	conj	14
opinion	意見	意见	yìjiàn	n	5
opportunity	機會	机会	jīhuì	n	15
oppose	反對	反对	fǎnduì	v	9
opposite side	對面	对面	duìmiàn	n	12
order (food)	叫(菜)	叫(菜)	jiào (cài)	v(o)	3
original; originally; at first	本來	本来	běnlái	adj/adv	11
other; else	其他		qítā	pr	5
otherwise	否則	否则	fǒuzé	conj	14
outstanding; excellent	優秀	优秀	yōuxiù	adj	19
overcast; hidden from the sun	陰	阴	yīn	adj	19
overseas; abroad	國外	国外	guówài	n	20

English	Traditional	Simplified	Pinyin	Part of Speech	Lesson
overseas; abroad	海外		hǎiwài	n	19
owe	欠		qiàn	v	8
P					
palace	宮殿	宫殿	gōngdiàn	n	18
panda	熊貓	熊猫	xióngmāo	n	14
parents; guardian of a child	家長	家长	jiāzhǎng	n	9
part; section	部		bù		10
participate; take part; attend	參加	参加	cānjiā	v	13
(particle used to emphasize the obvious)	嘛		ma	p	11
passenger; voyager; traveler	旅客		lǚkè	n	13
paste; glue	貼	贴	tiē	v	11
pay attention to; attention	注意		zhùyì	v/n	14
people think of food as important as heaven	民以食為天	民以食为天	mín yǐ shí wéi tiān		12
perform; act; performance	表演		biǎoyǎn	v/n	14
performance; achievement; result; score; grade	成績	成绩	chéngjì	n	15
perhaps; maybe	説不定	说不定	shuōbudìng	adv	6
person of ability, integrity, and talent	人材		réncái	n	9
personality; character	性格		xìnggé	n	6
persuade; advise; urge	勸	劝	quàn	v	17
persuade; convince	説服	说服	shuōfú	v	17
petroleum; oil	石油		shíyóu	n	16
Ph.D.; doctor [academic degree]	博士		bóshì	n	9
phenomenon; appearance	現象	现象	xiànxiàng	n	15
philosophy	哲學	哲学	zhéxué	n	5
piano	鋼琴	钢琴	gāngqín	n	9
pillow	枕頭	枕头	zhěntou	n	13
Ping-Pong; table tennis	乒乓球		pīngpāngqiú	n	15
plain	平原		píngyuán	n	10
plastic bag	塑料袋		sùliào dài		16
plateau	高原		gāoyuán	n	10
poet	詩人	诗人	shīrén	n	18

English	Traditional	Simplified	Pinyin	Part of Speech	Lesson
poetry; poem	詩	诗	shī	n	18
point of view	看法		kànfǎ	n	9
pollute; contaminate; pollution; contamination	污染		wūrǎn	v/n	16
population	人口		rénkǒu	n	10
portion; part	部分		bùfen	n	18
position; status	地位		dìwèi	n	15
pressure	壓力	压力	yālì	n	8
price	價格	价格	jiàgé	n	7
price	價錢	价钱	jiàqian	n	4
product; merchandise	產品	产品	chǎnpǐn	n	19
professor	教授		jiàoshòu	n	5
profound; deep; dark (color); intimate (of relations or feelings)	深		shēn	adj	13
protect; safeguard	保護	保护	bǎohù	v	16
proud; arrogant; full of oneself; pride	驕傲	骄傲	jiāo'ào	adj/n	15
provide; support financially	供		gōng	v	8
province	省		shěng	n	10
provincial capital	省會	省会	shěnghuì	n	13
public place	公共場所	公共场所	gōnggòng chǎngsuǒ		16
publish	出版		chūbǎn	v	7
pure cotton; 100 percent cotton	純棉	纯棉	chúnmián	adj	4
push; shove	推		tuī	v	16
put down in writing; record; record; account	記載	记载	jìzǎi	v/n	18
put; place	擺	摆	bǎi	v	2
pyramid-shaped dumplings of glutinous rice wrapped in bamboo or reed leaves	粽子		zòngzi	n	11

Q

English	Traditional	Simplified	Pinyin	Part of Speech	Lesson
Qin Dynasty	秦朝		Qíncháo	pn	18
Qing Dynasty	清朝		Qīngcháo	pn	18
quality	質量	质量	zhìliàng	n	4

English	Traditional	Simplified	Pinyin	Part of Speech	Lesson
quarrel	吵架		chǎo jià	vo	6
R					
railway carriage	車廂	车厢	chēxiāng	n	13
really; truly	真的		zhēn de		2
reason; sense	道理		dàoli	n	4
receive	受到		shòu dào	vc	8
recycle	回收		huíshōu	v	16
red envelope containing money to be given as a gift	紅包	红包	hóngbāo	n	11
reduce; decrease; lessen	減少	减少	jiǎnshǎo	v	16
reform and open up; Reform and Opening-Up	改革開放	改革开放	gǎigé kāifàng		15
regard males as superior to females; privilege men over women	重男輕女	重男轻女	zhòng nán qīng nǚ		15
regardless of…; whether it be…	無論	无论	wúlùn	conj	4
regulate; specify; rules and regulations; provisions	規定	规定	guīdìng	v/n	16
relation; relationship; connection	關係	关系	guānxì	n	18
relatively; comparatively; rather; to compare	比較	比较	bǐjiào	adv/v	1
remain as before; retain	保留		bǎoliú	v	12
replace; substitute	代		dài	v	11
reply; to answer	回答		huídá	v	19
Republic of China	中華民國	中华民国	Zhōnghuá Mínguó	pn	18
residential district; residential complex	小區	小区	xiǎoqū	n	11
respect	尊重		zūnzhòng	v	9
restaurant	餐館兒	餐馆儿	cānguǎnr	n	2
retire	退休		tuìxiū	v	14
return; come back	歸來	归来	guīlái	v	19
reunite (as a family)	團圓	团圆	tuányuán	v	11
revolution	革命		gémìng	n	18
ride	騎	骑	qí	v	12

English	Traditional	Simplified	Pinyin	Part of Speech	Lesson
(of water, prices, etc.) rise; surge; go up	漲	涨	zhǎng	v	17
risk; danger; hazard	風險	风险	fēngxiǎn	n	17
river	河流		héliú	n	10
river	河		hé	n	13
road	馬路	马路	mǎlù	n	2
room	屋子		wūzi	n	7
roommate	同屋		tóngwū	n	2
route; itinerary	路綫	路线	lùxiàn	n	10
row or line of people; column; (measure word for teams and lines)	隊	队	duì	n/m	14
rumbling sound	咕嚕	咕噜	gūlū	ono	12

S

English	Traditional	Simplified	Pinyin	Part of Speech	Lesson
sad; hard to bear	難過	难过	nánguò	adj	12
safe	安全		ānquán	adj	1
salary; pay; wages	薪水	薪水	xīnshuǐ	n	15
saliva	口水		kǒushuǐ	n	3
salty	鹹	咸	xián	adj	3
save (money, time)	省下来	省下来	shěng xia lai	vc	5
save money; economize	省錢	省钱	shěng qián	vo	1
save up; deposit	存		cún	v	8
scary; frightening	嚇人	吓人	xiàrén	adj	19
scatterbrained; forgetful	丟三拉四		diū sān là sì		6
scenic landscape; scenery	風景	风景	fēngjǐng	n	10
scenic spot; tourist spot	景點	景点	jǐngdiǎn	n	10
scholarship money	獎學金	奖学金	jiǎngxuéjīn	n	8
school of engineering	工學院	工学院	gōng xuéyuàn	n	5
school of management	管理學院	管理学院	guǎnlǐ xuéyuàn	n	5
schoolfellow; alumni	校友		xiàoyǒu	n	20
science; scientific; rational	科學	科学	kēxué	n/adj	14
score	比分		bǐfēn	n	15
sea turtle	海龜	海龟	hǎiguī	n	19
sea; ocean	海		hǎi	n	10
seas and oceans; the ocean	海洋		hǎiyáng	n	19
(see) with one's own eyes	親眼	亲眼	qīnyǎn	adv	13

English	Traditional	Simplified	Pinyin	Part of Speech	Lesson
sell; market	銷售	销售	xiāoshòu	v	19
senior high school	高中		gāozhōng	n	6
separately; respectively; to part from each other	分別		fēnbié	adv/v	13
serious; grave	嚴重	严重	yánzhòng	adj	7
set out; depart	出發	出发	chūfā	v	13
shake hands; clasp hands	握手		wò shǒu	vo	19
share (joy, happiness, benefit, etc.)	分享		fēnxiǎng	v	13
Shenzhen	深圳		Shēnzhèn	pn	10
shop	購物	购物	gòuwù	v	4
short	短		duǎn	adj	10
short term	短期		duǎnqī	n	19
shortcoming; defect; weakness	缺點	缺点	quēdiǎn	n	19
Sichuan (a Chinese province)	四川		Sìchuān	pn	3
sign; autograph	簽	签	qiān	v	17
sign up; register	報名	报名	bào míng	vo	13
silk; silk fabric	絲綢	丝绸	sīchóu	n	18
since	以來	以来	yǐlái	t	15
since; as; now that	既然		jìrán	conj	19
sincere; wholehearted	真心		zhēnxīn	n	6
sisters; female friends or co-workers who share a sister-like bond	姐妹		jiěmèi	n	17
situation; condition; circumstances	情況	情况	qíngkuàng	n	15
sleep	睡眠		shuìmián	n	14
sleeping berth or bunk on a train	臥鋪	卧铺	wòpù	n	13
small and inexpensive dishes; snacks	小吃		xiǎochī	n	12
small number; few; minority	少數	少数	shǎoshù	n	10
smoke a cigarette	吸煙	吸烟	xī yān	vo	14
smooth; successful; without a hitch	順利	顺利	shùnlì	adj	11
snacks; nibbles	零食		língshí	n	19
snore	打呼嚕	打呼噜	dǎ hūlu	vo	13

English	Traditional	Simplified	Pinyin	Part of Speech	Lesson
so; therefore; for this reason; consequently	因此		yīncǐ	conj	19
so; therefore; thereupon	於是	于是	yúshì	conj	4
society	社會	社会	shèhuì	n	9
soft	軟	软	ruǎn	adj	13
software	軟件	软件	ruǎnjiàn	n	7
solar energy; solar power	太陽能	太阳能	tàiyángnéng	n	16
solve; resolve	解決	解决	jiějué	v	5
someone who truly understands; soulmate	知音		zhīyīn	n	9
something weighing on one's mind	心事		xīnshì	n	6
son's daughter; granddaughter	孫女	孙女	sūnnü	n	17
son's son; grandson	孫子	孙子	sūnzi	n	17
Song Dynasty	宋朝		Sòngcháo	pn	18
sound; voice	聲音	声音	shēngyīn	n	12
souvenir; keepsake; memento	紀念品	纪念品	jìniànpǐn	n	13
speak; tell	講	讲	jiǎng	v	13
spicy	辣		là	adj	3
spinach	菠菜	菠菜	bōcài	n	3
Spring Festival; Chinese New Year	春節	春节	Chūnjié	pn	11
spring-like all year around	四季如春		sìjì rú chūn		10
stable; steady; to stabilize; to be steady	穩定	稳定	wěndìng	adj/v	20
station; stop; to stand	站		zhàn	n/v	12
stationery; writing supplies	文具		wénjù	n	2
stature; figure	身材		shēncái	n	14
stay	待		dāi	v	7
stay up late or all night; burn the midnight oil	熬夜		áo yè	vo	14
steam (food without heavy sauce)	清蒸	清蒸	qīngzhēng	v	3
stern; serious	嚴肅	严肃	yánsù	adj	19
stir-fry; sauté; speculate (for profit)	炒		chǎo	v	17
stock market	股市		gǔshì	n	17

English	Traditional	Simplified	Pinyin	Part of Speech	Lesson
stock; share	股票		gǔpiào	n	17
stone; rock; pebble	石頭	石头	shítou	n	13
Stone Forest	石林		Shílín	pn	13
story; tale	故事		gùshi	n	13
strange; odd	奇怪		qíguài	adj	11
street	街		jiē	n	12
student studying abroad	留學生	留学生	liúxuéshēng	n	3
study; look into; research	研究		yánjiū	v/n	10
study abroad	留學	留学	liú xué	vo	9
succeed; successful	成功		chénggōng	v/adj	11
such as	像		xiàng	v	4
sudden; unexpected	突然		tūrán	adj	17
suffer from; be troubled by; make a noise; noisy	鬧	闹	nào	v/adj	16
suggestion; to suggest	建議	建议	jiànyì	n/v	5
suit	適合	适合	shìhé	v	8
suit; a set of matching outer garments	套裝	套装	tàozhuāng	n	19
sun	太陽	太阳	tàiyáng	n	16
Sun Yat-sen	孫中山	孙中山	Sūn Zhōngshān	pn	18
sunny	晴		qíng	adj	19
supermarket	超市		chāoshì	n	16
supplement; replenish	補充	补充	bǔchōng	v	14
surpass; exceed	超過	超过	chāoguò	v	15
surplus; spare	餘	余	yú	v	11
sweat	出汗		chū hàn	vo	16

T

English	Traditional	Simplified	Pinyin	Part of Speech	Lesson
tai chi; a form of traditional Chinese shadow boxing	太極拳	太极拳	tàijíquán	n	14
take a walk; go for a walk	散步		sàn bù	vo	14
take care of; look after	關照	关照	guānzhào	v	20
take pictures; shoot film; clap; pat	拍		pāi	v	12
take someone on staff; employ	錄用	录用	lùyòng	v	19
takeout	外賣	外卖	wàimài	n	7
talk; discuss	談	谈	tán	v	5

English	Traditional	Simplified	Pinyin	Part of Speech	Lesson
Tang Dynasty	唐朝		Tángcháo	pn	18
taste	嚐	尝	cháng	v	12
taste; dietary preference	口味		kǒuwèi	n	3
taste; flavor	味道		wèidao	n	3
tax	税		shuì	n	4
teahouse	茶館	茶馆	cháguǎn	n	13
team member	隊員	队员	duìyuán	n	15
tease; play with; amusing	逗		dòu	v/adj	13
technology; technique	技術	技术	jìshù	n	18
temperature	温度		wēndù	n	16
Temple of Confucius	夫子廟	夫子庙	Fūzǐmiào	pn	12
tender	嫩		nèn	adj	3
term of address; to address as	稱呼	称呼	chēnghu	n/v	18
terracotta warriors and horses	兵馬俑	兵马俑	bīngmǎyǒng	n	18
terrain; topography	地形		dìxíng	n	10
terrible; formidable	厲害	厉害	lìhai	adj	9
Thanksgiving	感恩節	感恩节	Gǎn'ēnjié	pn	11
thick tube-shaped object	筒		tǒng	n	16
thing; matter	事情		shìqing	n	8
think; consider	認為	认为	rènwéi	v	9
think deeply; ponder over; contemplation; cogitation	思考		sīkǎo	v/n	17
thinking; ideology; thoughts	思想		sīxiǎng	n	18
thousands upon thousands	千千萬萬	千千万万	qiān qiān wàn wàn		18
thriving; flourishing; fire; flame	火		huǒ	adj/n	20
throw; toss; throw away	扔		rēng	v	16
Tianjin	天津		Tiānjīn	pn	10
toilet paper	衛生紙	卫生纸	wèishēngzhǐ	n	4
(of consequences) too ghastly to contemplate; unimaginable; extremely bad or dangerous	不堪設想	不堪设想	bùkān shèxiǎng		16
toothpaste	牙膏		yágāo	n	4
tourist	遊客	游客	yóukè	n	12
towards; in; on; at; (indicating comparison)	於	于	yú	prep	16

English	Traditional	Simplified	Pinyin	Part of Speech	Lesson
towel	毛巾		máojīn	n	4
tower; pagoda-shaped structure	塔	塔	tǎ	n	13
tracheitis	氣管炎	气管炎	qìguǎnyán	n	15
trade	貿易	贸易	màoyì	n	18
tradition; traditional	傳統	传统	chuántǒng	n/adj	11
traditional Chinese lunar calendar; lit. "agricultural calendar"	農曆	农历	nónglì	n	11
train	火車	火车	huǒchē	n	10
translate; interpreter; translation	翻譯	翻译	fānyì	v/n	7
transnational; multinational	跨國	跨国	kuàguó	adj	19
transportation; traffic	交通		jiāotōng	n	13
travel; travel	旅遊	旅游	lǚyóu	v/n	10
tree	樹	树	shù	n	14
t-shirt	T恤衫		tīxùshān	n	4
turn upside down; go backwards	倒		dào	v	11
turn; shift; change	轉	转	zhuǎn	v	19
tutor	家教		jiājiào	n	8
TV drama; TV series	電視劇	电视剧	diànshìjù	n	20

U

English	Traditional	Simplified	Pinyin	Part of Speech	Lesson
understand	理解		lǐjiě	v	9
understand; know about; be informed	了解		liǎojiě	v	10
unexpectedly; contrary to one's expectation	竟(然)		jìng(rán)	adv	12
unfamiliar; strange; unknown	陌生		mòshēng	adj	12
unify; unite; unified; centralized	統一	统一	tǒngyī	v/adj	18
unit	單位	单位	dānwèi	n	15
upper outer garment; jacket	上衣		shàngyī	n	19
use; utilize; take advantage of; exploit	利用		lìyòng	v	16
useful	有用		yǒuyòng	adj	7

English	Traditional	Simplified	Pinyin	Part of Speech	Lesson
V					
very	十分		shífēn	adv	6
visit; look around	參觀	参观	cānguān	v	18
vitality; energy	活力		huólì	n	14
vocal concert	演唱會	演唱会	yǎnchànghuì	n	6
W					
wages; pay	工資	工资	gōngzī	n	8
wall	牆	墙	qiáng	n	11
wardrobe	衣櫃	衣柜	yīguì	n	2
wash	洗		xǐ	v	2
washing machine	洗衣機	洗衣机	xǐyījī	n	2
waste; squander; wasteful	浪費	浪费	làngfèi	v/adj	11
water heater	熱水器	热水器	rèshuǐqì	n	20
way; method	方式		fāngshì	n	17
way of doing things; course of action	做法		zuòfǎ	n	9
we; us	咱們	咱们	zánmen	pr	4
website	網站	网站	wǎngzhàn	n	7
week	週	周	zhōu	n	20
West	西方		Xīfāng	pn	18
wet	濕	湿	shī	adj	19
what on earth; what in the world; in the end	到底		dàodǐ	adv	6
why; why on earth; whatever for	幹嗎	干吗	gànmá	qpr	19
wife	妻子		qīzi	n	15
wife controls (her husband) strictly	妻管嚴	妻管严	qī guǎn yán		15
wife of mother's brother	舅媽	舅妈	jiùmā	n	11
win	贏	赢	yíng	v	15
wind	風	风	fēng	n	16
wish somebody a happy Chinese New Year; pay a Chinese New Year's call	拜年		bài nián	vo	11
with	以		yǐ	prep	11

English	Traditional	Simplified	Pinyin	Part of Speech	Lesson
without extra effort or motion; conveniently	隨手	随手	suíshǒu	adv	16
women	婦女	妇女	fùnǚ	n	15
woods; forest	樹林	树林	shùlín	n	13
woolen sweater	毛衣		máoyī	n	4
work overtime; work extra shifts	加班		jiā bān	vo	19
world	世界		shìjiè	n	5
worry	着急		zháojí	v	2
worthy; worthwhile	值(得)		zhí (de)	v	20

X

Xinjiang	新疆		Xīnjiāng	pn	10

Y

Yangtze River	長江	长江	Cháng Jiāng	pn	10
Yellow River	黄河		Huáng Hé	pn	10
yoga	瑜伽		yújiā	n	14
young	年輕	年轻	niánqīng	adj	20
Yunnan	雲南	云南	Yúnnán	pn	10

Z

Zhang Tianming (a personal name)	張天明	张天明	Zhāng Tiānmíng	pn	1

Acknowledgments

Selected Illustrations (p. 26, 61, 277): 洋洋兔动漫

Café photo (p. 44), Lijiang Old Town photo (p. 84), Shijie Wenhua sign photo (p. 84), teahouse (daytime) photo (p. 84), Yunnan minorities photos (top left, bottom) (p. 85): Courtesy of Anne Greenleaf

Nanjing Temple photo (p. 48, top): Courtesy of Duanduan Li

Nanjing Temple photo (p. 48, middle): Marc van der Chijs

Nanjing Temple photo (p. 48, bottom): Mark Nan Tu

Skyline photo (p. 54): Courtesy of Kristen Wanner

Hard sleeper photo (p. 74): Courtesy of Tiffany Iliadis

Dining car photo (p. 74): Courtesy of J. E. Taylor

Kunming train station photo (p. 75): flickr/barkertrax

Photos on p. 78, 79, 83, 84, 94, 96: Courtesy of Zhijie Jia

Siheyuan photo (p. 117): Courtesy of Jonathan Brooks

Tai chi photo (p. 118): Craig Nagy

Fan dancing photo (p. 118): flickr/feserc

Turtle photo (p. 203): Courtesy of Julian Damashek

Terracotta soldiers photo (p. 248): David Wiley

Terracotta soldiers photo (p. 249): flickr/palindrome6996

Sun Yat-sen statue photo (p. 251): David Schroeter

Silk Road map (p. 256): Courtesy of Jean-Paul Rodrigue

Sun Yat-sen photo (p. 257): Library of Congress, LC-USZ62-5972

Map of China (p. 277): Mapping Specialists, Inc.